# THE
# ETHNOGRAPHY
# OF
# FRANZ
# BOAS

LETTERS AND DIARIES OF FRANZ BOAS
WRITTEN ON THE NORTHWEST COAST FROM
1886 TO 1931

# THE ETHNOGRAPHY
# OF FRANZ BOAS

COMPILED AND EDITED BY
RONALD P. ROHNER

*With an Introduction by*
Ronald P. Rohner and Evelyn C. Rohner

*Translated by*
HEDY PARKER

The University of Chicago Press
CHICAGO AND LONDON

Standard Book Number: 226-06238-4
Library of Congress Catalog Card Number: 70-77152

The University of Chicago Press, Chicago 60637
The University of Chicago Press, Ltd., London

To
the
Memory
of
REGINALD PARKER
*Humanist, Scholar*

# CONTENTS

### APPENDIXES

# ILLUSTRATIONS

# PREFACE

While conducting field work in a Kwakiutl village from September, 1962, through August, 1963, I attempted to use some of Boas' major ethnographic reports as an aid in assessing problems of culture change. I had difficulty using his data. Some of my older informants who might be reasonably expected to remember or know about the questions I raised said that Boas was wrong; sometimes they told me that Boas had been misled by George Hunt, Boas' principal Kwakiutl informant for over forty years; some of them simply said, "I guess things have changed a lot since the old days"; and not infrequently they told me that Boas' data related to some other Kwakiutl group, but not to themselves.

I became increasingly puzzled about why Boas' data should be controversial and difficult to use; so my wife and I returned to British Columbia the following summer and I attempted to systematically interview some of the oldest and most knowledgeable Indians about their recollections of Boas and his activities on the Coast as well as about some of his data. How often did he go to the area? What did he do when he was there? How did the people feel about him? What kind of work did George Hunt actually do for him? How did Hunt collect his data? These were among the many questions I asked in an effort to make better sense out of Boas' monumental ethnographic output about the Kwakiutl. The answers I received were interesting but incomplete.

The American Philosophical Society has almost the entire Boas collection, including several thousand pages of unpublished field notes, letters, and diaries. Almost seven hundred pages of letters and diaries written by Boas in German from the Northwest Coast are included in this collection. I hoped that this material would give more satisfactory answers to these questions, especially from Boas' own point of view. Consequently I applied for and received a grant from the University of Connecticut Research Foundation in the summer of 1965 to examine this collection of materials. The Boas collection proved to be so rich that I applied for a second grant that summer, from the American Philosophical Society, to initiate the translations of Boas' North Pacific Coast letters and diaries. Subsequently I have been awarded two further grants from the American Philosophical Society to have the translations completed and to prepare them for publication. I acknowledge my great appreciation to both the American Philosophical Society and the University of Connecticut Research Foundation for their support.

I wish to thank Mrs. Gertrude D. Hess, Dr. Richard H. Shryock, and the other staff members of the American Philosophical Society for their very generous and cordial assistance during the past three years; Mrs. Marjorie M. Bentley of the University of Connecticut Research Foundation, for typing the final manuscript; Mrs. Nancy Mazzoni, my editorial assistant, for painstakingly polishing and retyping the translations before I submitted them for final typing; and Miss Susan Jankot, my research assistant during the summer of 1967, for performing the invaluable service of helping me identify many of the names mentioned in Boas' letters and diaries as well as helping with a number of other editorial tasks. I particularly wish to express my gratitude to Miss Franziska Boas, who graciously supplied the photographs of her father used in this volume and helped me identify her kinsmen cited throughout the book. In addition, I thank Robert L. Bee, Anthony D. Fisher, Seth Leacock, Dennison Nash, and Wayne Suttles for their critical reading of an earlier draft of our introduction. And I particularly wish to acknowledge the very careful and detailed criticisms that George W. Stocking, Jr., made of the entire manuscript.

For more reason than I can say I thank Dr. Hedy Parker for her unfailing patience and enthusiasm over the past two years, while translating Boas' handwritten German letters and diaries. I also warmly acknowledge the assistance of Mrs. Helene Boas Yampolsky, who translated the 1886 and 1888 diaries before her death. All other translations were done by Dr. Parker. Unfortunately we did not have access to Boas' original 1886 and 1888 diaries. Mrs. Yampolsky was uncertain of her translation in a few places, but because we did not have the originals we were unable to make an attempt at clarification.

Despite the invaluable and gracious help of all these persons and organizations, I remain responsible for any deficiencies in the volume except in the Introduction; for that section my wife, Evelyn C. Rohner, shares full and equal credit or blame with me—especially for the parts dealing explicitly with the development of North American ethnology and ethnography.

RPR

INTRODUCTION

# Franz Boas and the Development of North American Ethnology and Ethnography

Ronald P. Rohner and Evelyn C. Rohner

Even today, a quarter of a century after his death, Franz Uri Boas remains one of the most controversial figures in the history of anthropology. Anthropologists have tended to take a categorical stance approaching adulation or condemnation regarding the value of his work. In 1943, for example, Benedict rhapsodized, "He found anthropology a collection of wild guesses and a happy hunting ground for the romantic lover of primitive things; he left it a discipline in which theories could be tested." White (1963), on the other hand, recently charged that "Boas came fairly close to leaving the 'chaos of beliefs and customs' [in the ethnological enterprise] just about where he found it."

Part of the controversy raging over the value of Boas' work centers in his field research and especially in his ethnographic publications. But until recently (Rohner 1966a, b), scholars have known almost nothing about his field research. Consequently, they could do little more than speculate about Boas' field techniques or his attitudes toward field work. These and other questions such as how often he went to the field, why he did the kind of work he did, where he worked when he was on the Northwest Coast, and how he financed his field trips were unanswerable until a short time ago. Answers to these questions are essential, of course, in order to appraise the nature of this ethnographic research, and ultimately, to evaluate the overall significance of his monumental ethnographic and ethnological output. Now that the intensity of opinion has mellowed regarding his place in American anthropology, a more impartial assessment of these questions can be made in the light of the evidence contained in this volume, which presents a full and self-expressive account of Boas' field work on the North Pacific Coast from 1886 to 1931.[1]

In this brief and highly contracted introduction we also attempt to place Boas' field activities and his conceptual orientation toward ethnological and ethnographic research within the broader context of the work of his nineteenth-century North American predecessors and contemporaries. Several questions guide us in this aim: What was the climate of scholarly thought among Boas' predecessors and contemporaries when he came to this country in 1886? How did Boas react to this? What were the general characteristics of nineteenth-century American field work, and what contributions did Boas himself make to the development of field research?[2]

## THE DEVELOPMENT OF NORTH AMERICAN ETHNOLOGY

A dominant but by no means the only late nineteenth-century ethnological perspective in North America and Europe was that of unilinear cultural evolution—the belief that all cultural systems, or specified parts of culture, progress slowly and unalterably through the same invariable stages of development. Students of early man and comparative customs formulated grand laws of cultural development in an effort to explain human progress over time. After placing educated, industrialized, nineteenth-century Europe and America (representing civilization) at the top of the structure, evolutionist

1. Some of Boas' field work in British Columbia is not within the conventionally defined boundaries of the Northwest Coast. Part of it, for example, is in the Plateau culture area. Strictly speaking, therefore—because this volume focuses on Boas' Northwest Coast field trips—some of his work in the interior of British Columbia should not be included. We do not exclude it, however, for two compelling reasons. First, no clear distinction can be made in terms of goals, purposes, or procedures between Boas' research on the Northwest Coast and his work in the interior of British Columbia. Second, Boas himself did not view his work in the two areas as being different.

2. We believe that Boas' work cannot be fairly appraised without understanding the formative context in which it developed, although we are very much aware that an exclusive focus on the early development of North American ethnology and ethnography as it influenced Boas does not do full justice to the problem. Other scholars, however, have already described the general developmental outlines of European ethnology, and a few have traced some of the lines of influence on Boas' early career in Europe (see, for example, Stocking 1965; Kluckhohn and Prufer 1959; Benison 1949). But to our knowledge no one has attempted to contextualize Boas in the development of nineteenth-century North American anthropology.

We recognize that this presentation does not clearly differentiate all the various lines of thought current in nineteenth-century ethnology and ethnography, but our goal here is more to give a sense of some of the critical contours and characteristics of late nineteenth-century American anthropology than to attempt completeness.

scholars sequentially scaled the customs and societies of other people around the world into hypothetically earlier stages of development. Nonliterates such as the Australian aborigines were usually firmly secured to the bottom of the structure. Primitive peoples such as these were assumed to represent the earliest stages of civilized man's development. But as Daniel Brinton (1896) observed, present-day savages are not as rude or brutish as the hypothetical primeval man; they merely stand nearest to his condition.

These early scholars did not mean to imply that living non-literates are in any way biologically inferior. To the contrary, most of them explicitly disavowed this. In fact one of their cardinal principles of cultural evolution, the psychic unity of man, clearly postulates the common humanity of man—the idea that all men share the same basic potential at birth for action, thought, and belief. This concept assumed the uniform working of men's minds as a basic explanation for the recurrence of similar institutions in widely separated areas. Without this assumption there could be no science of man. The presumed validity of psychic unity, then, not only supplied one of the necessary minimal assumptions for the study of man, but it was also a critical conceptual device for explaining the repetition of similar traits in noncontiguous and noncontemporaneous societies. Moreover, psychic unity was part of the evolutionists' conceptual apparatus used to fight church doctrine regarding man's fall from Grace.

Comparison of specific aspects of custom among tribal groups around the world—the comparative method—was the technique most frequently used to help evolutionists formulate laws of cultural development. Scholars believed that, because human nature is constant, nonliterates today live the same kind of life as their forefathers. By comparing societies and arranging them in order of complexity it became possible to reconstruct the history of our own society as well as of man in general. Once an evolutionary sequence was established, the comparative method became essentially a procedure for classifying new information.

In their attempt to give comprehensive answers evolutionist scholars often documented their theories through the arbitrary selection of evidence without regard to historical or geographic context. Features of a society which seemed out of place or inconsistent with what evolutionists thought should be there were often viewed as remnants of an earlier period surviving into the present. These survivals were interpreted as both examples and proof that society had evolved from an earlier stage of development.

Some societies, however, patently had customs that could not be reasonably explained in any way other than through cultural borrowing, or culture contact. Evolutionists—especially American scholars such as John W. Powell (1881)—recognized, for example, that some American Indians had learned to use metal through culture contact but that the Indians had not accordingly risen to the level of civilization. In general, these exceptions to their theories presented only minor problems for evolutionists because they minimized or discounted cultural borrowing as an important explanation of progress whenever any standard conceptions such as psychic unity or survivals could be used. Cultural borrowing implied to these early scholars that man is a passive, uninventive accepter of existing ideas, and this notion was incompatible with their assumption that all men are rational, creatively inventive beings striving for self-improvement.

By no means, however, were nineteenth-century ethnologists concerned only with total cultural systems. Indeed, the major interest of a number of students was in the origin and development of what we today call aspects of culture, such as art, folklore and mythology, and social organization. In their investigation of aspects of culture we see an emergent interest in historical explanations and an increasing interest in inductive, empirically based theory construction rather than speculative or deductive theory and evolutionary interpretation. Some nineteenth-century scholars were interested in other issues as well, including linguistic studies, the influence of environmental factors on culture growth and stability, culture contact (acculturation) and diffusion, the migration of Indian groups, and the origin of race—especially of the American Indian.

These interests represent some of the principal areas of concern among North American ethnologists when Boas moved to this country in 1886. What was Boas' position in relation to these issues? To begin with, he was the only nineteenth-century scholar in America who consistently attacked the deficiencies of unilinear evolution, as well as some of the other ethnological perspectives of that time. As described more fully below, he published a number of articles between 1886 and 1896 questioning the deductive reasoning behind theories of cultural evolution; he attacked the use of the concept psychic unity as an explanation for the appearance of cultural similarities among distant societies; he argued against using the comparative method for arranging societies into hierarchical sequences; he attempted to demonstrate that the notion of geographical determinism is invalid; and he pointed out that much of nineteenth-century ethnology was ethnocentric. In addition, he acutely felt the need for more fact and less speculative theory. Thus he emphasized both an empirical and an inductive approach to data collection and analysis. This need, however, was also recognized by a few other scholars before Boas moved to the United States. Samuel Haven (1856), for example, had already denied that all cultural similarities could be explained by psychic unity; Horatio Hale (1882) warned against the danger of believing one's own cultural system to be superior to others; Daniel Wilson (1878) pointed out the need for more fact to test theories.

As suggested above, the concepts of diffusion, culture contact, borrowing, and acculturation were present in American ethnology before Boas' arrival, but he stimulated a shift of interest from the *fact* that diffusion occurs to an interest in the *process* of diffusion— even though he himself did not study process as such.[3] He took the position that the widespread occurrence of diffusion invalidates theories of cultural evolution, but that, in turn, a study of diffusion itself is incomplete. More importantly, Boas asked, *how* do cultural systems change? Why do people accept some elements and not others under the conditions of culture contact and diffusion? One must look at real people, he urged, to understand such dynamic processes. Thus, the study of culture contact and diffusion must be psychological, and above all it must be empirical and inductive. Simply employing the assumption of psychic unity to explain the presence of cultural parallels among different tribal societies is insufficient.

Furthermore, he warned, the study of diffusion must work from the particular to the general. Investigators who are seriously concerned with problems of diffusion should plot the distribution of traits in small, delimited areas before mapping their distribution on a continental or worldwide basis. Attempts at what he called historical reconstruction, or the study of the actual historical contact of nonliterate peoples, should begin at a modest, empirically defensible level and not become involved in grand, sweeping schemes of universal reconstruction. Boas recognized that a catalogue of similar culture traits across diverse societies can never itself offer sufficient evidence of historical contact. Rather, the similarities must include traits that are interrelated in similar ways to offer adequate proof of diffusion. In addition, he concluded, we can reasonably assume contact only among geographically proximate societies. He reiterated these points many years later in an exchange of letters with A. L. Kroeber: "I call it an attempt at historical reconstruction when I assemble the available data that throw light upon the agents that have shaped a culture. I think you have to acknowledge that my analysis of Northwest Coast culture is based on that attempt" (1935).

---

3. Indeed, Boas does not make it clear what he means by the term process.

Boas (1896a) also challenged the evolutionists' use of comparison for arranging societies into unilinear sequences. He accused his evolutionist colleagues of attempting to establish, without the proper research tools, the existence of grand laws guiding the progressive development of man's culture from simple to complex. The then current use of the comparative method, he pointed out, was based on the investigator's assumptions that Western society is superior to Indian society and that primitive peoples necessarily move toward the same technological level as Western peoples. Boas (1896a) accused most nineteenth-century scholars of approaching the data with the preconceived notion "that ethnological phenomena developed everywhere in the same manner" and then forcing these data into prefabricated theories—instead of going inductively from fact to theory as he felt they should.

Boas (1896b) used a book by his first student, A. F. Chamberlain, to illustrate the nineteenth-century abuse of the comparative method. In his review of the volume Boas criticized ethnologists and ethnographers of merely collecting samples of similar culture elements in different societies in the hope of advancing science, rather than assuring comparability of the material and using the more defensible concept of diffusion. Concluding his review, he suggested that ethnological investigations should examine the history of a particular society and should search for general psychological laws governing the growth of society. Only after discovering these laws can one know if societies are comparable, because only phenomena coming from common psychological or historical causes can be compared. He does not make it clear what he means by psychological laws, however.

Continuing with this approach, in another article he (1896a) reproached anthropologists who spent all their time searching for laws governing the development of man. He suggested that the fault with their search for a grand system of progressive development as well as for the existence of great universal laws was based on their circular reasoning that the similarity of customs or inventions among societies serves as proof of the existence of these laws. That is, Boas did not object to a belief in the existence of developmental laws, but he did object to this belief being based on what he considered to be an utterly tautological argument. Boas also disagreed with the assumption that primitive tribes are living examples of earlier stages of culture through which more advanced societies have passed. Cultural improvement is relative, he (1888) explained; it is not an absolute, with Western man representing the apogee.

Ethnologists in the 1880's and 1890's arranged museum specimens according to a sequence of types to demonstrate the evolutionary development of man's culture from simple to complex or from homogeneous to heterogeneous. The displayed items were often ordered without regard to time or geographic area. Boas (1887b) pointed out that this approach to museum arrangements does nothing more than perpetuate nineteenth-century theories of cultural evolution. He and O. T. Mason, an outstanding representative of nineteenth-century museum work, engaged in a dispute over the proper organization of museums. Mason arrayed museum items in a progressive sequence to portray the historical development of material traits, although he did recognize that museum exhibits cannot entirely disregard geography. Mason was aware that societies within a given region share more traits among themselves than they do with groups outside that region. But he (1887) insisted that these commonalities are the result of psychic unity, and he accordingly arranged his specimens in a simple-to-complex sequence—based on the deductive rationale of unilinear development.

Boas disagreed with Mason's approach. As an alternative he (1887b) proposed that museum collections should be arranged to demonstrate principles of diffusion operating within geographic provinces, or what we today call culture areas. According to Boas, museums should function to display the cultural items of societies and show how these diffuse to neighboring societies. Powell, representing the traditional, conservative position, became involved in this controversy. He (1887) argued that Boas' idea of revealing diffusion by arranging artifacts according to tribe and geographic area was impossible because of the vast number of specimens that would be required. Furthermore, he dismissed Boas' notion that similarities in widely separated areas are due to diffusion, and he concluded his argument by stating his belief that Mason's classifications were much more reasonable than Boas' suggestions based on diffusion.

Many nineteenth-century ethnologists explained cultural similarities and differences through the mechanism of geographic determinism. That is, they believed that climate and other environmental conditions affect the cultural development of a people and in this way determine their rate of progress. Lewis Henry Morgan (1876a, 1877), for example, explained cultural diversity and the lack of progress in many human societies as the result of historical accident, borrowing, or geographic isolation. Daniel Brinton maintained a comparable position. He (1896) wrote that cultural parallels should be explained through borrowing or derivation from a common source only when there are special reasons to indicate this to be the case. When these reasons are absent, the explanation should be either that the two groups were at the same cultural level, or that their physical surroundings were similar. Frank Cushing (1896) also used geographic location as an explanatory device. The Indians of the Southwest developed toward civilization, he wrote, because of their need to overcome the difficulties of living in an arid waste. He also employed the concept of "adaptation to a wasteland" to explain the development of the Key Marco (Florida) Indians, who, he said, lived in a desert of water. The geographical environment (wasteland) of both areas, he continued, fostered rapid and high development of the people. The necessity of close and intimate living helped them develop their agriculture, which in turn required well-developed forms of social organization and government.

Boas (1896*a*), on the other hand, argued that ethnologists should not try to discover cultural origins or search for geographic or environmental determinants of culture. He maintained that geographical determinist philosophies are vacuous for theory construction, but he did concede that environment may play a part in influencing technological or economic development. If two groups live beside a body of water and both have developed a fishing economy, they probably have done so not because of psychic unity or even because of diffusion but simply because this was one real possibility open to them, given that kind of environment.

Boas was a major contributor to the nineteenth-century study of linguistics. He urged, for example, that languages should be studied from the point of view of their own structural characteristics and that they should not be cast into an Indo-European mould. This principle, however, was not a novel contribution, because it had already been well enunciated by Hermann Steinthal, a German philologist whom Boas knew as a student. Leading pioneers in language studies such as Albert Gallatin and J. W. Powell were already familiar with the inductive approach. Powell (1891), for example, credited Gallatin with founding the inductive study of philology. Later, through his own efforts (having been stimulated by Joseph Henry), and by directing the work of others as head of the Bureau of American Ethnology (BAE), Powell systematized the inductive linguistic classification of western North American Indian tribes. Both of these men, however, classified languages according to the number and complexity of words used by a people to describe certain concepts. Gallatin's (1848) classifications were based primarily on similarities of words used to describe edible foods. Following this tradition, Powell (1877, 1891) too based his language taxonomies on vocabulary, despite the fact that he was primarily interested in the structure of grammar.

Boas took a significantly contrasting position. He (1893) argued that linguistic classifications should be established by morphological criteria. Moreover, regarding other linguistic issues he said that ethnocentric taxonomies based on the presumed superiority of Indo-European languages would not withstand the test of scientific analysis, and in 1893 he flatly rejected the notion of Hale and Brinton that race can be defined by linguistic criteria. Furthermore, he maintained that as important as linguistic classifications are for the scientific study of man, they should not be an end in themselves. He (1888) encouraged investigators to study language change because he believed the resulting knowledge would illuminate the history of a language, which in turn would reflect the history of that society. Later he (1897) advocated tracing the distribution of languages to facilitate the study of historical changes.

Boas' conceptual position on a number of ethnological and ethnographic issues in the late nineteenth century is often at variance with the scholarly and scientific research he himself actually did. His position regarding the collection of texts—verbatim ethnographic reports in the informant's own language—is one illustration of this fact. He pointed to the potential bias of using texts collected from a single informant. The idiosyncratic style of an informant can obscure the real grammatical form and phonetic elements of the language, and to avoid this pitfall he recommended training several informants to write texts in a given language. As revealed in his letters and diaries in this volume, however, he did this infrequently in his own field work.

At a more general level it is apparent from Boas' publications between 1886 and 1896 that he favored a three-stage plan to determine man's place in the universe. The first step was to explore in detail the customs and traits of a single tribe. He recommended that field investigators collect and minutely describe every detail, every aspect, of culture including such disparate activities as canoe building and food preparation. A field worker's most valuable skill, according to Boas, is a knowledge of the language. He emphasized the importance of learning the language of a group well enough to keep notes and collect texts in it. In this way the almost inevitable descriptive distortions of customs and beliefs occurring through translations can be minimized, and safeguards are provided against describing Indian culture in terms of one's own. In addition to studying the cultural history of a group, the scholar should study the physical environment and the group's relation to it, including man's relationship to man. And field workers should utilize archaeological methods to investigate prehistoric remains.

The second step was to investigate a number of neighboring tribes in a small, geographically limited area. A comparison of what Boas calls tribal histories, or the geographical distribution of culture traits or customs, leads to information regarding historical causes of the formation of these customs.[4] This in turn leads to knowledge concerning the influence of environment on cultural development as well as to an understanding of the psychological factors creating the common customs among neighboring tribes (1896*a*). Investigators should look for origins of similar traits in a carefully delimited geographic area, and they should describe how these traits develop in each of the societies within that area. This method of comparison avoids the evolutionist pitfall of interpreting slight similarities of culture as proof of psychic unity, and instead it provides a means of tracing the history of the growth of ideas.

Boas recommended collecting museum specimens, collecting folktales, and investigating native languages to facilitate tracing the distribution of cultural elements in a small area. The study of comparative linguistics and comparative mythology was important to him (1889) because here one can find a clear expression of primitive thought. Furthermore, myths furnish clues to the religious ideas of a people, and Boas believed that a careful investigation of mythological elements in tales reveals customs missed by other methods of observation.

Finally, after the first two stages have been adequately treated, one can begin the careful search for general laws of cultural development. The final goal of anthropological investigations should be to discover the psychic laws governing the growth of ideas (1887*c*). Boas (1889) believed that the existence of these laws would be evident when the social life of different peoples was compared. To find these laws one must be aware of the way in which they are expressed among different tribes. That is, one must know the processes by which individual societies grow before one can lay down universal laws. Boas' own research, however, never really went beyond the first two stages. In fact the greatest part of his ethnographic production is inextricably embedded in the first stage. But what are some of the broader characteristics of his ethnographic output, and what is his position within the development of nineteenth-century field work in North America?

## NINETEENTH-CENTURY ETHNOGRAPHY

Boas worked with Northwest Coast materials for almost sixty years, but he also worked among the Eskimo of Baffinland as well as in New Mexico, Puerto Rico, and Mexico. The Indians of the North

---

4. Most of Boas' writings on such concepts as tribal history and historical reconstruction contain a number of ambiguities. In this case Boas does not indicate what the relationship is between tribal histories and the distribution of culture traits.

Pacific Coast, however, were his first love, particularly the Kwakiutl Indians, about whom he wrote well over five thousand pages (Rohner 1967*a*). About one-quarter of his total publications deal wholly or in part with the Kwakiutl, but almost half of what he wrote during his life deals with the Indians of the Northwest Coast in general. George Hunt, Boas' principal Kwakiutl informant for over forty years, contributed the data for something more than two-third of Boas' major Kwakiutl reports. These facts reflect Boas' extensive involvement with the Kwakiutl.

Anthropologists have remarked many times that despite Boas' vast ethnographic output he never produced a complete, integrated ethnography of any Northwest Coast group. Part of the reason for this, no doubt, lies in his philosophy of field work: he insisted that ethnographers should collect all the facts about a people and only then allow themselves some cautious generalizations. Boas was never satisfied that he had all the facts about the Kwakiutl, and indeed he did not, because, as reflected in this volume, he gave his major attention to the more symbolic, or expressive, aspects of culture such as language, mythology and folklore, art, and religion. He was less concerned with, and as a result collected less information on, the structural features of Northwest Coast social systems such as economic organization (including the precise nature of the potlatch) and social organization (including problems of class-rank stratification and social structure).

Also amply documented in this volume is the fact that Boas was less concerned with what people *do* than with what they *say* they do or say they *should* do. He took this position because he felt the most important task in ethnography is to present the culture of a people from their own point of view, as perceived by the people themselves. His repeatedly avowed purpose in ethnography was to study man's mental life, his subjective world. For this reason the greatest part of his North Pacific Coast publications are in the form of texts. These texts include interlinear translations but no explanation, interpretation, or analysis to make them more comprehensible to the reader. Resulting from his belief in the importance of texts are several thousand pages of ethnographic description that are exceedingly difficult to use. Moreover, Boas' texts and other ethnographic materials over time contain many inaccuracies and inconsistencies (Rohner 1967*b*). He was aware of these difficulties, but he never corrected them in print.

Boas' field methods were essentially the same as those used by his nineteenth-century predecessors and contemporaries, except that he covered a broader range of issues than most of them. He did standard nineteenth-century ethnological research during his Northwest Coast field trips, such as collecting museum specimens and studying folk-lore; graphic arts; techniques of collecting, preparing, and using plants; and other aspects of customary behavior. He also collected texts and vocabularies, analyzed the grammatical structure of different languages, and worked on problems of physical anthropology. His research in physical anthropology was largely in the form of anthropometry—making bodily measurements and plaster casts of faces, collecting skeletal material, and photographing body types. Archaeology was the only area of anthropological inquiry that he missed in his research on the North Pacific Coast, and this he did during his trips to Mexico from 1910 to 1912.

The principal difference between Boas' ethnographic research and that of many of his peers is a matter of perspective. He did not approach field work with the same naïve ethnocentrism that some other enthnographers did, nor did he arbitrarily select facts to fit some predesigned theory. Furthermore, whereas his associates only infrequently learned the language of the people they were studying, Boas argued for the necessity of learning the native tongue well. This injunction to learn the language constitutes another minor inconsistency, however, between what Boas wrote should be done and what he himself did. He learned the Chinook Jargon and used this lingua franca in his research along the coast, but he did not become fluent in any indigenous Northwest Coast language, including Kwakwala, the native language of the Kwakiutl.

But what are some of the other central characteristics, aims, and content of nineteenth-century North American ethnographic research? Who were some of these early ethnographers? How did they become involved in field work? What did they do in the field? And what comparability and differences are there between Boas as an ethnographer and his predecessors and peers?

In the first place almost all field workers in America until the closing years of the nineteenth century were involved in some non-anthropological profession such as geology, law, the military, medicine, or government administration. Boas was no exception. He came into anthropology from a German background in geography, mathematics, and physics. Ethnographers were recruited from outside anthropology because formal disciplinary training was nonexistent in this country until the turn of the century. Despite this, a cadre of dedicated scholars emerged before Boas' arrival in North America who believed that their obligation to humanity was to record as much as possible about the American Indians before their customs disappeared. Thus, North American field work developed, for the most part, out of a tradition of diffuse, nondirected, unsystematic, individualized, and often ethnocentric descriptions of Indian life by enthusiastic but untrained observers. By the end of the century field research was more systematic, organized, and focused, and professional training became a reality.

Washington Matthews (1897), an army surgeon during the Civil War, serves as an illustration of one whose field investigations were secondary to his major professional involvement. He devoted much of his spare time to collecting information on Navaho language and culture, and he produced poetic translations of their chants. George Dawson (1887), a geologist, collected field data between 1877 and 1890 while on geological surveys in the interior of southern British Columbia. And in the process of doing his own work among the coastal Kwakiutl in the summer of 1885 he collected information on their "traditions, myths and way of life."

Some of the people who began observing and recording Indian customs on a part-time basis later became full-time ethnographers and ethnologists. Henry R. Schoolcraft was an Indian agent when he became involved in ethnology and ethnography. Unlike Matthews and Dawson, Schoolcraft (by the 1830's) eventually became totally immersed in ethnology, perhaps because of his intense field experience. He became increasingly involved with the Ojibwa as he gathered data on their magic, taboos, social organization, and folklore. Powell provides yet another illustration of a convert to ethnology and ethnography, in this case from geology, in the 1870's. In the 1860's he began taking his students on summer field trips to give them firsthand experience with the geological world around them. He developed an interest in native customs from his Indian pack guides. While traveling through the West on a geological expedition in the winter of 1868, for example, he interviewed his Ute guides on their language, social organization, customs, and myths. He also collected vocabularies and grammars and recorded their songs. His interest in American Indians continually broadened throughout the decade. From 1870 to 1873 he studied the Paiute and other Indian tribes, including the Hopi who adopted him into their tribe. By the time he became director of the BAE in 1879 his geological career was greatly overshadowed by his interest in ethnology.

Morgan was a professional lawyer who became deeply committed to ethnology. He, among others, appreciated the fundamental value of field work, and he believed in the importance of firsthand contact with nonliterates as an antecedent to drawing theoretical generalizations. As a result of his personal involvement with the Iroquois he (1851) wrote the *League of the Iroquois,* in which he carefully distinguished between direct observations and verbal reports of others. He went into the field every summer between 1859 and 1862 to gather additional data. During this time he was adopted into the Seneca tribe and he became a close personal friend of several Iroquois. Morgan (1876*b*) also pointed out the necessity of using a nomenclature consistent with the life of the Indians. He believed that as long as the terms of Westerners are used to describe primitive social organization the result will be a caricature of the Indian and a self-deception. Morgan himself, however, was later criticized by Powell (1879) for using the culture-bound terms "nation" and "national" to describe Iroquois institutions.

As more people became involved in field work, scholars became increasingly aware that aboriginal Indian customs and languages were disappearing. The desperate cry could be heard that soon no unacculturated Indians would be left to study. This realization created an urgently felt need to record everything about the Indian as rapidly as possible. In 1849, for example, Joseph Henry, secretary of the Smithsonian Institution, asked the American government to continue supporting the research of Schoolcraft. "The learned world looks to our country for a full account of the race that we have dispossessed," Henry (Gruber 1967) declared, "and as every year renders the task more difficult, it is hoped that the investigations on the subject now going on under the government will not only be continued, but that means may be afforded for their active prosecution." He emphasized the need for haste again in the Smithsonian report of 1857. It is the sacred duty of the country, he (1858) said, to relate the manners and customs of Indians to the civilized world.

This agitated concern to study the American Indian before it was too late prompted government support of ethnographic research in the second half of the nineteenth century. The BAE was the greatest governmental organization in America for promoting the science of man in the last century. Its original purpose was to aid in grouping Indians on reservations, but its scope later expanded to include the investigation of tribal relations more generally. Attempts were also made under Powell's direction to systematize the spelling of tribal names and, most notably, to coordinate the field work being done by different investigators. The major contribution of the BAE, according to Boas (1887*a*), however, was to put an end to the dilettantism that had previously existed in American ethnology. Boas attributed the appearance of the first sound ethnographic and ethnological publications based on continued research in American ethnology to the BAE's broad and systematic plan for research. In short, government support contributed to the development of professionalism in American ethnology.

The survey approach to field work intensified both because of the increased field research opportunities through government aid and because museums such as the American Museum of Natural History and the United States National Museum wanted to expand their collections. Investigators spent two days to a few weeks at a given location collecting museum pieces, recording myths, eliciting texts, and describing Indian customs—usually without knowledge of the language. They then moved on to a new site and began the procedure again. This pattern continued until they returned to their homes, sold their artifacts to the organization under whose auspices they had conducted their research, and wrote up their field data. The resulting monographs consisted of a compilation of observations often heavily colored by value judgments; little attempt was made to do other than describe the strange customs of diverse Indian tribes.

Men who engaged in this type of survey research include John Powers (1877), who traveled among groups of Indians in order to study their customs during the summers of 1871 and 1872. Jeffries Wyman (1875) traveled to Labrador, Florida, Surinam, Chili, and Peru to gather museum specimens. W J McGee (1898) worked among the Seri. Anita McGee (1889), wife of W J McGee, visited several non-Indian American communities such as the Amana. She later gathered additional information from informants through correspondence with former community leaders. While he was still a graduate student, George Dorsey went to South America on a collecting expedition for the World Columbian Exposition at Chicago in 1893. And in 1895 Walter Fewkes was doing reconnaissance work in heretofore unexplored areas of Arizona.

The survey approach was also a significant feature of Boas' field work on the North Pacific Coast. Even though he acknowledged the need to intensively study a single people in the field, he did this infrequently in his own work. As revealed in his letters and diaries in this volume, he usually traveled from location to location for brief visits working on specialized problems and then moved on. Part of the reason for his extensive use of the survey approach was outside his immediate control. Relatively little was known about the area when he went to the Northwest Coast for the first time in 1886. Consequently the emphasis of his first trip was largely on general ethnogeographic reconnaissance—mapping the distribution of languages and cultural systems along the southern coast of British Columbia. This emphasis, however, also reflects his university training as a cultural geographer. His next seven field trips to the coast were guided by the aims of the British Association for the Advancement of Science (1888–94) and by the Jesup Expedition (1897–1901). In none of these was he completely free to engage in the type of intensive research of a single people that he might have liked to do. Oddly, however, he continued to do the same type of research during the last five trips, when he was free to do what he wanted independently of any sponsoring organization. In fact Boas' field procedures remained essentially unchanged throughout the half century that he worked with Northwest Coast materials.

A second factor that could account for his lack of extensive field involvement with any single people was the fact that nine of his thirteen trips to the coast were during the summer. Summer months were (and are today) poor times to do intensive research in villages along the coast because the Indians were heavily involved in different aspects of the fishing industry. Many of the men and women were away from their villages; consequently community life was truncated from late spring to early fall. With minor exceptions, however, even during his four winter trips he did not become personally involved in tribal affairs.

With some outstanding exceptions such as Frank Cushing, nineteenth-century field workers seldom actually lived with the Indians, participated in their daily routines, or learned their language. This was most notably true before the time of intensified government support. Boas is illustrative of this trend, even during the 1900's. As revealed in this volume, he rarely participated in the daily lives of the Indians (although he spent a considerable amount of time on different occasions observing and recording significant aspects of customary behavior), and he seldom lived in Indian households or communities unless circumstances required that he do so. He typically stayed at a boarding house, hotel, or other public accommodation within walking distance of the community where he was working. After he came to know George Hunt well, however, he usually lived with or near Hunt and his kinsmen in Fort Rupert and Alert Bay.

Most nineteenth-century ethnographers obtained information regarding Indian customs through the employment of selected Indian informants who spoke both English and their native language. Informants were often recruited by the resident missionary or government official with whom the investigator lived. Typically, the informant arrived at the field worker's residence and was interviewed. After the interview had been duly recorded, the informant returned to his village and the investigator moved on. As an alternative to this procedure, informants were sometimes brought out of the field to the ethnographer's home. When Mathilda Stevenson, for example, accompanied her husband, James, on his collecting expeditions, she became interested in the activities of women and children. After her husband's death her field work among the Indians of the Southwest became more extensive. In 1895 she brought a

Zuni woman, Wai Weh, out of the field into her home. The woman taught Stevenson Zuni art, language, and myths, and when the appropriate season arrived for certain religious rites, Wai Weh performed them for Stevenson, Mason, and other interested ethnologists.

Boas, too, tended to work with single informants, but he made no attempt to select only Indians who were bilingual in English and their native tongue. Indeed the majority of his informants knew little or no English. Boas also occasionally brought Indians out of the field to his home. After his last trip to the Northwest Coast at the age of seventy-two, for example—when he thought he was too old for more field work—he brought several informants to New York. When he did not have direct access to informants in the field or in his home, he worked with them (especially George Hunt) by mail. In fact Boas' ethnographic research cannot be adequately appraised until his massive correspondence with George Hunt from 1894 until Hunt's death in 1933 has been analyzed (Rohner n.d.). It seems probable that one of the reasons why Boas had such difficulty understanding aspects of Kwakiutl social organization, for example, is that he devoted little time to studying it himself *in situ*. Consequently he had no overall perspective in which to contextualize the minute details supplied in writing by Hunt and Boas' other informants.

Despite the apparent deficiencies in Boas' own ethnographic research he did make positive contributions regarding field methods in his writings. These contributions are largely in the form of recommendations, many of which are central to contemporary ethnography. In the first place, as we have already noted, he stressed the fundamental importance of empirical, inductive field work. He also insisted that the ethnographer learn the language of his people; he stressed the importance of collecting and interpreting field data from the viewpoint of the Indians themselves; and he acknowledged the value of intensively studying a single people over an extended period of time—although he did not mean participant observation type of research. Moreover, he was among the first to emphasize the value of training informants to record field data in their own language. And he was the first person to systematically identify the language and tribal groupings on the Northwest Coast as well as something about their historical relationships.

To conclude, Boas' work must be assessed, at least in part, from the perspective of the formative context in which it developed—not simply from the perspective of today's anthropology. One conclusion starkly emerges from this point of view. Boas did not *create* an intellectual tradition in either North American ethnology or ethnography, as some scholars have claimed. Rather, as Gruber

(1967) suggests, he *joined* a well-established, ongoing but changing enterprise when he came to this country in 1886—although he did reshape a large part of American ethnology and, to a much lesser extent, ethnography, through his own personal influence. In other words, he clearly played an instrumental role in reorganizing American anthropology as a distinctive intellectual discipline, not so much by creating new concepts and approaches, but by effectively challenging and reformulating old ones. This appraisal does not reduce Boas' role in anthropology to that of a bland rethinker of old ideas, but it does indicate that many of his principal contributions are really the reformulation and espousal of preexisting ideas rather than the introduction of new ones.

# THE ETHNOGRAPHY
# OF FRANZ BOAS

# BOAS' INTRODUCTION

EDITOR'S NOTE.—*The following notes were published under the title "Herr Dr. F. Boas: Über seine Reisen in Britisch-Columbien" (Gesellschaft für Erdkunde zu Berlin, Verhandlungen 16 [1889]: 257–68). They provide a clear and coherent description of Boas' perception of the Northwest Coast during the late nineteenth century. As such, they constitute a fitting introduction to this volume.*

Today I want to make a brief report on my trips and observations along the north Pacific coast of North America, especially in British Columbia. I visited there in order to study the natives, and therefore you must forgive the fact that descriptions of the life of the Indians compose an unusually large part of my report.

When the northern Canadian Pacific Railroad was completed, British Columbia became more accessible, and every year the beauty of the country attracts a stream of tourists who visit the accessible parts of the Rocky Mountains, the Selkirks, or the picturesque coast. Yet the whole territory remains wide open for the explorer because neither the topography, nor the geological structure, nor the fauna and flora, nor the inhabitants of this vast mountain chain are sufficiently known.

The railroad brings us to the coast, and from there Victoria, the capital of the province, can be reached by a short sea trip. It is situated on the southern tip of Vancouver Island. Let us briefly examine the coastal territory. From Victoria one can observe the snow-crowned peaks of the Olympic Range which forms the south shore of the [Juan de] Fuca Strait. To the east we see the beautiful lines of Mount Baker, and to the north and the south many openings to the winding waterways of the coast. Whereas farther to the south the Pacific coast of America stretches out in an almost uninterrupted, inaccessible line, here it forms an inextricable net of channels and fjords. Numerous islands form a narrow passage of water, from the southern tip of British Columbia up to Alaska, through which the ships glide as if on a river. The wreath of islands is thinner only at a few places where the open sea reaches as far as the coast.

Far to the south, Vancouver Island, which in places rises to a height of 3,000 meters, closes up an elongated body of inland water. Farther to the north a great number of low islands lie parallel to the coast, forming narrow channels. Everywhere the coast is very steep and the traveler can see beautiful snow-covered crests and peaks. Narrow fjords with steep walls cut deeply into the mountain range. Rivers flow into the upper ends of the fjords which roll partly through inaccessible canyons and partly form usable passes into the interior of the country. A plateau of medium height stretches east of the Coast Range. Owing to the strange formation of the mountains, intercourse between the coast and this territory is restricted to a few routes. In the south the Fraser River forms an old traffic artery. In older times a well-kept trail led along the steep walls of the riverbed. A railroad goes down into the valley now. Farther to the north a trail which is quite difficult and dangerous winds through the dark gorge of the Bute Inlet. Intercourse is very good between the coast and the interior on the Bella Coola River, which connects the valley of the upper Fraser River with the coast. Finally, the Skeena and the Stikine rivers permit another access to the interior. Thus there are only four routes connecting the long drawn-out coast with the interior. Because of this the coast forms, geographically and economically, a closed-off piece of territory which has little in common with the interior of the country.

The southern part of the interior, the mountainous country between the Selkirks and the Coast Range, belongs to the driest parts of the western highlands of North America. The rivers cut deeply into the boulders which fill the valleys. Agriculture is possible only with artificial irrigation; animal husbandry, however, is highly developed, centering in the area around Lake Kamloops. The higher parts of the country are covered with woods which become more dense and extensive farther to the north where there is more precipitation. Here some fertile land can be found at the eastern foot of the Coast Range from the Fraser River to the Skeena. The climate of this highland is completely continental, with short, hot summers and cold winters. Settlements are restricted to the eastern marginal mountains, which contain gold, and to the southern part of the plains.

The quality of the soil and the climate of the coast are vastly different from those of the interior. The land is rocky and everywhere so steep that very little lends itself to cultivation. The climate is even, with cold summers and mild winters. The outermost line of the coast belongs to the most rainy parts of North America. Hence, the country is covered with impenetrable virgin forests, consisting chiefly of Douglas fir and Alaskan cedar. Only the alluvium of the rivers is fertile ground, and it is almost everywhere covered with virgin forests, causing great difficulties for the settlers. The southern parts of Vancouver Island and the delta of the Fraser River are climactically fit for growing oats, barley, and hops, but the summer in the parts directly on the coast is too humid and cool for the production of grain. In the northern parts of the Province the summer is so wet that not even potatoes can be grown. Accordingly, the cultivated and more densely settled parts are restricted to the Gulf of Georgia.

There are only four cities along the British Columbia coast today, and each of them is known for a separate industry. New Westminster, at the delta of the Fraser River, is the agricultural center and also the center of the spectacular salmon fisheries of the Fraser River. Victoria, the capital of the Province, owes its growth to the discovery of gold in British Columbia. Today it is the seat of trade with the United States. The import and export of the Province is centered there because the fisheries of the northern coast are located there and the important trade with the natives gets its supplies there. The little mining town of Nanaimo, which owes its existence to the coal mines, is connected with Victoria by a small railroad. It is an important coal station of the northern Pacific, exporting especially to San Francisco. To the north of the mouth of the Fraser River, the city of Vancouver was built after the Pacific Railroad was finished. The railroad takes care of the traffic across British Columbia. Steamboat lines to east Asia originate there and the planned cable to Australia will start from there.

The northern part of the coast is almost entirely unsettled. Occasionally one can find lumber camps and small sawmills. There are salmon fisheries and also salmon canneries on the larger rivers, and missionaries work with more or less success in various Indian villages. Recently there have been attempts to utilize the coal deposits in the northern parts. These stretch north from Nanaimo along the eastern coast of Vancouver Island and can be found again farther north on the Queen Charlotte Islands. They are in mining condition in Comox and on the Queen Charlotte Islands. Up to now the fisheries have been mostly restricted to salmon. The sea, however, contains enormous riches of other fish which will be a source of income for the Province in the near future. Recent research has proved that the northern Pacific fish banks surpass those in Newfoundland, and already successful experiments have been made to introduce Pacific fish into the states along the Mississippi River.

After this short survey of the conditions of the country, I will turn to a discussion of the native population. The total number of Indians in British Columbia is estimated at 38,000, the majority of whom live on the coast; there they outnumber the white inhabitants.

The stranger coming for the first time to Victoria is startled by the great number of Indians living in this town. We meet them everywhere. They dress mostly in European fashion. The men are dock workers, craftsmen, or fish vendors; the women are washerwomen or working women. Some just hang around on the street. These are squat figures whom we meet here; the color of their skin is very light; they have prominent cheekbones, straight, short-cut hair, and dark eyes. They remind us so strongly of the east Asiatic peoples that throughout British Columbia there is the indisputable opinion that they are descendants of Japanese sailors.

Walking around the suburbs of Victoria, we come to that part of the town exclusively inhabited by Indians. They live in miserable, dirty wooden shacks or even in light tents. Visiting the Indian suburb in the evening, we find the inhabitants in gay, sociable gatherings. Friends are treated, the happenings of the day discussed, memories of the faraway native country exchanged, and gay songs can be heard everywhere. The Indians who live close together here belong to the various language groups of the coast. And since they do not speak any English, they use a mixed language, the Chinook [Jargon], in which the conversation goes along easily. The visitor who leaves the much-traveled tourist roads in British Columbia has to depend completely on this means of intercourse.

Victoria, however, is not the place to learn much about the Indian. We have to seek him out in his own country where he lives according to his old customs, not influenced by European civilization. There are only a few trading posts, missions, and fisheries along the northern parts of the coast, and they do not exercise any great influence on the Indians. The fisheries on the coast are operated chiefly with Indian help. The owner is at the same time the trader from whom the Indians buy the European goods they need. The salmon fisheries and the canning plants are all situated in the larger Indian villages because the Indians do the fishing. They are paid in script with which they pay the trader for their necessities. This makes it possible to operate the fisheries with a minimum amount of capital. These centers of civilization exercise a much greater influence on the Indians than the missionaries do. A number of tribes, however, have even escaped this influence, as for example, the Kwakiutl of northern Vancouver Island.

The native population of Indians is divided into an immense number of tribes, and the reigning confusion of languages is as great as in the valleys of California and the Caucasus.

The Tlingit live in the northernmost part of the coast. They have been extensively and perfectly described by Krause. Their immediate neighbors are the Haida, who inhabit the Queen Charlotte Islands. The Tsimshians live along the Skeena and Nass rivers. They also can be found on the western islands off the coast, as far as Milbank Sound. The language of the Tsimshians is divided into groups which differ little from each other. Farther to the south live the Kwakiutl, between the Skeena River and the Gulf of Georgia. This nation is composed of numberless tribes, which can be placed, however, in three groups according to their language, the dialects of which are vastly different from each other. On the west coast of Vancouver Island live the Nutka [Nootka], while the southern part of the coast is inhabited by tribes of Salishan origin. The great dialectic fragmentation of this language group is very striking. The Salishan dialects reach across the Coast Range into the interior of British Columbia and into the neighboring parts of Montana, Idaho, and the Washington Territory. Along the coast they are spoken almost as far as the Columbia River. In the interior of the country there are only two main dialects, Shushwap [Shuswap] and Kalispelm [Kalispel]. On the coast, however, the language is splintered into a great number of dialects, eight of which are spoken in British Columbia alone. To these can still be added the Bilchula [Bella Coola], a part of the Salishan language which is spoken on the Bentick Arm and the Dean Inlet.

From the fact that the peoples of this territory belong to such a large number of language groups one can deduce that this apparently uniform culture is the outcome of a long development, and an intensive study reveals that the traces of this development can be followed.

As is known, the coastal tribes are distinguished by their highly developed artistic taste, which manifests itself in numberless carvings and paintings. They are all very careful in the construction of their houses and boats, which exhibit their characteristic artistic skill. The houses of the northern tribes form a square about twenty meters long. The walls consist of boards tied to a strong scaffold. The pillars which carry the roof are beautifully carved and represent the crest of the owner of the house. Along the walls runs a platform on which small compartments are built which serve as bedrooms. One family lives in each corner of the house, the partitions being made of hanging mats. An immense wooden chair, big enough to seat an entire family, stands in each of these partitions in front of a high flaring wood-fire. The whole house is filled with smoke, which escapes slowly only through a small hole in the roof. The houses of the southern tribes differ from the ones just described only by their greater length.

The manifold origin of the culture of these tribes manifests itself most clearly in their different social organizations, which stand out clearly in spite of the continuous influence upon each other. As among most of the Indian tribes, the inhabitants of the Northwest Coast are divided into clans, which usually have animals as their crests. The above-mentioned highly developed art which distinguishes the Indian tribes is restricted to the presentation of heraldic animals, heraldic spirits, or mythological descriptions in connection with their clans. Therefore the art of the North American Indians is not understandable without a knowledge of the organization of their clans and their mythology. The entire life of the individual Indian, as well as of the whole tribe, is governed by regulations which are based on the organization of the clans. Every clan is the owner of a part of the tribal territory in which it has the exclusive right to hunt, to fish, and to collect berries. In addition, certain clans have important trading privileges. Thus a certain Tlingit clan has the exclusive right of intercourse with the tribes of the interior. Only two years ago the Hudson Bay Company acquired a similar right concerning the Skeena River from a Tsimshian clan. The clans have different ranks, and the privileges arising from them are strictly enforced. Such privileges especially cover certain feasts which may be celebrated only by certain clans, the order of seating and of being served at common feasts, the services and tributes that have to be rendered, and similar things.

The coastal tribes can be divided into two groups, the northern one consisting of the Tlingit, the Haida, and the Tsimshian, with Milbank Sound as their southern border. The tribes of these nations are divided into two, three, or four clans which have animal names, and employ certain animals in their coats-of-arms [crests]. These clans are exogamous, which means that members of the same clan may not marry each other; so the members of the Raven Clan of the Haida may not marry members of the Raven Clan of the Heiltsuk, even though they are, of course, not related. The child always belongs to the clan of the mother and stands under the protection of its uncles on the mother's side.

The social organization of the clans of the southern tribes is very different. Every tribe is divided into numerous clans. A particular clan, however, belongs to only one tribe. Only a few of these clans have animals as their heraldic figure; most of them derive their origin from mythical ancestors, and their coats-of-arms [crests] deal with certain heroic deeds of these ancestors. Farther south the conception of clans and village communities is almost the same, since the descendants of one ancestor live jointly in one village, exercise sovereignty over a large portion of land, and have the exclusive privilege of using certain masks and carvings. In all these tribes the child belongs to the clan of his father. These facts prove most clearly that the culture of the nations of the American Northwest Coast is of manifold origin, and herein derives the interesting task of examining what the sources of the parts of this culture are.

An examination of the languages reveals that they can be divided into three groups, according to their form. Haida and Tlingit form the first group, which manifests itself by the great lack of inflection. The Tsimshian forms the second group, which is characterized by the fact that essentially all conceptions are taken verbally. The third, the southernmost group, comprises the Kwakiutl, Nutka [Nootka], and Salish. Custom and usage have everywhere broken through the linguistic boundaries, and we find that one nation, the Kwakiutl, has both kinds of social systems which we have mentioned above. The northern tribes of the Kwakiutl still belong to the group with the matriarchal system, while the southern tribes have the patriarchal system, although a peculiar form of it. The child inherits from his father; when the son marries, however, he acquires all the privileges of his wife's clan and becomes a member of that clan. Therefore his children belong to the clan into which he married, although they inherit from their father.

One of the most important privileges of the Kwakiutl clans is membership in certain secret societies, of which there are a great number. The right to become a member of a secret society is acquired by marrying the daughter of an older member and by subsequent initiation into the society. The tribe considers the existence of the secret society a most important distinction, and great care is taken that the societies are sustained by the right marriages. If the chief of a secret society, who is the only one initiated into all the secrets, does not have a daughter, a make-believe marriage between one of his sons and the son of another chief is arranged, and the latter then will be the next in line as the chief of the secret society. Since these societies are of utmost importance in the life of the tribes on the Northwest Coast, I shall, if I may, try to describe some of them in a few words. During the the winter festivals the whole Kwakiutl tribe is divided into several groups. Each of them has its own ceremony. The most important of these groups is the Mēemqoat, which comprises five secret societies. The Hāmats'a, the Haokhaok, the Hāmaa, the Grizzly Bears, and the Nutlematl. Members of the tribe who do not belong to a secret society are divided in classes according to age and sex: the old men, the old women, the young men, the young girls, the children. The chiefs form their own class. The winter is spent with gay dances and songs, which, however, are interrupted by the gruesome feasts of the secret societies. The houses in which they take place are taboo and are recognizable by posts covered with cedar bark. Every secret society has its own way of winding the cedar bark around the posts. The most feared one is the Hāmats'a, which means the ones who devour. After a Hāmats'a has reached a stage of ecstasy by a strange, slow dance, he rushes upon one of the spectators and bites or cuts out a piece of flesh of his arm or of another part of his body. At another dance of the Hāmats'a human bodies are torn apart and devoured.

There is no doubt that these secret societies originated with the Kwakiutl and spread from them to the neighboring tribes. This is proved by the fact that only parts of them are known by the other tribes and that almost everywhere they have names which come from the Kwakiutl. Thus the Catlotlq of Comox have the secret society of Hāmats'a and they even call it by this name. Instead of tearing apart human bodies, however, they introduce artificial corpses at their dances by tying the flesh of fish to human bones. The Tsimshians have four secret societies. That of Hāmats'a is borrowed from the Kwakiutl and is restricted to a few clans which acquired the right from the Kwakiutl by marriage about two hundred years ago. Parts of Kwakiutl dances can be found under the Kwakiutl name as far south as the Columbia. From these facts it appears very clear that the Kwakiutl exercised an essential influence on the development of the custom and usages of the North American coastal nations. All other ceremonies are also closely connected with the social structure of these nations. Feasts connected with dancing are given throughout the year. They are the means of raising the social status and the prominence of the giver of the feast.

Permit me to describe such a feast which I attended in Nawette [Nawiti], a village near the northern tip of Vancouver Island. The preparation started early in the morning. Young men left at daybreak and returned at about nine o'clock dragging behind their boats heavy logs, which were cut into firewood. In the house of the chief the mats which were used as partitions were removed and the floor was swept. A large pile of wood was stacked and lighted in the middle of the house. Dried halibut and fish oil were brought from the supply room and prepared in large wooden bowls. Finally the men gathered—women are excluded from feasts and gatherings. They were wrapped in their best blankets; their faces were painted red and black. Their hair was carefully arranged and covered with eagle down. The seats of honor were in the back of the room behind the fire. The most honored guests took their seats there, while other guests sat in front of them according to their rank and dignity. The common people sat near the door.

At first decorous silence reigned, until the most distinguished chief gave the signal to begin. In one of the back corners of the room a man sat whose duty it was to beat the drum. The drum is a multicolored box of cedar wood which was beaten with the fist and has a deep dull tone. The drum started; all guests joined by rhythmically clapping their hands. The chiefs carried beautifully carved sticks with which they beat time on the planks in front of which they sat. Then the song leader, whose task it is to rehearse and direct the songs, began to lead the melody, and after a few beats the entire chorus joined. Just imagine this scene! The Indian house with its queer carvings, blackened by the smoke, the corners completely dark, while the blazing fire threw a strange light on the people sitting around in a circle. The men, wrapped in their best white blankets, sat on the ground; their long hair was tied back with colorful head scarves. Their faces were painted red and black, according to the clan to which they belonged. They all sat bent forward, beating time with the greatest effort and apparently to their greatest satisfaction. The song leader shouted the text of the verses above the reigning noise, and these were repeated by the chorus. It was surprising to see how exactly the chorus, which consisted of sixty to one hundred men, repeated the difficult rhythms. This is possible only because the song leader practiced every morning with the boys and young men, while the older men are kept in practice by the frequency of the feasts.

Four such songs, which is a required part of all council meetings, are sung before the festive meal may begin. Four is a holy number for the Indians. While the men were singing the food was prepared by a slave under the supervision of the host. It was put in prepared bowls and served to the guests in accordance with their rank. The meal was eaten in silence. If there is no special agenda and the feast is only a social one, one of the guests gets up after the meal and praises the deeds of the host, his rank and nobility, and the greatness of his ancestors. Then the host gets up and expresses his thanks to the guests. The following peculiar custom was observed: at the left of the door of the house stood a carved figure with a hollow back and an open mouth which had the shape of a speaking tube. The figure represented one of the host's ancestors. The host stood behind the figure and spoke through its mouth as if he were the ancestor himself. With some families it is the custom to have the owner of the house wear a mask and, after performing a dance, speak through the mouth of the mask.

The festive meal is often followed by a dance, especially when a very important guest is feasted. On such an occasion the hostess will sit at the fire, which she constantly feeds with blubber [fish oil] so that the house will be well lighted. The dancers convene in the open and beat time with their fists and sticks on the house walls. Then they slowly approach, singing the dancing song. I vividly remember the impression such a dance makes. Suddenly the door of the house is opened, the dancers appear, led by the chief. The walls trembled from the heavy blows of the fists. The dancers entered singly. The chief was followed by two dancers, their woolen blankets around their waists, the upper parts of their bodies bare. As belts they wore a wood carving representing a doubleheaded snake [Sisiutl]. Around their heads and necks they had wreaths of fir boughs. In their right hands they carried sticks ornamented with colorful ribbons, and in their left hands bows and arrows. Their hair was tied back with sealskin and ornamented with red feathers. Their faces were painted black. They were followed by two men dressed in white woolen blankets, their heads decorated with stuffed otters. Next came one dancer in a dancing apron trimmed with little metal bells, and under the apron a rattle was hidden. Then the rest of the dancers broke into the house and formed a wide circle around the men with the snake belts. A wild song started, in which the chorus joined. Now the spectators became very excited and started in turn to dance around the real dancers.

After the dance was over, there was another kind of noise outside. The door opened and twelve boys entered. They were naked; their little bodies were covered with chalk and painted with red and black figures. Their hair was smeared with a mixture of oil and chalk and looked like the bristles of a brush.

Now I would like to say a few words about the myths of the nations of British Columbia in order to show that traces of the past, in which each of the nations had its independent culture and schools of thought, still exist. As everywhere in America, we also find the sun to be the center of veneration here. With the Tlingit and the Haida the Raven plays the most important part, next to the sun. The Raven created the sun, the moon, and the stars as well as the earth and man. So many stories are told about him that they have a saying that human life is not long enough to tell all of them. The farther south one goes the less important is the part of the Raven in the legends of the Indians. Therefore, I believe that the Raven myth originated with the northern tribes. The Tsimshian also have a number of Raven legends, but research into their mythology has proved that they originally worshiped the heavens and that the stars, the trees, and the animals were considered intermediaries between the heavens and men. The Raven myth is intermingled with these concepts, and everywhere attempts can be found to unite these contradictory notions and to equally emphasize the divine power of the heavens and the Raven. Therefore, here the Raven is believed to be the grandchild of the heavens. The myths of the Kwakiutl deal mostly with their above-mentioned secret societies or their ancestors. Also in this respect they differ greatly from the ones of their neighboring tribes. In addition, they have a strange tale about a son of the deity, Kanikila [Q!aniqilaqᵘ, "Transformer"], who wandered through the whole world and delivered it from monsters. The same tale is found in the south with the Salishan tribes, but they believe that the wanderer [transformer] is the deity himself. Their main myths cover the sun and the moon, which are usually considered to be brothers.

A knowledge of the legends lends a special attraction to travel in British Columbia. How often do we hear a tourist complain that the lack of historical tradition impairs interest in the beautiful countryside. The traveler who makes an effort to penetrate the train of thought of the natives will not join in this complaint. I remember with the greatest pleasure many trips in colorful canoes with Indian guides who did not stop telling tales: it was that mountain peak which alone reached above the waters during the great flood, and from this peak the earth was populated again. Here, the battle took place in which the stone giants were outwitted and killed by the brave Indians. A dangerous rapid, formed in prehistoric times in a narrow strait, reminds us of the Son of God, who killed and sank a dangerous sea monster into the ocean at that place. Each strange place is woven into a legend.

I wish to close with a few words about the anticipated future of these Indians. We find here very gifted people fighting against the penetration by the Europeans under comparatively favorable conditions. Their ethnographic characteristics will in a very short time fall victim to the influence of the Europeans. The sooner these aborigines adapt themselves to the changed conditions the better it will be for them in their competition with the white man. One can already now predict that the Kwakiutl, who have so completely shut themselves off from the Europeans, are heading for their extinction. Certain Indian tribes have already become indispensable on the labor market, and without them the Province would suffer a great economic damage. If we can succeed in improving their hygienics and thus lower their ruinous child mortality, and if the endeavors of the Canadian government can be successful in making independent producers out of them, we can hope to avoid the sad spectacle of the complete destruction of those highly gifted tribes.

FRANZ BOAS

June 1, 1889

# PART
# ONE

---

# INITIAL
# FIELD WORK
# ON THE
# NORTHWEST
# COAST
# (1886)

EDITOR'S INTRODUCTION.—*Boas began working on Northwest Coast materials in 1885 while he was an assistant to Adolph Bastian at the Royal Ethnographic Museum in Berlin where several Bella Coola Indians were being exhibited. He became intrigued with the Indians of the North Pacific Coast from his contact with these Bella Coola, and he was able to arrange a leave from the Museum to conduct field research along the coast of British Columbia, Canada, in 1886. His purpose was to make a general reconnaissance of the coast and to collect museum specimens, but he also made limited linguistic studies, compiled an ethnographic map of Vancouver Island, and collected skulls. He apparently financed a large part of the trip himself, although his uncle, Abraham Jacobi, offered him $500, of which Boas accepted only $400. Boas also appears to have received additional funds from friends, and he was able to solicit free train transportation to and from British Columbia. He stayed on the coast for almost three months during his first trip.*

*His family letters during this time clearly reveal his acute preoccupation, worry, and occasional depression about his future. He wanted very badly to stay in the United States, and he saw this field trip as his entrée to a museum position in America. His most cherished hope was to become an ethnologist in the American Museum of Natural History in New York. He was also lonely and unhappy about being separated from his fiancée, Marie Krackowizer. His unhappiness was compounded by the fact that he could not marry her until he had some form of job security. Moreover, field work was hard for him because of the irregularity of mail delivery—he maintained an active correspondence with his family in Germany and with his fiancée in New York.*

*The position with the American Museum of Natural History did not materialize, but Boas felt his future was potentially much better in the United States than in Germany; so he resigned from the University of Berlin and accepted a position as assistant editor of* Science *in January, 1887—several weeks after returning from the field. That same year he married Marie Krackowizer.*

17

# I

## Letter-Diary to Parents
## (1886)

*September 18—Victoria:* In contrast to previous days my first one here was interesting. We arrived at 2:30 P.M. But first I should mention that starting at Port Wilson, at the end of Puget Sound, the smoke gradually lessened and we saw clearly before us heavily wooded, mountainous Vancouver Island. The water was as smooth as a mirror; in only a few places the surface was somewhat rough, showing that there was a strong undercurrent. Behind us the Olympia Range with its snow-capped mountains slowly emerged. Toward the southwest overpowering Mt. Baker gradually became visible. It is as imposing a sight as Mt. Rainier. At one o'clock, owing to the clear atmosphere, we were able to see the houses of Victoria. They are on a small peninsula. The sea was alive with gulls and seals. The latter had emerged to breathe or to sun themselves on the driftwood. Taking a very tortuous course the small *North Pacific* entered the harbor, which presented a lovely picture. At its entrance are very pleasing homes. Soon the scenery changes as the steamer pursues a winding course. There are many scattered rocks at the entrance of the harbor. On one of these is a lighthouse.

At last the city lay before us. We soon reached the dock, and I had enough to attend to, seeing to baggage inspection and its transportation to the hotel. My traveling companion from Nanaimo, Mr. Sabitson, who will probably appear often in my letters, immediately met so many friends that he was of no more use to me. We went to the hotel together, but then he vanished from sight until evening. He was in high spirits; the celebration had started this afternoon in Fort Townsend, where we had stopped over for an hour. It is a very pleasant place at the foot of a curious cliff at the entrance of Puget Sound. We were able to wander through the town a bit. Steps and steep streets lead up to the cliff. We immediately met many acquaintances so that "drinks" were called for. After I had made my baggage and myself respectable, I set out to look about a bit. Strangely enough I discovered pictures of my Bella Coolas everywhere and soon found their source—an Indian trader who had had them rephotograped.[1] I went into the store and became friendly with the trader, who turned out to be a German. I immediately asked about the Bella Coolas and heard that two were still here but intended to leave for home that evening. It happened that two Bella Coola girls passed by who, of course, knew where the men were staying. I went with them, and after searching for a while I found my good friend Alkinous in the small house of a Bella Coola woman. He was of course very much surprised when he recognized me and said I must be a "smart man." It amused me to see the astonishment of the women when they heard me talk their language. Unfortunately I had forgotten almost everything in these months. After searching some more we found Itlkakuani, the other Bella Coola who is still here. I gave him a letter to Captain Jacobsen and then said goodbye after giving him greetings for his fellow tribesmen.

In the meantime I became hungry and went for my dinner. After eating I returned to the store, obtained a number of good addresses, and saw endless Indians of various tribes. I was just about to pick one out, a Tlingit, when the fire bell began to ring and everyone ran away. A big wooden mill near our hotel was on fire, and immediately three houses caught fire. There was no wind and so it was possible to control the fire. Fire is a terrible thing with these wooden houses. I then bought a few maps which I had been unable to get in New York. I think I spent my first day very well.

I am anxious to know how I shall fare when I really get to work. There is nothing to be gained from these tradespeople, but one must listen patiently and be polite because they can be very helpful in finding the right Indians. I hope I shall soon be able to decide how to arrange matters. Perhaps I shall stay here for a month and then go to Nanaimo and Comox, but I shall have to see. I have not yet been able to visit the settlement here.

*September 19—Victoria:* I was restless and could not sleep last night. I got up at six, breakfasted, and went down to the harbor. I got into conversation with an old miner, here on a visit, who told me much about how things had looked here in former times. He accompanied me to the Indian village on the other side, a walk of about fifteen minutes across a bridge which crosses the pretty harbor. Only

---

1. Boas is referring to the Bella Coola Indians with whom he worked while he was an assistant under Adolph Bastian in the Berlin Royal Ethnographic Museum in 1885 and the early part of 1886.

a few of the old houses are still inhabited. The Indians have built themselves others according to the European plan.

The people were quite reserved at first, but I showed them half a dollar and they became willing. A man from the Songis tribe [Straits Salish] who lives here took me to his house and showed me his father, an old grey-haired man. The houses look very old. They are built of large planks which the Indians had cut, with much labor, from monstrous trees. There was great sorrow because the child of the chief had died that morning. The relatives sat together in their part of the house and began at a given time to sing the death chant in unison. Early in the morning all the "medicine instruments," rattles, . . . , etc., had been burnt, according to the demands of custom. I shall have to describe the houses at another time. The people held my attention this morning. One, who had been born in Nanaimo, was half drunk, but he is a clever man and soon understood what I wanted. I hope to learn much from him.

I began to ask about the language. In the beginning it is always hard work. But I soon found the pronouns and a few verbs. That is usually sufficient to break the ice. I did not stay long this morning because I wanted to go to the Indian church, but I was too late. After some questioning I discovered the existence of a very religious Tsimsian, whom I looked up. I had been told that he speaks English and is well informed about the myths of his people. I arranged for him to recount some to me tomorrow. He did not wish to do so today because he wanted to go to church. He said he had left his home, Metlakatla, because the missionaries quarreled too much during confession. I only fear that he may no longer know much about his traditions, but a few old women who live here may be able to help me out. I then visited a Bella Coola woman from whom I hoped to learn something, but she was not in the mood for talking because she was engaged in cooking dinner. So there was nothing for me to do but take a recess and eat my lunch too. I shall try my luck with this woman again.

*Evening:* She was in no mood for talking. It appeared that my old friend from Berlin, Itlkakuani, is still around, and she preferred that I go to him. So I went to his tent and began talking at once; I showed him my drawings from various museums, and it was soon apparent that they will be very useful. I am now convinced that this trip will have the results I desire. Today I have made many notes about masks and such things. A few spirits have wandered into my diaries. I hope I shall accomplish a great deal! Tomorrow I shall have to pay calls. I have mapped out a whole campaign in order to interest as many people as possible in my work. Tomorrow I shall visit Dr. Tolmie, whose name I have mentioned a number of times, the Indian agent Dr. Powell, and the Catholic priest. I must further try to interest photographers and perhaps the school teacher, whom I wish to enlist for some matters. Since I have so little time I want to have as many coworkers as possible.

I intended to take a walk this evening, but it got too dark to see anything more. I am glad to be finally working at something worthwhile and new, because I became tired of the Eskimo.[2] Victoria is a strange place. I have never seen such a mixture of peoples among such a small number of inhabitants. Besides many whites there are a very large number of Chinese, who occupy one section of the city exclusively. There are also many Negroes and Indians. Many Indians must have been accepted into white families because their typical facial form shows itself in many of the inhabitants.

*September 21:* I was so tired last night from running around all day that I went to bed at 9:30 after I had finished copying my notes for the day. I had breakfast at 6:30 and then walked to the small peninsula which separates the Juan de Fuca Strait. Unfortunately it was foggy and I could not see much. Magnificent, tall firs, knotty oaks, and another tree whose name I don't know grow there. It was a very beautiful walk. The ground was covered with lush ferns, and naked grey rock showed here and there. Only here does one find nature free and untamed so close to the turmoil of a city!

I returned at about 8:30 and called for the Tsimsian with whom I wanted to work. He is very intelligent and tells me more than I expected. He immediately recognized one of my drawings from New York and told me a long story that goes with it, first in Chinook and then in his own language. The session lasted until one o'clock and I was satisfied with the results. I wanted to pay calls in the afternoon, but Dr. Tolmie was not at home. I was no more successful with the Catholic priests, because the one who knows the languages of western Vancouver [Island] had left for there last night. I had no better luck at the English church. The people were all very kind, but there was no one who could really help me. I must still go to the High Church; perhaps I can find what I need there.

I also went to the Songis [Songish] settlement, whose inhabitants all seem to be terrible drunkards. I wanted someone to give me words, but I had great difficulty because everyone was drunk. Unfortunately I had taken a map with me. There was great excitement because they believed that the railroad was to be built through their reservation. Because of the map they thought I belonged to the railroad and regarded me with suspicion. Everyone asked whether the railroad

2. Boas did field work among the Eskimo of Baffinland in 1883.

would pass through their territory. They did not become any more friendly when I wanted to write down their language. Not until I became a little rough with them and showed them money did their attitude improve. By this time it was about six o'clock and I went for my dinner. I had enough to do in the evening to copy the results of my day's work. This morning I hurried to my friend Mathew and engaged him for every morning, starting at eight. In this way I hope to learn quite a bit about his language. I am afraid his knowledge of folklore is not very great but he knows quite a number of things. In half an hour I shall go to see Dr. Tolmie, and I hope that he will be able to help me considerably. I also asked Mathew to try to interest a Bella Coola in telling me things in his way. I hope that can be arranged. Besides, yesterday I went to see the Indian agent Powell, but he was out of town. He is to return in a week. So far I have gotten something every day, but I am not yet satisfied with the results.

*September 21—Evening:* This morning the son of the hotel proprietor drove me to Dr. Tolmie's. His farm is about two and one-half English miles from here. The son remained there with me. I found a kind-hearted, talkative old gentleman, but it was very difficult to keep him to the point. His learning is not very great, and in addition he is deaf and therefore not very trustworthy as far as language is concerned. He is not much interested in ethnology, customs, masks, etc., and knows little about them. Fortunately Dawson (from Ottawa) got him to publish what he knows of mythology, so that we can learn something from him. He has a very nice collection which I shall draw tomorrow. Maybe I shall get a little more information when I am alone with him.

On the way back the son of the "hotel" gave me valuable information about a Bella Coola who lives here and who is supposed to know a great deal. By the time we returned to town it was twelve o'clock. After lunch I went to my Bella Coola and obtained a lot of useful information about folktales, but I did not quite understand everything; I hope to learn more tomorrow. In the evening I went over to the village. Today I made a friend over there. It seems that the women are always more intelligent than the men, and from her I obtained good material on language. I dare not appear with my maps for a while lest they again become suspicious. I regret every lost hour, but unfortunately in this kind of work it is necessary to lose many in order to find suitable people with whom to work. I do not think I shall try to work with the people of the west coast [of Vancouver Island]. They are too different from the people here and should be studied by themselves. I definitely want to study the

Kwakiutl. After I have been over there a few more times I want to describe their village. I am not ready to do it yet as my impression of it daily becomes clearer and more complete.

*September 22:* My friend Mathew, the Tsimsian, came again this morning and told me a long story of the origin of the cannibal. He recognized another one of my pictures and wants to tell me the story today. (It is now the morning of the twenty-third.) He says it is a nice story and very long! I am looking forward to his arrival. In the afternoon, as I had promised, I went to Dr. Tolmie and copied a few of his things. It is not worthwhile to question the old man, since it is impossible to keep him to one subject, but he owns some very fine objects. On the way back it was raining heavily, but fortunately a wagon passed by and the driver was kind enough to take me back to town. The road to Dr. Tolmie's is very pretty. It passes a number of homes and goes through a primeval fir forest and fields with magnificent cattle. I have seldom seen orchards as heavily laden with fruit as these here. The roads around the town are good and it is a pleasure to wander over them. When I got home I had to copy some things.

After dinner I went to my Bella Coola woman to learn the details of yesterday's story. Since I did not understand her well enough, I took her to town to an Indian store, whose owner had promised to help me. He understands Chinook very well. Fortunately he was able to understand something of her tale, and I found out a little more than before. I hope I can find the man of whom I spoke yesterday, so that I may become well informed about these matters and above all about the important Bella Coola language. I am finding out quite a bit about Tsimsian and with some good luck should also learn about the Bella Coola and Comox, and perhaps about Cowichan. Such a confusion of dialects and languages exists here that it is very difficult to accomplish anything in a short time. The material overwhelms me. I am very curious about the story I am to get today. Each day brings so much that is new and so many surprises. I discovered yesterday evening in making comparisons that a dance which occurs among the Bella Coola is similar to one among the Citlattang[?]. Intercourse and transference must be very great between individual tribes.

*September 24:* Here too my mood changes with the weather. We have had rain since the day before yesterday; this does not improve my stay here. I am cross because my Tsimsian has deserted me, and so far he has been the best one I have had. From experience I should know that such things happen, but it is easier said than done not to be angry about it. I told the good man, who, by the way, is one of the most religious, that he was the greatest liar I had ever known since he did not keep his word. I told him I would tell his pastor about it. I immediately went in search of another and hope I shall be successful tomorrow.

I must now relate what I have done since yesterday. In the morning my Tsimsian, Mathew, the one who disappointed me today, was here. For six hours he told me a long story which I of course copied. I had hoped to obtain it in Tsimsian, but now I shall be unable to do so. The stories are in part completely senseless, and I became quite stupefied. Basically, however, they contain so many interesting religious and social facts that I want to hear them.

In the afternoon a card was brought to my room inviting me to a dinner party given by McDonald, the Victoria representative in Ottawa's parliament. I do not know how it happened. I put on my dress suit and went. They had accidentally heard of my presence and had invited me as a favor to themselves. Of course the newspapers get wind of everything and follow my doings. The evening was quite pleasant, but rather formal English. The general tone in the city appears to be quite different from that in America (U.S.A.). It has a greater similarity to Europe. Lady and lord play the chief role in the newspapers, the military is a favorite topic of conversation, etc.

This morning I waited in vain for friend Mathew. Then I went to a good acquaintance, a trader of the Hudson Bay Company. With his help I got to know a wild-dance story. It relates to a mask which is in the Berlin Museum and the museum in New York. The explanations are so lengthy that I shall not get very far with them. I also learned much about the mythology of the Bella Coola and the Bella Bella. I am afraid I am mentioning names that are of no interest to you, but since this is a diary I cannot omit them. I hope I shall find another good Tsimsian tomorrow to replace Mathew, whom I cannot curse enough. He was able to dictate very well. It reminds me so vividly of the Eskimo—they also ran away in the middle of a tale.

*September 25:* Today was the worst day since I have been here. I learned practically nothing because I spent the entire day running about in search of new people. This morning I looked for some Tsimsians who live in another part of the city. After a long search I finally found them but could get nothing from them. All I got was a few notes about their family lines and the patterns of their clothing. A woman started to tell me the story of the thunderbird, but she did not get very far. She claimed to have forgotten the most important part. I then went to the trader of the Hudson Bay Company and had his wife, a Wikiano [Wikeno] Indian, retell the cannibal story I had got yesterday. I wanted to verify it because parts were not clear to me. Her husband showed me the homes of several Indians, but I was not very successful in finding out anything.

A Bella Coola arrived the day before yesterday, but I have not been able to find him. Maybe I can learn something from him. He does not seem to be the one of whom I have frequently heard. I finally found a Newetti [Nawiti] from the northern point of the island. He claims to know all sorts of things and promised to tell them to me. He is supposed to come tomorrow, and I wonder whether he will appear. If things continue to go so badly I shall hurry away from Victoria; I do not wish to hang about in vain. I was very tired at night from running about so much and went to bed in a bad humor. That was a profitless day's labor!

*September 26:* Today things went a little better for a change and I am very glad. The man whom I had asked to come was useless. He was impatient, could not express himself, and was unable to give me the information I wanted. I then went to the Tsimsian woman where I had been yesterday. At first she knew nothing, but after we had talked all manner of nonsense for an hour she suddenly told me a wonderful family story. The tribes are divided into so-called totems, each having its representative animals. As I discovered yesterday and today, all masks and rattles are used only by certain families. I left at twelve, ate lunch, and then took a walk, since I could find no Indians. It was a glorious day and the scenery is very beautiful.

When I returned I crawled into a Bella Coola tent and obtained a few nice facts from two women. I have the least trouble with this tribe because I know their language a little. The results are not as good as I should like, but better than yesterday's. Toward sunset I took another walk to Beacon Hill Park, a beautiful expanse along the seashore. It is in part a dense forest, but along the ocean all the trees are gone. An unbroken grassy slope rises to a hill close to the shore. This affords a fine view over the Olympic Range and the entrance to Victoria harbor. I am unhappy for every moment lost, but one cannot butt one's head against a stone wall; I must bear these fruitless hours patiently. I hope it will be better after I leave here. After this I shall have to deal with only one tribe.

*September 27:* This diary affords little variety. It always tells the same story: that I went to visit Indians and that I returned home; that I am told stories and that I copy them, etc. Perhaps it will become a little more interesting after I get to Nanaimo. I have decided to take the steamer *Boskowitz* to Alert Bay either Saturday or Sunday. I have [letters of] introduction. There is to be a great potlatch festival there at the end of the month. I shall be able to see dances and buy masks.

It will be cheaper to live there because the hotel is less expensive. This morning I visited the Tsimsian woman, who told me a long story, and in the afternoon the Wikiano [Wikeno] woman told me the story of the origin of the sun. I have not obtained much concerning the mythology of these tribes. It is very difficult to get them to talk. This week I shall have to buy all manner of things and visit Dr. Tolmie, who looked for me in vain yesterday.

*September 28:* Today the Tsimsian woman was quite unapproachable and was unwilling to tell me anything. I had to give up after several attempts and left in anger. After that I visited the two Bella Coolas, who quite unexpectedly and without my asking told me the story of the origin of the salmon, a tale for which I have been looking for a long time. They told me a few other things besides. In the afternoon I went to see Bishop Hills of the Anglican Church, with whom I had an appointment. I was there yesterday but he was engaged in some sort of church conference at the time. He lives in a handsome wooden house in the midst of a beautiful flower garden. At first he seemed very formal and condescending but turned out to be quite approachable and gave me all the information I needed. He even gave me an old book which he owned in duplicate.

Then I went to the Wika'no [Wikeno] woman but did not discover a great deal. I met a man there who had just arrived from New Westminster in his canoe. He is a big chief in Fort Rupert, was very talkative, but for some strange reason I could not get much from him. He believed I would buy all kinds of articles and as a result claimed to own everything about which I asked. I wanted to go to the Bella Coolas this evening but could not because of this stupid fellow. The books from Philadelphia finally arrived today. I had ordered them while I was still in New York. I also received letters from Minden.[3] I had been quite worried until the [boat] arrived. The weather has been very fine the last few days.

*September 29:* This has been the best day since my arrival, I think. I have at last succeeded in explaining to the Bella Coola women how they must dictate their language to me. Now I really hope to learn something. I went to the Wika'no [Wikeno] woman this morning. She greeted me with an endlessly long tale. Scarcely had she finished when she started on another. It was very interesting to find certain traits of the Tsimsian tales accurately repeated by her. She kept me over three hours. Then I met the Kwakiutl man, who brought me

---

3. Boas' parents, with whom he corresponded extensively until their deaths, lived in Minden, Westphalia, Germany. His reference is to their correspondence with him.

strange paintings. I shall see him tomorrow morning and have him explain everything to me. I ate my lunch and afterward, on my way to the Bella Coolas, met the Catholic priest whom I had visited the other day. We greeted one another. I told him I had been unable to find a Tlingit whom I was very anxious to see. He offered to take me to a woman tomorrow who speaks this language, as well as Haida.

I then proceeded to the Bella Coolas and heard the end of yesterday's story as well as some new ones. Four Bella Coolas and a Kwakiutl were there, sitting peacefully together. I must describe their home. Picture a small wooden house, its narrow side facing the street. Along either side is a long verandah-like passageway leading into the living quarters, which consist of an entrance hall, kitchen, and living room. The room farthest back is the bedroom. In each house there are about twelve units. This is one of the more elegant. Most of them have only one room, which serves for everyone. On my visits to these homes I usually find the women busily engaged in household duties or busily being lazy. Today was a beautiful day, the kind of day found only in June in Germany. They all eat in negligee[?] on the verandah. They squatted in front of their doors on cedar bark mats and ate pea soup from a large pot with their homemade wooden spoons. It seems that these wooden spoons, the mats, and the boxes are the only things they will not give up.

Conversation among the Bella Coola is of course in their own language. I generally understand just about enough to know what they are talking about. As soon as friends from other tribes are present, conversation is in Chinook [Jargon]. I am gradually learning to understand this language quite well. Unfortunately the language is incomplete, even more so than the jargon among the Eskimo, although the latter contains fewer words. The people speak very rapidly, a rapidity which I can by no means approach. I understand everything that is in any way to be understood, however. It is characteristic of Chinook that one must guess the meaning of a sentence; one never knows what is subject and what is object. Even verbs and nouns can often not be distinguished, and one has to be very alert in listening to their mythical tales. When I get to Alert Bay I shall try as quickly as possible to pick up something of the language so that I can make myself understood. A mixture of Chinook and the native language is quite useful for purposes of communication.

*September 30:* It is strange how "luck's scale moves up and down." In the last few days I have been overwhelmed with material, so much so that I can scarcely handle it all. I wrote yesterday that I had met the . . . on the street. The man is the soul of kindness. He was waiting for me this morning when I arrived with my usual promptness. He hitched his horse to the wagon and drove me to the Indian woman of whom he had spoken. He really is the kindest man I have ever met. The Indian woman is married to a white man. She was very pleasant and helpful because of the manner of my introduction. "Papa," as he is addressed in Chinook [Jargon], seems to be highly respected by these people. I asked only one question, and the entire myth of the origin of the world descended upon me. The priest offered me his house, in case I should wish to continue with my work. He will ask the woman to come there, so that I am very fortunate. I hope in this way to get the entire nature [?] myth of the Haida and Tlingit. Today, although I just started, I discovered new and valuable traits, and also the first Tlingit text in existence. Afterward I went to the Wika'no [Wikeno] woman, who told me a strange story which almost sounds word for word like the story of Phaeton. This afternoon she told me the story of the origin of mosquitoes.

This mass of stories is gradually beginning to bear fruit because I can now discover certain traits characteristic of the different groups of people. I think I am on the right track in considering mythology a useful tool for differentiating and judging the relationship of tribes. I have made some progress with the masks, but I expect to do more with them after I get to Alert Bay. I do not think I have ever enjoyed as glorious a fall as this one. The weather is mild and beautiful—just like our summer. Unfortunately it is not quite as clear as it was a few days ago after the rain. The distant views are again shrouded in smoke from the forest fires.

*October 1:* This morning I finally visited Dr. Tolmie. I have had it on my conscience for some time. I stayed there about three hours and told the old gentleman what I was doing. He was much interested and is very alert for his age. It is strange how all the Scotchmen with whom I have so far become acquainted are alike in certain respects. They are all primarily interested in questions on religion and all seem to solve them in a similar way. They must have a very deep emotional life. I cannot believe that it is mere accident that all the Scotch I know and who are unknown to one another should be so much alike. Then I went to my Wika'no [Wikeno]. She told me a story about the origin of the frogs and gave me information about death customs. I am not at all clear about the latter, however. At noon I went to the Bella Coolas but they were so drunk I could get nothing from them. Most of my Indians are not of the very best sort! In the afternoon I wrote a few letters and caught up with some of my copying. I have become so far ahead in these last few days that I have been unable to write up the material as it has accumulated. The long-promised Bella Coola arrived today, but because of a misunderstanding we missed one another. I am curious to know whether he will turn out to be as useful as has been promised.

*October 2:* Yesterday evening the steamer *Boskowitz* docked again, with Bishop Ridley from [Metlakatla] as a passenger. I shall certainly visit him. I heard today that the steamer would probably remain here for two weeks. That would be very unpleasant for me because it would shorten my trip to Alert Bay considerably. I shall have to look into it the day after tomorrow and make my plans accordingly. This morning I obtained exactly the same story from a Bella Coola woman that I had been told by the Wika'no [Wikeno] yesterday. She also told me a story of the origin of the stars. From the Wika'no [Wikeno], however, I learned more about death customs and about the invention of the coppers, which are valuable articles of trade; also about shell ornaments.

This evening I saw the Bella Coola whom I have sought so long. He is quite intelligent. "Auf Anhieb" (as we used to say as students) he told me the story of the son of their highest being. Is it not strange that, as far as I know, two entirely different tribes designate him as "Our Father," without, it would seem, the influence of missionaries? I think I am on the track of some very interesting matters but it still remains uncertain whether things will develop the way I now suspect. At any rate these people have a highly developed religious system. I find it strange that in spite of the great differences in language there should be so great a similarity in the myths and beliefs. I have a rendezvous with two Bella Coolas for tomorrow and this man will visit me again tomorrow night. It sounds odd to hear him talk German. It is impossible for the Indians to pronounce quite a number of letters. The other day I made a beautiful mistake. I wrote down "*Nī'tlkal*" believing it to be a name, but. . . .

[*October 5. On board the Boskowitz:*] I am taking only one box of books, a case of tobacco, and a bolt of cotton for the Indians; the rest money. In this way I expect to get a lot, at least what I want. I returned to my room and packed the trunk which is to remain in Victoria. I am storing it at the hotel. At ten o'clock I went to the bank to get money and to the steamship office to find out when the steamer sails. To my horror I discovered it was leaving yesterday afternoon, and I had to hurry to get ready. I rushed to the stores and bought all I needed, then finished packing, with barely time to write and mail a few lines. Just before the steamer left I grabbed letters from Marie and Toni and from home. Of course I accomplished nothing yesterday, since all my time was taken up in getting ready. The weather was beautiful when we left at 5:30. Victoria is situated beautifully, stretched out along the harbor. The sun spread a warm light over all and everything looked quiet and peaceful. Outside the harbor there was a strong breeze, and our steamer, which crawls along, danced merrily on the waves. In another hour it was completely calm. The *Barbara Boskowitz* has schooner rigging.

When I boarded, they were still busy loading. About twenty Indians were sitting on shore, with their baskets, boxes, and bundles, waiting for her departure. When she was ready to sail, they all rushed on board with their belongings and made themselves comfortable on the lower deck. It was a colorful group and they were all very gay. The cabin passengers were friend Herigon the trader, his Indian wife, and I. In addition there were a grumpy captain, a talkative machinist, and a silent helmsman. The conversation at meal time was not very inspiring. I wandered back and forth on deck for several hours and enjoyed the beautiful evening. The moon shone and the stars were mirrored in the calm waters. The ocean glowed as the ship cut through, and a faint streak of light showed where we had sailed. In the moonlight the hills of Vancouver Island and the small islands, which leave only a narrow channel, stood out wonderfully against the night sky. I went down to my cabin at about ten o'clock. It had none of the elegance of the cabins on an ocean liner. Nevertheless I had a sound and healthful sleep. This morning at six I was awakened by much noise. We had docked a few miles above Nanaimo for coal. The heaps of coal and the barrows full of coal standing on the gravel roads looked strange in the beautiful wooded landscape. Everywhere the glorious forests of pine and spruce reach down to the water. Once in a while a small farm can be seen on a low rocky island. On the water the Indians drift about in their canoes, fishing. At 6:30 we sailed on.

The high mountains of Vancouver [Island] rise in the west, their ravines filled with eternal snow. To the east are the pinnacled mountains of the mainland. After breakfast I had the Indians tell me a story. I was told the long-drawn-out tale of Masmasalmix[?], the creator of all things. I had already heard the beginning of the story yesterday. We have just had lunch, and I must hurry and copy what I got this morning. Yesterday afternoon (the fifth) it began to pour. Nevertheless I ventured out to see the scenery. In the evening I wrote a few letters and copied the latest stories. The trip is very beautiful. The mountains are close to one another and the waterways between are very narrow. At three o'clock we were in Alert Bay but went on immediately to Newetti [Nawiti]. Here to the west was the ocean, while to the east were narrow passes and straits. At 11:30 we entered the strait which lies between Newetti and Georgiana Island. Before long we saw the Indian village. Pine forests stretch to the ocean.

Almost everywhere steep cliffs reach the water. Soon, however, we came to a flat spot. Behind this stood the Indian village, consisting of seven houses.

The steamer whistle blew and before long we saw forms who, wrapped in brightly colored blankets, had been sitting idly in front of their houses jump and up and run to the boats. Two boats were quickly launched and the men, wrapped in woolen blankets, rowed toward the steamer. The boats were loaded and we rowed to shore, while the steamer continued on her way. Each boat was made from a huge tree trunk which was nicely hollowed out and "gespritzt" [?]. There is a beak in front and back. Such a boat is hanging in the museum in New York. These here, however, are not as handsomely painted. They are the size of a whaleboat [?]. Just before we arrived here the weather had cleared and it was fine when we landed. The boat was pushed onto the sand and the bare-legged men carried us to shore and unloaded the boat.

On the way to the shore I heard them discussing me; since I looked relatively respectable they took me for a missionary. But I explained to them that I was no priest. I wished to go to an Indian home, and so we were taken to the home of the chief. Soon a large group had assembled in front of the bright wood fire. The house is about fifty feet long and is built of heavy planks. The rafters are held up by beautifully carved supports. The emblem of the owner's family is painted in black and red on the front wall of the house, which forms a flat gable. Platforms lying directly on the ground have been built onto the fronts of the houses. The lower ends are supported by posts and are surrounded by planks for protection. All day long the natives sit here on mats and gaze out to sea or converse with one another. The women wear the same kind of clothes as the men. Their hair is parted and in two braids which may either hang or be pinned up. Inside the house a slightly raised platform extends all the way round. On this, separate rooms have been erected. One of these will be my home for a few days.

In the afternoon I told the Indians what I wanted, and it seems they are willing to cooperate. The results of the first days are, of course, not very rewarding, since they must first learn what it is I want. An old man told me some stories and showed me the accompanying masks, which I intend to buy. There is a totem pole in front of one of the houses which I am going to draw. It has been explained to me. Last night, in a neighbor's house, I heard a medicine man at work. I went there to watch him. Left of the entrance to the house, a family was busy drying fish and baking cakes. A sick person, an old woman naked to the hips, lay in a room to the right. The doctor was bent over her, singing softly; he then apparently sucked the sickness out of the body. He blew it away, turned about and sang into his hands [did something in front of his mouth, back and forth (?)], and occasionally blew into it [?].

*October 7:* The evening was most interesting. There was a great pot-latch festival in the neighboring house, and of course I went to witness it. The people were very friendly and invited me to sit down. It was a weird sight. The house had been cleaned and the family partitions taken down, so that there was only a large square room. In the center of the room was a huge fire; on it stood a large kettle in which fish oil and halibut were being cooked. A man stood next to it with an enormous wooden spoon and stirred the concoction. The men and a few women sat on the platform which encircled the room. A man sat on the left holding a large drum on which the sun, the crest of the host, was painted. It all looked very weird lighted up by the wood fire. The Indians were all crouching with their backs against the plank which divides the . . . from the hall. They were packed closely together and sang to the beat of the drum. They clapped their hands and sang well in unison, while one man read the text. You should have heard with what intensity and enthusiasm they sang. The figures looked very strange. Their heads were bound in gaily colored cloths and they occasionally swayed backward and forward, while clapping their hands. The host stood alone in the middle and clapped his hands and sang. At the same time he looked after the food and tended the fire. The chief then arose and gave a long speech with raised voice and animated gesticulation. I was told that he praised the host, who, by the way, gave away about $200-worth on this occasion.

Finally I noted that I had become the subject of their speeches, but naturally I had no idea what they wanted. At last they sent a young man who had been in Victoria for some time to interpret for me. I must add that the natives were not too clear about why I was there and what I wanted and that they were making all kinds of conjectures. At first they thought I was a priest, and now, because I had bought nothing, they thought I might be a government agent come to put a stop to the festival. The missionaries and the Indian agent have done this, but the Indians have refused to take orders and continued to celebrate. The agent said he would send a gunboat if they did not obey, but they did not believe him and were not going to pay attention to the warning. Whether I wanted to or not I had to make a speech. So I arose and said: "My country is far from yours; much further even than that of the Queen. The commands of the Queen do not affect me. I am a chief and no one may command me. I alone determine what I am to do." (I was introduced as a chief as soon as I arrived here and am so introduced wherever I go.) "I am in no way concerned with what Dr. Powell (the Indian agent whom all the natives dislike) says. I do not wish to interfere with your celebration. My people live far away and would like to know what people in distant lands do, and so I set out. I was in warm lands and cold lands. I saw many different people and told them at home how they live. And then they said to me, 'Go and see what the people in this land do,' and so I went and I came here and I saw you eat and drink, sing and dance. And I shall go back and say: 'See, that is how the people there live. They were good to me and asked me to live with them.'" This beautiful speech, which fits in with their style of storytelling, was translated and caused great joy. A chief answered something or other, but unfortunately they mistook me for a very important personage and demanded a written statement from me that no gunboat would be sent. So I had to explain to them that the Queen was somewhat more powerful than I, but I promised to say that I liked to see them sing and dance. They were satisfied with this and promised to make a big celebration for me tomorrow. I think I managed the affair quite well. Until a few minutes ago all the chiefs have been coming to see me to tell me that the "hearts" of all their people were glad when they heard my speech.

I must now write all that went before. At noon gifts were distributed. Everyone received a few blankets and $2 from the host, which they then took home. In the afternoon the host, to show his importance, chopped up his new boat and used it to make a fire. In the meantime the chief talked another two hours. Of course I do not know what he said, but I hope to know tomorrow. Then everyone took a burning piece of wood, carried it to his house, and threw it on his own fire. The celebration ended this evening with a big feast given by the host.

I gathered much material today: two long, long stories from the two big chiefs. I have been looking for these stories for a long time. I also saw the masks which belong to these stories, but unfortunately they are not well carved or painted. It is unfortunate that earlier collectors carried away good material without obtaining the stories that go with it. In many instances this cannot be rectified, or rectified only with great difficulty, because it would take a very long time to get all the information about them. I wonder how they will take it when they find that I want to buy the masks. I will be satisfied with the results of this trip, if things continue as they have so far. The surroundings remind me so vividly of the time spent among the Eskimo—the natives with their original customs and habits, and among them only one white man!

# ILLUSTRATIONS

Franz Boas on His Way to Baffinland, 1883
(Courtesy of Franziska Boas)

Marie Krackowizer and Franz Boas' Engagement, *ca.* 1886
(Courtesy of Franziska Boas)

Franz and Marie Boas in New York, *ca.* 1896
    (Courtesy of Franziska Boas)

1911 in Teotihuacan, Mexico (*above left*, Franz Boas; *right*, Mexican assistants; *below left*, Marie K. Boas; *right*, Alice Krackowizer)

(Courtesy of Franziska Boas)

Franz Boas on Board a Steamer, *ca.* 1923
  (Courtesy of Franziska Boas)

Portrait of Franz Boas, *ca.* 1930
(Courtesy of Franziska Boas)

*October 8:* The days seem interminably long, and I could not get on without the aid of this diary. I see so incredibly much that is new to me. It would be better to record things consecutively as they happened today, but I prefer to give my impressions of the big dance I witnessed tonight while they are still fresh in my mind. I had announced that I would distribute food tomorrow if they would end today's celebration with a dance. Naturally they were more than willing. The chief came to me and said: "When a chief comes to visit we do not celebrate with a dance but because the chief from a distant land came to us, we shall hold a dance. Go to your house and await us." In the meantime the house was cleaned and all the [partitions?] for the family were taken out. A very large fire was made. Three old people were seated at the entrance on the left. They all held dance sticks and one played the large drum. Loud screeching was heard outside and a wild horde entered dancing. In the lead was the chief, a man certainly over sixty. He had been given a uniform by the Indian agent so that he could serve as policeman and keep order, and, especially, prevent the holding of large festivals. In order to carry out this duty he wore the uniform and carried the British flag, which he declared with the greatest pride had been given him by the king. A second chief followed, carrying a large flag. Singing and beating with sticks on the walls of the house were heard outside.

The first two figures to enter were naked to the waist, around which the fabled snake, *Sisiutl,* was coiled. Around their necks they wore large rings of hemlock branches. In their right hands they carried two sticks to which bright placards were attached; in the left hand of each was a gun. They had wound blankets about their legs. Their faces were completely covered with black paint, and on their heads they wore sealskin bands with bunches of red feather. Two Minks followed, wearing the stuffed animals on their heads. Their shirts were white, and white blankets were wrapped around their legs. Then followed a man with a horrible headdress. He was completely enveloped in a blanket, under which he carried a rattle which he shook. The next was most strangely attired. He wore a dance blanket trimmed with copper pieces, the kind that are highly prized for trade. These were the most important participants in the dance. The rest of the crowd were painted and looked equally strange and mysterious. Some wore enormously tall caps made of cotton which was stretched over sticks. All were painted black, some with red-painted eyelids, and they had decked themselves out with hemlock branches. As long as the two danced, the *Sisiutl* jumped about within a circle formed by the others. They danced either on one leg or jumped about while crouching. While dancing they swung their weapons and sticks wildly, without interruption. The *Tsogoala* (those with the dance blankets) jumped more wildly than any others. As soon as the chorus joined in and they all began to dance, the Minks jumped out wildly and became the chief actors. It is very funny to watch the tiny tots, who can scarcely stand, dance and imitate the grownups. A little two-year-old girl tried very hard to imitate the postures of the women. By the way, only men and children danced. The whole presented an indescribably wild picture. The dance in all its various phases, which are impossible to describe because they cannot be grasped at once, lasted about a half hour. They left the house singing, and danced away until they scattered. This dance is supposed to have been invented by the Nootka, on the west coast. It is danced here because the father of the chief comes from there. When Nootka Indians come to visit, the Indians from here go to meet them in boats which have been tied together and in which they dance.

Now we return to this morning. Early in the morning my host told me the story of his house posts, of which I have made drawings. But that was all, since there was a celebration out of doors. As I heard later, a little boy had fallen from his boat into the water. The father felt such shame that he had to make a potlatch, a present-giving party, in order to redeem himself. He therefore gave away $20 and many woolen blankets. Is it not a strange notion that, in order to make the awkwardness of his child praiseworthy, the father found it necessary to make a show of his generosity? I then wandered about in the houses to see what I could discover. I learned quite a bit because a young man explained everything to me. Above all I learned about the large ancestor figures which stand near the entrances of the houses. They have hollow mouths, and at a potlatch the chief stands behind the figure and talks through the mouth. It sounds as though spoken through a megaphone, and gives the impression the ancestor is speaking. My host then showed me masks which may be seen only by the initiated; boys may not see them. Since everyone was celebrating, I took the opportunity to draw the houses with their large paintings. It was a very good day for this because the sun was shining brightly after a day of rain.

*October 9:* I did not wake up very early today, presumably because I do nothing but draw and listen to stories. I was dissatisfied yesterday but I made up today for what I missed yesterday. I am unable to copy my notes evenings because the light is poor, and I am afraid I shall fall behind. First this morning I had the men tell me stories, and then I went out to finish the drawing of the house I had started yesterday. In the meantime the men again had a potlatch. Fortunately they were finished at noon and I had the opportunity to get a story, after which I drew the totem pole, the only one standing here, and then went for my mid-day meal.

I had been told that the third chief was most unhappy that I had not sought him out, so I had to remedy that. But first I held my own "potlatch" to pay for the dance held yesterday. I had a large fire built, in the middle of the house, over which two big bowls of rice were cooked and then roasted[?]. The house had been cleaned for the festival. Soon all the men assembled. The first to come were three greybeards who are always together and always to be found on the [platform?] in front of the houses. Gradually the others came and sat down on the platform which extends around the house. A drum was brought, and while the boy whom I had engaged as cook stirred the concoction the entire company sang their songs. So far I have transcribed only one melody. The melody is so foreign to me that I find it difficult to record, and I am very much out of practice. After four or five songs had been sung (I have already described this), the dishes were passed and everyone ate busily. When they were almost finished, the chief arose and gave a long speech, which was interpreted for me. "This chief," he said, pointing at me, "has come to us from a distant land, and all our hearts are glad. He is not like the other whites who have come to us. His heart is pure and kind toward us Indians. None of the King George men (English) or the Boston men (Americans) gave us . . . festival. But his people must be good and he shows that he has the heart of a chief. Whoever of us shall meet him, will be glad and recognize him as a great chief. We are glad he came and hope he will return. My heart is friendly toward him and if he wants anything from us we shall do our best to do what he asks." I accepted the speech with proper composure and gave some tobacco to every man. There were thirty men, one woman, and a few children. It seems women take part only if no male member of the family is alive. When all was over they got up and carried what was left of the food to their wives.

About a quarter of an hour later I went to the third chief, taking all manner of trinkets along, and told him that I knew he was a great chief and that he should tell me the story of his family as the other chiefs had done. He speaks no Chinook [Jargon] and I had to use an interpreter. It finally got so dark that I could do no more.

*October 10 and 11:* I was unable to get to my diary yesterday because of a mass of material, and I find it difficult to recapitulate. Yesterday was a fine day, and I spent some hours in the morning drawing, in different settlements. My ability in this line is not very great; I shall have to have everything redrawn later. The potato fields and the grass turned out badly. I must still try to make a drawing of a platform and then I should be finished. In good weather the natives spend all their time in the open. There they sit, wrapped in blankets, leaning against [platforms in front of houses?], talking, singing, or giving speeches. There is a small or large potlatch almost every day, which of course interrupts my work. But since I know what to expect, I make use of this time for drawing. Yesterday they came to me in large numbers and I obtained a great deal, so that I should be satisfied. Stories were told and objects were shown until nightfall.

Tomorrow I shall start to buy things. I wonder how I shall fare. This morning I rode out and visited a few spots in order to be able to draw a map of this place, also to visit the graves. I found them. ... I was interrupted by the arrival of Herigon, who I had asked to bargain for me because I am supposed to be too aristocratic to do any trading. In other words I would be cheated right and left. He said there were two masks I could get for 15 blankets; i.e., $7.50. I did not think I could get them for so little and am glad to buy them, since I have the whole story. Well, I found the graves decorated with flags. The corpses are in small houses which are covered with woolen blankets. Next to each grave is a wooden figure, decked in bright cloths, and beside it is an enormous spoon, which serves as a bowl. The location is very beautiful—the top of a cliff, rising from the sea. It is difficult to climb through the underbrush to the graves, which are among gorgeous firs. The old ones are covered with a green growth. In the evening I tried to scramble inland but soon gave up because the undergrowth is so thick that one cannot penetrate in ordinary clothes, and without knife and ax. I do not know whether I mentioned that we are situated near the northern end of Vancouver Island. The weather here is supposed to be, for the most part, stormy and rainy, but so far it has been very beautiful. I hope it will stay this way for the voyage to Alert Bay. I think I shall leave here on Friday so that I can work on the language [Kwakwala] at Alert Bay.

*October 12:* I had a miserable day today. The natives held a big potlatch again. I was unable to get hold of anyone and had to snatch at whatever I could get. Late at night I did get something [a tale] for which I have been searching—"The Birth of the Raven." It is unfortunate that the work here has to stop for a while, since I have such fine leads. It is especially curious that myth cycles do not seem to be alike among the different tribes speaking the same language, although I am not sure how much of this may be due to my ignorance concerning the myths. At present I am quite confused by the amount of nonsense to which I must listen. I expect to leave for Alert Bay the day after tomorrow. Except for two, I have bought the best masks available. These two they will not let me see because they are afraid to show them to an uninitiated person. Perhaps I shall still get to see them. I have bought quite a number of good articles and hope to get more. Life here is now quite montonous. This afternoon I put two women to work to weave mats and baskets for me. They are all intended for the museum collection.

*October 13:* The big potlatches were continued today, but people found time to tell me stories. This morning I had them describe the winter dances, and I wrote down the texts of the songs that accompany them. Everyone is most anxious to tell me something. I bought quite a number of things and also drew a few carvings which I wanted. I expect to get a large number of objects tomorrow. There was another big dance in the evening. These dances really present a wild picture. What must the large winter dance be like?

This evening the young men and children danced. We heard them approach from the distance, singing, and then heard the heavy, rhythmic beats on the walls of the house. The young men entered first and performed a wild dance, accompanied by their own song. The rhythms are so difficult that I am afraid I shall not be able to record one of them, although I very much want to. The young men were dressed either all in white or all in red, except the lead dancer, who wore nothing but a shirt. Their hair and eyes were sprinkled with eiderdown and their faces painted black. They carried nothing in their hands but moved them in rhythm. After they had danced the first figure, which was a slowly danced procession, the boys came leaping in, as naked as they were born. They were completely covered with flour, and all manner of figures had been painted in black on their chests and abdomens—one a face, another stripes encircling the body, or a cross in front and two big red spots in back on the shoulders. The hair above their foreheads had been heavily greased and stood straight up. The entire group of dancers now formed a circle, the boys standing with their backs to the entrance door. An older man stood on the steps that lead from the door into the house. He held two white cloths which he moved in accordance with the dance movements, now to the right, now to the left. A man with a drum stood to the left of the entrance.

A few figures of the dance were really beautiful. For example, the leader leaped forward, and following his lead the group, arms spread out above their heads, danced to the right, then to the left. Many of the dance forms end in a deep growling sound while the dancers bend their bodies toward the ground. The people have a tremendous fondness for the dance. The onlookers became so excited that they repeatedly jumped up and joined in the dance. The women, particularly, took part in this manner. They dance in a very curious fashion. Their hands are raised to the height of their heads, the palms turned outward. While dancing, both men and women jerk their heads from side to side in a lively fashion. One must admit that these dances are full of artistry. It is the head dancer's duty to organize the dances. One often sees him wandering back and forth in front of the houses teaching the boys to sing.

After the dance was over, all the dancers went from one house to the other. As soon as they were heard approaching, oil was poured onto the fire so that the flames shot up brightly. If this was not done it was taken to mean that they were not wanted. The dance was not finished until they had visited all the houses. In the evening my host told me another story. There is always quite a crowd around the wood fire. I sit with them on the big family chair, leaning against its back. The room is the size of a medium-sized Eskimo hut. It is bounded on the right and left by beautifully carved, slanting boards. The floor serves for mats on which the other people lie or crouch, or they lean against the rests. When stories are told or the conversation becomes lively, the women prefer to rest on their knees and elbows, with the heads propped up.

*October 14:* Another big dance was announced for tonight, but it did not materialize. I bought quite a number of things, however, and my collection is becoming valuable. I hope I shall have no ill luck with it.

*October 15:* I barely had a chance to write yesterday. I really intended to leave but was unable to do so because I still wanted to buy some things. I recorded nothing today except for a few little morsels I picked up here and there, but I completed my collection. I obtained all the ornaments that belong to one dance and am very happy about it. What I have now I certainly would not sell for less than $200. It is the only collection from this place that is reasonably well labeled. I, too, have not been here long enough to understand everything completely, but I have accomplished a good deal. Today I was a real businessman and [acted?] as though I had stood behind a counter all my life. I hope I shall be able to enlarge the collection in Alert Bay. The *Boskowitz* passed today, having left Victoria yesterday morning. I went out to her in a canoe and learned that she will return in about six days. If the wind is favorable I shall go to Alert Bay tomorrow. I hope the weather will be fine and I hope I shall find some letters there. I had the post office forward them and shall be very glad to have some news again. During this last week and a half I have felt as though I have been cut off from the world for an endlessly long time. In about ten days I will surely be back in Victoria. I am very glad, for I shall feel nearer to everyone!

*October 16:* It is Saturday evening, and still I have been unable to leave. This morning I could not get a boat; later the wind was from the east and we could not leave. Now the wind is from the west, and I hope it will stay that way so that we can get there and I can get to work by Tuesday. If the winds are favorable we could be in Alert Bay by tomorrow night. Of course we cannot leave if a storm should blow up, and the sky to the south does not look propitious. It is very unpleasant to be so dependent on the weather. The morning was spent attending to all manner of small matters. Since I did not have to spend much time in making purchases, I succeeded in filling gaps in a number of the stories. I have now procured about all I wanted. My collection is quite imposing: sixty-five articles. Today I obtained a few more facts about a dance and a handsome mask. I hope we can leave tomorrow. There is not much more that I can do here.

*October 19:* I must now write up the happenings of the last few days, and what days they were! Sunday morning the sky was clear and beautiful. Saturday I had made a few more purchases, and everything had been packed. Early, at 6:30, we finally started, and while we were loading the boat Ned's (that is what Herigon is called) Indian wife made coffee for us, which we gulped down hurriedly. We were ready to sail about 7:30. There was no wind and we had to row hard against the current. During the first hour we grew very hot because the sun was burning our backs and there was no breeze. Gradually we noticed that the water had become somewhat rippled, and we sailed eastward without effort, carried along by a gentle wind. After a few hours we had passed the chain of islands which separated us from the Gulf of Georgia. We then had to pass along the coast for about seventeen sea miles. Here there was no protection from the sea to the west. There was no wind and we had to take to the oars, but not for long. Soon a strong wind sprang up and rapidly became stronger and stronger. It was not too much for our boat, and we hoped to reach Alert Bay in the evening. We had to cross a deep bay, Hardy Bay, which is about three miles in width. We were about one mile from shore when the wind became bad and the waves began to break over our heavily laden boat. It was wiser to turn back; we sailed into the bay and sought shelter in a protected spot along the shore. It was about one o'clock. We ate a frugal meal of dried beans and fried bacon which was most excellent after all that hard work. Toward four o'clock the wind seemed to abate somewhat. The whitecaps disappeared and we decided to sail on. Barely fifteen minutes after we had left shore, the sky began to cloud over and the wind became stronger from minute to minute. It was a steady wind, not intermittent as previously, and so we were able to cross the bay easily. By midnight the wind was very strong, the trees on the shore along which we were sailing trembled and creaked, and we decided to spend the night in a well-protected cove.

We were about one and one-half miles from Fort Rupert. We could see it from the entrance of our little harbor. There seemed to be about sixteen houses, one of them enormous—the house of the chief. It is said that three years ago, in order to show his greatness, he gave a feast in which he gave away $3,000 in cash to his people and those of neighboring tribes. As a result he is very highly respected. I had decided, in the event of bad weather, to visit the settlement yesterday, but it turned out to be a very fine day. The night before, we anchored our boat and slept very well beside a warm fire, under the branches of a magnificent cedar. At six in the morning we packed up and, since the weather seemed fine, started out. It was calm outside of the harbor and we rowed for about one and one-half miles. After that a light breeze carried us to *Tlikse'na* in two hours. Since Ned wished to leave part of his cargo there, we landed in a small cove. There is no Indian settlement here, only a rather large spread-out farm which lies on flat land at the foot of the mountains. The soil is rich and black, and the owner, whom I had met during my first days in Victoria, raises potatoes and breeds cows and sheep. We built a fire on the beach and cooked our mid-day coffee. I pressed for departure because I was afraid the wind might grow stronger, but my friend Ned was not to be hurried.

It soon appeared that he preferred to stay there, so I took an Indian and a boat, packed my few belongings, and we continued on our way. More quickly than was to be expected, the wind rose to storm's height. All my life long, I think, I shall remember this canoe trip. First we had to pass through heavy seas, after which we reached calm waters under the protection of land. The wind, however, reached storm proportions. Heavy blasts, which could have easily overturned us, were especially dangerous. Fortunately the wind did not often strike our side so that we were able to keep the boat upright by sitting on its edge and bending far over. Because of the great pressure of the wind the boat was rapidly being pushed leeward, and to our horror we saw that only under the most favorable circumstances would we be able to pass by a small island which lay ahead of us. To complete our bad luck the rope of the sail became entangled during a gust of wind, so that we could not close up the sail. In less than half a minute the boat hit a rock with full force. The "Schoten" [?] were torn and the rudder behind which they had been caught was thrown on shore.

A rapid examination showed that the boat itself had suffered little injury. It was fortunate that we had been cast upon a flat rock. A few feet farther on, the rocks rose perpendicularly from the water, and I do not know what would have happened to us there. We could not remain where we were because the water was rising. The land rose steeply behind the place where our boat lay. We had to go on. With great effort we floated the boat and drifted on with the wind. It was most difficult to steer the boat. I helped as best I could, but I do not know much about sailing. The two of us held on to the sail so that it could catch the wind, and finally we came in sight of the settlement at Alert Bay. My spirits did not rise, however, until we were in the smooth waters of the harbor and our sail was down. This journey was just as bad as the one in Salmon Fjord on October 18, 1883 (the same day).[4] At that time the waves broke over our boat and we could hardly keep it from overturning because of the heavy ice.

Alert Bay is a well-protected cove on a small island which is about two miles long. The settlement is stretched out along the flat shore and is much larger than the one at Newetti [Nawiti]. At the west end, separated from the rest by woods, there is a pleasant house with a vegetable and flower garden. It is large and has a nice verandah. It is the home of Mr. Hall, the missionary. The church is on this side of the woods at the west end of the settlement. Then come the Indian houses, which do not seem to have been much influenced by the mission. Only one shows a painting, but there are many totem poles and the gables of the houses are gaily painted or ornamented with painted figures. Just as in Newetti, men and women were crouching on the platform in front of the houses, conversing and looking out to sea. When they saw our boat approaching they all ran to shore to help us. Here, too, the water was somewhat rough. I jumped on shore, and soon the boat had been pulled onto dry land. My Indian friend and I laughed about our trip, and he said to me: "*Maika kakoa manita, maika haiach kuli kopa eti!*" ("You were just like a deer, so quickly you jumped on shore!") I then went to the dock and the Indians showed me Mr. Spencer, who was busy making some repairs.

First of all I must continue to describe the settlement. East of the row of houses a stately dock has been built, together with a large storehouse. This is where Spencer stores and packs the salmon, and here the salmon is canned. His pleasant home is above the cannery, and a little to the east is a row of small cabins like the ones I described in Victoria. These are rented to friends, and I was housed in one of them. I found Spencer on the dock, and the first thing he told me was that my belongings would be locked up. I then asked for my mail. There was an enormous quantity and I went into the house to read it. It was a great joy to hear from you after an interval of two weeks. I

4. He is referring to an incident during his field trip in Baffinland.

was still in the midst of reading my mail when I suddenly saw a steamer round the point and steer into the harbor. Asking immediately for pen and paper, I had time to write two words to Marie before the steamer was ready to leave again. She stayed here only five or ten minutes. The steamer had been sent to carry salmon and wood from the north to Victoria, where some ships were awaiting the cargo. I was very glad to hear from Uncle Kobus that Aunt Phips is better and that they arrived in New York safely. Spencer then introduced me to his family, and I found his wife, whose mother is an Indian, to be very pleasant. We conversed a good half hour. I told him what I wanted to accomplish here and he promised to help me, which is worth a great deal to me, since of course he speaks the language.

By this time it was four o'clock. Since I did not wish to waste the entire day I went out and drew the houses and totem poles. When it began to get dark I went indoors, and soon it was time for dinner. I must say that I enjoyed the warm room and the good food for a change. Life in this "nest" is most strange. Just as I dropped in, someone or other appears almost daily, stays a few days, and departs. Only five or six white people live here, and they do not seem to have much to do with one another. Besides myself, the Indian agent from Comox is here with his eleven-year-old son, and a man and his wife who have bought some land. In addition, at mealtime Spencer's two brothers-in-law appear. I also met two men whom I had seen in Newetti. They have been commissioned by the government to look for fertile lands. I spent the evening with the [Spencer] family. Mrs. Spencer was very gracious and told me many stories, which I recorded later in the evening. I see I am quite well posted; it is difficult to find something new to tell me. Well, I have been collecting like mad.

It was not necessary to invite me to sleep more than once. I slept like a log. This morning, the nineteenth, I caught up with my diary. At ten o'clock I went to see Mr. Hall. I had to walk through part of a beautiful forest. Old trees lay on the ground to the right of me, and a new generation rose above them. There are huge cedars along the road. The handsomely carved boats of the Indians stand under them. It is now the time of great celebrations and the people go about gaily painted. Slanting red stripes are painted across their faces, or black circles around their eyes, or they are painted in any other way that custom or preference may prescribe. Soon they assembled, and, as I was walking toward the pleasant home of the priest, I heard the muffled sound of a drum, hand-clapping, and monotonous song. The mission seems to have little influence here; otherwise these festivals would be the first to disappear. There are many Kwakiutl from Fort Rupert here, who have been invited to a large potlatch which is to take place soon. By appointment I went to Mr. Hall's at ten o'clock. Several Indians and an interpreter were there and we spent a few profitable hours. But Mr. Hall has no conception of the methods and aims of ethnological work. I hope I opened up some viewpoints to him. I certainly know more about the people than he does. I have learned a great deal in these two weeks; even today I learned more, although not as much as I should like. At noon I went to lunch and then wandered about the village trying to get people to talk to me. During the first days, one wastes an awful amount of time in these places. I had the opportunity to buy a mask and hope to get more. I want the collection to be worth $500, preferably more, so that it will pay for the trip. I had an appointment with a young man this evening who told me a long story, parts of which I already knew. Later, until 10:30, I caught up with my diary. On these trips I usually go to bed at 9:30 because the light is very poor.

This morning, the twentieth, I went to the village to find someone to tell me stories. I collected two Kwakiutl family histories and then found a woman who related the heroic deeds of the Mink. In the afternoon I got some information about a fabled figure and about one of my masks. This evening the cannibal was explained to me. I have been looking for this for a long time but could never get it. As a result I want to buy quite a number of pipes that belong to the tale (I could not get them—remark from Victoria). I think the *Boskowitz* will arrive Saturday and I shall return to Victoria. I shall be glad to get the letters which I shall find there. Again it seems as though I have had no word for ages. I shall try to get hold of a Tlingit and a Bella Coola when I am in Victoria. I am afraid I will not be able to accomplish anything with the Songis of Victoria because they are always full of whiskey.

*October 23:* I have been unable to write these last few days, being always busy with something or other. During this time I have bought a rattle belonging to a long story, and a mask. My collection now consists of seventy pieces. I haven't much to tell about my life here. It is quite monotonous. I go about visiting and listening to stories, then write until my fingers are lame. It has become difficult to get much that is new because I am so well acquainted with the mythology. I shall have to work hard in Victoria, reread everything, and, if possible, copy it. Otherwise I shall lose control of my material. Thursday at noon I received an invitation to dinner from the missionary, Mr. Hall. I went there at six o'clock and spent a pleasant evening. The party included Mr. Hall and his wife; Mr. Price, who is Mr. Hall's assistant; the Indian agent from Comox and his small son and myself. After dinner we retired into Mr. Hall's pleasant study and had a long conversation about Indians. I hope I inspired Mr. Hall to make a number of studies. He promised to follow up certain matters of which I spoke. In the afternoon I visited Mrs. Spencer and had her tell me some tales. Unfortunately she is not well or I should really bother her. She relates well and is very gracious. I have obtained much about the usages of women from her. This is now an important part of my collection.

Yesterday morning at nine o'clock I again went to Mr. Hall to give him my texts. He will translate them, but I have discovered that he does not know the language well enough. It may be that he will be able to do something with the help of the natives. At any rate it is clear that I have transcribed the texts quite well, because the Indians always understand when I read to them. In the afternoon I got an accurate description of the distribution of the tribes. This is an important part of my work. Unfortunately, I can make only a beginning, for in order to do it properly I should have to travel about and would have time for nothing else. In the evening an Indian came to tell me stories after which I went to bed, expecting the steamer to arrive during the night. She did not arrive, however, and I am still here today. I went to Hall again and gave him the remaining texts. Now I can do nothing because the Indians are having a festival. This morning it rained heavily but now the sun is shining brightly. I wish the steamer would come soon. I cannot find much to do. If it does not arrive, I shall go and bother Mrs. Spencer again this afternoon.

# 2

Letter-Diary to Parents
(1886)
(*Continued*)

*October 26—Victoria:* I did not write for several days because it was very uncomfortable and crowded on the steamer. Saturday [October 23] afternoon I went to see Mrs. Spencer, and she was kind enough to tell me all I wanted to know. The information I obtained from her was the most valuable I received in Alert Bay. I spent the evening with a few Indians, who told me more stories. At night, at one o'clock, we were awakened by the cry that the steamer had arrived. Jumping quickly out of bed, we gathered up our woolen blankets. But the steamer took her time and we were on the pier a long time before she docked. We had an unpleasant surprise: all the beds were occupied. There was a place only for the one woman who was with us. Eight of us were leaving from Alert Bay. Provisional quarters were put up for us in the hold, and at about four o'clock we could lie down quite comfortably and finish our night's rest.

The weather was bad and our progress slow. This is the most horrible ship I have ever experienced. The *Ardandus,* on which I sailed from St. Johns to New York, was an angel compared to this one. Tuesday morning it took the utmost effort to advance half a mile per hour. The wind blew against us with all its force. The ship was very full, and I was quite amused to see that I was regarded as a stranger. The passengers all seemed to know one another, all seemed to be more or less related, so that the settlers from north of Comox all the way up to Alaska almost constitute one family. They know one another inside out and know what everyone's salmon, goats, cows, wife, and children are doing. There were a number of children on board who, together with their mothers, were miserably seasick on Monday. I suppose I should describe some of the people I met. The most distinguished and oldest of the settlers is Mr. Duncan from Mextlaqatla [Metlakatla] in the Tsimsian country. He is a well-known character, having gone there as a missionary in 1857. He told us that at the spot we were at that moment passing his boat had been attacked by natives and that he had to be very careful in the beginning. He is the strangest missionary I have ever met. Besides being a missionary, he owns a large salmon fishery and makes a great deal of money. He is very animated and talks without stopping, more about business matters than anything else. Originally he was a member of the English church, but when Bishop Ridley came to Mextlaqatla [Metlakatla], according to a letter which was sent me and forwarded from Minden, small difficulties arose and he finally left the church. Apparently his pride suffered because he was no longer first in the settlement. Since then bitter enmity exists on both sides.

Most Indians follow their old teacher, Duncan. Apparently conditions up there are very unpleasant at present. Instigated by Duncan, the Indians show great opposition to the surveyor who has been sent there to survey the land. People who understand the situation are opposed to Duncan and consider him a great humbug, but he has many friends here in Victoria.

In addition, there was on board a young girl from the Bella Bella mission. At her request, and so that I could learn the language, I taught her how to take down folktales, and she promised to collect some for me. There was also a Mr. Clayton, a nice man whom I had met up there. He has many interests and understands Bella Coola well, having lived among them for a long time. I talked to him so much that he promised to write down stories during his free time in the winter and send me copies. He really showed understanding of the points suggested. The rest of the company was not very interesting. I must mention the captain, the most unpleasant grouch imaginable. Everybody scolds and complains about the man and his ship. I have never heard anything like it.

Monday morning we made scarcely any progress. Toward noon, however, the wind died down and we sailed ahead. There was great excitement, especially among the seasick ladies, over whether the captain would take the inside or the outside course. The inner course is like a river, whereas the outside sea is very rough. At first we turned seaward but soon turned to the inner course. Before long we sighted Departure Bay, where we had taken on coal on the outward journey. Signs of civilization became more frequent, and soon Nanaimo lay in front of us. It was a friendly sight to see our first city. We continued on our way and after we had passed through some narrows, whose waters rushed furiously and threw the ship about, it became dark, and all the passengers assembled in the warm cabin. I really do not know how it happened, but I had to recount and after a little while I noticed that I was the only one speaking. This gave me a terrible fright, especially since I was speaking in English, but I could not very well stop, and I felt very uncomfortable.

Tuesday morning at seven we finally reached Victoria. I immediately went to the hotel and made myself respectable. My beard of three weeks' standing, which made me look like a monster, vanished, and I felt well again. Then I got my belongings and unpacked. At noon I went to the Bella Coolas and found them ready to tell me something new; I asked chiefly about language. Of course, the first thing I did in the morning was to get my letters. Later I lunched with Clayton, whom I like very much. I had much to do in the evening— letters to write, my diary to copy for Minden, etc.

*October 27:* I worked with the Bella Coolas and later wrote a long letter to Fischer, in Marburg. It is intended for publication in *Petermann's Mittheilungen.* I also wrote to Schurz about the museum, asking him not to forget me. My reports from here will probably be very meager; I shall have so much to write that I shall lose all desire to write them. Besides, I do not get to see much, nor to live like any other civilized person. I ate again with Clayton and Spencer. Clayton is going to make some inquiries for me in Bella Bella and get a few things which I need to complete my collections.

*October 28:* This morning I went to a photographer with Spencer (the business was formerly owned by Spencer) and borrowed a camera which I shall use in Comox. I hope the pictures will be better than the ones I took when I was among the Eskimo. Then I again wrote a long letter to Fischer in Marburg, for publication in *Petermann's Mittheilungen.*

So the poor "Flegel" is dead. The climate in Africa is horrible.

Afterward I went to the Bella Coolas. I am not very well satisfied with my results, although during these last three days the grammar of the language has become much clearer to me. But progress is slow. I want very much to collect folktales, but I have no opportunity to do so because there is no sensible person here. So I shall have to give it up. At noon I looked for Dr. Powell but could not find him.

I received a package of books today which had made a long journey. They were sent to me to Berlin by Bishop Ridley, from there to Minden, and then here!

All afternoon and evening I wrote for all I was worth. I see more and more that I must get a look at the myths of the Tlingit. The old records must have been edited, because they contain things I do not understand. Naturally the material [becomes more interesting? complicated?] the deeper one gets into it.

I expect to leave on Wednesday and will be in Comox on Friday. I shall then have a few days for Nanaimo. If I do not find anything I shall stay another week. The museum matter bothers me dreadfully. I wish it would end well, but it does not seem very likely, judging from Uncle's [Jacobi's?] letter which I received today. It is apparent that nothing will happen until I return; another reason why I should hurry. My work is well under way. The Bella Coolas tell me the most beautiful stories in their own language. The stories themselves are not worth much, but on the other hand the language is very worthwhile. Accompanied by my dear Catholic priest, I looked up the Tlingit lady, who told me things all morning long. I am occupied all the time.

Today as I was making up my accounts I became very much excited—$40 was missing! But fortunately I found it, in small silver coins in my trunk. I am very proud of the fact that my accounting up to now has been accurate. Altogether I have used up $280 since I have been here. How much more I will need depends upon what I buy in Comox. I am glad to pay out this money because I know it will be returned. According to prices in Victoria my collection should be worth $200 as curios. I paid $70 for it. Am I not a regular merchant?

*October 31:* This morning I went to the Bella Coolas and had them continue explaining the grammar of the texts I got yesterday. Only two more days, and I shall again be on my way, but this time into civilized regions. I hope to obtain another text tomorrow. The day after, I shall have to listen to a Tlingit tale, and then it will be time to leave. I am worried about my collection because fires are so common here. I am unable to send it to New York because of the duty. It would be much too expensive to store it in the customs house for any length of time. This afternoon I cannot find . . . so I shall visit Dr. Tolmie, as I have been intending to do for several days. Tomorrow night I shall go to see McDonald. I suppose I must show myself there some time.

Tonight I shall copy some of the material I have brought from Newetti. All that stuff is beginning to make me feel very stupid. The Eskimo tales are innocent compared with these. I have recorded one hundred and nineteen, among them a whole bookfull that have not been copied. At any rate the results of my trip will make a presentable book. I shall not be so stupid as to tear them up, as I did my Eskimo material [?].

*November 1:* I really do not wish to leave since my work is going so well, but it cannot be helped. I must go to Comox. I am putting off my departure for a week in order to see an exhibition. . . . This morning I went to the Bella Coolas and obtained a few stories and half of a text which I translated this afternoon. At noon I visited Dr. Tolmie, who wished to see an object from my collection, and I spent the afternoon until dark with the Bella Coolas. I wrote a few letters to Toni and Minden and then paid my long-postponed visit to McDonald. I told him I was going away again and would stay until Christmas. They do not load steamers during Christmas, but I hope I shall be on board the train by that time, traveling eastward. The evening was very pleasant and they were most gracious to me.

I also met Mr. Duncan, the missionary from Metlakatla. There is active warfare between the missionaries here. Duncan has done a great deal for the Tsimsian Indians during the twenty years he has been here, but when Bishop Ridley arrived he left the church. The Indians claim a large stretch of land as their own and used force to throw out the surveyor. Duncan is accused, and probably rightfully, of being the instigator. He is hated by the . . . inhabitants of the coast, who say he uses the mission only as a business to enrich himself. I know that he has done much for the Indians and in a more sensible way than most of the missionaries, by teaching the various crafts. But I am certain that these Indians [Tsimshians], in spite of appearing to be Christians, are as strange and crazy a group as all the others; there is enough proof of this. My personal impression of Duncan is that he is clever and ambitious, but one cannot judge from such a superficial acquaintance. It seems to me that the main question is whether the government has a right, without asking the Indians, to stake out reservations arbitrarily. In my opinion the difficulty lies in the fact that every Indian considers land personal property.

*November 2:* I shall not be able to leave tomorrow after all. I still have five pages of Bella Coola texts to translate, which I do not wish to neglect. I intend to go to Cowitschan [Cowichan] first, to learn a little about this tribe; then I shall go to Comox. I have a camera and plates and hope to get a few pictures. I shall be in Comox on the eleventh and remain four weeks so that there will not be much time left for work in Nanaimo or Alberni. But all that remains to be seen.

Today I finally made my much-talked-of visit to Dr. Powell. He told me that he had often been asked to organize the collection in New York but that he had not had the time to do so. He does not seem to know very much about Indian customs. At any rate I shall be able to do better than he. He was very gracious and gave me introductions to Cowitschan [Cowichan] and to Comox and promised to help me in every way possible. Fortunately I shall not need his help. I spent most of the day packing and making purchases. I was with the Tlingit in the morning and the Bella Coolas in the afternoon and am very tired from running and standing around. My collection from Newetti is packed and can be sent off as soon as I have written the address.

*November 4—Cowitschan* [Cowichan]: I have left Victoria at last, probably until December 10. Last night I did no more work because I had to pack. I had to buy several things yesterday morning, and afterward I went to the Bella Coolas and sat with them for four hours, without interruption! It was a dreadful session. In the afternoon I finished packing, had my cases secured with a few iron bands, took some fur-covered masks to . . . , and napped until six o'clock. I gathered my pack and took a cab to the very primitive Victoria railway station. The railway journey, which took about two hours, is almost more beautiful than anything I have seen as yet. The train passed through wonderful forests, along steep mountain slopes, over deep black canyons, and through lonely mountain scenery. Without doubt this landscape measures up to that along the Columbia River. This is primeval country in all its loneliness, and the train seems to traverse untrodden paths. For a European it is most interesting to see nature so free and untrammeled.

At 10:30 I reached Duncan and found myself standing alone on a small wooden platform—no station house or anything resembling one. I was surrounded by my six pieces of baggage (I travel like a lady, with endless baggage), and I looked about in vain for a kind soul to direct me to Cowichan. To the right I saw a house which was in the process of being built, but nowhere a living soul. After a few minutes some Indians passed by, driving a pair of oxen in an old-fashioned wooden yoke. They were pulling firewood to town in a boxlike trailer. Two white people followed them who told me it was seven miles to Cowichan. Upon asking about the Indian villages and explaining why I had come, I then learned that one of the men was the Indian agent to whom I had an introduction, and the other a storekeeper and boarding-house owner combined. So everything was *alright* (isn't that nice German?). The two men had come to pick up the mail which lay on the platform in a bag. I rode down with them and am now comfortably settled, in a whole house all to myself. I have not lived so well since I left New York. I have a large, pleasantly furnished room, and a bedroom. A bright fire is burning in the fireplace, and I am sitting at a small table, writing.

The Indian village is about two miles distant so that as soon as I have found the right people I shall be settled very comfortably. After lunch I went to the Indian agent, who promised to introduce me. There are three Indian villages in this neighborhood. All the villages I have so far seen were near the ocean; these are situated along a river which has its origin in a large lake. Scarcely one old-style house is left in the two villages which I saw today, but there are a few good ruins which I must draw or photograph. Lomas the agent went with me into one of the villages, where I obtained one story, quite a good beginning. I returned to this village but was not able to accomplish much because it soon grew dark. I hope I shall have good luck and get much that is new.

At 6:00 P.M. I went to dinner with my hosts, but I was a little early. Four children were playing in the room, the oldest about four, the youngest barely one year old. We soon became friends, and I spent the time until dinner playing with them, since my room was cold and uncomfortable. I had to tell them something about myself after dinner, because they wanted to know who their guest was. I then went to my room, found it lighted and a fire burning. I shall now copy my day's observations and then go to bed. It will certainly take me until eleven o'clock. Normally I go to bed around ten, rarely later.

*November 6:* I was cross last night and did not want to write. The Indians in the village were so suspicious and unapproachable that I could accomplish nothing. This morning I went to Somenos, the village two miles from my house, and obtained a few things, hoping to continue this afternoon. But for some inexplicable reason I could not get the people to talk. They evidently think I have come with some evil intent. As a result I wasted three hours without accomplishing a thing. This morning I had quite a scene in the upper village. I had my camera with me and photographed a handsome totem pole in front of a house. Shortly afterward the owner, a young man, appeared and demanded that I pay him, which naturally I refused to do so that I should not deprive myself of the possibility of photographing whatever I might wish. He declared that he was master of his land and would not permit me to leave until I paid. I replied just as quietly that I would leave when I felt like it. They always try to bluff strangers, and I know by this time how to counter them. I quietly proceeded to another house and continued with my work; lo and behold, it was not long before friend Indian followed and asked whether he might not interpret for me. I accepted, providing he would make himself useful, and today he sought out all the people who have the information I am seeking, and he helps me as much as he can.

I was here in the afternoon and wanted to photograph a painted house. Earlier I had held conversation with the owner, but he did not want to tell me anything. While I was putting up the camera he merely said it was his house and that he wanted a picture of it. The whites look upon the Indians not as humans but as dogs, and he did not wish anyone to laugh at things that were their laws, such as painted houses and articles used for celebrating their festivals. In spite of anything I could say, I could get nowhere with him, and, since I want something from this man, I did not insist. I said I cared nothing about the picture and spoke of other things. In this way I learned a great deal by subterfuge. A young man came with a stag and wanted me to take a picture of it. I placed him in front of the house I wished to photograph and so attained my end. But I have obtained nothing from the Indians out here. My host promised to accompany me to the village tomorrow, and since the people trust him I hope the ice will be broken. Last night I was completely out of sorts.

This morning I again took my camera to Somenos, photographed a nice post, and heard much of interest. I went back in the afternoon and stayed until 6 P.M. It is quite a lot to walk those two miles four times a day, and it takes too much time. I shall be surprised if I do not get fat—yesterday afternoon much sleep and fresh air! The road to Somenos is very pretty. It passes through woods or by farms on recently deforested land. The villages are situated in the broad valley of the Cowichan River. This valley can be seen stretching upward for twenty miles to Lake Cowichan. When I got there this morning the natives were occupied in catching salmon. They pushed two boats upstream, stretched a net between the two, and then came downstream as quickly as possible. For this they use extremely small boats, built like kayaks but open on top. The shape of the large boats here is also different from the shape of those farther north, and I must draw one before I leave. I must get busy and copy my day's material.

*November 8:* I find that my notes are very scant these days owing to the slow progress I am making. I must admit that this week has been the most unpleasant one I have spent in this region. I have to run about all day—twice a day two miles to the settlement—and there is very little to be found there. At least I know that the people here have an entirely different cycle of myths from those in the north, and this strengthens me in my belief that the myths here originate from two different sources. I was up there again yesterday and almost became impatient because of the long-drawn-out manner in which they told the stories. It really was a test of patience. In the afternoon I tried my luck in the other settlement but was unable to accomplish a thing. I persuaded my host to talk to them, since he knows them well; perhaps that will make things easier.

This afternoon I was in Somenos again and could do nothing, for the strangest reason. An old man who usually tells me stories was in best form when an equally old woman interfered. He said a man had lain dead for nine days and she said ten, whereupon he became so angry that I could not get another word out of him. These sessions are most amusing, but not that one. Yesterday two young men appeared and laughed when they heard the old man tell stories. He was ashamed because of it and said he would refuse to talk if others were present. Every five minutes he assures me he is the best among all the men here and knows everything. In the meantime screaming, dirty children run about; sometimes a meal is eaten. Dogs and chickens force their way between the people; the fire smokes so badly one can scarcely see. The old man watches to see that I write down every word he says, and, if I fail to do so, he takes it as a personal insult and holds a long speech of which I do not understand a word.

This evening I went to the settlement of Cowichan, which is in front of my house. My landlady's talk really helped; the old rascal who had forbidden all to tell me anything gave me a long speech, saying that he feared the chief but that now he would tell me some things because he knew I was a good man. But I was to repeat nothing. I already know these big lies! I also had trouble in Somenos this morning because I wanted to make a drawing. The Indians always try to bluff strangers with their impudence. Nowhere have I had such trouble as here. There is supposed to be an old cemetery up here. I shall go there tomorrow and try to get some skulls. At dinner this evening I met two men who had been on a wagon trip with my host Mr. Jaynes, and they were full of whiskey. I have rarely heard such elaborate speeches and such good advice, but the men were harmless and merely poured tea into their soup and put meat in their cups. Although this valley is very beautiful, I do not think that I shall return. Tomorrow is my last day here. I shall wait for . . . at the train in Nanaimo and go on to Comox.

*November 9:* It is unfortunate that I must leave tomorrow because I have just made a good beginning. An old man related so well about the first people that I shall try, if at all possible, to stop here on my way back. Perhaps I shall get the linguistic material which I need very badly in Comox; otherwise I should prefer to remain in Nanaimo. This morning I went down to the village, as arranged, only to find that my new friend, who goes under the name of Bill, was not at home. His wife gave a long speech of which I did not understand a word, and so I left and asked for him outside. I did not have to ask long, for I heard his stentorian voice issuing from one of the large houses standing on the steep bank of the river. He was giving a long speech. I climbed the stairs [a euphemism] which led to the house and found a large number of men assembled, crouching around two fires. A kettle in which half a freshly slaughtered pig was cooking was suspended over each fire. Beside the fires, sides of bacon hung on ropes and were being tried out into containers.

These houses are curiously constructed. Imagine a huge Westphalian barn, the roof constructed of heavy planks. The sides are made of planks tied horizontally to posts. Of course, the whole thing is a drafty hole and in order to prevent this, the walls on all sides are covered with rush mats. A platform about two and one-half feet high on which there are mats used for beds runs around the house. When several families live in one house, they separate sections with mats and wooden walls. In front of the houses stand posts, eight feet high, joined by beams. Poles are laid on top of the roof, places have been built for storing food and for seating guests who have come to watch a dance. In front of the house there is a stage on which the festival-giver stands and distributes presents to the guests.

Well, I found them all assembled in front of the fire discussing the case "Boas," or just about to begin. I understood an occasional word and gathered that they were discussing my wishes. The result was that Big Bill, who up to now had forbidden them all to tell me stories, said in the best Chinook [Jargon] that he would help me, and he has really kept his word. But there was nothing to be done then, since the big, warm dinner had first to be eaten. If I had understood their language, it would have been an excellent occasion for me to learn to make "after dinner" speeches—one may not say "drinking toast" here. The Indians make prepared speeches which last about two hours, apparently with great satisfaction to themselves and their listeners. I am afraid the content of the speeches would not be very pleasing to our society, for in them the Indians mainly take the opportunity to speak of presents they have formerly given and to boast that they have the heart of a chief [?].

After the meal I went home and wrote a long letter to Dr. . . . [in Berlin] in which I put on paper my heroic deeds here, in their best light, and told of some of the results I had obtained. The mail had arrived, but I received only a letter from Toni. I had expected three—from Marie, from Minden, and the one from Toni. Now I must be patient until Thursday.

At 11:30 I went down (to the village) and let them talk until 2:30. By that time I was hungry and ate my lunch. The teacher had promised to show me an old burial ground. She kept her promise, and I went down there at about 3 P.M. I picked up two especially well-preserved skulls because they showed [deformation?] of the head very well. I then asked Mr. Jaynes, my host, to buy a few things for me after I left, hoping thus to get them more cheaply. I also did some copying. Unfortunately it took so long to get the skulls that I did not get back until 4:30 and was unable to do much more. The days are very short; the sun disappears behind the mountains by four o'clock. My manuscript is now one hundred and sixty pages long. I hope it will make good progress in Comox! I think I have gotten the two most important stories from here; only the Raven is missing. It is very striking that I have obtained no hero stories.

*November 12:* Now at last I have arrived in the much-talked-of Comox and I wonder how I shall get on here. The day before yesterday I got up early, packed my belongings, and prepared for the trip. About ten minutes before it was time to leave I discovered that my wallet was missing, and although I searched frantically I could not find it. Perhaps someone will find it; otherwise I shall have lost about $35. I cannot understand how this happened unless it fell out of my pocket while I was chopping wood. There was no use staying here any longer, since I had only lost drafts, and so, in a bad humor, I got into Mr. Jaynes's wagon and rode to the station. A journey of one and one-half hours brought me to Nanaimo. It was a very fine bright day, and the landscape is magnificent. The train passes through dense forest, but often a view opens up on the right over the countless islands in the Gulf of Georgia, onto the wild forms of the Cascade Mountains. We were in Nanaimo at noon, and I went to Sabitson's Hotel. I greeted my old fellow-traveler and his wife and we wandered through the town of Nanaimo. It exists mainly because of the coal mines which are situated on the coast; the big steamers take on coal directly from the mines. The city is prettily situated on a slope and affords a view of Mt. Baker and the entire Cascade Mountain chain. I spent the afternoon writing letters and the evening with Sabitson at the bar of his hotel. I enjoyed watching the people there as they came and went.

One of the chief figures is the . . . old P——. He is usually somewhat drunk and likes to tell of his adventures with the Indians and about the time when there were no white settlers in this locality. There is also the farmer who complains that the Indians have all the best land, etc. At ten o'clock I went on board the steamer to sleep, since we were to sail early this morning. I woke up just as we were leaving Departure Bay. This vessel can boast of neither size nor speed, but the captain is friendly so that we had a pleasant journey. There were heavy seas in the Gulf of Georgia and a big storm blew up behind us, but since we were passing through narrow channels we were in good spirits and not seasick. Nothing was to be seen; all was veiled in clouds and occasional rain. At the dock here I met my old acquaintance Cliff from Newetti and of course went to his hotel. I inquired about conditions among the Indians and shall try my luck today. I got my letters ready for the steamer, which is going back today, copied the data of my last days in Cowichan, and went to bed. The sun is shining this morning and there is no wind. I am getting ready to go down to the village, which is about one and one-half miles from here.

*November 12—Evening:* The first day is over and I feel in an entirely different mood, because this time I have accomplished something. Mr. Cliff went to the Indian village with me this morning as he had promised. It takes about twenty-five minutes to get there. It is the saddest-looking village of any I have seen so far. It is apparent that the inhabitants are dying out rapidly. There are ruins everywhere, and beautifully carved totem poles stand in front of empty shells. The village is situated at the mouth of a small river. There is a good road from here which crosses some hilly country and then descends to the flat river valley. Opposite are the mountains of Vancouver Island; looking through a deep valley, high snow-covered mountains and glaciers are to be seen. Descending to the village, one passes a large cemetery with especially fine carved figures.

When we arrived the Indians were having a great feast. The Le'quittig [Lekwiltok], who speak the same language as the inhabitants of Alert Bay, lived in the first villages. These and the Comox were formerly open enemies, and the Le'quittig [Lekwiltok] frequently attacked the Comox, took them captive, and sold them to the north as slaves. As a result the southern tribes never go farther north than this place. The Comox live in the last houses of the settlement. Mr. Cliff, who has lived here for many years, introduced me so that they were very friendly. I have already written that I was under the impression that the Comox spoke two different languages. After some fruitless questioning I discovered that they have combined with the Penntatish [Pentlatch]. There is only one family of these left, the last of the tribe. I immediately made friends with them and am now learning this newly discovered language.

From the few words I have obtained in one day, I know that it, too, belongs to the Salish, but it has apparently been very much influenced by the language of the Comox. Pure Penntatish [Pentlatch] seems no longer to exist. I shall spend the next week learning the language and recording the myths. My ethnographic map of Vancouver Island will then be pretty good insofar as I have seen the country. The people at the hotel are very nice to me. You must not picture this hotel as anything like the Hoffman House in New York or the Central Hotel in Berlin. It is a large farm house, several rooms of which the owner has given up to boarders. It is more comfortable than at Cowichan. The small rooms are warm and we are well taken care of.

*November 13:* I made the unpleasant discovery today that I had forgotten my photographic plates in Nanaimo. It will be two weeks before I can get them. I went down to see the Comox today and made an attempt with connected sentences, but since I could not get the man to talk slowly I had to give up. I think I shall soon be able to find someone else. I then went back for lunch and worked on Pentlatish [Pentlatch]. I am hopeful that I shall get on well and that the people will also learn to speak well. This is always very difficult to accomplish.

I have obtained two stories and am again very busy. I feel much better here than I did in Cowichan, since I know that I am accomplishing something. This newly discovered language is affording me much pleasure and contributes much to raising my spirits, which had been very low as a result of Cowichan and the money I lost. I have much to do now as I have to prepare questions for the language study; that takes me at least two hours every day. Then I have to work up my results daily and walk for twenty-five minutes four times a day. So it is permissible to be quite tired by evening.

*November 14—Sunday:* I did not accomplish much today because the Indians had a great celebration. The Pantlatish [Pentlatch] family had invited everyone to a large feast, and so, of course, I could do nothing. I used the day for drawing, which, because of the cold, is no longer a very pleasant occupation. The ice formed at night does not melt during the day even when there is sun. It is quite pleasant in the sun however. I have finally succeeded in finding another Comox Indian who suits me better because he talks more slowly. Yesterday a hunting party returned from the north. Among them is a doctor who stays in this hotel; he apparently intends to remain for some time because he is thinking of settling here. I am quite pleased to have someone with whom I can occasionally converse. Today to my surprise I found a moundlike heap of shells near the Indian settlement. I shall have to take a shovel and dig a bit, but I must first find the owner.

*November 15—Monday:* Today I found something worthwhile: a very old, well-preserved skull. I discovered it in the mound I spoke of yesterday. I hope to find more tomorrow. This morning I walked along the beach in order to determine the extent of these shell-heaps and found that they extend for miles along the river and the seashore. There were human bones everywhere. I spoke to my neighbor Mr. Duncan about it this afternoon, and he told me that a farmer had dug up quite a number the day before yesterday. I secured one of them and hope to get the others. At any rate this one skull shows that the Indians who are living here now have made the shell mounds, because it is somewhat deformed, in the same manner as theirs are today.

This morning and afternoon I spent with the Puntlatish [Pentlatch]. I now have about four hundred words in both the Comox and Puntlatish [Pentlatch] languages. I still have no texts but hope to get some soon. It is always quite difficult to get started in a language, but I shall be very happy if I can get one thousand words and a few texts in both. Then I drew a pole and came home very tired because I had been running about endlessly. I also got a story today. As long as the weather remains so pleasant I will be very well satisfied. The walk to the village twice daily is nice, the people are kind and friendly, and I am having a real rest from my experiences in Cowichan. I wrote a letter to Virchow yesterday and again reported my results. I think I report about myself to Europe often enough!

*November 16:* I really have to work very hard. I don't understand the structure of the language very well as yet, and I want so very much to learn a good deal. I hope to have a good ethnographic map, and the people here are well informed about the neighboring tribes. At last I got my first text today, but progress is slow, slow! I am awaiting the arrival of the steamer most impatiently, since I have had no letters for a long time. Yesterday an acquaintance from Alert Bay arrived, with his wife and seven children. These, together with my landlord's five children, make this house a lively place. Mr. Petrock is an Indian agent and is moving to Fort Rupert. It must not be overly pleasant for the family to have to move into the wilderness. Aside from a few Indians, only one white trader and one other white person, whose occupation I do not know, live in Fort Rupert. I should certainly prefer Comox. There really is no village here, but the white inhabitants live on farms scattered throughout the extensive valley. The whole aspect is pleasant and well-to-do. The roads and the cattle are well kept, and as I walk along I continually meet some one either driving or on horseback or following work horses. It looks as though there might be a storm tonight; I hear the sound of the surf down by the harbor, and I suppose soon the wind will be here.

*November 17:* I am getting into real trouble because of the time left at my disposal. I wanted to stay here until December 8 and then return to Nanaimo. I have heard of another tribe in the vicinity of Vancouver which I must visit if it is in any way possible. But my difficulty is time. I want to get the ethnographic map into good shape, but I do not wish to give up the two languages I am now studying. I am afraid I shall have to leave December 2 because otherwise I shall not be able to be back in Victoria until Christmas, and I need another week in Victoria. I do not know what I shall do. I think I shall let it depend upon what I can accomplish here in the next two weeks and whether a stay of an additional week would be worthwhile. I am very sorry that the results of my trip are so contradictory to those of the good, old Dr. Tolmie. I have occasionally mentioned this old Hudson Bay man; I find that, although he is considered the chief authority in this region, he knows very little. He has lived here for fifty-three years! The *Boskowitz* has not yet arrived, and the Petrock family and their seven children are still here.

*November 18:* I am today sending off my schedule of lectures for next summer. I shall announce the lecture as Ethnography of Northwestern America. I do not know yet whether I shall announce the same subject for my student course [Privatkolleg], or Geography of America. The latter would cause me a great deal of work, which I dread, because the organization of the results of this trip is going to require much time.

I was greatly disappointed yesterday. A Comox woman narrated to me for two hours in Comox, and I thought I had obtained a nice text. While I was writing I wondered why there was so little narrative, only questions and answers, but this often occurs in tales and I did not worry much about it. But it turned out to be a made-up conversation: "How are you? Shall we go and look for berries? No, I do not feel like it, etc." Well, maybe now I shall get a text. They tried yesterday to raise their price but I did not agree. Fortunately they are nice enough not to cause any unpleasantness.

*November 19—Evening:* If ever I have been tired it is tonight. I must nevertheless record my activities of yesterday and today. I am so impatient for the steamer to arrive that I make myself especially busy to pass the time. The Indians were in good humor and so I got a good deal. As a matter of fact I get so much material that I cannot possibly work it over every day as I should like to. Fortunately for me the Puntlatish [Pentlatch] language has turned out to be closely related to Comox, which somewhat shortens my labors. I have found a Comox woman who dictates very well and am therefore taking the opportunity to learn Comox well. The old Puntlatish [Pentlatch] people understand this language, and hence I progress in both languages. I was most industrious yesterday.

In the afternoon, when I heard the steamer's whistle, I became restless and rushed to the post office as it grew dark. It seemed a long way, though I had never before walked so fast. In almost three weeks I had only once received a letter, from Toni. I did get an enormous mail, and it took me almost two hours to read my letters. The business with the museum gives me no rest. I have to force myself to think about it as little as possible, otherwise I cannot work properly. (This is really not the place for this, but I think about it every day, although as I write of my small daily doings it unintentionally escapes me.) I could not continue with Comox yesterday. The wide road was filled with carts and wagons, and men and women wandered to the pier, some of them carrying big baskets of food because their farms are quite far from the post office. An unbelievably large crowd of people stood about reading letters or studying newspapers. The weekly edition appears on Fridays and so cannot be sent here; the most recent news to reach us is in the local paper from Nanaimo, which appears twice a week. I retired to my room with my mail and, after reading it all, sat down and wrote a dozen letters. This time I shall arrange to spread it (my writing) over the week.

I made my announcement for Berlin: Geography of North America, 3 hours; Ethnography of North America, 1 hour with practice in making itineraries [?]. If only I shall not have to give the lectures and can stay in New York! I announced the first course because I do not think it wise to hold the same course twice. I can prepare for the course at the same time I make my annual report for

Petermann. My manuscript has now reached page 212, but I still have about sixty pages to copy. My Puntlatish [Pentlatch] has gone deer-hunting today, and so I had to content myself with Comox. After a long search I finally found a Sisa'atl [Sechelt] and can now get a vocabulary of this tribe. I shall also get a Nanaimo vocabulary and a Squamish in Vancouver. That will end my work. The beginning of the Raven myth turned up today. I wonder how much of it is known here. But I must get back to work! I am wildly industrious at present.

*Saturday—November 20:* My life here is really quite monotonous. I had intended to visit a lake not too far from here, but I already know that I shall not take the time to go. I am getting on so well that I begrudge every minute lost. I know how miserable I shall feel when there is no getting ahead in Nanaimo and Vancouver. It is too bad that I am so hard pressed for time that I have a bad conscience whenever a moment is lost. I shall be in this country twenty days longer and then return east! Unfortunately the Puntlatish [Pentlatch] work is progressing slowly. They are celebrating many festivals, and I have to depend on the women; but there are no more Puntlatish [Pentlatch] women. It is not too bad, however, since the two languages are related. I got another nice Comox text today. One thing is unfortunate—the myths are so very coarse, to put it mildly, that three-quarters of them cannot be retold. I find very great differences between these myths and the ones farther north, and I am coming more and more to the conclusion that originally there can have been very little intercourse between the two groups.

I am always very tired evenings because I really have to work very hard. I get up at 6:45, have my breakfast, and work in my room until 8:30. I then go to the settlement and start work there at about nine o'clock. I return at 11:45 and am out again by 1:30. By five o'clock I am back here and work over my material as well as I can and prepare myself for the following day. By that time it is 10:30 or eleven and I am really tired. Nevertheless, I am getting quite stout. There is nothing much more to relate. Unfortunately, owing to the loss of that $35, my purse has become very slim and I may buy nothing at all.

*November 21—Sunday:* I did not write today because I was too tired. This seems to be my only song: "I am tired." But the Indians have so much to tell me that I am scarcely able to keep up with the transcriptions. I did not get as much as usual today because I missed meeting one man. It was a little late, snow began to fall, and it grew very dark; so I had very little material when I returned home in the afternoon. However, I talked to my next-door neighbor Dr. Duncan for half an hour. The English and we Germans seem to have very little in common. Only here have I found so many people of the same type as my neighbor—very tall, exceedingly quiet, lazy, with very few interests except horses and guns, and possessed of the gift of sitting for hours, self-satisfied and dreaming. The doctor typifies this class of people. The other doctor, whom I mentioned earlier, is an entirely different kind of a person. There are even fewer like him among us.

I always have to think of Dr. Sl. (I have forgotten his name) in Pickwick. He has a red nose (no exaggeration), is unusually short and quite shabby. His sentiments are expressed by the following: He asked me whether there was anything of interest to be seen among the Indians, and I do not know how it happened, but I told him that formerly the crest posts had been erected on slaves who had been killed. "Oh what a pity I didn't come earlier! I fear there is nothing as interesting now!" I had already had enough of the red-nosed bum, who was always armed with horrible pistols. But this was too much, and I did not accept his invitation to visit him. The good Petrock, with his roly-poly lively wife and his seven offspring, is still here, patiently waiting for the *Mrs. Marianna Boskowitz,* who may perhaps make her appearance tomorrow. That reminds me, I have to write to Spencer; I left something behind. I used the rest of last night to finish up my transcriptions of the material I have collected here and fortunately am up to date with them. The material from Newetti and Alert Bay has not yet been worked over. It will be impossible for me to do anything about it until I get to New York.

This morning, November 22, I awoke with the pleasant feeling that I shall be leaving Victoria in four weeks. The twelve young ones were making such a terrible hullabaloo that I quickly got out of bed and sat down to work even though it was still dark. As a result, I find myself in the pleasant position of having only today's data to copy. But it is a great deal, and I am afraid I shall again not be able to finish. Tomorrow and the day after I shall ask only grammatical questions in order to find out more about verbs. It was quite wintry today, snow and ice everywhere.

*November 23:* Again a day's work is over. I am confronted with the fact that once again I cannot keep up with my transcriptions because I get too much material. I do not like it at all, because as a result quite a number of questions remain unanswered. I have a real horror of writing this book; it entails an enormous amount of work, and it is going to take a long time to work it out completely. I am afraid that the journals will have to serve first. You cannot imagine how I worry all the time lest I lose my manuscript. That would be something! I shall send everything that I do not need with the steamer to Uncle Jacobi in New York—unfortunately not as much as I should like to send. Two more days and the mail will arrive—a holiday for Comox! Everyone here counts the week from Thursday to Thursday, not from Sunday to Sunday. The time passes quickly for me because I have much work to do and am getting on well with it. Nevertheless I shall be glad when the time to leave arrives. Then four more weeks and I shall be back in New York.

I cannot report much about my day's work, since one day is like another. I have gotten another long Puntlatish [Pentlatch] text and at last, with great difficulty, discovered some pronouns in it. It took me an hour to distinguish between "I" and "you." They are so nearly alike that I could not hear the difference. I always have them tell me myths in the afternoons. I must go to the Sisa'atl [Sechelt] man a few times more; I also wish to make a Lequiltag [Lekwiltok] vocabulary. It will take me only a few hours for three days and it is worth getting. The thirty-eight Flathead tribes will drive me to distraction.

*November 24:* Last night a dreadful storm raged and the wind blew through the wooden walls of the house. When I went out this morning it was still raining and storming, but it cleared while I was with the Indians, and at noon the weather was fine. The *Boskowitz* has not yet arrived, but the Indian agent Lomas from Cowichan, whose name I mentioned when writing from there, came. A missionary from Kuper [?] Island, near Tsimenes, came at the same time and invited me in a very friendly way to visit him. If I should see him again tomorrow, I may decide to go there instead of to Nanaimo because that place is easier to reach. It is only a mile from the railway station. I shall decide that tomorrow. In any case I must go to Vancouver. I intended to visit them this evening on board their boat, but it was anchored so far out that I could not get there. If they have not left by tomorrow morning, I shall go out to them. Otherwise today was like all other days. The Indians had a big feast this afternoon so I did not get much. But I made up for it by copying and am now only two days behind. The same thing is happening to me now as has happened before—I forget what is *new* of the things I have learned and cannot know until I have the opportunity of telling someone about my findings who knows about these matters. Would you like to know how large my manuscript has grown?—up to 257 pages! I wish it were tomorrow afternoon and I had my letters.

*November 26:* I should have preferred to leave today, but it would have been shameful desertion had I allowed my feelings to run away with reason. I was in the village yesterday and collected stories. In the afternoon I got a number of very nice ones. I then rushed home as fast as possible, but there was no letter from Marie, and since I can hear nothing for another week I was very unhappy. I sealed my letter and sent my . . . to New York. As a result I felt somewhat unsettled. I woke up in a little better mood this morning and went to the village. The weather is unpleasant, with continuous rain and fog; i.e., since yesterday. I worked until noon but was forced to be lazy this afternoon because the Indians are having a big celebration. A man wishes to build two houses and the chief does not want to permit it. He has called a big meeting at noon today to discuss the matter and make a decision.

Lomas left this morning. His presence caused great disturbance in the village and therefore interfered with my work. I have six days more and much must be accomplished in that time. I am particularly concerned about the Liquiltag [Lekwiltok] vocabulary. Yesterday I received a letter from Gatschet, who is in Louisiana. His letter was forwarded repeatedly ever since September and finally returned to him. This afternoon I was a bit lazy, and now I shall get back to work. For safety's sake I sent another copy of my lecture announcement to Berlin. I always think there is nothing to write, but there always seem to be a number of letters. A week from today I shall be in Nanaimo. Thursday is always an exciting day here. There are endless vehicles in town (which consists of seven houses), and the people amuse themselves to their hearts' content. I have been invited to the weekly ball this evening, but I am not going because I do not want to waste the whole evening.

*November 27—Saturday morning:* I had been working about an hour when the whistle blew and *Mrs. Boskowitz* appeared. Since I had a number of acquaintances on board, I wandered down to the boat. To my very great surprise, I met Jacobsen, the Bella Coola man from Berlin, who is on his way home. We were both delighted to meet and spent several hours in conversation. I was very glad to speak German again. It is nice to meet unexpectedly an old acquaintance in another corner of the world. Above all it is refreshing to meet someone who is glad to see you. We talked of Berlin, and he told me of his intentions and points of view. He lives all alone among the

Bella Coola and has started a fishery and animal breeding station. We stayed together until about 10:30 when I took him down to the boat and said goodbye to him and the Petrock family. Ned did not buy the things for me in Newetti, and so I had him return the $50, which came in good stead after the loss of the $35. I asked Jacobsen to buy certain masks for me in Bella Coola and he has promised to do so, but I cannot have them before March.

*Afternoon:* I heard the most interesting story of the Raven, on which the separation of the sexes among the Tlingit is based and which appears here only occasionally. In some ways the myths of the Comox are very interesting, and I am glad that I have found so many of them. I am beginning to understand something of what the people say and try to say something myself once in a while. I shall not be able to work this evening because, after having been urged many times, I promised earlier in the week to visit someone down here and it is for this evening. I am going with Mr. Duncan. Until it is time to go I shall do some copying. I am glad to know the maps which I forgot at Spencer's are now in Victoria. I had put much work on them. They must be the first four which will be published by Petermann and will appear in April or May. I dread writing. The long-expected [winter] weather has arrived: rain, rain, rain and wind, but it is not too bad. It is possible to go everywhere in raincoat and rubber boots. Tomorrow is Sunday again, everyone is shocked that I do not interrupt my work and go to church. In two weeks I shall be in Vancouver and in four in St. Paul or nearby! I am ashamed of myself to be so eager to leave this interesting country, but nevertheless it is true. I am already counting the days until next mailing day, Thursday!

*Saturday—November 28:* Yesterday after dinner, which is at six o'clock, I went with Mr. Duncan to visit the Rabbs, the farmer family I had promised to visit. Saturday seems to be their regular card evening. There were quite a number of guests present, and soon two tables of whist were arranged. The family consists of an old man and his wife, who represent a past generation; at least they would amongst us. The woman wore a cap and had long curls at her forehead, such as were in style I don't know how many years back. They came here when their children were small, and now the children manage the farm. After a while I sat down and played chess with the old man and we beat one another to both our satisfaction. Then there was singing, which I accompanied on the harmonium. We spent a pleasant evening; it was 11:30 when the party broke up.

Today, Sunday, breakfast was very late. I did not get to the Indians until 9:30. When I got back at 12:30 for dinner it was not ready, and so I conversed with Mr. Duncan. He happened to tell me that he is thirty-one years old, and I had thought he was twenty-five. He as well as others have taken me to be thirty-five! So you see how old I must look. To everyone's consternation I went to work again this afternoon, and my day was the best I have had in a long time. The Indians tell me a great deal and I get very many grammatical notes, so that it takes me all evening to copy the linguistic material. I am so far behind with the myths that I shall give up trying to transcribe them while I am here. Only four more days! I really dread all I must do in the next three weeks—the distribution of the Cowichan and Shoamish [?], and the vocabularies of the Lequiltag [Lekwiltok], Nanaimo, and Squamish! That will be difficult in the time available to me, but I hope very much that I shall be finished by the seventeenth so that I may have two days to finish up in Victoria, where I have to pay a few visits and pack.

*November 29—Monday:* I am very lazy this evening. I have been writing so much all day that I no longer feel like doing a thing and shall go to bed and sleep. My work here is rapidly drawing to a close, if I can only finish the Lequiltag [Lekwiltok] vocabulary. The orthography of a printed translation of the Bible into this language is quite incomprehensible to me. Three days more and I shall go into new regions. I have seen quite a bit of the country in this short time and have learned much—if only the trip will bring me the desired result! I can follow the conversation of the people, with some difficulty, but shall, of course, forget everything very quickly after I leave.

Three weeks from today I shall be in Tacoma and in four weeks in New York. The walk to the village is now anything but pleasant; in this rain and fog it takes me a half hour. I must go twelve times more and I won't be dry. So far this has been the best place I have visited. From the very beginning the Indians were friendly and willing to talk. I have not found them so anywhere else. There is not much more to tell; life is very monotonous, as I have already told you. I am very curious to know whether the Squamish language is a dialect of [Cowichan?], or what it may be. I shall know about it in two weeks.

*November 30:* I did not get much wiser today. I tried my luck with the Sisa'atl [Sechelt] again but was unable to get anywhere with him because he speaks too quickly and cannot understand what I want. I think I had better stop with my vocabulary instead of continuing to be annoyed and not discovering anything with certainty. I am slowly progressing with the Lequiltag [Lekwiltok] vocabulary and today got some Puntlatish [Pentlatch] texts and a few Comox stories, but nothing much worthwhile. The Comox and Puntlatish [Pent-latch] vocabularies contain up to this time about 1,000 words, and I can make myself quite well understood by using the small number of these that I know. At least they can no longer speak without my knowing what they are talking about. I was lazy this afternoon and did not work from noon until dinner time, but I shall get started im-mediately. I have become tired from working steadily these last three weeks and am glad that I shall have a few days of rest. I wish I had another week in order to learn something of Squamish. I am afraid a very meager vocabulary will be all that I shall have. I should like very much to have a few texts, if I can get them. The day after tomorrow will again be the longed-for day, mail day. It seems to me it was scarcely two days since the boat was here. My reports are very meager, but there is nothing to write. One day is like another.

*December 1:* I did not have a chance to write because I went down to the Rabbs in the evening to say goodbye; now I see the steamer emerging from the dense fog, and you can imagine how happy I am that I will have my letters in a few hours. Yesterday passed as all other days. I was in the village all morning and afternoon, listening to stories, etc. I did some copying in the afternoon, and in the evening Dr. Duncan and I went down to the Rabbs. I had to play chess with the old man again and afterward accompany the singing.

*December 4—Saturday:* Now I am in Nanaimo again. I was inter-rupted the day before yesterday (December 2), and there was too much to do before leaving Comox. Thursday, the day before yester-day, was unusually stormy and rainy so that the walk to the village was most unpleasant. I ended my work at noon in order to pack and write letters in the afternoon. I think I may be very well satisfied with the results obtained in Comox, because I have learned much that is new and am better informed than the oldest people here, who have spent all their time with the Indians—Dr. Tolmie and others, for example. I got up very early yesterday because the steamer was leav-ing early. All the hotel guests accompanied us (there were quite a number of travelers) to the steamer, and we sailed away. Old Mr. Rabb was also a passenger, and the time passed quite quickly as we conversed.

I am very well known by this time, having visited in so many places, and am always in touch with all the different groups of the population. The country population is very nice, but I do not like the city dwellers. The difference between American and Canadian cities is strange. The ties that bind the inhabitants of the [Canadian?] cities to England are much stronger than I had thought. However, the influx of so great a number of foreigners must certainly influence the relation of people.

We did not arrive here until four o'clock because of strong head winds, and I made Mr. Neptune a very small offering. On arrival, I put myself in the hands of a beautifier (i.e., barber), bought a pair of shoes, and proceeded to the missionary, Mr. Good, from whom I want to get a treatise on the Salish language. I found my way to the door in deepest darkness and landed in a brightly lit living room where Mrs. Good sat, writing busily. I introduced myself; soon the grown-up children appeared and, at last, father Good. Unfortunately he was just about to hold services so I had to be patient until today. I shall see him at two o'clock. I am living at Mr. Sabitson's hotel, of course, but I could wish for a better place because I have only one room, no meals. But it does not really matter, since it is only for a few days. I shall make use of this morning and transcribe as much as possible. I shall mail these words today; otherwise the time between letters will be more than a week, and I know how unpleasant that is.

Mr. Good is not very cooperative; he claims to be busy but talks endlessly about his own work. He kept me for two hours yesterday afternoon showing me his Salish translation of the prayer book, although I asked him a few times to go with me to the Indians. He declared he did not have the time. It would be interesting to listen to him if I did not have work to do. I do not wish to go to the Indians unaccompanied because of my past experiences, which were not good. At last he went with me, and we met one of the people, who serves as interpreter for the church. I arranged for him to help me, but of course I will not be sure of him until he appears. At noon (it is Sunday morning), I shall go and look for him. I am sorry not to have accomplished anything these last two days, but I really could not help it. Presumably I shall stay here until Saturday morning and then go to Victoria or Vancouver, whatever seems best to me. I have made use of my time and have transcribed and have caught up a bit. It is, however, quite out of the question that I shall be entirely caught up. I am about 80 pages behind, and my manuscript has reached page 306.

I obtained the address of a missionary in the interior from Good and have asked him for notes on the grammar of the language. If these people will answer all my requests, my book will gain in value. I have asked Bishop Ridley for a sketch of the Tsimshian, a certain

Collins for one of the Haida, a Mr. Small for . . . , and Hall for translations from the Kwakiutl. I hope very much that they will honor my requests; the most doubtful is Hall, who seems to be very lazy. If I get to Vancouver, I shall try to get the Squamish [?], and perhaps through the Catholic mission one or two other inland tribes. I tried as much as possible to compare the orthography of the missionaries with mine. Now I shall start working again, that is transcribing. I consider it the duty of a field worker to obtain as much additional material as possible in this way. Everywhere I go I am asked whether it is not true that the Indians come from Japan. This notion is so strongly ingrained in the people here that I do not even take the trouble to answer. I am not very much inclined to propose such theories and support them. Nanaimo appears much more unfriendly than when I passed through on my way to Comox. Fog and rain are the rule, the streets are unspeakably dirty, and everything looks most dreary. There are no people on the streets; in short, it looks dead.

*December 6—Monday morning:* Yesterday morning I was busy transcribing. At noon I went to the settlement to make arrangements with the Indian. He is one of the most civilized people, but he did not wish to talk business on Sunday; so I shall have to wait until morning. I hope I shall also find a Squamish here in Nanaimo so that I will not have to go over to Vancouver. I was doing some writing yesterday afternoon, but at 3:30 it cleared and I threw my papers aside and took a walk through town. It is a strange sight to see the impenetrable primeval forest right next to the houses. Nanaimo is very prettily situated. There are countless sandstone islands beyond the shore line and these are separated from one another by narrow channels. Some of these are filled with slimy mud and have water at high tide only. Nanaimo is situated on such an island near the coast. Wooden bridges cross these gorgelike channels. It is very hilly and the streets very steep. The chief interest lies in the coal mines to which Nanaimo owes its existence. In clear weather the view over the Rockies and Mt. Baker is very beautiful.

Yesterday, however, it was clear for scarcely an hour. So I returned to the hotel, but because I did not feel like copying I composed a few New Year's letters for Europe. I wrote to Hete, Martha, Haller, and Grünwedel. Then I had a long conversation with a man from Victoria who is here on business, but he was not very interesting—an Englishman, not an American. In the evening there was a big fire; I helped the Nanaimoans pump water and pull down the house, then went to bed well satisfied. Now I shall go to the village and hope to get started with my work. I am beginning to grow impatient. Everything looks very unpleasant again today—fog and rain, rain and fog. They told me at the hotel that the weather had been unusually pleasant, but that seems to be at an end now.

*Evening:* Unfortunately my hope of finding a Squamish is not to be realized, and so I must go to Vancouver. The man with whom I am working is good, and I have learned more during this one day than during the week in Cowichan. I expect to get everything I want during this week. Since I must waste two days in traveling, I am afraid I shall not finish here in less than two weeks, unless a Squamish should turn up somewhere. It can only be a question of two days, because I must leave on account of my pass, and I wish to be in New York New Year's Eve. This morning I went to my friend Cushing. He and his nephew were expecting me and we worked hard. We paused at noon and then worked until five o'clock, when it grew so dark I could see no more. Today's results consist of a vocabulary of a few hundred words, a small collection of sentences, and a story in the language. This is the fifth language in which I have gotten texts. I think I shall also succeed in getting the distribution of the tribes. If he only knew something of the Squamish dialect so that I would not have to go to Vancouver. It would take four additional weeks to formulate the needed questions.

*December 9:* It is very pleasant to go to the post office every day and ask for letters and be able to receive some! The great event today was letters from Dawson and Marie; hers had been drifting about for *only* sixteen days. I was somewhat irritated by Dawson's letter. He asks me about a small matter which he wishes to use for publication and makes a big business about not wanting to take anything away from me, as though I were guarding everything jealously for fear someone would make use of it before me. We are not used to treating such things as a business matter in Germany, and I wrote him that in a friendly manner. I suppose he meant to be very polite about it, but it went against my grain.

My Indians here are very nice. They talk well, and I have gotten a large quantity of material in the last few days. I think that in order to save time I shall go to Vancouver directly from here. The steamer leaves Saturday morning, and so I shall be there Saturday afternoon. It is not so good that the next day is Sunday, but I would not be able to do anything in Victoria either. I can probably leave Vancouver by Wednesday and finish up in Victoria from Thursday to Saturday. I do not wish to stay up here longer than two weeks. I have a great deal of work to do now, and I work for six hours with the Indians without interruption. Of course, I am again very far behind with my transcriptions. My manuscript has reached page 326. Now I must go to bed; I am murderously tired. Two weeks from today I shall have passed beyond Portland, I hope.

*December 8*[?]: It is definitely nice to be in a city where one can get mail every day, and consequently I feel very well. But it will be very unpleasant later, on the train, when there will be no news for such a long time. If the days were only longer! I should like to write a paper for Petermann while on the train, but I am afraid I shall not get very far with it. By four o'clock it is quite dark. My Indian is quite a success, and I have obtained a great deal in these three days. In the next two days I hope to grow much wiser. I had a letter from Bastian today in which he puts $250 at my disposal. Unfortunately it is too late. Three months ago I would have accepted with thanks. He writes, "In order to facilitate the purchase of objects for a collection you may count on us for a preliminary sum of 1,000 marks. It will not be difficult for us to come to an agreement about what should be definitely included in the collection. I shall of course be very glad if, while carrying out the aims of the museum, we can find support for scientific researches such as yours." That is fine, my dear sir, only unfortunately a little too late. Ten horses will not keep me here longer than I need to finish up.

Today I learned much about the social organization of the Snana'imox [Nanaimo], but neglected the language somewhat. I have about 800 words and a few short texts, as well as a collection of phrases for working out the grammar. This evening I went to . . . , the Comox-Vancouver steamer, to inquire about the best connection to Vancouver. It seems to be cheaper and more practical to go to New Westminster and from there take the omnibus to Vancouver. I shall be there Saturday afternoon and hope to be in Victoria on Thursday. I made an important discovery about the distribution of the tribes today, namely, that on the mainland the same language is always spoken as on the corresponding part of the island. Because of this the distribution takes on an entirely different aspect. I must get busy and copy because I am much too far behind.

*December 9:* This morning I again worked with the Indians until noon. The newspaper from Victoria usually arrives while I am having lunch, and today I saw to my sorrow that old Dr. Tolmie died. I would have gone to the funeral had I been able to get away. His death imposes a very unpleasant duty on me. Tolmie was about to publish his observations on the Indians, and I shall have to see to it, as soon as I get to Victoria, that they go to either Dawson in Ottawa or to me. I wrote to Dawson immediately and asked him to take steps in the matter so that either he or I can see to their publication, since we are the only ones who understand something about it. Is it not curious that so soon after my letter to Dawson the day before yesterday I should have occasion to show the genuineness of my protestations? If these notes of Tolmie's are saved, I shall care little which of us edits them. I shall return to Victoria as quickly as possible to do something about this, no matter how unpleasant it may be.

*December 10—Victoria:* I really hurried back here. I found out at noon in Nanaimo that the funeral is to be the day after tomorrow, and so I boarded a train and came here. I shall go to the Indian Bureau tomorrow, and if Powell will let me have the papers I shall be able to finish the work there in three days. I hope there will be no difficulties. This part of the work is very important to me. I always feel very well when I get back to Victoria—it is quite a decent city. I should be satisfied with my results in Nanaimo. I obtained much grammatical material and important ethnological notes. I hope things will go well in Vancouver. If Dr. Powell is friendly, I shall probably go over on Wednesday. I am glad I spent so much time on this southern tribe because the work has really been worthwhile. I may as well continue with these pages until Sunday, since I shall not leave until Monday morning. It is almost unbelievable that letters posted in Comox on Thursday do not leave here until Monday! The trains always leave just before the arrival of the steamers and the steamers just before the arrival of the trains. I wonder whether I shall be able to do something about Dr. Tolmie's work?

*December 12—Sunday:* I spent all day yesterday running about. In the morning I went to see Powell, who had no time to give me the papers because the mail for California was to leave at noon. But he promised to give me most of the papers and I was very glad about it. I hope I shall find his data useful and get my map into good condition. This geographical part of my work has been about the most difficult. The names of the tribes were unknown, and, after I had found seventy tribes with the greatest difficulty, I had to arrange them according to language and dialect and determine their locations. In spite of the short time, I have succeeded quite well. I then went to the office of the *Boskowitz* to call for a package of maps which Spencer had sent me from Alert Bay. They contain a portion of the geographical notes. To my dismay they were not there, and I rushed to all the places where they might possibly be. I then returned to the office of the *Boskowitz* and there found out that the owners of the *Boskowitz*, thinking the maps belonged to them, had appropriated them. I have been promised their return tomorrow. I had my lunch and then ordered a wreath for Dr. Tolmie, which is not so simple to do here in Victoria. In the afternoon I copied something that had been left over from Nanaimo and shall continue today. I then colored my map of various tribes and shall take it to the Indian office tomorrow in order to make the remaining entries. It is pouring; I suppose the funeral at noon will not be very pleasant.

*December 16—Victoria:* Dear Parents: This is the last letter you will receive from here. I have wound up my work, and all I must do is write a few letters, ask a few people for certain information, pack my belongings, send the last of the Kish [?] collections, and then leave—and what a pleasure that will be! It is a strange feeling to have again completed this type of work. Now for a year or longer I shall have to live on the memory of this quarter of a year. I came back from Vancouver this morning and worked at the Indian office for the last time, getting all the information I desired at this last moment. I think the last page of my diary was written on the Sunday Dr. Tolmie was buried. At that time I packed the book in my trunk, hardly expecting to find time to write in Vancouver. I must make up for lost time. I shall not write to Marie because I will be able to tell her about it at the same time [as she would receive my letter]. When you get this letter you will probably have received my telegram from New York, perhaps even a note of greeting from there. If we are not detained by snow drifts I shall be in New York in a week, at what time I of course do not know. I shall have to stop in Chicago, at least for a few hours, on account of Julius and Alice. After this the time it takes to receive answers from you will seem very short to me. It took an eternity for them to reach me here!

Now I shall start to tell you what I have done. On Monday [December 13] I went to Dr. Powell and worked in the office for a short time. He gave me the papers that I needed and I was able to busy myself all day, so that I was ready to leave in the evening. I did not leave my room all day and wrote and drew until about twelve o'clock. Then I went to the steamer, which left at two, and slept very well all night. When I awoke in the morning the weather was beautiful and clear and I had a view of the wild, mountainous landscape, which before I had admired only from a distance. It was very foggy in Burrard Inlet, where Vancouver is situated. It was impossible to see anything, and it took us quite a long time to dock. I went to the hotel immediately and inquired about a few people to whom I had introductions. I ran about unsuccessfully all morning trying to find someone who knew the Indians. I finally found a Methodist minister, who went to the settlement with me. Fortunately he knew a very good Indian, and I learned a great deal in two days. Vancouver makes a very strange impression. It is scarcely a year since the city arose from the wilderness, the moment it became known that the Canadian Pacific would have its terminal here. Where there are no houses, even in the middle of the city, there are burned or burning tree stumps. People from all lands, no one really seeming at home, swarm about the streets, which are covered with wooden planks. The streets are not yet completely finished, and where there are no wooden side streets, as well as other streets not covered with wood, there is nothing but impassable swamp. A white collar is still an event in Vancouver, but all this seems to be disappearing rapidly. The landowners believe the city to be a second San Francisco, but I am afraid they are mistaken. So far British Columbia has not enough tillable land. The forests can only be conquered in the course of time, and the small amount of gold is insufficient to make the land valuable.

The city will soon become important, however, as a harbor city and railway terminal. So far Victoria is the only tolerable place on the coast. The harbor is good, except that the entry is somewhat difficult. The city is situated on the flat south side of Burrard Inlet, which is the delta made by the Fraser River. It is the only flat land along the entire coast. The center of the district is New Westminster, which also has its railroad. Of course, I do not claim to know this city, having been here only two days. Reverend Hall, the Methodist minister, took me to the Indian settlement which is next to one of the large saw mills. The Squamish, the Indians of this region, do not live there; the inhabitants are a mixed company from this district together with whites and Negroes. I find it very unpleasant to visit this kind of place. Nowhere else is there so much dirt, dirt of all kinds. The man I wanted to see lives there, and so I had to spend the day in that place. Picture to yourselves a number of wooden huts, crowded together along the shore, some deserted and in ruins, poorly put together, all the rubbish heaped in front of the houses, the ground so swampy that one must balance oneself on boards carelessly strewn about, and you have a picture of this place. The real Indian village gains much by comparison. It is situated on the north coast. The Catholic church stands in its midst and is surrounded by friendly-looking white houses. The mission *appears* to have really improved the condition of the natives, but a hasty impression is easily misleading. I collected busily during the few hours that were left as well as on Wednesday and Thursday.

Wednesday, December 15, in the evening, I was suddenly cor-

nered by a reporter, supposedly for an English paper, and to my
unpleasant surprise I found a glowing account of myself in yesterday's Vancouver paper, which I suppose will be reprinted immediately. That is typically American! It was also reported that I would
return to Victoria yesterday. To my great amusement I heard people
sitting next to me on the boat discussing the German doctor. Thanks
to the notice in the paper I was able to spend hours on the steamer
in pleasant conversation with a couple who had lived in Berlin for a
half year. This morning I again went to the Indian Bureau and
worked there until I had all the information I wanted. Dr. Powell
has invited me for noon tomorrow, and I shall lunch with him. I am
planning to go to McDonald's tonight, an unpleasant walk in this
weather. Now farewell. You will hear from me from New York.

My best love,

Franz

# PART TWO

RESEARCH
PRIMARILY FOR
THE BRITISH
ASSOCIATION
FOR THE
ADVANCEMENT
OF SCIENCE
(1888–1894)

EDITOR'S INTRODUCTION.—*Boas' research on the Northwest Coast from 1888 to 1894 was guided and financed by the Committee of the British Association for the Advancement of Science for the Study of the Northwestern Tribes of Canada. More specifically, his work was directed by Horatio Hale, editor of the committee, who gave him explicit instructions regarding the nature of his research.*

*During his 1888 field trip, for example, Boas was instructed to confine his linguistic research to the collection of limited vocabularies and brief grammatical sketches. He was requested to prepare an ethnographic map of the region and to make anthropometric measurements of the different tribes. Moreover, he was told to make a brief description of the country insofar as it helped to understand* "the condition and mode of life of the different tribes" (Hale 1888a). *Hale later summarized his directives in another letter.* "As I understand the matter, what is specially desired from you, in your present mission, is not a minute account of two or three tribes or languages. We wish to learn from you a general synopsis of the ethnology of the whole of British Columbia, according to the linguistic stocks. We do not expect you to visit every part of the Province; but we think that with what you have already seen of it, and what you can learn from the natives and white residents and from books, you should be able to give an ethnological description of the whole region, from north to south, without omitting any stock" (Hale 1888b).

*Boas felt extremely constrained by Hale's particularistic directives, and the following year he offered an alternative plan of his own:*

My suggestion for this summer's work would be the following: I should go as soon as possible to Alert Bay on the northern part of Vancouver Island in order to settle a number of doubtful points on the sociology of the tribes of that region, but principally to obtain translations of a number of songs of members of the secret societies which, as I think now, will shed a new light on this important problem. Then I shall proceed to Bella Bella and devote my attention to the little known tribes of that district. I chose them because I feel convinced that we shall find here important information on the history and development of the social organization of these people and particularly regarding certain religious ideas and the original concept of totemism. I should visit the settlements of Chinaman Hat, Bella Bella, Talung, Rivers Inlet, and, if I could possibly arrange so, of Gardner Inlet. I also hope to ascertain some facts

81

*regarding the conventionalism of art which I consider of importance.* [*Boas 1889*b]

*Boas also suggested that he move his family to Victoria for a year or two to facilitate his research plan.*

*Hale responded to this proposal with an upbraiding letter:*

> *I must earnestly enjoin you to follow implicitly the instructions you received from me. If you had done it last year—if you had kept the linguistic portion of your work strictly within the limits prescribed, and had made your ethnographic map to conform to my Oregon map (as I requested)—you would have saved yourself and me a great deal of trouble, and would have produced a more satisfactory report.*
>
> *I cannot understand why you should persist in causing me an immense amount of useless trouble, as well as much annoyance, by objecting to my instructions, which you are expressly engaged to carry out. Kindly go on hereafter with your usual energy and ability, in the course which, after much experience and careful consideration, I have marked out for you.* [*Hale 1889*]

*Boas' reaction to this and other such letters is recorded in his letters to his wife.*

*Boas' 1890 field trip was financed by the Bureau of American Ethnology. He was given $1,100, of which $450 ($150 per month) was allotted for salary and $650 was set aside for traveling and research expenses. Hale markedly relaxed his control over Boas' research schedule during this trip: "As regards instruction, I need only say that the object of your present trip, so far as the work of our Committee is concerned, is to fill up, as far as practicable, some of the Lacunae which was unavoidably left in your former investigations. You, of course, are the proper judge of what proceedings will be best for this purpose. I will not hamper you with any specific instruction. You will consider yourself entirely at liberty to act in your own judgment" (Hale 1890).*

*Boas does not appear to have written a diary during his 1891 field trip, or if he wrote one it has been lost. The few letters that are available about his work on the coast contain very little relevant information. He was in Portland, Oregon, on July 5; he went to Bay Center, Washington, July 9–21, back to Portland on July 25, and he returned to Bay Center from July 29 to mid-August. He then went to Victoria, British Columbia, from August 19 to early September. Most of his efforts seem to have been devoted to collecting Chinook texts.*

Boas continued to work under the direction of the BAAS in 1894, but he was also given support by the American Museum of Natural History and by the United States National Museum. Apparently he received a total of $1,900 for his field trip, but after he arrived in British Columbia he requested an additional $200 from George M. Dawson, one of the BAAS committee members, so that he could continue his field work for an extra month during the winter. Hale responded that the Committee could send only $100, and so presumably Boas had a total budget of $2,000 for this trip. Before leaving for British Columbia Boas received a set of instructions for field work from Dawson:

We feel inclined naturally to leave the general character of the work largely to your own discretion. As a good deal of space has already been given to linguistic matter and as Mr. Hale thinks we now have a good basis in this respect for philologic comparison, the investigations of this summer might profitably be directed chiefly to customs, etc., with perhaps such folk-tales as may appear to be important as historical traditions, and whatever you may consider to be necessary to complete the general anthropometric data for comparative purposes. [*Dawson 1894*]

# 3

## 1888 Diary

*May 31* [*Vancouver*]: The region through which we passed yesterday was so beautiful that I did not take the time to write. It would
be useless to try to describe the high mountain chains, the Rocky
Mountains and Selkirks. I have never passed through a high mountain chain before. The pass through the Selkirks is most imposing. The
train crawls between two mountains, rising upward to about 8,000
feet. I was very unlucky; as we reached the glacier house something
flew into my eye and I could see nothing for hours. You must excuse
me for not describing the trip.

When we arrived here today I was dreadfully tired. I immediately went to the . . . , got some money, and made the necessary
inquiries; then I crossed the harbor to the Indian reservation, looked
up the missionary, and had him introduce me to the Indians. I have
an appointment today with an old chief who knows something of
their old traditions. I find my Tsimshian[?] has become somewhat
rusty. I was so tired last night that I lay down on the bed and fell
fast asleep. I woke up at eleven and of course went to bed. This
morning I shall start to work. I shall leave here Sunday noon for
Victoria, where I shall stay one and one-half weeks.

I hope I shall get letters today. It seems an eternity since I have
had word. It is raining quite a bit, and the trip across the harbor will
not be very pleasant. I must not stay here long because I wish to
hurry to the unknown tribes. It is June 1 already. I really have very
little time for work. The latest I wish to leave is July 25. In July my
headquarters will be in Kamloops, but I must leave it uncertain where
I shall go from there. The bell is ringing for breakfast. I must hurry
and cross the harbor.

*June 2:* I stopped writing rather suddenly yesterday. The coal dust
which got into my eye prevented me from doing anything, and I
had to go to a doctor to have it removed. He finally succeeded,

causing me much agony. Since then my eye has been all right again. You have been deprived of descriptions of the wonderful countryside, which really is the most beautiful I have ever seen. On Wednesday I rode with the engineer in the engine for a while in order to get a better view. It was of the valley of the Kicking Horse River, which flows through a deep gorge. The Columbia is wonderful. The valley looks somewhat like the Rhine Valley at Bacharach and the Loreley. But the river is swifter, and everywhere there are snow-covered mountains. I shall pass there again on my way home and probably spend two weeks there. I am glad that on the way home I shall have to travel only five days in succession. It is a dreadful trip.

Yesterday I went to the doctor in the morning and reached the other side at about eleven. I hired a boat and traveled over the approximately three-mile-wide inlet in the pouring rain. I have already written that I met the bishop over there, who fortunately was here on a tour of inspection. The Indian village is very well kept, better than any I have seen. It is situated in a clearing on the north side of the inlet and is called Slaa'n. A small wooden church, painted white, stands in the center, and around it stand the small houses, most of them also white. The canoes lie on the shore. The Indians are all *very* ardent Catholics, and so I cannot work tomorrow, Sunday. The bishop was very friendly and immediately got hold of the old chief for me, who, in the presence of the bishop, of course knew nothing of their old traditions. But afterward he told me much of great value. The Indians here are all alike. First he got out all his "papers," which I had to admire. He said, "It is not good to proceed too fast. First I must show you that Chief Joseph is a good man." And then I had to make some flattering remarks about his papers, which he subsequently wrapped up carefully in a handkerchief.

Then we had the following conversation: "Who sent you here?" "I have come to see the Indians and to tell the white people about them." "Do you come from the Queen's Country?" "No, I am from another country." "Will you go to the Queen's country?" "Perhaps." "Good, when you get there go to the Queen and tell her this. Now write down what I say: Three men came (i.e., the Indian agent and two commissioners) and made treaties with us and said this is the Queen's land. That has made our hearts sad and we are angry at the three men. But the Queen does not know this. We are not angry at her. God gave this land to my ancestors, and it is not right that the three men take it. Now read what I have said." I read it and said everything as he had spoken. But he corrected me so that I always had to read: "Chief Joseph says so and so, etc."

I hoped I could in this way get to my affairs, but Chief Joseph was in no hurry. I still had to write, "When you see the Queen tell her Chief Joseph has little money or he would go and visit her." It is useless to cut short such outpouring if one wishes to find out anything. I stayed there until five in the evening and found out a lot of what I needed to know. The bishop sent me a young man who speaks English well and is unemployed. Several years ago he lost an arm in a sawmill. He gave me words and grammatical material. By yesterday afternoon I had trained him so well that I really hate to leave. He understood very well what I wanted. But I must not spend more time here.

*June 3—Sunday:* If I do not get fat on this trip, I will not know what is wrong. The lighting is so poor here that I cannot write at night. So I went to bed at 9 P.M. and slept until seven this morning. This morning I must copy everything I have so far obtained. The ship I am taking to Victoria leaves at two o'clock. I must find out there when the *Boskowitz* and the *Maude* are sailing. I'll make my plans accordingly. I hope to be back here by July 1, but I will go right on. I will probably stay two days in Harrison and then go right on into the interior. It is clear except that there are some clouds on the high mountains on the north side of the inlet. These will probably disappear by noon. The next news will be from Victoria.

*June 8:* I must now think where I stopped—I think it was when I left Vancouver. It was a beautifully clear day, with hardly any wind, at least until we reached Victoria. It gave me great pleasure to see again all the places I had known. When we left at one on Sunday, the mountains were still covered by a few clouds, but it cleared up entirely while we were on the way. At first we sailed close to land through the muddy waters of the Fraser River and then through the charming narrow strait, "Cowitchin [Cowichan] Gap" into the narrow waters between Vancouver Island and the islands lying before it. We arrived here at eight and went again to the old Oriental Hotel; I was greeted everywhere as an old friend. Monday morning I wandered through the streets and met I do not know how many old acquaintances. I then went to the Catholic Mission. Unfortunately the head father was not there, but I hope he will be back tomorrow. They had expected him yesterday.

Next I went to the Indian Office and got information for my future trip and procured the services of a Tsimshian woman from whom I learned a great deal yesterday and today. I am hoping to find a Kwakiutl and a Haida here. Then I inquired about boats and found that I have to go to the west coast by land, probably next

Tuesday, since there is no ship. I have made no plans beyond June 20. This morning I went to the mayor of Victoria to obtain permission to measure the Indians who are in prison. I got permission and must now also go to the provincial prison.

*June 6:* Yesterday and today I was very busy. Last night I called on McDonald, my Tsimshian donna. Dr. Powell makes more promises than he keeps; he had not found a Haida for me today, although he had promised that he would. In the morning I looked up a doctor who is supposed to be interested in Indians. He was willing to make measurements if I would give him the formulas. Unfortunately I have them only in German. In the evening I looked up a man from Cowitchin [Cowichan] who has a large collection of skulls. We have arranged to go there on Sunday to see them. Later, by appointment, Mr. Hastings, the photographer, came to show me a place where there are Indian skulls. We took a boat and went out. The wind was very strong in the harbor, and it was difficult to get ahead and to land. We discovered that someone had stolen all the skulls, but we found a complete skeleton without head. I hope to get another one either today or tomorrow. (It is now Thursday morning, F.B.) It is most unpleasant work to steal bones from a grave, but what is the use, someone has to do it. I have carefully locked the skeleton into my trunk until I can pack it away. I hope to get a great deal of anthropological material here. Yesterday I wrote to the Museum in Washington asking whether they would consider buying skulls this winter for $600; if they will, I shall collect assiduously.[1] Without having such a connection I would not do it.

Cariboo Fly arrived yesterday afternoon. It is competing with the *Boskowitz.* I shall probably change my plans and go to Port Essington, at the mouth of the Skinar [Skeena] River, on Tuesday. Then I can go back to Bella Bella and be back here about July 1. Then I could be on the west coast by the tenth and would have about fourteen days for the interior. Well, we shall see. Now I must go and find out about the *Cariboo Fly.* Up to now I have not been able to learn when she is to leave, but it might be Monday morning. Then I should certainly take this ship. I dreamed of skulls and bones all last night. I dislike very much working with this stuff; i.e., collecting it, not having it. I shall of course defer all measurements on dead material until some time later. I am as well known here in Victoria as a mongrel dog. I look up all kinds of people without modesty or hesitation. Today I am also going to call on the lieutenant governor of the Province.

1. Apparently his reference is to the United States National Museum in Washington, D.C.

*June 9:* I hope you take it as a good sign that I have so little time here to write. My hands are full. I have now returned from Cowichan, but I do not feel like working because I am tired. Unfortunately it is raining today. Mr. Sutton, the owner of the collection, disappointed me yesterday because he suddenly had to travel to the interior. But he gave me a letter to his brother, who called for me at the dock at Cowichan. This morning at 8, I left on the Nanaimo train, which is really good. At ten I was in McAkerson [?]. From there it took about an hour to reach the dock on a road leading through a most beautiful forest. The elder Mr. Sutton met me there, and we sailed across the bay to the house, which is situated in a pretty cove. It is connected with a sawmill.

There is a *hotel* there which we would call a *shanty*. Since I did not know about it I went in. There I found an old fellow with whom I had to sit by the fire. (In this country only wood is used in open fireplaces in which the cooking is also done.) Even though I was very hot he insisted I join him at the fire. The old fellow gave me his raincoat so that I should not get wet. Mr. Sutton came in and sat at the fire for a while and then we sailed across. It is near the Quamitchin [Quamichan] where I was last time for about a week, only about seven miles to the east. I was immediately taken to the collection and measured frantically all day long—about seventy-five skulls. We left at 3:30, and I went back to the station and got a train at five o'clock. By the way, that must be a pleasant life. The man lives all alone in the sawmill, which has stood still for months because of the poor condition of the market. I had lunch with him at twelve. He himself prepared it quickly.

Most of the collection was very instructive. I hope I shall receive an affirmative answer from Washington so that I can buy it. In Washington I would place its value at about $700. An unexpected result from the examination of these skulls shows that the individual tribes, speaking the same language, vary considerably from one another. I hope I shall have the occasion to investigate the Kwakiutl, to better understand this phenomenon. Yesterday and the day before I spent a profitable day talking to a Haida. I also had him photographed because of his handsome tattooing. I have discovered that the Haida and the Tlingit belong to the same language group. This is an important point about which I am very happy. I suspect that the Tsimshian also belong with another group and that the great confusion about the languages here may be quite simply solved. Yesterday and the day before I sat at home all day learning Haida. There would not have been much for me to write about. I have engaged a Kwakiutl for tomorrow. Whether he will come is another question.

*June 12:* You must be surprised that I am still writing from Victoria, but traveling is difficult here and I cannot get away. The steamer on which I had taken passage was suddenly chartered by another company and is not leaving until next week, so I shall not leave until Friday on the *Boskowitz* and will have to shorten my trip north whether I wish to or not. Sunday I was in Cowichan, but I have already written about that.

At 8 A.M. on Monday I waited for my Kwakiutl in vain, and in desperation I went to the jail. There I measured a Tsimshian and then went to the Catholic Mission. Father Jonkan [?], my old friend from earlier times, had returned at last and I had a long conversation with him, which was very profitable. It is good that I have not gone to the west coast, because the famous grammar of which I have spoken is on its way here. That is the main thing I have been looking for. I am to meet the grammatical father here on July 8. The good father also told me of Stikine [Tlingit] Indian women, who are very important for my work. Unfortunately they were occupied yesterday, and I could not do much, to my regret. So I measured and described the skulls which I had stolen and made arrangements with my photographer friend to return to the graveyard in order to obtain one or two additional skeletons. We went out there again at eight and now I have three skeletons, but without heads, which in all probability are in the Cowitchin [Cowichan] collection. Before I leave I shall get two more. At ten o'clock we were back from our expedition.

This morning I first went to the prison and got permission to drag the Indians to the photographer. It may be that my anthropological [anthropometric] observations will turn out to be the most valuable results of my trip. I am very glad about this. I now have photographs of three men, two Haida and one man from west Vancouver, the last a splendid fellow. I am having them all photographed nude to the waist. Since I also have the measurements, the photographs are very valuable. Not being able to get hold of any Indians for this afternoon, I cleaned the first skeleton and packed it up. They take up more room than I thought, and I shall have to acquire larger boxes. Besides having scientific value these skeletons are worth money. I expect to ship them the middle of July. I had asked my Haida to come this evening, but he was so drunk that I had to send him away. So I took a walk to Beacon Hill, from which one gets a beautiful view over San Juan de Fuca Strait. A Kwakiutl came this evening whom I had wanted very much, and so I am "fixed" for tomorrow.

*June 13:* At least so I thought yesterday, but I have been very much disappointed. I first went to the jail, but after waiting half an hour I learned that no new Indians had been brought in. Then I went to my Tlingit lady and got along well for three hours, but then she began to mutter. My Kwakiutl, George Hunt, came at 1:45 to tell me that he had been called as interpreter to a court sitting but would come to me at 4 P.M. He is an interpreter. I busied myself copying until four, but George Hunt did not appear. At eight I finally set out to look for him and was able to find his home after a long search, but he was not there. I must try to catch him tomorrow morning. The only way I can get people is to drag them in by the hair.

This week was the most unsatisfactory one I have spent on the coast except for the time at Quamatcin [Quamichan] when I was here before. I cannot help it. I am doing the best I can. Yesterday I passed through the ordeal of an interview. It seems that the attention of the newspaper men has been directed toward me from Toronto. Today there was a long story about my former trips, etc., but it is all nonsense. I wish I had two weeks longer at my disposal so that I could finish up properly.

*June 17—Sunday:* We are now nearing Alert Bay, and if I do not start writing soon everything will go helter-skelter and I shall not be able to write a sensible letter. I must recapitulate beginning from Thursday [June 14]. After much trouble I finally succeeded in getting Mr. Hunt for a morning and obtained all kinds of worthwhile information from him. In the afternoon I went to my Stikine Indian; in the evening I went on an expedition and obtained three, not-quite-complete skeletons. Besides that, I looked up some musicians in Victoria and tried to interest them in Indian music. Friday I was very busy packing my skeletons. After that I went to the Stikine woman for a few hours and packed my belongings for the trip north.

The steamer left at six in the evening. I greeted the captain and helmsman as old acquaintances and at last we left Victoria. We arrived in Nanaimo at four in the morning, where the ship took on coal, and six hours were wasted in the most pleasant manner. It rained a little all during the day, but otherwise it was pleasant and I walked about on deck. There are only a few passengers: a missionary going to Bella Bella, a few wood-choppers [loggers?], who were put on shore last night, a policeman going to Port Simpson, and I. There is also quite a nice fellow, a Mr. Anderson, who has lived in Port Simpson for several years and who is now going there to wind up his affairs. I asked him to get me some skulls and he has promised to do so. It looks as though I might possibly be back in Victoria by July 1. This morning we met the *Cariboo Fly*, which was to have left Victoria last night, in Nanaamo; I hope I may be able to go back on her. I should be very glad if that were possible because I could then still see the Kootenay, which would be of great importance. Maybe I can still go to the west coast. It is too bad that traveling is so difficult here. One loses so much time. My friend Jacobsen, you know whom I mean, is in Rivers Inlet I hear, and I shall probably see him late tonight or tomorrow morning. He will be surprised to see me here again.

*June 18:* I wonder whether it is true that the poor Kaiser is dead. It was reported on the day we sailed, but it was impossible to find out definitely. I think the domestic affairs on the other side [Europe] will become very strange. Yesterday at three o'clock we arrived at Alert Bay. I greeted Mr. Spencer, whose poor wife is sickly and was in bed. We were there only about a half hour, and in the evening we passed by my old Nawette [Nawiti]. I heard to my sorrow that the chief, who on my last visit made a beautiful speech, had died. I went to bed when at night we turned northward through Queen Charlotte Sound. It was the first time that I had seen the open Pacific Ocean.

I got up at 5:30 this morning. We had reached Rivers Inlet, where I hoped to see Jacobsen. I met him two hours ago and we were delighted to see each other again. I should have liked to stay here a while, as there would be work for me, but it is not possible. We are now in the long stream which leads to Alaska; it is broken only once, at Bella Bella. Up to now we have had pleasant, quiet weather, but it is still quite cool here. There is a lot of snow on the mountains although they are not very high. The forests are unbelievably dense. Every small cleft in the rocks is full of tall spruce, so that in the long run the landscape appears gloomy. I hope we shall reach the Skinar [Skeena] by tomorrow night or at the latest very early Wednesday morning. This letter is going back on the *Boskowitz*.

*June 14* [19?]: We have had very good weather and have almost reached the Skinar [Skeena] River, my goal.

*June 21—Port Essington:* I could write a great deal today if I had the time, but fortunately I am very busy here; above all, I haven't the peace of mind to write because I never know when I can work and when not. We arrived Tuesday, the nineteenth. Here the Skinar [Skeena] River is a wide arm of the sea, but it soon narrows farther upstream. Port Essington is larger than I expected. There are two salmon canneries. During fishing time there are at least twenty whites here. There are about forty Indian houses and two churches, one Methodist and one High Church. The town is on a narrow, flat strip of coast.

Mr. Anderson, my ship's companion, introduced me to Cunningham, who put me up in a cabin at first, but today took me to live in the residence. Tsimshian is about the only language spoken in this house, and Mrs. Morrison, the interpreter whom I wanted, is also here. I have never had a better opportunity to learn a language; I learned more yesterday than in a week elsewhere. Today I shall try to find out something of the old customs. I met a doctor from New York who teaches here in order to study the medical customs [?] of the Indians. After speaking with him for a while and finding that he really is an educated man and a doctor (which I doubted from what I had heard), I asked him for an abstract from his casebook and some statistical data, which he promised to give me. That will be a welcome addition to my work. I try to get as much cooperation as possible.

*Evening:* I learned a great deal today; in reality, enough, according to the program planned. I am quite certain that I can leave with a clear conscience, having accomplished what I had to do. I hope I shall find the priests from the west coast in Victoria and can stay there until about July 10. Then I will also be able to include the tribes of the interior.

*June 25—Monday:* I believe I last wrote on the twenty-second. I shall have to tell my story backward. Yesterday was Sunday, the worst institution ever in this part of the country. The natives, who are all Christians, keep a regulation English Sunday, and of course I can do nothing about it. The *Cariboo Fly* had arrived the night before, and there had been much noise and ado; so I slept until after 8 A.M. I was by no means the last one to appear at breakfast, however. I then went for a long walk to avoid being questioned about why I did not go to church. It was a beautiful, clear day. I climbed a small hill below the village and followed a path through the woods which led to a sawmill, about one mile away, and wandered about in that place. It is of course only possible to follow trails that have been cleared. The ground is swampy and the underbrush almost impassable. I returned at about noon, slept about two hours, and wrote a little, secretly, in my room.

To my great surprise I discovered a photographer as I was wandering about in the evening. He had come from Victoria to photograph all the sawmills and salmon fisheries. I got hold of him right away and had him photograph five beautifully tattooed Haidas. They were in Adamo civil costume [*sic*], and I had front and back views taken of them. In the evening, while everyone went to church, I amused myself by playing the harmonium, which one finds everywhere. All day long on Saturday we were waiting for the steamer. I stopped collecting language and got a few old men and women to tell me about old customs and practices. I am quite well satisfied with what I have accomplished here. I have not measured many people, because they do not like to be subjected to it. I hope to acquire a skull today but am not quite certain that I shall succeed—the grave is very near the village.

I am sure you want to know what kind of place this is. It is situated on the south bank of the Skinar [Skeena] River, which flows through a narrow valley, hemmed in by high mountains, out into the inlet. Mr. Cunningham's canning factory stands on a promontory, and there is a second one in the small bay. The little houses, or rather shanties, are as here indicated [a small sketch included]. There must be about six hundred Indians here, all of whom fish. Those who have enough money to rent a cabin live quite well, that is, for Indians. According to our standards, of course, they are dirty inside, but according to the Indians, nice and elegant. Outsiders live in larger cabins, in which several families are usually packed together. The fireplace is in the middle. Salmon hang above it to dry; foodstuffs, cans, or rather boxes of fat, and clothes are scattered all over; in short it is not exactly attractive. Others live in tents on the beach. Cunningham's store is the center of the settlement, and there are always many Indians standing about. Stamps are used for money, so that the capital needed for trading is diminished and at the same time the Indians are forced to buy in one store. They are paid for the most part in stamps.

There are two churches here, one English and one Methodist. Of course I had to visit the missionaries.

Work starts in the cannery at 7 A.M. Two hundred Indians are used for processing the salmon, and Chinese solder the cans. It is quite interesting to watch the processing of the salmon. At the first table women cut them open; at the next table heads and tails are removed. Then they are drawn and thrown into a bath where they are washed. They are then put into a machine which cuts them into seven parts and throws them into a trough from which they are distributed to be stuffed into cans. The lids are placed on top at another table and then they are placed in a soldering machine which fastens the lids. They are then placed on a large iron frame. The soldering is not checked in any way. The entire frame is then placed into boiling water for twenty minutes and then cooled. Finally the cans are packed into boxes. About forty fishing boats leave here, according to tide conditions. The salmon are caught in nets.

*June 29—On board the Cariboo Fly:* You must not wonder why I have not written all these days. I had much work to do in Port Essington; then, too, it is not much fun to write when one knows the letters will not leave for days. Now we have reached Comox and will probably reach Victoria at about four o'clock tomorrow night. I shall be happy to have letters again. The two weeks I have been away seem like four. I finished my work on Monday. I bought an entire doctor's outfit and a few other things for the museum in New York.[2] The ship returned on Tuesday and was to leave toward noon. But it was low tide, and so we did not sail until evening.

The photographer had returned, and I persuaded him to go with me to a small island in the vicinity and photograph the village while I tried to get a skull. I wanted him to do this in order to distract their attention. At low tide one can reach the island, which is about a quarter of a mile distant, on foot. Of course I did not tell the photographer (a stuttering idiot) what I wanted until we were there. I took a skull and the entire lower portion of the man. Mr. Anderson had returned from Port Simpson on the ship but had not had time to get the skulls he had promised me. It is very sad that I haven't more Tsimshian skulls. I have made another attempt with a traveling watchmaker who earns his living repairing Indian watches, but I have no idea whether he will be able to accomplish such a thing. We left Tuesday evening against a strong wind and are going along monotonously.

There are a number of Indians on the steamer, and I have found a Bella Bella who is willing to tell me things, so that my days are not entirely wasted. I hope I shall be able to find George Hunt tomorrow so that I can get to work immediately. I also hope that Professor Hale will be satisfied with my work; if not, I cannot help it. I intend to stay in Victoria until about the twelfth and then go to the interior. I should be in Kootenay on about the sixteenth and work there for a few days. Then I shall go back home. The Bella Bella turned out to be pretty good. Through him I have been able to complete the list of tribes and am acquiring quite a good vocabulary. It is good that I was forced to study the skulls. As a result I have gotten an insight into this subject about which up to now I knew little. I must say that I did pretty well in this. I do not think that there is a single Tsimshian skull in the collections I know. The weather has been nice practically all the time since we came to Skinar [Skeena].

*July 3—Tuesday:* I believe I ended my story with my arrival here from Port Essington. We arrived here [Victoria] at 4 A.M. and at

2. This reference is apparently to the American Museum of Natural History in New York.

seven, as soon as the post office was open, I went to get my letters. There were many letters from Marie and from Germany that had been forwarded from Lytton, and in addition there were letters from Hale and Dawson. The latter is in British Columbia in the neighborhood of the Kamloops, so that I may see him. It took me quite long to read all my letters. After breakfast I went to the prison but found no Indians there; I then went to the Catholic mission and was very much disappointed to hear that the west coast Indians had not yet arrived. Next I searched for George Hunt, the man from Fort Rupert, but did not find him. So I wandered back to the Stikine woman, after having spent a useless morning.

At noon I went to Sutton, the skull man. Having had word from Washington that I could get rid of the skulls, I told him I wanted to buy his collection. Yesterday was a holiday—"Dominion Day," an aping of the Fourth of July; since the Indians celebrate most dutifully, I thought it best to use Sunday and Monday for packing. We therefore arranged to go out there on Sunday. Mr. Sutton went Saturday afternoon and I followed Sunday morning. Saturday afternoon and evening I worked with my Haida. Sunday morning at eight I was again on my way. It was the loveliest, most delightful rainy day that you can imagine. My train ride lasted until 10:30, and then I went down to Cowichan Bay where Mr. Sutton was waiting for me. (I had to walk for about an hour.)

We crossed the water to their sawmill. I think I have already told you what it looks like. The mill is out of operation, presumably because capital is lacking. The two Sutton brothers live in a small house and pursue "phrenologie" besides their business. Of course I refrained from saying anything about the nonsense of phrenology. In the course of years I have acquired the curious habit of listening to all manner of opinions without agreeing or opposing. We worked hard on Sunday and Monday. Sunday afternoon I had a half-blood Indian come to the house so that I could learn something about the language, but I could do nothing with him. Therefore, when we had finished packing on Monday, we left, crossed Cowichan Bay, and went up the river to visit a real Indian, from whom I was able to find out most of what I wished to know. At three o'clock we went up to Duncan (the railway station) and on the way spoke to my old friends, Jagner [?] and Lamar. At 7 P.M. we were back here. I was so tired that I went to bed at 8:30 and slept through until this morning at seven. I must try to meet the people from the west coast today. I am still working with the Haida and Stitkin [Stikine] today but I think I shall be through with them.

*July 3* [4?]: This morning I first went to the police, but in vain; there were no Indians in jail. Then I went to the Stitkin [Stikine] woman, and at noon I inquired whether the west-coast Indians had arrived. They had, a short time before, but the father had left his grammar at home, and unfortunately the fellows are staying only two days. I have bad luck with these people. I do not seem able to reach them.

*July 4:* Yesterday I got a little . . . but that was all. Now I longingly await the arrival of the Indian in order to start work. Last night I accidentally met some traveling companions—Mr. and Mrs. Morris—who are on the point of sailing to California because they are very much disappointed with British Columbia.

*July 5:* I have now completed my travel plans. If nothing intervenes, I shall go to New Westminster on Tuesday to learn a little more of west coast language. Thursday I shall go to Kamloops and stations in between and will arrive in Golden the following Monday. From there I shall take a steamer on the Columbia to the lakes and will go to Kootenay Ferry. I shall turn back from there and travel home. I shall probably be in Golden on the twenty-fifth and will get to the farm [in New York] on the thirty-first. I am not quite clear about the timetable; perhaps I cannot reach Golden before the twenty-seventh. Hodge will have to be satisfied if we arrive August 4. I am about finished here.

Monday evening I returned from Cowichan. I believe I have already written that I met the Catholic priest from the west coast. I was able to work with the Indians one afternoon. Then they went on to New Westminister. That is why I want to go there; here I cannot get hold of these people. Today and yesterday morning the priest gave me Indian language lessons, and in addition I learned more Tlingit and Haida. Last night my Haida was to come, but he was so drunk that there was nothing for me to do but take a long walk. It was finally clear after weeks of rain and was really pleasant. I walked for about one and one-half hours along the shore. Today it was very fine. The people of Victoria are really nice. They celebrate not only Dominion Day but also the Fourth of July. There was a huge picnic outside the city, and all stores were closed to celebrate the day.

This afternoon I visited the museum and made several sketches. Tonight I again expect the Haida. Tomorrow morning I shall pack my skeletons so that I can send them away on Monday. On Saturday

I am going to Sanitch [Saanich, Straits Salish] to hunt skulls. Sanitch [Saanich] is an agricultural region northeast of Victoria. My diary is not very entertaining this time. That is because I am in the city most of the time, learning languages and measuring people. I must go and eat now in order to be on time for my Haida. I was almost desperate this evening because my Haida did not come, and I was about to go out when he appeared.

*July 9:* It was good that I said I shall leave on the nineteenth *unless* something interferes. Something *did* interfere, and I shall stay here a few days longer. Last night I was not very tired. I had no Indian and was busy writing up my notes for Hale. While I was so occupied it suddenly occurred to me that Haida and Tlingit did not have the structure of Indian languages, but that of the Asiatic. You can imagine that this thought caused me a great deal of excitement because that would be an important discovery. I could not go to sleep for a long time. The idea kept turning over and over in my mind. Isn't it funny that it should have happened on my birthday! I immediately decided to stay here longer, to find a basis for this idea. I worked some today on this matter but do not yet dare say whether my idea is right or wrong. There certainly is something to it, even if it is not more than that the two languages belong together.

This morning I was very busy sending off my collections, which are going to New York in bond. There are twelve boxes, which I have addressed to the museum. I was busy with packing and customs until two o'clock. Everything has been attended to, and I hope the things will arrive safely. It *should* not take more than three or four weeks. This afternoon I began to study Tlingit again and engaged a Haida who knows English well. When I leave depends somewhat on the results I get. In all events I wish to be in New Westminster for one day. Up to now my idea about the languages seems improbable to me, but it is not entirely impossible that it may be correct.

*July 10:* Today I had a good morning because I had letters from Berlin and Marie. I run to the post office every morning as soon as it opens and get my letters. But now there will again be about two weeks during which I shall hear nothing.

*July 12:* I have stayed in Victoria so long that I must hurry east as fast as possible. Yesterday I did practically nothing but learn Haida and Tlingit, and in the evening I packed. I am now in Vancouver and will be in Lytton at ten tonight. I shall stay there two days, then go on to Golden. On Monday I shall take the boat to the Columbia

... and from there the bus to Kootenay. I wish I were on my return trip to Golden because then I would be through.

Yesterday I had a letter from Hale saying that the Committee would like to print a preliminary report for this meeting. That means he would have to have it by August 18. I must hurry back to New York to get my manuscript ready as fast as possible. From Golden I will probably be able to write more definitely when I will be back. I telegraphed congratulations to Berlin this morning, and now I am cross because I have just heard that the wires are broken and no telegrams will be sent before tomorrow. Now I suppose my telegram and letter will arrive at the same time. First I was going to send a telegraph to Toni separately in Minden, but it is too expensive, especially since I do not even know whether she is there. The last few days have seemed dreadfully long. I no longer feel like working and shall finish up as quickly as possible.

*July 13—Lytton:* I am still here and am not sorry, because I must know something of the language to get ahead. I slept miserably during the night, on the way from Victoria to Vancouver—I really do not know why. Yesterday I felt all in, especially after having been shaken up in the train. In the morning I tried to write as much as I was able to. The train left at 1 P.M. It was pouring, but clear enough that I could admire the Fraser Valley. I had not been able to see it the last time because something got into my eye. The valley is very narrow and the river is wild. I had of course not taken a Pullman for those few hours, and the company was dreadful—singing Salvation Army people, etc. We arrived here at ten. The donkey of a conductor did not want to let me get out—he said I had to go all the way—so I was out of sorts when I arrived here. Someone at the station promised to take me to the hotel, which was supposed to be *"way down."* It was pitch black, and I was most surprised when in two minutes we stopped at a house, which was also pitch black. It was nine o'clock. He knocked, and soon a form in underpants appeared. It was the hotel owner. The address books of the C.P.R. list Lytton as a city of three hundred inhabitants but does not mention that two hundred and seventy of them are Indians. You can imagine what kind of a hotel this is. I went right to bed and slept quite well.

At seven this morning I breakfasted and then went in search of a suitable Indian. After some trouble I found one. Before that I visited all the graveyards and gathered a few bones, but nothing of great value. I also found a bone dagger and a stone hammer. I shall visit these places again tomorrow morning. Since I was unable to find an Indian right away, I went to the pastor of the Church of England

and found him to be very helpful. You can tell what sort of people they [the missionaries] are from what he said when he was told about a sick woman: "The best thing that can happen to them is to die, if they die believing in Christ!" The man, Reverend Smith, was curious to see what I was doing and got the people to come to church, where they told me stories. I did not get very much, but a little. I collected a small vocabulary this afternoon and shall continue with it tomorrow. These pages will go to Golden with me tomorrow and then continue on their way. I think I will be in Winnipeg two weeks from today. I am in a hurry to get home.

The Indian village here is not nice. The people unfortunately have been Christians for a long time, and that stands very much in my way. I hear little about olden times. Well, I must be satisfied. I am sorry I could not stay at Harrison Lake for two days. A dialect is said to be spoken there which is unknown to me. Of course, I can get very little of this language, but it is better than nothing at all. It will save my successor trouble. The Indians are not able to make much use of canoes on this swift river and so have many horses. These are the first "horse Indians" I have seen. The river valleys have been cut into the mountains for 1,000 feet or more. About 300 feet above the river there is a wide layer of terraces which one can see for many miles. In some places there are snow-covered mountains. At the junction of the Thompson and Fraser rivers there is a bridge across the river, on the old road to Cantro-Seit [Canford?].

*July 16—Golden:* I sent off my last letter from Lytton yesterday afternoon, packed the bones I had collected, and left at 10 P.M. Lytton is a very small place of about thirty or forty whites and many Indians, who have large farms and herds. Many of them have more than one hundred horses. A mule path branches off to the north (Lillooet), and the packing of supplies for these and their transportation on pack horses are the sources of livelihood for Lytton. At night I took a Pullman and arrived here last night at 6 P.M.

Golden, on the Columbia, is situated in a wide valley between the Rocky and Selkirk mountains. The population consists of innumerable mosquitoes[?], a few wooden houses, some of them inhabited, and two hotels. The population consists exclusively of gold miners, who lie about in the parlors of the hotels evenings, when full of sweet whiskey. They are mostly young fellows, eighteen to twenty years of age, but there are also a few old ones. Their most frequent expression is "God damn" used in all manner of combinations. Otherwise there is nothing special about this place, except that the surroundings are very beautiful. The shapes of the mountains on either side are very handsome, and the weather is glorious. Agriculture is only possible by means of irrigation.

I immediately went to the steamer yesterday to find out when it leaves. The steamers are flat and have wheels in back. I was unpleasantly surprised to find that it takes five days to get to Kootenay Ferry, not three or two and one-half as I was told in Victoria; so I shall get no farther than the Columbia [Lake?] where it widens.

*July 18:* I am now in Windemere, which is very pleasant; I am staying in a nice hotel and am hard at work. It is expensive but interesting. I am very happy at the thought that I shall have letters in another week and will be home in two. So far I like this place very much. It is very hot during the day but cool at night, and I am glad, in spite of the heat, to see blue sky for a change. There never was any at the coast. Windemere consists of three [or eight] log houses, scattered about. One of them is the hotel. It is two stories high. The upper story is a kind of attic, which has five bedsteads and one partially walled-in corner, the prize room which I occupy. But it is so nice and clean that it is really pleasant after all those horrible "hotels." The hosts are an "awfully nice" young couple, who make every effort to be pleasant; as a result I am also very pleasant and in a good mood. Of course it is very quiet and lonesome here, but you should see how nicely my hostess entertains me at dinner and supper—I am always late.

The steamer arrived here yesterday afternoon. The food on the little boat is very good, and [the cabins] are arranged comfortably, except that they are very hot and full of mosquitoes. The Kootenay Valley is about one and one-half German miles wide. On either side the mountains rise to seven or eight thousand feet, the highest peaks being snow-covered. They are for the most part steep and jagged. The Selkirk range is to the west, the Rocky Mountains to the east. The valley floor consists of terraces, made of sand, rising up to 3,008 feet above the river. Because of the dryness the sand appears in the most grotesque shapes—steep cliffs, peaks, and towers. The valley is open for the most part. Along the brooks that flow down from the mountains, there are dense stands of deciduous trees, and here and there a spruce, which lend a strange appearance to the entire countryside. On the green heights of the Selkirks there are dense forests, while the topmost regions are bare or covered with snow.

I know now why the scenery along the coast began to appear monotonous to me. It is due not only to the lack of human habitation but also to the absence of open grassland and deciduous trees. The light green of the dense growth of willow and oak along the Columbia is really refreshing. The Columbia flows along quietly and has many windings and tributaries. In some places the curves are so sharp and the river so narrow and swift that steamers get through only with great difficulty. One curve is especially bad. The captain tried to make it three times and finally succeeded by fastening a rope to the center of the curve, which helped to swing the steamer around it. As we approached the lake the water became beautifully clear and green. Earlier the river had been so shallow that we grounded frequently and got through with difficulty. At night we lay at anchor under the. . . . In the afternoon as we approached the lake we occasionally saw Indians riding proudly along the shore on their horses. After a short run on the lake we arrived here.

A large number of Kootenay were here to receive us. These are the first real Indians that I have seen: red skin, eagle noses, the famous blanket, moccasins, rabbit [?] apron, and deerskin jacket, with hair hanging loose or braided, more than six feet long. I introduced myself immediately, and after a conversation with a French hybrid who had a Kootenay wife I engaged an interpreter, who was to come this morning. Since he did not appear at seven o'clock, as had been arranged, I went to the Frenchman at ten and engaged him. It worked out very well because he is the best interpreter I can get here. With his help I quickly found the right people and am now in the midst of work. Fortunately he lives only two English miles distant so that I can reach him easily. But it is no pleasure to walk the distance in this broiling sun. In the sun the thermometer reads 125 degrees, and 98 in the shade. Last night it was 26 degrees [—3 cold Reaumur and 29 Reaumur heat, F.B.].

I have quite a respectable vocabulary and hope to get a good number of folk tales. I shall then have material about all the British Columbia tribes, except the T——, which have been known for a long time. This morning I had a wonderful swim in the lake. The water is wonderfully clear and very warm. I intend to have this pleasure every day. At night it is impossible on account of the mosquitoes. In a week I shall again be on the train and then speedily eastward!

*July 19:* I have been very fortunate with my interpreter; I am getting very good results. As a matter of fact I shall have about everything that Hale wants by tomorrow evening, and I am seriously considering leaving on Saturday. My stay here is too expensive. I pay the interpreter $3.50 a day, and I am not so very much interested in these tribes, because they have very little relation to all my former work. I shall not decide yet but wait until tomorrow evening to see what I have gotten. If I should get on the track of some important points, I will stay, but otherwise not. The language is very unfamiliar to me and the interpreter does not understand well enough to make it worthwhile to stay another week. Therefore I half hope to be at Lake George in a week. I am sorry now I did not stay at the Fraser River a few days longer, but I had no way of knowing how things would be here. I work nine hours daily in the sweat of my brow without interruption. Of course I can learn something in that length of time. Tomorrow I shall have reached the point where I shall have no more questions and will have to allow myself to be guided by the Indian. This is usually the point at which a brief survey becomes unprofitable unless you are dealing with very intelligent people. It is very hot again today. I do not feel it so much because the air is very dry, but I have become very sunburned these last few days. I think I am more black than brown.

*July 24:* We will at last be in Montreal the day after tomorrow, in the morning. I shall send these words from there. Dear parents, now I can address you directly, since I shall soon be able to tell Marie of the happenings of the last days. You cannot imagine how glad I will be to get home. Perhaps it was not quite right not to stay in Kootenay three days longer and wait for the steamer, but I thought that I would get only very meager results and so turned back. I learned more there than I had expected to, especially about folk tales and old customs. While in Windemere I finished my report for Hale which is to appear in print in September. The boat left late in the evening, so I had trouble catching the train in Golden and getting my mail. I had hoped to change into better clothes but did not have time to open my trunk. There was therefore nothing else to do, though I did not like it, but to continue as I was, dirty and messy, to Winnipeg. But I did not look too different from my traveling companions. I was able to get at my trunk in Winnipeg and make myself respectable. A train ride is very boring; time just crawled. We reached Port Arthur on Lake Superior at 1 P.M. You have no idea how dreary the prairies are west of Manitoba, as well as here, where there is nothing to be seen but small crippled spruce and birches. It was a pleasure to see fields and houses in Manitoba.

All in all I am satisfied with the results of my trip, although I have accomplished only about one quarter of what I did last time. This is due to the fact that I had to travel back and forth so much and had to deal with so many different tribes. I am at least glad that the work will be published so soon; it will be printed by September. I am glad that the reports of my three trips will appear this year: the Eskimo, the German report in Ascher [?], if I get the money from Boston, and this one. It is terrible how much I scribble these days. Our train arrives in Montreal Thursday morning, and I shall have to continue on the Grand Trunk, although I do not know about connections. I shall probably have to spend Thursday night in Baldwin, at the northern end of Lake George, and then get a boat in the morning. I have telegraphed Marie to reserve a cabin on the steamer from Albany to New York for the thirty-first. We will arrive Wednesday morning at 7 A.M., and I shall have had three days at the farm, during which I shall be lazy and happy again to be with Marie. It was very hard for me to be away from her so long a time.

# 4

## Family Letters (1889)

Victoria, July 18, 1889

Dear Toni,

I want to answer your question about the alphabet right away as follows:

$$x = q$$
$$\chi = q$$
$$\dot{x} = h$$
$$tl \text{ or also } tl = \mathscr{l}\,{}'$$

ų rather copy the way it is written

The non-English position of the words has to be retained of course. As I told you before, it is unimportant how you translate the particular words on the slips of paper because this only serves the purpose of exploring the meaning and the proper form of every word. The most important thing is the right arrangement of the words and the statement of the place where they occur. This should serve to ascertain the meaning and the grammatical form. It is really a great help to me that you relieve me of this work. It lightens my burden for next winter. I hope you can finish it soon enough so that Marie can take it with her or that I can find it on my return in New York in October. There is time enough however, if I get it by the middle of October. Would you please ask Lehmann to get me the two pages of . . . history? I also need the newest edition of Gute-Wagner, *Textbook on Geography*, and Nann, Hochstaetter & Pokorny, *General Geography*, which Marie should bring back with her. I am so glad that baby is finally getting teeth. I wish I could see the sweet little child just once! Well, one month has already gone by. The worst is coming, however, when I go from here. We are having the most beautiful weather. I hope I will see Jule here on Sunday. I wrote to him last night and asked him to come. I am going to leave these lines until the day after tomorrow because the steamer does not go until then. Since I have nothing to do, I shall write this afternoon to Lenz and Leiser.

Cordially, your old

Franz

Victoria, British Columbia
July 19, 1889

Sweet Wife,

How happy I was about your letter and your telegram! So the little Bublichen [Helene] finally has one, or rather several, teeth. I am so impatient for your letters and have to wait so long for them all the time. Unfortunately I now have to go to a place where connections will be very bad and from where I can't even send telegrams. I will have to send my telegrams by letter to Victoria and have them sent on from there, and you will have to send them to this place. Thus I won't even be able to send you a telegram for your birthday. I am going to Alberni and from there to Barclay Sound. Both are in the southern parts of the west coast of Vancouver Island.

Today I finally received my definite instructions. As before, I sit between the two chairs, Dawson and Hale. I had a letter from Dawson the other day, who apparently thinks I should visit only the west coast, while Hale commissions me with the west coast, the Kwakiutl, and the Salish. This is really crazy. Fortunately I already have the material on the Salish and some on the Kwakiutl from my first trip. I am going to send Hale's letter to Dawson this winter so that he will not think I am fooling around so much on my own. Moreover, Hale writes me that the secretary of the Indian Department in Ottawa has suggested to Dawson that he avail himself of my services as ethnologist. Officially nothing will come out of it again.

*July 20:* I have to close this letter today so that it will reach the boat next Saturday. Sweetheart, I feel much happier today because I have accomplished something during the past days, but I will be really glad only after I have finally left Victoria. I don't think that Jule is coming today. Maybe he was not really in Tacoma. I did not get any answer from him. Sweetie, now I will go to work again. Do you know that I have no little photograph of you? When I look at Bublichen I would like to see you also.

Adieu, sweet wife, take all my love.

Your husband

I can't send you any kisses; they will have to wait for New York. Do you love me sooooo much?

Victoria, July 23, 1889

Sweet Wife,

Tomorrow I will finally leave here and will stay away for about five weeks. I will be able to write you, but the letters will arrive very irregularly. There might be an interruption of two weeks, although I am not sure about it.

Darling, yesterday I had another letter from Hale, and I pondered long after reading it, about what I should do. I had written him and Dawson and Tylor but had torn up the letters again because I thought it would not be the right thing to do to write them while I am here. And I also do not like to complain about him behind his back because this would look so much like intrigue. Therefore I have resolved just not to answer his letters except in the event of his wanting some information on something. When I come back I shall make excerpts from Hale's most juicy letters and send them to Tylor, explaining that I cannot go on working with Hale. If a new offer comes from him, I will write him the same and hope that Tylor will back me up. The old man is simply so forgetful that he forgets from letter to letter what he has said before and then accuses me of having not followed his instructions. I might also send my grievances to Wilson and Dawson and ask them to decide. Besides, his special instructions are very childish and show clearly that he knows nothing about general ethnology. I am not even angry any more about these things. Since I have agreed to work here I will carry out my agreement. I will see how this can be done despite his pestering me. It is clear that the only logical way out would be to write that I can't go on this way. This, however, would destroy the whole matter, which has just started to work out. And yet I tell myself again and again that I am taking too much of a beating. Hale's vanity, pedantry, and sensitivity are at the bottom of everything, and, because I realize this, I do not want people to think that my difficulties are due to the same traits. I don't see any other decent way out than to let the people in question decide whether I have followed my instructions or not. Well, we can talk about this later.

I hope that for the sea trip tomorrow we will have the same beautiful weather we have had all week. Do you know where the voyage goes? We leave the San Juan de Fuca Strait and turn into the very large sound on the west coast of the island. From there a long fjord goes to Alberni, a rather large, agricultural settlement, where I shall probably stay for some time. The mail arrives there every Thursday from Nanaimo and is back here on Saturdays. The telegram you will receive August 31 will have been sent on the 21st and your answer will be in Alberni September 7 or 8. The latter will be my headquarters. Traveling is unfortunately very expensive.

Darling, it is a month now since I left Berlin, and it will be two months and two weeks until my return to New York. You know, it is a good thing that with my present instructions the report will be finished in a rather short time. I won't have too much linguistic work. Owing to the present fussing he is simply not going to get the skull [collection?]; I am going to keep them for my own purposes, especially since the pay is so low that I do not want to have extra work.

Today I want to write a few lines to Virchow because of my Kwakiutl essays, to which I want to add the vocabulary. In the winter I shall be very busy at first. I have to make Wagner's report, the one to the Canadian Committee, the article for Virchow which I just mentioned, and first of all the geography. I hope it will be possible for you to start sorting things out before I come, but without working too hard, so that we won't lose too much time.

Your husband


Victoria, July 26, 1889

Dear Parents,

Isn't it ghastly that I am still sitting here? And heaven only knows when I will finally be able to get away. They now say on Monday, but that is highly doubtful. Today I got your kind letter of July 9. At that time I was still in New York. I am really very dissatisfied with this trip now. The only reason is my unfortunate instructions.

Your Franz

P. S. I think you know that you should keep the meager diary. I have a copy here for Marie and myself.

Victoria, July 28, 1889

Sweet Wife,

The day before yesterday I wrote home so that not all the letters go to you. Isn't it terrible that I am still sitting here? An especially unlucky star seems to hover over this trip. Yesterday the
steamer on which I was to sail went aground, but fortunately it was
freed after twenty-four hours. Now it probably won't leave here
before Tuesday. I really have absolutely nothing to do here any
more. I have completely pumped all information out of my [Indian]
lady and can do nothing more with her. You cannot imagine how
angry I am with Hale's instructions. Apparently he is not familiar
with the existing literature on the coastal tribes, otherwise he would
not state that the tribes of the west coast are the least known. The
opposite is the fact. The outcome of this trip will be very meager,
I am afraid, just because I have to follow useless instructions.

Well, I don't want to write about this. I left Berlin five weeks
ago today, but it seems much longer. It will be nine or ten more
weeks until I will have you and Bublichen again. I think I am leading
a healthy life. I don't work too hard, am outdoors a great deal, and
eat a lot. But I find that I am not as thin as before. You definitely
have spoiled me.

The weather is strangely beautiful here; it is like it was in Berlin
in the spring but not as hot. Today I took a little walk to the reservation and made a drawing of the [entrance?] of a large house. I had
tried to do it each time I was there before, but the owner had prevented me. Today he permitted me to do it for one dollar. It took
me about three hours. Yesterday I again heard of a funeral plot, on a
farm about seven miles from here. The farmer allegedly has several
skulls, and I want to try to get them. Otherwise I am not concerned
with skulls this time.

In the past days I discovered that the shamans here also use a
special language. It appears, however, that no one knows a word of
this language any more. I wrote down a little song yesterday which
an old woman gave me. Now I will have to go to Nanaimo once
more to see whether I can get something on it, because they would
have had the same song. I live so quietly here that there is very little to tell you. I find that Victoria has become busier within the past
two and one-half years; I don't think that the city has grown, but
I think the people here have become busier and more enterprising.
I have not visited McDonald yet because every day I have thought
I would be leaving. If the boat does not go tomorrow I might still
go there.

Sweetheart, do you want me now to say how I love you? Next Saturday I shall especially long for you. Do you know that then it will have been one year since I came back? Darling, I am so tired of all this traveling and wish I could stay at home with you next year. I hope that the geographical part of this matter will finally peter out this winter. I am leaving this letter unsealed until tomorrow, until I know that the mail will leave.

*Tuesday, July 30:* I am really going now to Alberni. The boat finally came yesterday and will leave in two hours. I had already given up the trip. Now I do not think I shall be back here until August 22 or 23, and Anna will probably be cheated out of her birthday letter this way.

Adieu, darling, I hope I can send you a telegram for Saturday. I don't know if my letter will arrive on time. Today we are having the first clear day. The sun is shining but the air is filled with smoke as a result of the forest fires. This morning I opened a little . . . and it was all clear. If I don't get seasick I shall have a very nice trip; I think we should be there tomorrow evening. Adieu again, sweet wife. Give Bublichen a kiss from me. See you in two months.

Your husband

Alberni, August 12, 1889

My sweet Wife,

I prefer to send these lines to you at Southampton because they might not reach you at Bremerhaven any more. This evening the government steamer *Douglas* arrived unexpectedly and will take this letter. Unfortunately I am not finished here and can't go on it myself. The fires on the way to Nanaimo are so terrible that one cannot go there now. I shall go to Kwalekum [Qualicum] instead, to take the boat to Comox from there.

I am not satisfied with this trip. As I expected, the tribe that I am with now got all its customs from the Kwakiutl. I hope you will have a good trip. You must send me a telegram as soon as you have arrived. Early in September I can write you where I shall be. Greet . . . for me. I am so glad that she takes care of you. Sweetheart, I am afraid of all the work this coming winter; afraid it will be like last winter. At present, though, I only look forward to being with you again. It will be some time still, but almost half of our separation is over, and seven weeks from today I shall be with you. I only wish that I would not have to leave you again. I think I have fulfilled my duty toward this kind of work and hope that I can turn again to . . . work.

Alert Bay, August 25 to<br>September 3, 1889

My sweet Wife,

Today, Sunday, I can't work very well so will take the time to write you. I have already sent a letter to you to New York from Victoria, but these lines will also arrive before your return, since I shall be in Victoria again on September third or fourth. Sweetheart, I am very happy now because I achieved good results in the past days, in my opinion. I made the interesting discovery that Nutka [Nootka] and Kwakiutl belong together. This is even clearer than the connection between Haida and Tlingit. Through an extraordinarily lucky coincidence, members of many tribes have come together here, and therefore during these two days I have accumulated quite a lot of material.

Darling, but I should write you about other things! I wrote Hall on August 30 and probably will have an answer on September 5. Probably it will take some time until it reaches me. If the answer is definite, however, I shall know even before you arrive whether the Worcester matter has materialized.[1] It is unfortunate that Hall did not indicate whether he wants me as anthropologist or as geographer. I will let you know right away, of course. If the matter becomes final, then you will have to move into a boardinghouse in New York where we can live until October. You should make sure, though, that I have a study, because I shall have much to do before we leave. You know that we must not spend more than $150 a month; the moving will cost us enough. There is nothing else to write. Of course I have not told Hale anything. I shall wait until a final offer comes, then see him in the fall and hope to have a reasonable talk with him. I do not think, though, that I shall tell him anything about this offer. In October I shall get after the matter with Bien [?] and hope that the position in Worcester, if I get it, will be of advantage to my negotiations with Gissen [?] and company. In any event I will go to Washington in October to see if I can do anything there. Sweet wife!

1. Boas was negotiating a position with G. Stanley Hall, president of Clark University, Worcester, Massachusetts. He received the position at Clark in 1889 as a docent in anthropology at about $1,500 a year.

Now that I address letters to New York it does not seem so long before I will see you again. It will be five weeks from the day after tomorrow.

*August 29:* Today I am more than angry. As you can see from the diary, my interpreter was taken away from me, and so I cannot do much today but must try first to get the new interpreter going. I have to completely give up the work on the grammar. It is too bad; I could have learned so much more during these three days. Hall, the missionary here, was unfortunately very . . . , a thing I could have guessed from his so-called grammar. I have stumbled upon a few problems which were very obvious but which he did not recognize during all the twelve years he has been here. But he is very friendly, and helps wherever he can.

Now that it is almost September I am getting very impatient to get away from here. I have little confidence in the progress I am going to make in the next weeks because not much time is left and the area is completely unknown to me. Darling, you can write me on September 15 once more to Kamloops, British Columbia (general delivery). I will leave from there either on the twenty-second or the twenty-fourth. On the seventeenth you could write to Medicine Hat, North West Territories, Canada; on the twentieth to Winnipeg, Manitoba. The letter would have to go by evening train to Montreal. In any event I will also inquire there for mail. I am definitely expecting a letter in Winnipeg. I cannot tell you exactly when to mail it, but you can inquire and get a time table, to see when I shall arrive in Winnipeg and when your letter could be there. You must of course consider that the post office needs time to sort the mail, and then you should write as late as possible. I will be in New York on the twenty-ninth or the first of October. Oh, if the day of my return would only arrive! After today there are still thirty-three days to go, just one-third of the period I shall have been gone. Sweet wife, if I could only be with you; I am sick and tired of traveling.

*September 1:* I have been waiting all day for the arrival of the steamer *Boskowitz.* It was supposed to come last night, but the weather was so bad that it was delayed. I do hope it will come tonight because I would like to be in Victoria on Tuesday. The remaining four weeks don't seem so long any more, compared with the long time I have been away from you, but I wish they were over. My stay here was very successful after all. I thought it would be, because I was well prepared for it, which was not the case on the west coast. I am positive now that Nutka [Nootka] and Kwakiutl belong together. I wonder what will come of the Worcester affair? I really hope that I will see Dawson in order to urge the Canadian society . . . , and also see about my collection. I bought very nice pieces and am only sad that I will have to pass them on right away. I also think that I have fulfilled Tylor's wishes. I have a few not very [old?] but interesting pieces for him which are what he wanted, I hope.

Your Old One

Kamloops, September 8, 1889

My Sweetheart,

What do you say to my accepting Hall's offer? I wish I could have talked the matter over with you! But there was nothing I could do about it. I hope you will like it there and soon make friends. I hope they will be satisfied with me and that the position will become a permanent one. Now that everything is settled you don't have to keep it a secret any more although I hope it will not get out too early because of the. . . . I should like Otto Buehler to become secretary and therefore do not want it to become known that I have to resign. Darling, how will you feel about going back to Worcester? Will you recognize the city again? Are any of your old acquaintances left there? You know I don't like to build castles in the sky, but, I feel now that the position will be permanent, with a decent salary. And sweetheart, in Worcester we will be able to rent a little house! We will have $1,850 for the next year and that will go far there, especially with the cheaper rent.

*September 10:* I don't think that I will get too much done here. But I am trying my best. Now the weatherman has upset my plans, so that I could not do anything this morning or this afternoon. Adieu, darling. The letter has to go out.

Longingly,

Your Old Man

Kamloops, September 14, 1889

My dear, sweet Wife,

The closer it gets to the time to go home, the more impatient I get and the harder the work, which is not very satisfactory here anyway, becomes. Yet I am working ten hours a day and hoping that this year's report will please old Hale. The last two weeks were not very fruitful. To my great distress a Lillooet Indian who had promised me the evenings has gone again, and I had wanted to learn something about their language. When you get this letter you will be all settled again in New York.

Darling, I don't think that you will get any more letters from me until my return. There is no more postal connection available. I still have to make the Lillooet . . . and then go for a few days to Okanagan. Maybe I will get a letter from you in Sicamous on my return. Otherwise I will expect one in Medicine Hat and Winnipeg. I wonder whether you really had a good trip? Darling, don't be cross that I am writing such a short letter, but the closer the end of the trip comes, the harder it is to write. I long so much for Ernst. This morning I was thinking how hard it is for an old married man to bear being so far away from his family. Do you love me? Are you looking forward to seeing me again in two weeks?

**Your old man**

# 5

## Diary to Parents and
## Family Letters (1890)

EDITOR'S NOTE.—*The first twenty-three pages of Boas' 1890 German diary are illegible. Unfortunately it is not possible to tell accurately when he first arrived on the North Pacific Coast in 1890 or what he did at that time.*

### DIARY TO PARENTS

*Monday, June 9:* Finally the end of my railroad journey approaches, or at least the end for the time being. This morning we went through Tacoma and in six hours will be in Portland. It is just too bad; I could have been there with the Union Pacific yesterday morning. I doubt that I can finish everything in one afternoon. If I accomplish all I have in mind, I can leave for the Siletz reservation [Oregon] tomorrow morning.

There is not much to tell about the trip. The landscape is not half as nice as along the Canadian Pacific. The mountains don't impress me much. The people on the train are tolerable, and occasionally we have even had a good time. One evening stories were told and there was some singing. It is dreadful, however, to sit for eight days on a train. One is completely stupid at the end of it. In Helena I saw our former Marie. She looked really great. She apparently was very glad to see me and was sad that I could not stay over. They are getting along very well and seem to be quite happy in Helena. They asked of course how Helenchen was and were disappointed that I did not have a picture of her.

I read in the paper yesterday that it was terribly hot in New York. I only hope that Bubbel was not there. Since the day we came into the mountains it has been terribly hot, but it cools off agreeably at night. I really don't know how I have passed the time. I hardly read anything. I bought Pushkin's Memoirs but found them uninter-

115

esting. I do hope I will find some letters in Portland. Letters mailed in New York could be there by now. Today it is refreshingly cool. We are riding between the Cascades and the Coast Range through a wide valley. The landscape changes from dense woods to lovely grasslands. In a few weeks I will be coming through here again because I will have to work here. I am really anxious to see my [report?] of the Chinooks. I hope my Canadian report will arrive all right and will be printed as nicely as the previous one. Even if the setup is not as nice, the important thing is that the print should be readable. I still have not written Chamberlain in Toronto; I think I will do it this afternoon.

*June 14:* I have now been here in Siletz for two days and have started to work. I am finding it very difficult because I do not have a good interpreter. On the twelfth I sent you a few lines about my experiences in Portland and about the fact that when I arrived in Toledo that night I found to my dismay that there was no means of going on right away. I spent the evening as well as I could and started to pester them the next morning at six o'clock to move on. But it was eight o'clock before the carriage was ready.

*The same evening:* The trip to this place was very nice. The road goes along the Coast Range, through hilly country, and is very steep and winding. The first part traverses territory which burned twenty years ago; there is now a young and very lovely forest. Later on one rides through deep forest. At the end, the road leads deep down into the valley, apparently the ancient bottom of the ocean, about two English miles wide. Here lies the main part of the Siletz reservation, extending to the ocean with the Siletz River, a quite small, torrential mountain stream, running through the center. The road leads down to the valley and then fords the river. At about ten o'clock we arrived.

There are about six hundred Indians on the reservation. The officials consist of an agent, who lives in a rather nice home; a secretary; two teachers, one a crafts teacher; and a doctor. There is also a store. The agent was away on an inspection tour, but the secretary was very gracious. It appears that there are very few left of the tribe for which I am looking. Here there are three, two of whom are away right now; eventually others will be found. This makes me wonder about my work, insofar as I am in doubt about spending more time on these few fellows.

The secretary took me promptly to one of these Indians and I started to work. It seemed at first that I would have trouble finding a place to live, but finally I was taken in by the crafts teacher, who lives in a rough-looking little house. I have a partitioned-off corner, with all the windows nailed shut, but there is a bed! I eat with the owner of the store and go into the school when I want to write my notes. If it rains I work with my Indians in the attic of the agency; when the sun shines we sit in the open. The Chinook spoken here is very different from that in British Columbia, and therefore I experience difficulty in talking with them. This morning the agent came back and sent for an Indian who knows English. He lives about fifteen miles from here. I really hope he will come so that I can work with him. The old man I have now is quite good from the ethnological point of view but otherwise of not much use. One difficulty I have with him is that, when I want to work out a grammatical form, he says, "That is exactly the same," and he refuses to speak it aloud. I could just about explode! Most of the young people speak English. The number of languages is really large. I don't know how long I am going to stay here. It depends chiefly on the young man whom I am expecting now. That makes me hope that I will be successful.

*June 15:* The young man has arrived, and he speaks English well. At first everything looked very bad for me here, but now I have regained a little confidence. Perhaps I will even be able to take body measurements again, starting tomorrow. If this turns out all right, I will be really pleased. I especially want to measure children. I have also heard four stories, three of which are from Tillamook; now I shall see whether the young fellow can explain my texts.

Last night we all gathered around the agent and were up until nine o'clock. Yesterday morning it rained, and I worked in the agent's house. He placed a room at my disposal. During the day I usually write in the school, mornings from seven to eight, and in the evenings from 5:30 to 8 P.M. after I come in from my outside work.

*Portland, July 4, 1890:* I have behind me a series of most disagreeable days and have the feeling that the coming weeks will be just as disagreeable. I left Siletz last Sunday afternoon after getting good material there. I finished what I wanted in the linguistic and ethnological fields and measured ninety-eight persons. The officials were all very gracious. The agent took me down to Toledo. The trip was a great pleasure; the weather was wonderful and the woods very beautiful. Monday morning I left Toledo by train, arriving in Corvallis at 10:30. There I had a three hours' wait, which I passed as well as I could. I had to go to a place called Sheridan, which is not on the railroad, and nobody could tell me how to get there. I finally went through the whole train and asked everyone. It turned out that if I got out in . . . there would not be any transportation until the next

morning, and there was no house near the station at all. But if I rode
on to Amity, a station two miles farther, I could stay over night,
so this I did. In Amity, while getting my luggage from the baggage
car, I found that I could go on to Grand Ronde, about twenty-five
miles farther, the same evening; hence I rented a carriage and rode on.
About two miles along, we came to a river which we had to ford
because the bridge had been torn away by a flood. The water was
very high, and I had a difficult time saving my bundle. We then
went on, stopping at 7 o'clock for dinner in a small dark inn in a
little place called Willemina.

At 9 P.M. we arrived at Grand Ronde, where there is an entrance
to the reservation, and there I spent the night. There I found, to my
horror, that the cover of my bundle was open. The worst, however,
I noticed the next day. The agent had ordered another carriage for
me, and at 6 A.M. we rode on. I had written him to get an interpreter
for me, and he had done so for Monday. When I unpacked my bundle I found that the sack with my instruments had slipped out. You
can imagine how distressed I was! The agent was ready to go to
Sheridan himself. He is a real old-time Yankee who lives there with
his family and a couple of Indians. He is apparently an old settler
who got the job through political pull. The agency is in an old dilapidated shack. The agent is also the secretary. He was very gracious
in his way and let me work in the "court building," which was even
more dilapidated.

It was of little use to get angry over my lost instruments, especially since I was able to borrow compasses and other tools from a
cabinetmaker shop with which I could get along. I started to work
immediately but found after about ten minutes that my interpreter
was no good. He did not know the language well enough. I then
found out that . . . the relationship between the Clackamas, which I
wanted to learn, and the Chinook . . . and that there was no Chinook
on the reservation; it would be necessary to go to Astoria. I could
not leave the next day and therefore ordered an old man to work
with me so that I could at least get something out of staying there.
I also found out about the existence of a language, the name of which
I didn't know, which was spoken there. I quickly wrote to Washington to find out whether the language is already known there. If
it is not, I will have to go back to Grand Ronde once more. (On the
twenty-second I heard that a farmer had found my instruments, but
I have not yet heard anything directly from him.)

Since matters stood this way I packed my things and returned
yesterday morning to this place. The school in Grand Ronde is run
by the Catholics. It just so happened that the bishop was there, and
the children performed for him, with singing, theater, music, and

recitations; it was delightful to see these little Indians playing like this. I measured seventeen Indians in Grand Ronde, children and men. I was promised the use of a government car yesterday morning, but when I came down at 5 A.M. the car had just left without me. The agent sent a rider after it who brought it back, since it had gone only a half mile. Thus I was happily on my way and arrived here at 4 P.M. I needed money, but the banks were all closed because it was the Fourth of July. Fortunately the owner of the hotel cashed a check for me so that I can leave again tonight. I shall go to Astoria and maybe to Oysterville. For how long, I don't know. I spent today preparing my bills for Washington; that is a big job. I must also copy several of my writings which I want to mail from here. I came back to the hotel early to take a bath and to sleep. After a whole month on the road, one really longs to freshen up a bit. To-night I move on.

*Seaside, July 6:* The last time I wrote was the day before yesterday from Portland, a day which I used to copy many of my things and to write letters. In the evening I packed and made ready to take the boat at eight. Unfortunately these boats belong to the Union Pacific, and I had to fill out all sorts of "transportation orders," which cause endless trouble. (The railroad has borrowed money from the state, and all services it performs for the state are deducted from its debt.) I then heard that the boat was not leaving until eleven so that the passengers from Astoria could celebrate the Fourth in Portland. On the boat I asked about my Indians and learned that they were not in Astoria but somewhere closer to the coast. Yesterday morning at six we arrived in Astoria. It was an unfriendly, rainy morning. I went around in the harbor, asking everyone for advice, and found that I had to go on. By coincidence a railroad line was opened the day before yesterday, and so I arrived here comfortably at 10 A.M.

This place lies about seventeen miles south of the mouth of the Columbia. It will one day become a big resort for the people of Portland. The Indians I visited are quite civilized, mostly half-French. There are altogether ten adults, the remainder of what was once the largest tribe in this part of the country. I am staying at the post office, which is also a boardinghouse. By the middle of July the house will be filled with guests, but now I am the only one. The innkeepers are Swedes and apparently very nice people. The Indians live only about three-quarters of a mile from here, and I went to see them right off. I was soon disappointed. The younger people don't know their language well; most of them are not from here at all but speak Tillamook, which I had learned in Siletz. Only one old woman understands the language, but she does not speak English, so that I have to rely on my Chinook. I really get along all right with it, but unfortunately it is hard to get people to speak slowly. There is another woman who speaks the language, but she lives in Astoria. I think I will probably go to see her. I worked yesterday until 6 P.M. with the old "aunt," whose husband is a French half-breed. Today I shall continue but will probably leave again tomorrow evening because I don't think that I will be able to learn much more from the old woman. I don't know yet where I shall go from here—perhaps upstream again. I don't know whether I should go to Chinook to get more information. If I go I won't stay long. Here the Indians essentially live by digging clams, which they sell in Astoria. They live like the white people but are a little more dirty.

*Wednesday, July 9* [*Ilwako?*]: The few days at Seaside were really quite agreeable, and my work was successful. My hosts were Swedish. She was a really nice woman, so that I enjoyed my stay. There were also two small children, five and seven years old. In the evening when I came home, we all played together and then sat around the fire. It is quite cold in the evenings, and it rains all the time. I also played the organ, an instrument you can find in every larger house, and the children sang. I am getting along fine with my old woman, I think. Her husband is a French half-breed from Arkansas who has been working for the Hudson Bay Company for about twenty years. He was a great help to me. I now have quite a good vocabulary in the language and am using the last days of my stay to learn more about the language I learned in Siletz. I heard that a Tlaskanagu [?] the last of his tribe, was still living—in Nehalim [?], about thirty miles north of Seaside. If I can find the time I should like to go there, of course.

This morning at six I left in an open carriage during a very heavy rain lasting three hours. After breakfast I had to wait two hours for the boat to Astoria. In Astoria I bought boots because mine had fallen to pieces. Then I lunched. At two the boat left for this place. Ilwako lies on the north side of the mouth of the Columbia. I am about to go to Bay Center on Shoal Water Bay, where I want to see a few men. I don't know whether I will get anything out of them, but I must try anyway. I had hoped to find a connection here, but there is none until tomorrow. The trip from here to Astoria can be very stormy because here the current runs into the Columbia. I don't know yet how long I shall work around here. It won't be much longer than one week.

This morning I was made very happy by receiving a mountain of letters. Birthday letters. They came just on time. Mother's last letter went from Tacoma to Portland, from there to Grand Ronde, back again to Portland, and then to Astoria. I also received a nice long letter from Toni, and two from. . . . These were the best birthday gifts I could have had.

*Bay Center, Washington:* I think this is the prettiest place I have seen so far on this trip. Yesterday morning, the tenth, I mailed some letters. I had spent the night mainly in killing fleas which jumped around on my bed by the dozens and fed on my blood. In the morning at ten the train was supposed to leave, but nobody was around so I could pay my bill, and I had to go into the kitchen in order to get rid of my money. At ten the train was still standing on the street, and . . . drove it into the dirt. It took two hours to get the cars back on the rails so that the trip could begin. The train goes twelve miles over a very narrow peninsula which separates Shoal Water Bay from the ocean. After lunch, at the end of the train trip, I took a small steamer to this place. The water was very low, and after navigating around for a long time, we arrived here at four. The big place called Bay Center lies at the mouth of a small river. There may be twenty houses scattered along the shore. The "hotel" stands right at the landing. It is a wooden shack with a few partitions dividing the kitchen from the bedrooms. A ladder leads upstairs.

After some searching I found a man who told me where the Indians live; I was fortunate to find the Indians so quickly. By that time it was five o'clock and not worthwhile starting to work, so I went back to the hotel, following the "road" along the shore. Then I found that I had the wrong time. All clocks here are three-quarters of an hour slow. So I had no dinner until 7:45. I used the interim to make notes. There were four people at dinner. Although by now I have had four meals here, I have not heard a sound out of anyone. Oh, if only my nice hostess from Seaside were here, and her two brats! Fortunately my Indian is very intelligent. His English is not very good, but he quickly caught on to what I wanted, and he understands his own language. Thus I learned more about the Chinook language today than I had during all the time I worked so hard on it before, and that is since June 30! This man is the only one left who really knows the language. I hope to be finished with him by Sunday and then I will return to Astoria. That is, if no good Tsihelish [Chehalis] interpreter shows up. I wish I were one hundred miles away from this dreadful place. I have never in my life been in such a dull spot.

*July 15:* Despite the dullness I am still sitting here, and probably will stay another week. This Indian here is too valuable to let go before getting just everything out of him. I think I shall work with him on the Chinook until next Sunday and then start with the Tsihelish [Chehalis]. I might leave next Wednesday or Thursday, the twenty-second or twenty-third. The place itself is really awful. The only person who has talked to me is the priest, who wants me to come to church. He came here a few evenings to hold prayer hours. I politely refused to go. The one Sunday School class I attended in Siletz was enough for me for a long, long time. I finally ordered my letters to be forwarded. Up to now I did not ask that they be forwarded here because I didn't know how long I would stay.

The people here seem to be a truly poor lot. If you address someone you will get an answer, but then he sits down again and continues whittling, without speaking another word. Sometimes you can see three or four together playing chess [?] and . . . without saying one word. That seems to be their way of having fun. This game seems to be characteristic of these people; it is their favorite occupation. My work here is very successful. I finally have a notion what the Chinook language is all about. Now I have to close and go to work again. As I said before, the clocks here are all three-quarters of an hour slow but the day before yesterday they were set ahead and now breakfast is earlier.

*July 16:* Today was a full day; I got letters and postcards, and just now my instruments were returned. The man wanted $5 for his trouble, and I finally gave it to him. I can't tear myself away from here because my Indian is worth more than his weight in gold, he knows so much. I think I will stay another week to get as much from him as possible. Then, however, I must hurry back to Grand Ronde. If I had enough money with me, I would slowly go north, but I have to get the checks that are waiting for me in Astoria. I obtained very interesting material from this man and I want to pump him for more information, but this won't be possible I am afraid. Today I found an important legend which has its origin on Lake Superior or thereabouts. Here on the coast it is known only in Bella Coola and in this place. It throws a peculiar light on the way legends get around. I also got a very interesting version of a visit to heaven [?], a migratory legend which is known all over America. I can find relatively little about old customs. From everything I hear it appears that California culture has spread as far as the Columbia; that east of the Columbia . . . came, whereas north of here there is a group of tribes with whom I have had no dealings up to now. My measurements make it clear that here on the Columbia a migration from the east took place.

Well, this does not interest you, because it is only a detail, but for me it is of greatest importance. I am anxious to know what Powell will say about my measurements; he does not want to hear about this sort of thing. And yet it is of the greatest importance. I am working so hard chiefly to prove it to him. I won't reveal anything about it until I have digested it; then I will see what can be done with it. There is no money in it, of course.

The good weather seems to be over. Three whole days were beautiful. I could sit with my Indian on the shore of the ocean from morning until night. I hope the weather will improve again, but tonight it is raining. Since yesterday I started to exercise again, because I move around so little. I think I must look very well these days because in the past few weeks several people guessed my age to be twenty-seven, whereas last year some people thought I was between thirty-five and forty years of age. I have a very good tan and am a little rounder. I don't work as hard here as in Siletz because my old Indian cannot stand too much work, and he is the only one with whom I can work.

*Friday, July 18:* I have news from Washington and will have to go once more to Grand Ronde. The time that I have reserved to spend in Washington is running very short now. I will stay here until Wednesday and then go for six days to Grand Ronde. I want to come back here on August 12 [?]. Then I will have twenty-three days for the man from Washington, six of which I shall spend at the crossing of the Columbia with the Northern Pacific [?], maybe with the Tsihelish [Chehalis], or in Grays Harbor. After that I want to go for three or four days to Chemawa, near Salem. How I will work this out I don't know yet, but I have to do it in such a manner that I can reach the boat to Victoria. I plan to go to Bella Bella for the Canadians or maybe to the Nass River but don't know yet what I shall do. I think I shall finish with my Chinook tomorrow morning and then go straight to Tsihelish [Chehalis]. I have already busily used my recaptured instruments. During the past few days I measured eight "homunculus."

*Sunday, July 20:* Now I am glad to get away from this terrible place. I wish I could go home instead of going deeper into the wilderness. The fodder here is ghastly, especially the awful American bread, which lies in your stomach like a brick. And the beans! Meat is rare, and the people look it. Wednesday morning I leave directly for Portland. The connections are bad. I will leave here at 10 A.M. and arrive in Portland the next morning, if everything goes all right. I will rest for a day there and then go for about one week to Grand Ronde. My bedroom here is completely boarded up, and I have no air at all. In addition the fleas and flies are thick, especially now when the sun is very hot. I cannot use the room for anything but sleeping.

Yesterday I started still another language with my Indian—Tsihelish [Chehalis]. It is not easy, and that might be the reason why I will leave here early on Tuesday—but that is not certain yet. Anyway, the language is very difficult; its vowels and consonants are much more difficult than the Chinook. My measurements are now luckily up to one hundred and thirty. There are many people here, but it is hard to get hold of them because they are out gathering oysters most of the time. Today I worked as on any other day, to the horror of the pious population, who even go to church on week-days. The only newspapers they have here are religious ones. A few days ago I wanted to buy stamps [?] but found the entire . . . singing hymns and had to sit it out until they were finished. Well, it seems to me tonight I can't do anything but fuss. That's because the language is so unexpectedly hard. I would rather continue later when I am in a better mood.

FAMILY LETTERS

Victoria, July 30, 1890

My dear Wife,

I have never spent such an unhappy week as the past one. The last time I wrote you was from Tacoma, where I measured thirty-five people. Monday night I went to Port Townsend to find the Chemakum. It turned out that there are still three of them, but I could not find any; they were out fishing somewhere but no one knew where. What could I do? I learned that a steamer was going north the next day, and came here to take it. I want to use the time to do the Canadian job. When I went to buy my ticket, I found that the steamer had left early and that there was no way to go north for two weeks.

After looking around for a long time I found a few Haida last night from whom I wanted to get some information. It is allegedly a dialect of the language, and I also wanted to collect things. When I went there today it appeared that the difference was so great that I could not do anything with the language. One man wanted to explain tattooing to me, but when I came back from town, where I went to buy paper, he had started drinking; so here I sit and can't do anything! All the Indians seem to be in North Westminster, and I want to go there now. I hope I will find something to do there. For one week now, since last Wednesday, I have not accomplished anything. I am so angry that I can't write reasonably.

Darling, in nine weeks from today! I wish the calendar were that far along. Darling, you never wrote that uncle invited you to go to Europe with him. Mama wrote me about it. The distance between us is already very great. It is bad enough that I am six days from you. I could hardly stand the constant worry if you were in Europe. I hope my next letter will be more cheerful!

Your husband

New Westminster, August 2, 1890

My dear sweet Wife,

I must write you tonight so that this letter can leave tomorrow. In the morning I will have an Indian here so that I won't be able to write then. I wish I could be with you tomorrow and could kiss you, and also Bublichen. Darling, I haven't heard from you for so long that I feel awful. Something is wrong with the mail. The last letter I have from you was dated the 19th. I got it in Tacoma. I hope there will be another before Tuesday, because then I go for a week and a half to Bute Inlet and won't be able to get letters during that time.

You can well imagine in what a bad mood I have been. Since I left Bay Center I have hardly accomplished anything. Everywhere I went I had bad luck. I wrote you last from Victoria. I finally measured five Indians there. Here everyone is busy in the salmon fisheries. Yesterday morning at 7 A.M. I went up the river about thirty miles to measure children in a mission school. The priest who ran the boys' school was very friendly and I measured twelve boys. He then brought me to the girls' school, which is run by nuns. The head of the school almost scratched out my eyes. She said such a request was never made before and that it is outrageous for a man to want to measure girls. "How can science dare thus to deal with the work of God," she yelled at me. Very sadly we had to leave. This morning I measured a few more persons, and I finally found an interpreter who seems to be good. Today I obtained some valuable information, and I hope to get more tomorrow. Tomorrow afternoon he has to go fishing again, but I have another one lined up. Tuesday the boat leaves, probably in the evening. This summer I will have to endure a lot of church services! Yesterday I was taken almost by force into the Catholic church and had to get down on my knees during benediction, and so studied European ethnology instead of Indian. The trip up the river was very nice; it takes about four and one-half hours. The countryside is flat, but one sees the Coast Range in the background. It so happens that a larger party went up on the boat to accompany the minister of the interior, who is visiting here just now. I knew a few of them, and so the trip was quite enjoyable.

Darling, insofar as I can foresee, you should write me to New Westminster until August 10, then to Victoria until the fourteenth, and then to Tacoma. I will probably send you a telegram in the middle of the month giving you exact dates and places. I feel very fidgety when I don't get mail. And what is our Bublichen doing? Yesterday I was about to give up the whole job in Canada and come home in September. But that of course is impossible. Adieu darling.

Your husband

New Westminster, British Columbia
August 7, 1890

My dear, sweet, good Wife,

At last a letter from you again, the one of July 12. When no letter came from you yesterday I was desperate but then I realized it must have been sent to the wrong address. You can't trust the mail here. I know now of three letters—from different people—which did not reach me, or were very late. I hope you got my telegram of August 2. I am staying here until Monday and then will go down to the mouth of the river. My stay there depends on what work I find.

Darling, we have to make more money this winter. I am serious about this. I am not sure how much we will have. These mean cheats deducted $19.40 from my July–August bill as "not admissible." I am angry, because I am so thrifty. I received the letter with the three enclosures: Sutton, Gustav, and. . . . About Sutton I wrote you before. I have been afraid for a long time that I would have to pay him $150; I will just have to sell part of my collection. Things like this are repulsive to me. I received a nice circular from the university from which it appears that. . . . They want more details, but that is not possible because I have nothing to tell them. Darling, I long so much for you. How can I stand seven and one-half weeks more? In two or three weeks I can tell you when I will be back, or rather when I will leave Portland.

Your husband

I am making good progress now.

New Westminster, Hotel Douglas
Sunday, August 10, 1890

My sweet, dear, good Wife,

I have nothing special to write you. I have finished my work here with the exception of a few little things which I will wind up today and tomorrow morning. I will go, or rather steam down to the mouth of the river. I hope I will be all right there. Yesterday I wanted to measure the Indians again, but one of the salmon fishermen was mean enough to turn the Indians against me so that they refused to be measured. I measured only a few. Because the Indians are all Catholics I went immediately to the bishop and asked him to put in a good word for me. That will help, I am sure. I should like to measure more Indians this afternoon. I have never had as many difficulties as these I am having here because of the disgraceful [?] behavior of the white man.

I have really spoiled you these days by writing so much, even though I have had nothing to tell you. Just imagine, it is ten weeks today since I left you, and there are seven and one-half more to go. At times I feel like giving up the whole trip and letting all the Indians run off, and I myself would run back to you. The Indian I have here is a prize. He is a chief and has a genealogy going back nine generations. He is of course very conceited, and at least once a day I have to listen to a speech about how great he is. He does not work but lives on what the tribe gives him as payment for former potlatches. The main topic of his conversation is the fact that his wife once gave Princess Lenore [?], the wife of the former Governor of Canada, five cows which she did not even acknowledge, thus proving herself to be most unworthy.

When I visited the bishop yesterday he invited me to go with him to visit Jervis Inlet on the twenty-fifth. I should have liked to accept very much, but I don't have the time. I hope I find everything I want at Ladners Landing. If so I will stay there for two weeks, then return here. After that I want to go south along the east coast of Puget Sound to visit the Lummi and Tulalip [?] reservations. When my work is successful, time always passes rapidly; otherwise it drags.

Little by little my winter lectures on geography are shaping up in my mind. Those will be really hard weeks of work. My winter plans are still very incomplete. I intend to work seven or eight hours for the university and then write my Canadian reports there after that. In October or November I must write the small geography book. It may have to be delayed even longer because I have to collect the material, and I may not find it easily in Worcester. I think I wrote you that I changed the plan of the book so that it will become more comprehensive: trade routes of primitive peoples in antiquity and in the Middle Ages. Everything will be second hand, of course, except for a small part of the first section. Therefore it should be well written and. . . . I wonder if I will find time to draw the map which P——wants to have printed. After that I could do some work in late winter and in the spring for Powell, to make money for the summer. I hope something like this will work out.

Goodbye, darling; I wish I were with you in spite of the 92 degrees. Here it is rather warm too, but one can stand it more easily. When I make measurements I always perspire a great deal.

Your old man

Ladners Landing, August 12, 1890

My sweet Wife,

Yesterday at noon I left New Westminster to come here. In the morning I was still working on the genealogy of the family of the chief of . . . Lake, which I had him tell me. It goes back nine generations and is very interesting. When I go to a new place, I am always afraid I won't find enough work. I feel the same way here. The steamer took only one hour from New Westminster. The countryside is completely flat. There are many farms and fisheries—a whole new village sprang up within the past few years. I arrived here at 4 P.M., and the first person I saw was the photographer Brooks [?] whom I had met two years ago on the Skeena River. I let him show me around a bit, and soon I also met one of the local . . . Bella Coola, who had also been in Berlin. I found out that three of these people are here, and thus I had a good introduction to the Indians quickly. They all work in the canneries, however, and have free time only in the afternoon.

The hotel is ugly and dirty; the bed is so dirty that I kept all my clothes on when I lay down for a little time. I don't think that I am going to be able to work here more than one week. I don't know yet what I shall do then. The salmon are becoming scarce, and I heard that the Indians will soon go up to Puyallup. I doubt that I can do much more here. At any rate I will go from here to Victoria. Shall I bring back something for you . . . ? It appears now that I won't be able to work for Canada with success for more than two weeks; then I will have thirty days for the people in Washington—altogether forty-four days. Thus it is possible that I shall be back home on September 25 or 26. Couldn't you stay that long in New York so that we could come home together? I could then also buy the things I need in New York. This we could do together, darling. In six weeks we will be together again. How I look forward to this! I hope I shall get a letter from you tomorrow via New Westminster in answer to my telegram. The mail comes only two or three times a week, I think. It is much cooler here than up the river, because we are so close to the ocean. It was very hot these past days up there, and here it was only 73 degrees.

The Indians are very nice and gracious here, and I can get many of them. Yesterday at noon I set up my measuring shack and didn't even have to urge them. After I started they came of their own accord, one after the other. Such a thing has never happened to me before. Unfortunately, they are working so much of the time that I can't have them many hours, and never in the mornings. I heard the fisheries will close the middle of next week. I don't know yet what I shall do then. Up to now I have measured two hundred and forty-eight people. When you consider that all our knowledge is based on seven hundred persons who were measured during the war [?], none of them from the Pacific coast, you can imagine that I am very happy about the figure. I am curious to learn what the result will be when I am finished with my research.

I hope I will get a letter from you this morning. I won't close this letter until the mail arrives. Now it has come, and nothing from you. Just a few lines from Hale; that was all.

Your husband

Ladners Landing, August 14, 1890

My sweet Wife,

Do you know, I am very unhappy? Again no letter from you! I have not heard from you since the thirty-first, in spite of my telegram of the second. A letter could have been delivered today. It is held up somewhere, I am sure. The mail is most unreliable. I am not accomplishing very much here. I am measuring a lot of Indians, but that is all. I would like to do other work too, but there is nothing else here. At this point I hardly know what I shall do all next week. The canneries are all closing this week or next. I think I shall go to Victoria, which is a good place for measuring because everyone goes through there.

Darling, I did a lot of figuring yesterday. Now I have to pay Sutton, and we must see whether I shall have to sell the collection this winter. It would be wiser to keep it because it will gain in value. Today I paid him $150. I am afraid that I will have to pay about $9 or $10 out of my own pocket every month for the Washington Indians. I am sure that when I pay Sutton the $200 after my return there won't be anything left from the trip but the $450 which will be in Worcester. In the spring we had $370 in the savings bank which I withdrew for the trip. After my return I shall get $150 from Canada and, according to Hale's last letter, another $100 for my report. If we don't count the latter sum, we have altogether $600, plus $1,500 from the University, which makes $2,100. This is what we have to live on until next fall. I fear I shall have to sell the collection. It is not good to have nothing in the savings bank. I still hope that I will get all kinds of items here, and then I am sure I will get $1,800 for the collection. Some doctors [?] promised me a few skulls.

Sweet wife, write me often. Last week passed quickly, but now time is crawling again. Still six more weeks! There won't be any letters until Saturday.

Your impatient husband

Ladners Landing, August 17, 1890

My sweet Wife,

A week has gone by again, and it now appears that my working time here will be short. To think that eleven weeks have passed already since I have been away from you! And that I still have to wait five to six weeks until I will be with you again, darling.

Regardless of the fact that my hotel is filthy, I am very well off here. This week I measured thirty Bella Coola, and now I have engaged one with whom I am making good progress. He is of the group which was in Berlin. With what I am getting now and what I got before, I can see that I have learned a great deal. Much of the confused knowledge I had then is being straightened out now. The Bella Coola now fit better into the pattern of the neighboring tribes. I also got several very good drawings which will be valuable for my next report. They are strange crests. The day before yesterday I was annoyed. When I went into the camp to make measurements, the boss of the cannery came and told me in a rude manner to "clear out." I could not protest because the buildings belong to the cannery. I went straight to the office but the owner was not around. The boss is a stupid ass, a very simple, uneducated man who had no idea what I was doing. One cannot argue with people like that. The bookkeeper fortunately was a very nice man and told me that the boss had no authority; that he was only boss over the Indians and Chinese. He succeeded in changing the man's mind. To make up for the trouble he caused, I asked them to let me have one man, which they did. So this ass unwillingly helped me to have a good, productive day. I hope now that I can stay here until next Saturday, the twenty-third. I will stay a few more days in Victoria and then return to the Sound [?]. I play Skat with the doctor every evening. Even if the man is a boor, he has some sense of science, and one can reasonably talk with him. The third player is a German merchant.

My schedule is now: eight to five, the Indian; five to seven, walking; eight to ten, card playing. So the days pass quickly, and this week will soon be over.

Your husband

Victoria, August 24, 1890

My dear sweet Wife,

I never had such a bad time with respect to letters as this year. I don't know why, but the letters take six days from Port Townsend to here; I got your letter of August 7 only today. I was so worried that I telegraphed you Thursday from Ladners Landing. It went with a prepaid answer, but no reply came. If I had not surmised from your wrong addresses that you did not get my birthday telegram, I should have died of fear. You should inquire quickly about those telegrams and then write me about them on a separate sheet. I shall try to get my money back. This is really unheard of, two telegrams which did not arrive!

I am now finished with my work for Canada. Little by little I am beginning to feel that the time of our separation is coming to an end. Yet it is still five weeks! I leave here tomorrow evening, will stay a few days in Port Townsend, and then go to Seattle and Tacoma. From Tacoma I will probably go to the Chihalish [Chehalis] Reservation and to a place called N——. This will take up the remainder of my time; after that I will make ready for my return. Address your letters from now on to Tacoma.

Adieu, darling, I can't write you any more today because I am a bit peeved at you for not writing more often. The last time I heard was two and one-half weeks ago.

Your dumb<br>Husband

Victoria, August 24, 1890

Dear Parents,

Last night I gladly returned to this place and am recovering in a clean bed and with decent food. Tomorrow evening I will go back to the American side, I hope. How happy I shall be! I was very busy in Ladners Landing and will be able to deliver a really good report to the Canadians next year, although I worked for them only four weeks. I will devote a few more days to them in Seattle, however.

The Congress is probably over by now and Uncle Jacobi back in New York. When you get this letter Toni will be back with you, I am sure. Helene's baby is born by now, I hope. I should like so much to hear about it, but the letters are so very slow. It takes six days from Tacoma to this place! The trip itself takes only eight hours. Here in Victoria there is nothing for me to do, and so I shall stay only until tomorrow night. I will visit a few people tomorrow during the day. I have already hired an Indian for Tuesday in Port Townsend. I hope he will be there. Wednesday or Thursday I will go to Tacoma and maybe stay there for a few days. Today I ran into young. . . . I want to go there once more tomorrow to see whether they still have my . . . from last year.

There is little to tell about myself. In Ladners Landing I spent a good deal of time with the doctor of whom I wrote you before. This way the evenings passed quite nicely, whereas they are usually boring, especially in dirty little places like that. I worked there especially on my Bella Coola and used an old friend from Berlin for that. All the Indians left Ladners Landing yesterday to go to Seattle to pick hops. I will get some more out of them there, I think. All in all I got quite a lot of material this summer. I should like to go straight home now. I will hardly recognize Bublichen; she must have changed a great deal during these four months. And she probably will have no idea who I am.

Take my most sincere greetings for today.

Your Franz

# 6

## Family Letters (1894)

Glacier, British Columbia
September 12, 1894

Dear Wife,

Now only a greeting before I leave here. My suitcase plus key arrived yesterday. I did not even open it, and I hope there is nothing missing. I don't think it was opened in Banff. Yesterday I sent a great deal of written material back to Donaldson and hope to send the rest to him soon. It is so beautiful here that I should like to stay. Oh, it is so repulsive to me that I must start work now, or rather start coaxing the Indians. I don't even want to think of it. Well, it is not until tomorrow.

Yesterday morning I took a wonderful hike through dense forest to a little lake. There the trail ended, and I climbed up the mountain without a trail. Soon I passed the tree line and went on over a meadow bordering the snow. I went up to the ridge which forms the top, but I could not go on; it would have been too dangerous all alone. The view was magnificent. At my feet lay the immense glacier, about a half hour's walk above the hotel. Above it lies Mt. Sir Donald, and far away the huge summits with their immense glaciers. On the other side one huge summit is next to the other. I rested about an hour and then ran down the mountain in one hour; it had taken me three hours to climb up. I bought a few photographs which are very beautiful and which will give you an idea of the beauty here. For Helenchen I also have something from Papa. Just imagine, up on the mountain there was a glen which looked exactly like the glen where the little rose grew in the song. When I arrived here I went straight to the glacier, which I knew from my first trip.

133

But now I hear my train coming and I have to make ready. I hope I shall find letters from you tomorrow morning in Okanagan. Adieu, darling. Kisses from your

Husband

Enderby, September 13, 1894

My dear Wife,

Now the misery with the mail is starting right in again! I looked forward so much to getting letters from you today, but it turned out that the post office at Okanagan was not where I thought it was. When I arrived here in Sicamous last night it was already dark and it was still raining. The old owner of the Hotel "Colonel Forester" [?] was at the station, and I recognized him right away. I started to chat with him about the innovations in Sicamous since I was here last, and about all kinds of things. They have a new station and the side railroad to Okanagan, and the place now consists of three houses instead of two. He warmed up a bit and I asked him about the Indians. He is a very nice old chap and very sure of himself, as behooves an old settler. He once was a slave trader in Africa, has lived also in China, Japan, and the South Seas.

Well, the Colonel gave me information concerning the Indians in general, and he sent me to a man here who could help me and whom it would be good for me to know, a Mr. Fortune. So today I rode up the valley to this place, about twenty-four miles, and went immediately to this man, who lives two miles from here on a farm. I found him to be an amiable man greatly interested in everything connected with science. He went to college for a half year and knew Sir Daniel Wilson and many others. Because he had hurt his back and could not leave the house, he sent a carriage after an influential Indian. He explained to the Indian what I needed. I engaged this Indian and am going to try my luck tomorrow. We will take a carriage and ride all over the country; then I will go by steamer down Lake Okanagan, and, finally, I will come back here. After that I plan to go to Kamloops, arriving in one week with, I hope, many measurements in my bag. I hope that I will be successful with my Indian.

Tomorrow I will go to the post office in Okanagan to pick up my mail. I hope that it will really be there. I haven't heard from you for a week. Mr. Fortune was so hospitable that I could hardly get away. Today I finally got around to opening my suitcase and I packed for the pending [?] tour. On this occasion I also looked at your dear pictures.

Adieu now. Many kisses from your husband. Tell the children to write also. I wonder how the negotiations with S—— turned out?

Sicamous, September 16, 1894

Dear Wife,

Last night I returned to this place and found that the train was eleven hours late, so that I had to spend the night here. Since a few Indians do live here, I shall also stay for the day and try to measure them. My Okanagan trip was a great failure. During the two days I was there I measured only five Indians and simply could not get any more without staying much longer. I came to the conclusion that my time is much too valuable to spend on fruitless attempts to measure Indians. There are younger people who can do this. After this trip I shall never do it again. All this measuring, or rather the talk connected with it to win over the Indians, is really repulsive. I wrote you about the nice old gentleman I visited in Enderby? I could have gone to him again to ask him to exercise his influence, but that would have taken too much of my time.

Friday [September 14] I went with an Indian to Lake Okanagan in pouring rain to measure Indians. Unfortunately he took me to the chief first instead of letting me go from house to house. We had to parley a lot, and then the chief told me to wait, that he was going to talk it over in the evening. From the way he acted I could tell that the good chief was afraid and that I wouldn't get what I wanted. When all the Indians had scattered in all directions in the evening, I left, arriving in Enderby very late and very angry. I was so cold that I could not move my fingers. The chief told me that he was descended from many great chiefs and that the Indians wanted to make him chief when his father died but that he did not want to be chief because he wanted to be humble. In all matters he had to ask the advice of the old people who helped him, and this he had to do in my case too. And they all live within a radius of about ten miles. Well, there was nothing I could do about it. He then also told me, as an example of his humility, that the government once gave saddles, bridles, and tools for farming to all the Indians but that he did not accept them because he wanted to have only things which he had earned on his own property with his own hands and with the help of the dear

God. It is interesting to learn how these people think, but this does not help my work.

Yesterday I got five people in Enderby. I met a missionary there who had come from the Lake. I greeted him politely, he asked me what I was doing, and I explained everything to him as well as I could. He answered very politely (he is French), "That seems very foolish. What do you want to do such nonsense for?" The Indians ask his advice, which he freely gives. And that is the reason for my lack of success in Enderby! I will be glad when I am back on the coast again!

I have only one letter from you, September 4. The copies of the magazine you sent have not arrived yet either. It seems that the letters addressed to Okanagan were sent to four different offices. I wrote to all four and probably will get the mail together soon. I wonder what you are going to do in the fall? I am anxious to find out. Do you think about Helenchen's instructions? That she has to start to learn something? Little Ernst will also have to get some . . . soon. Well, darling, in October you will surely get around to it. How I hate to be so far away from you all!

Mother is probably also back in town now. My suitcase is so terribly heavy that I shall send a few things which I don't need any more from Kamloops to New York. I hope it won't be too much trouble for you. I am afraid, however, that the suitcase will break in two. Yesterday I finished the review of Parker's address to the . . . in St. Louis and am mailing it today.

Goodbye now. I want to try to measure some Indians today. Please kiss the little ones for me. Do they sometimes talk about me all of themselves? Make them write me once in a while. With all my love,

Your Franz

Kamloops, September 17, 1894

My dear Wife,

I just wrote to Seler and asked him whether I couldn't be his substitute if he really. . . . I told him that I wanted to spend some time over there [Germany] in order to refresh my knowledge. This way we could mutually help each other. I wrote him also that I can't be sure I could do it because I can't make any plans until I have a permanent position and until I know how my future here will develop. I think it was worthwhile to ventilate this question for once. Don't get excited about it! The eggs have not been laid yet, and I am writing nothing about it to those over there. Well, the future will tell!

Unfortunately all the Indians are hunting now and I won't be able to do much. This is the reason that I am going to make a little tour to Lillooet and then to Chilcotin, and will ride down the river to Victoria where I shall arrive on Monday or Tuesday, the twenty-fourth or twenty-fifth. Then I will take the next steamer north; first to Metlakatla. Please address your letters to Victoria. How I long for a letter from you. I can't tell you how angry I am about the Okanagan mail delay.

Your husband

Kamloops, September 17, 1894

Dear Parents,

The last letter I received from you was that of August 27. The connections to this place are very good, if one considers that the letter went first to Victoria and then had to travel back two days. My trip to Okanagan valley was a great failure. I did not have much time to spend and wanted only to measure. The Indians were very contrary, however, and I could do nothing. I wrote you that I visited an old settler there who was very nice. The following day I rode on an old hay wagon with an Indian through pouring rain, and also great cold, to the Okanagan Lake. It took three hours! When we arrived, however, it stopped raining, and the people made a huge bonfire for us where we could thaw our frozen bones and get dry.

Then the question about the measuring was brought up. The chief, to whom unfortunately the question was submitted, was a timid old fellow. He made a long speech in which he emphasized his perfection and also said how humble he was: "God gave me these arms and these hands, and everything I have I owe to him. The government once wanted to give us farm implements, but I refused. What I don't earn with my own hands I don't deserve and don't accept and don't want. I was supposed to be chief, but I refused and said that they should assign to me two old men to rule with me." He said all this only to pass on the responsibility to the two old men and to chicken out. I was to wait a few days, and then do what I wanted. I didn't have time to waste, however, and therefore gave up; but the next day I quickly measured five people.

Then I returned to Sicamous. The train arrived eleven hours late; so I had to spend Sunday there and arrived here only today, Monday. Today I visited the missionaries, who are very amiable and well educated. This morning I went out to the Mission, a half German mile from here, and met a missionary making hay. It turned out that he was the missionary for the whites, and therefore I had to return to "town" where I saw the other one, Father Le-Jeune, who already knew who I was, and he was very obliging. I had to have lunch (dinner) with him, and we went together to the Indian school in the afternoon, again a half mile off. There I measured twenty-five children. So you see, I had quite a fruitful day. Tomorrow I want to try my luck in the village. Unfortunately almost all the Indians are out hunting and won't be back until the end of November. Such a poor priest really leads a miserable life. His house is poor, and he has no quiet time all year round because he has to go from village to village. Since the Indians speak so many different languages, a personal relationship can never develop with any of them. In short, I can't see what these people get out of their lives except religion.

Mama, you write as if you feel that I am withholding something from you concerning my [plans?]. But you really know everything that has happened and what is still pending. I keep on the alert and sometimes try to get information on some matter, but I don't write about it if there is nothing special to say. Now, of course, I cannot look around and therefore will give all my time to the Indians. Today it was very cold and stormy, and I am tired and worn out. Goodnight now. Give many greetings to the family and yourself. Your loving son,

Franz

North Bend, September 21, 1894

Dear Wife,

I am definitely resolved not to return this time before I have finished. This will be hard on me toward the end, but since this will probably be the last visit for a long time in British Columbia, it would not be right to break off early. I will stay here another two days and then go to Victoria. The disagreeable feeling I had that I don't get along with the Indians is slowly wearing off now, and I am hopeful that I will have good results. Tuesday night I left Kamloops. I took a Pullman, thinking that they charge by the mile. I was aghast when I left the train at 4 A.M. and found that I had to pay $3 for four hours' sleep—the same price I should have paid had I gone all the way to Vancouver. Well, no more sleeping cars for me.

I left the train at Spences Bridge, which is a little dump of three or four houses and a hotel right at the station. I had to make a lot of noise before I was heard, only to be offered a dirty bed shared with a drunken workman. I would have run away right then if it had made any sense. It was worse than in an Indian house. I objected so energetically that they gave me a "lady's room" which was tolerable. No fresh linen, of course, because they had only two sets and the other was in the wash. I had to sleep both days with my clothes on. In the morning everything looked quite hopeless. I took a ferry across the river because the bridge had been washed away in the spring. On the other side I went to see a man, a Salvation Army Warrior and big farmer, who raises... fruit and is supposed to know the Indians very well. He sent me to another young man, who lives three miles away up the mountain and who is married to an Indian. So I started up the mountain in the great heat and finally found the house, where he lives with a number of Indians. He was not at home. I waited, entertained by his wife and an old man, and after an hour he came. The young man, James Teit, is a treasure! He knows a great deal about the tribes. I engaged him right away.

With his help I measured all the Indians who live there. Since I didn't know that Indians lived on the mountain, I did not have my instruments, so that I had to go down, cross the river, and go up again. In the evening I was terribly tired and slept well in spite of everything. Yesterday we left at 5:30 and rode horseback to the various camps. Since the Indians are scattered all around, I cannot finish here but hope to be able to come back later. This depends on what I find in Fort Rupert.

Last night I slept only until 3:30, which was when the train left. Nobody was up in the "hotel," of course, so I found my way noisily in the dark to the station. In the station block-house all the employees were lying around on the floor, snoring. I had to climb over several to find a place to sit down. Fortunately the train was not late and I arrived here at 7 A.M. I took a bath immediately and let them bring my suitcase; I changed and felt like God in France. The last two days I had worked so strenuously that I was really exhausted. Goodbye, I had better start work now.

Your husband

North Bend, September 21, 1894

Dear Parents,

Today I received your dear letters of August 31 and September 3. How fast time flies nowadays. Monday I hope to be in Victoria; then the time will go even faster. I wish I were really sure that we can come over in the winter. If nothing completely unexpected happens, we shall be over there not later than March, but I am still hoping for January. I don't know what I wrote you to give you the impression that I could find a permanent job at the convention. As things stand here I don't expect to find anything before next June. It is nice to think that then everything will be more propitious. At any rate I am not worried. If I think of . . . bad luck, I could tear my hair that nothing came of the Chicago business. When I think of the $7,000, and how nicely I could have helped them— instead of having to count every penny! Well, something better will come up soon. One cannot always have bad luck in everything one touches. The most important thing is that everyone we love is in good health.

[I met] a red-headed Scotsman [James Teit] who is married to an Indian woman. He knows a great deal about the Indians and was especially kind. I engaged him right off. Around him live a great number of Indians and a man called Oppenheimer, who is a German Jew and is also married to an Indian. His sons were half-castes— Rachels, Davids, Osckars, and Isaacs.

Yesterday morning the Scotsman came down with horses, and we visited the Indian tents. The Indians here irrigate the land and raise horses and cows on the irrigated pastures. The last tent we visited was the medicine man's; he was just. . . . His white hair and face were painted. Unfortunately they interrupted the procedure when we came. The Indians were scattered all over the countryside, some hunting in faraway fields, and therefore I could not do very much.

Goodbye now. This letter has to leave here tonight. Many heartfelt greetings, and write often to

Your son

North Bend<br>Sunday, September 23, 1894

My sweet Wife,

Although I received your letters only the day before yesterday, I should like to have more today, but must wait until the day after tomorrow. I like it here very much in the handsome, clean hotel of the Pacific Railroad, especially after the filth in Spences Bridge. The travelers take their breakfasts and dinners in this station. The hotel is a resort hotel in the summer and very nice. The tables are decorated with colorful branches and flowers. At the moment I am the only guest and am therefore treated very well. The hosts are a young man and two sisters. There is also an Englishman here with his wife. He is an employee of the railroad.

Yesterday I played a piano which is in the hotel. I also wrote a letter to Putnam and copied my notes. Then I measured Indians. Strangely enough I could not get any men, whereas I had no difficulty with the women. I measured eighteen women and children. When I was all finished and had my dinner, I went to the missionary, Father LeJeune, and asked him to explain to the people in church what I wanted. He not only promised to do this but told me to come right after the mid-day service and measure the people in church. So I hope to get some men this afternoon. I stayed last night until ten o'clock with the missionary, and we discussed the Indians. He makes a "hobby" of teaching the children writing in shorthand, and strange to say they learn it much more quickly [than by longhand] because the signs are much simpler. I had studied the alphabet the day before and read something to the Indians; they enjoyed it very much.

When I came home I found the three ladies and two gentlemen still up; they said they had heard me play the piano that morning and that they would like me to play something. One of the ladies played quite well and the others sang. Whether I wanted to or not, I had to join them, not to make a bad impression. How dull this was, you can imagine. We played and sang until midnight. As a consequence I slept until 7:30 today, whereas you know I usually get up at 6:30. At last I could have my clothes washed again. I am afraid that I will have to buy hose out here. Darling, don't forget to send me a financial statement by the end of the month, your part of it. I will fill it out here and send it back to you.

I have discovered some interesting points working out here which have confirmed my former observations on the population in these parts of the country. I am slowly getting into the mood for "field work" again. I don't let myself worry and just do what I can. If there is no work to be found, I don't mind and take it easy. You will see how fat and healthy I will return. Yet I would rather be with you now! Today the weather is beautiful, and the Fraser River valley looks very pretty. The landscape is pleasing, although not gorgeous. The mountains in the distance have some snow already, although it often melts again. The valley is covered with a deep layer of loam which is really. . . . There is a hotel in addition to other buildings.

Adieu. How much I would like to be with you.

Your husband

Vancouver, September 25, 1894

Dear Wife,

I was disappointed not find letters from you here. I had written to Victoria to forward the mail here but had forgotten that there is none on Mondays. Therefore I have none here, but I hope to find letters in Victoria tomorrow. I stayed here to do some errands. At the moment it is pouring cats and dogs and I don't feel like going out. I shall wait and see whether it is better tomorrow. But I shall have to get used to the downpours; I am on the coast now and this is the worst rainy period. Yesterday morning at 7 A.M. I left North Bend and stopped over at the Mission, two hours from here, in order to measure the kids in the Industrial School there. The priests and the nuns were very amiable and cooperative and I started right in to measure. But I couldn't finish yesterday. Altogether I have now measured one hundred and fifty-eight Indians, but I have done nothing else.

I am going to send you the original and keep the copies of the measurement notes here. I don't want anything to get lost. I will write on the package "1–158," and then you won't have to open it at all. Tomorrow noon I plan to go to Victoria with the steamer and shall be there by evening. I am glad to put decent clothes on for a change, a clean shirt and suit! In the mountains I always wore the old brown ones. Did I write you that in Spences Bridge I lost my watch through a hole in my pocket, and that I found it two hours later on the road? It had fallen out before, through the same hole, in Kamloops, and that time the glass was broken. Now I have mended the pocket.

There is nothing else to write. Yesterday and this morning I really worked hard. I wish I could cover as much as this every day. The results of my measurements confirm very nicely my previous findings, which were somewhat doubtful at the time. To be really satisfied, however, I need more material. My darling, you are lucky that you hear from me so regularly. I wonder whether this letter will be in time to reach you at the farm? What are you going to do all these coming months? Kiss the children for me. I wish my trip were over.

Your husband

Victoria, September 27, 1894

Dear Wife,

Today I received your letters of the fourteenth and the eighteenth. The printed matter you sent has not arrived as yet. I hope it is not lost.

I also received a letter from Donaldson, who informed me that the collection was finally sold. He will probably send you $2,300. Put $1,000 in your name in a savings bank, send $700 to Uncle Kobus, and put the rest in a joint account in both our names. I am happy that the collection was sold and that our trip over there [Europe] is now sure. I am glad I was so tough and did not give in.

I arrived here last night. It was really quite stormy on the water. The boat to the north left yesterday. Isn't that too bad? Well, it cannot be helped. That's all for today.

Your husband

Victoria, September 29, 1894

Dear Wife,

Today I had hoped so much for a letter from you but none came. Now I must wait until the day after tomorrow. The *Boskowitz* finally arrived yesterday. Tuesday it starts north, and I will go with her, of course, and stay on the Nass River until about November 5. As I see it now, there will be three boats leaving here—one on the ninth, one on the eighteenth, and one on the twenty-fifth. These boats will return here on the fifteenth, the twenty-first, the thirtieth, and November 6. I can also write you from the boat which I am taking north now. You probably will hear from me every week, unless I am not there when the boat leaves. Therefore, don't worry if one of the letters does not arrive. I am much worse off because I won't get letters more often than two or three times during that period.

I hope that I will meet the people whom I want to see in the north. If I don't find them, I won't stay long but will go to Fort Rupert. You should always write me at Victoria until I give you different instructions. Yesterday I saw the [Indian] woman and the little child who were in Chicago.[1] She had lost her husband, whom you may remember. He was the one with the side whiskers. He suffered from the heat in Chicago. I cannot do anything here, although the place is full of Indians. It is too bad! This afternoon I want to try to make a cast of one in plaster of paris, if I can get one. I am very eager to do this because it would be a beginning for the work for the museum in New York later on.

Darling, I am so glad that I am rid of the collection. I don't think I will buy anything for a long, long time. Or at least I won't invest much money in anything. I have to write Mann one of these days to find out when the Washington job should be done. If not before the summer, I should like to go with you over there [Germany] as soon as I come back. I would like to be back again in June. If something should come of the San Francisco business, everything would have to be changed, of course. We just have to be patient. It is really terrible that I have been away for four weeks now and have not done anything yet, but this can't be helped. A week from tomorrow I shall be on the Nass River, and then the real work can start.

I am very anxious to know what you are going to do. I don't even know where to send my letters. Don't forget, when you make your arrangements, that we want to go over there upon my return. It is, of course, uncertain when I shall come. My money from the B.A.A.S. won't last longer than December 1, but I should like to

1. Boas resigned from Clark University in 1892 and was appointed chief assistant in the anthropology section, under F. Ward Putnam, at the World Columbian Exposition in Chicago. In 1893 he brought a group of Kwakiutl Indians, led by George Hunt, to the Exposition.

stay about ten days longer. Ten days for the New York museum and ten days in southern California will bring me back about January 1. Oh, how far away that is! Wherever I go after this, you shall go with me. In the event that I have to stay in Washington for two months, you shall go with me; or if I should have lectures in Cambridge for four weeks, we will both go. Well, things will develop some way! Darling, I think I am looking well now. I must weigh myself some time. Please write in detail about everything concerning the children.

I wrote Rudolf and asked him to find out whether I have the right to lecture on these things in Berlin. The reason for this is that I want the opportunity to work on my statistical book, and also to make Mama happy. If possible, we would arrange our visit to include the entire summer semester. I am also thinking of course of the money our visit will cost the old ones, and I will insist, if we stay for a long visit, that I pay them for it. Don't you think I should? Especially now when they have to take care of Anna. Even so, this insecurity concerning the future is terrible. I am so happy that we can go over there, but of course all kinds of things might still turn up. Well, we won't talk about it any more today.

My dear little kiddies! Is this not a funny flower Daddy found and is sending you? It is teeny-weeny and has no leaves, only a little round stem and stingers. It is called "cactus." Daddy found it on a mountain a few days ago. It was completely dry and dusty there, and the people said that it never rains. Daddy is now on the shore of a huge ocean, and in a few days he will go on a big steamer and return to you children. Will you be happy then? The Indians will tell me beautiful stories which I can tell you later, of the Raven and the Wolf and many others. Here is some space left for a kiss for each of you. Who will get the biggest?

Your Daddy

Victoria, September 30, 1894

Dear Wife,

This morning I got your letter of September 21. Before writing anything else I want to talk about money matters. I am sending you an explanation of all my various accounts. You don't have to bother about anything but the first page "statement." There you will find on top, "Cash on Hand, Franz Boas, $535.80 for Sept 1." Of course the October amount should now appear in this place. Please write how much you had on October 1, or rather when you get this letter, both cash and money in the bank. Then I can make a statement for the month of October by the end of the month. When you send the money to Uncle Kobus write me about it, and I will send you a corrected statement which will take the place of the present one. Please pay the enclosed bill to Shubert [?] by check. The following are my expenses from last month which I want you to enter:

| | |
|---|---|
| Ticket to Albany | $ 3.68 |
| Storage of . . . until Sept 28 | 13.00 |
| Book for children | 1.35 |
| Photographs—Sept. 12 | 2.00 |
| Glacier Hotel | 6.75 |
| | $26.78 |

I don't think that I will spend more on this trip with the exception of Chicago expenses on the way back. Please don't forget to pay for the safe for our silver. I will leave all my railroad tickets and bills at the British Columbia bank because I don't want to carry them around with me in the wilderness.

I figure as follows: I didn't work the three days in Glacier and Banff, yet I started to work for the [BAAS?] on September 4. I arrived here Wednesday night and will charge three days to the American Museum of Natural History; therefore my time for the [BAAS?] will start on September 7, and the $150 will have to be paid on October 7. From New York I will get $30 for the three days. I spent these days getting photos and casts for New York and was also lucky enough to get one. . . . Maybe I can get some more.

Yesterday afternoon I went with equipment and a photographer to the prison and got photos and one [plaster] cast of an Indian. I hope to get more tomorrow and the day after so that I will have good things for the Museum so they will hire me to make their [exhibits?], if there is nothing better. I forgot to tell you yesterday that I asked Rudolph not to say anything about my inquiry, in order not to disappoint Mama if nothing comes of it. Please don't mention anything about it either. At present I am hopeful again, as if all our troubles had been solved. I am so tired of this kind of wandering life I lead. Goodbye for now. I still have to copy Fillmore's melodies before I go north, and this takes a great deal of time.

Darling, I wish I could be with you.

Your husband

Victoria, October 1, 1894

Dear Parents,

I have been loafing around for a whole week here in Victoria, accomplishing nothing until Saturday. I had hoped to be able to make casts here for the New York Museum but could find no Indians until yesterday. The day before, I went to the prison and made a cast of a Fort Rupert Indian. The next day I met by chance a woman whom I had met on my first visit here and who had also been in Chicago. I promptly made friends with her, of course. Naturally she knew me well, and after working on her for a long time, Sunday morning she agreed that I could make her cast today. I prepared all my material, but when I went to her house she was afraid and did not want me to make the cast. After lengthy negotiations I persuaded her finally, and I made the cast of her face. With her help I got two others today and hope to get two more tomorrow. My time here was used well after all.

The boat leaves tomorrow evening at seven o'clock. It is the same boat on which I made my first trip—the *Boskowitz*, an ugly schooner with a small steam engine. Yet it is the best boat to make this trip. Saturday I visited my old friend James Deans, who was also in Chicago, and we had a long conversation. Yesterday I had dinner with another acquaintance, a Mr. Hastings. Saturday night I visited Senator McDonald, who had invited me at various times. I killed time very nicely, as you can see.

Your old son,

Franz

On Board the *Barbara Boskowitz*
October 3, 1894

Dear Wife,

We are stopping over in Vancouver, and so I can quickly send you some greetings. If only this ship were not so terribly slow! We have been under way since 9 P.M. last night; it is 8 A.M. now, and it will still take two hours to get to Vancouver. One Haida, two Tsimshians, and several Fort Rupert people [Kwakiutl] are on the ship. I am able to talk with the latter and am hoping to get some material before we arrive in Newette [Nawiti]. I don't know how the other Indians will behave. Last night I talked to the Indians, and they agreed to tell me stories today. But these fellows sleep late, and I have only two days to work with them. Well, I just have to take what I can get.

The *Boskowitz* is still as uncomfortable as she was before. The beds are so short that one cannot even stretch out; the deck is so full of cargo that there is no place to even turn around. I am addressing this letter to Mohigan House. The next I will probably have to send to New York because it is so uncertain where you will be. I learned that this boat takes two weeks for the round trip, not twelve days as I thought. You will therefore not hear from me for two weeks, because I can't find out where you will be. Please also notify my parents, since I will hardly have time to write them today. I want to start work as soon as I can. I dug up the Indians already and have to show myself to them again. Adieu for today, my sweet wife. Don't be too impatient about the long intervals between letters.

Your husband

On board the *Boskowitz*
October 3, 1894

[To Marie]

Today was rather disappointing. We left Victoria at 9 P.M. last night and went first to Vancouver, where I mailed a few lines to you. I also wrote my parents once more. When I came back the boat was about to go to another dock and I had to walk there. At eleven we finally left again. In the front part of the ship there are several Indians: four from Newette [Nawiti], two from Alert Bay [Kwakiutl], two Tsimshians, and one Haida. I had hoped to get something out of these six [*sic*] men, but it soon became apparent that I knew as much as they and I knew their legends and songs better than they. Yet I obtained a few not very important corrections in my old material, and a few additions. I want to make another attempt tomorrow; maybe I can get a few of their legends in their own language. That would really be something! I also should like to measure them. The boat is terribly slow.

I just read a book by Tolstoi which I am going to send you: *The Romance of Marriage.* It is another expression of Schiller's words, "Passion leaves, love remains; the flower wilts and the fruit ripens." Darling, the idea in this book is the right one. There are always traces which remain from the agony of the soul which no wish can remove, and no one can make us the way we were before. Neither is our relationship the same as it was eight or seven years ago. Passion was replaced by peaceful mutual trust. We are not strangers any longer, and a new day does not reveal new qualities in us, but we know each other perhaps better than we know ourselves. Each of us has adopted some of the thinking and feeling of the other.

Darling, before I started to love you it was your straightforward and free nature which captured me—and the truth in you, which always remains dear to me. We have become older during these seven years because life has not been easy for us, but we have had much joy in life, for which we should be grateful. In my case, at least, the time of hot reaction is over and has given way to a quiet, even feeling which creates a less intensive happiness but a more satisfying frame of mind. For this reason I may not suffer as much as before because of our separation; I just give in to the unavoidable.

I want to say one more thing, a point the book has taught me. Do you remember the ugly words I said to you at the end of the summer which made you cry? These words still lie heavily on my soul today. Why do we have to make each other unhappy when there are enough problems from the outside to do it for us? How was it that I could have been so unkind to you then when I could not have done it a few years ago? Darling, you will never find me so ugly again, and I hope that no little disturbances will ever influence me again in this manner. Perhaps a short separation from you is beneficial, giving me time to find myself and increasing the happiness of our being together again, Marie. Our inner and outer life bring us closer and closer together. Well, enough now! I had to express these thoughts which the book gave me.

*Noon:* We are still lying at anchor here. The counterwind is so strong that the poor *Boskowitz* cannot even think of fighting against it. I spent this morning with the Indian again and hope to get some more out of him this afternoon. Our enforced stay here probably will mess up the schedule of the boat. Don't be surprised if my letters don't arrive on the dates I gave you.

*Evening:* At 2 P.M. we left and moved on. It was clear, and we had a wonderful view. I worked three more hours with my Indian and walked around a bit on deck. Now I shall close and walk some more. The wind has calmed down quite nicely now.

Goodnight, sweet wife. Have a kiss, and kiss the children for me.

Your old Franz

On Board the *Barbara Boskowitz*
October 3, 1894

Dear Parents,

This was a disappointing day. We left Victoria last night at 9 P.M., going first to Vancouver. The boat is very slow. At five o'clock we arrived in Nanaimo, and now we are on our way again to Departure Bay, where we will take on coal. Tomorrow at midnight we shall be only as far as Alert Bay. Tonight I want to read over some of my legends in order to find out several things. The whole day was quite dreary: rain, fog, and the deck so full of wood, coal, and oil barrels that one could hardly walk a few steps. There are only three passengers on the boat. One gentleman is from Esquire . . . , near Victoria; he is going to set up a meteorological station in Rivers Inlet for the government. I know several people he knows, and so we can have a good conversation together. The other is a settler from near Alert Bay whom I know. The engineers, whom I know from former trips, sit at our table. Even the captain is the same one, but he is an old bear, and as grumpy as he was before. I figure that I will not arrive north before Tuesday.

*October 4:* We spent last night comfortably in the Bay because it was raining so hard and was so terribly dark that one could not see a thing. At 5 A.M. we steamed on, but not very far. It was very foggy, and the slight wind subsided completely after a while. We are now at the entrance to the mass of islands which lie between Vancouver Island and the continent. Because of the fog the captain ordered the anchor lowered, and we shall probably stay here all night! I really could explode. We are out of Victoria two days, and haven't made more than 120 miles. I let my Indian tell me stories in his language today and have collected a good bit of material. I hope that we can continue tomorrow. There is nothing else to tell. If I didn't have the Indians I would be bored to death. With this bad weather there is also nothing to be seen of the beautiful landscape around us. The barometer is falling rapidly now. There will be wind again and with it seasickness.

*October 5:* Until 1 A.M. this morning we lay at anchor at Cape Mudge. Then it started to clear and we continued. The wind is northwest now, but this morning at 6:30 it came directly toward us, forcing the captain to anchor again, in a little bay where we are still lying at noon. If I were not so accustomed to these delays, I really should despair. At the moment, however, everything is all the same to me, especially since I have the Indian with whom I can work, even though not much. I am afraid this long delay will disturb the entire schedule of the boat. Don't be surprised if the letters do not come on the dates I gave you.

It is wonderful weather today and I am spending the time on deck when not working. We are protected from the wind and the sun is very warm. The little bay is surrounded by rocks, and the trees descend to the water. If only the deck were not so full of stuff and one could walk around a bit!

This afternoon at two o'clock we moved on, against a very strong northwest wind. It had cleared up completely, and we could enjoy the beautiful view. Nevertheless, I worked with my Indian for three hours. He will probably leave the ship by morning. I just took another walk on deck (five steps each way), and now I will close this letter.

Much love and greetings to all of you, dear parents and brothers and sisters.

Affectionately yours,

Franz

On Board the *Barbara Boskowitz*
October 6, 1894

Sweet Wife,

Now we are near the north end of Rivers Inlet, and in about one hour shall arrive. We went through the dreaded Queen Charlotte Sound in beautiful clear weather, with no wind. I did not get seasick. Last evening the wind subsided completely, and it was a very beautiful night. I went to bed at nine o'clock because I heard that we will land at Fort Rupert and I wanted to get up early. I wanted to see George Hunt, if possible. At eleven we came to Alert Bay and stayed there about four hours before moving on. When I heard the whistle at 5:30, I arose quickly. We were entering the harbor of Fort Rupert.

A few Indians came out in one canoe. Among them was my old

friend, the Chief Wanuk [?], who had been head of the Chicago group. But George Hunt was not there. In Alert Bay an old Hudson Bay trader, Mr. Blinkinsop, whom I have known for a long time, came aboard. I gave him a letter to George Hunt in which I said I would be back there the beginning of November. I was a little sad that I couldn't stay there right then. My work in the north is so important, however, that I do not want to miss it. We next went on to Nawette [Nawiti]. I stayed on deck the whole time because I was so interested in the country in which I spent some time eight years ago. I know every promontory, every bay, and the legends connected with them. After about two hours the village of Nawette [Nawiti] appeared, and two boats with Indians approached. Among them was Tom, my old . . . and interpreter, who was one of those who had been in Chicago. The village is as primitive as it was before. The people still wear nothing but woolen blankets. Their faces are still painted. Everything invoked old memories. A bad wind came up in the meantime and so I lay down on my bed to make up for the lost hours of morning sleep, and also in this way I might avoid seasickness. I slept two hours and went on deck only after lunch. Although I had a little headache I did not become really seasick. At the entrance of Rivers Inlet we met the *Danube* [?] on her way back to Victoria. I now know that my letters which I had left in Alert Bay will go on. The meteorologist, the last passenger besides me, is leaving the boat here in order to hang up the barometer. At this time the captain again showed all his nastiness. He refused to promise to stop for the man on his way back, and only agreed when other people promised him some freight. The night is very beautiful. This afternoon we had a wonderful view again of the snowy mountains and wooded slopes. Tomorrow we shall probably be in Bella Bella, and Monday night or Tuesday at the Nass River. I hope I will find the Indians there for whom I am looking.

*October* 7: This is a bad day. It is storming and raining cats and dogs. Just now we are dropping anchor at the bay of "Chinaman Hat," where a little Indian village is situated. Just when the storm was at its worst, we had to pass through Milbank Sound, the second completely unprotected place on the coast, and the ship danced and rolled. All my belongings and the tables, chairs, and dishes were rolling around, and had it lasted only a few minutes longer I should have become seasick. I already felt upside down or something, but just in time we turned into the protection of an island. So I put on my raincoat and went on deck. There is nothing else new today. The day's work was quite pitiful. I worked only one hour in the morning with a Haida. It will surprise me if the captain proceeds at all. Of course, here we are protected again. The night, however, will be so dark and stormy that he won't move. We had gone with the wind before but now that we are anchored, we can hear it howl. Where we can see the steep shore, we see waterfalls coming down from every little creek formed by the rain.

*October 8:* Last night the wind subsided, and since we are now going through the protected channels again, there is no danger of my becoming seasick. The weather is dreary, however, and it is raining. Up in the mountains it is already snowing. I will have to get used to this during the next few weeks. Today at one o'clock we came to Gyitkans [?], a Tsimshian village situated west of the Skeena River on a little island far off shore. I should like to go there if time permits, which I doubt very much. The ship stopped there for two hours, and I went ashore with an Indian in his canoe. There is a row of very old, very interesting houses with beautifully carved posts, especially one post with a bird on it. It has an immense beak which is carried by two men. I sketched as quickly as I could the plan of the houses, which deviates considerably from that of the houses of the Haida and the houses in the south. Then I went back to the boat. The chief has had a kind of coat-of-arms [crest] carved in stone, probably in Victoria. This looks quite strange amidst all the old wooden posts. In front of one of the houses stands a tall rock about six feet high. I could not find out its meaning in our hurry, but it is apparently very old. The roofs and walls of the old houses are covered with moss and ferns and look very beautiful.

We then went on to the Skeena River, where we will stay over night to wait for the next high tide. Tomorrow night we shall finally arrive at the Nass River. My Haida turned out to be quite impossible, I am sorry to say. He cannot translate, and he speaks much too fast. This letter will leave tomorrow. I hope the next boat will come in ten days, but this is uncertain. I finally found out the name of the tribe I am looking for. I do hope I shall meet people of this tribe in Kinkolith! Today I have to write father a birthday letter. Oh, darling, I should like so much to go over there as soon as possible; I don't even know yet how I can arrange it in the best way, after my return. I should also . . . because I don't like Putnam's ideas at all.

*October 9:* Now we are in Metlakatla. Since the trip from here on goes through the open sea I probably will not feel like writing any more, nor like working, for that matter. So I will close this letter now. In three hours we shall be in Port Simpson, and at 10 P.M. we shall arrive in Kinkolith. I have figured out my trip very carefully now and think that possibly I shall be in Fort Rupert in twenty days, which would be the twenty-eighth. That depends, of course, on whether I can get everything done that I want in Kinkolith, and whether I forget about measurements in Port Simpson. I cannot definitely make up my mind yet until the next boat arrives. If possible, I should like to be back with you about New Year's. Goodbye for today, dear wife. How I will enjoy your next letters. Kiss the children for Papa.

Your husband

# 7

## Family Letters (1894)
## (*Continued*)

My dear Wife,

I received your letter the day before yesterday. This seems to me an eternity ago because I am in new surroundings now, and have seen a lot and made new decisions and plans. When we left Port Simpson it looked as if we would arrive here that night, and I made ready for it. When the whistle blew at midnight I thought we were already here. The captain, however, had passed the place, and he blew the whistle, for reasons unknown to me, constantly between twelve and two o'clock. Again the captain wanted to pass it without stopping, which would mean I should have to go back by boat about six miles. Of course I did not want to do this, and I asked him to take me ashore. Then he turned and lowered anchor about a half mile from here, and I came ashore by boat.

A few boats came near, one of them carrying Mr. Collinson, the missionary who was to help me. I asked immediately whether the tribe I was looking for was here, and I was told that everyone was away hunting. I wondered if it would be better to turn around and leave. I deliberated awhile and came to the conclusion that, since I wanted to learn the Nass [Niska] dialect anyway, I would go ashore. I dragged my trunk over the never-ending low-tide beach, with the help of an Indian, and went straight off into the mission, where I introduced myself to Mr. Collinson. From him I learned that one man of the tribe was still here, but that this Indian excelled in stupidity. I finally learned that the people were camping about thirty miles from here and were about to go on up the Portland Inlet. The young man was ready to follow them. Because no one understands the same Chinook [Jargon], I decided to hire an interpreter and follow the Indians with him.

In the afternoon the interpreter came, and, after making an agreement with him, I went out to buy food for the trip. I must say I was not looking forward to this because the people there don't have a house; they sleep under tree branches. After some time the Indian finally admitted that the others had planned to go eight days ago and that he did not know where they were at this time. Under these conditions I should have spent the whole time looking for these Indians. Instead, I tried to get as much as I could from my Indian this afternoon. I collected a little vocabulary, just a minimum. I learned for sure, what I had presumed, that this tribe was really Tinneh.[1] With this fact, the main question was settled. They are really Tinneh who have reached the ocean here. They are not even very much isolated from the other Tinneh. Thus I could examine the question with greater ease, since the most important question was settled and the tribe was really not as isolated as might have been possible. I tried to persuade my Indian to stay here, but he had set several traps a week ago and had to go to look after them. I asked him to send back an old man—the best informed of all the twelve people—and promised to pay well for him. The Indian promised to do this.

Then I found that there was a fifteen-year-old boy of the tribe here, and I wanted to get information from him in the meantime. Today I questioned him, while the other Indian, "Timothy," rode away to Portland Inlet with my message. I think he will find the old man soon because I have a hunch that he knows where the people are and that they were stalling only because the interpreter didn't want to go so far. This became clear to me only today, but I made the best arrangement I could. I can use my time with the boy until the old man comes, and I do think he will come. The boy on the other hand does not speak the language too well any longer; yet I got some important material, including information on their old sites. It is difficult to get information from a boy who is not used to this kind of interrogation and has never thought about the kinds of things I want to know. These people are a strange type. They are very light and have large heads, unbelievably flat noses, and thick lips. I am curious to see whether the old man looks the same. Tomorrow I will have to let the boy rest and will take measurements in the meantime.

The first day I was the guest of Mr. Collinson, who is very amiable. Apparently, however, his wife doesn't want to have me because it is too much work for her, and I can't blame her. On the

1. The Tinneh are one of the now extinct Athapaskan groups.

boat he said I could live with them, but nothing came of it. The first night I did stay with them and then I picked out the neatest-looking Indian house (they all have quite civilized houses here) and took up quarters there. How the food will be, only the gods know. I have a nice, small room for myself, with a mattress on the floor. Fortunately I took a blanket with me which will be sufficient together with my travel robe from Berlin and my grey coat. Until today I had meals at Mr. Collinson's. They have four children at home; three boys between eight and four, and a girl in between. He also has a grown-up son who is not here. The children talk almost more Indian than English. I will describe his house another time. I am tired now and want to go to bed.

*Saturday, October 13:* Darling, I could not sleep because I constantly thought of our little baby which we lost nine months ago.[2] There is almost no day in which I don't think of the dear little one. It is so hard to get adjusted to such a loss.

Yesterday and today I worked very hard and am relatively satisfied with results. I am glad I stayed here because the Indians here represent a completely new type, or rather they represent more clearly the characteristics of the northern tribes. I never before saw such huge faces or heard such tall stories. I am very curious to compare them with the Tsimshians of Port Simpson, where I am going from here. Naturally work progresses quite slowly. Yesterday I measured forty persons, today twenty-five; the remaining fifteen men I will get on Monday. I may go to a village a little north of here to get more material. The winter here is, as I expected, ghastly—constant rain, wind, and fog. I am glad I am not forced to camp outside. This village reminds me in some respects of an Eskimo village. The Indians also have many dogs, which are used for pulling sleds, and which are as noisy and terrible as Eskimo dogs. I never leave without my cane because the beasts bark at one all the time and make for one's legs. They are a real nuisance.

The scenery, what can be seen of it now, is very beautiful. The river, or rather the bay into which the river flows, is surrounded by high, steep mountains. A small, narrow side valley leads from here to the north. The mountains are already covered with snow. One can see quite far upstream on the river where the mountains are all white. On the other side is a little bay on which a salmon fishery stands, now deserted of course. To the west one can see the high mountains on the other side of the observatory and, farther out, Portland Inlet. The latter already belongs to Alaska.

2. Their third child, Hedwig, who was born in 1893, died in 1894.

Now I want to tell you about the missionary's house. It is a kind of rambling building which has a small store and is connected with the school and the church. I must draw a floor plan to make life in this house understandable. In front of the house is a yard in which potatoes and cabbage grow. A porch runs along the front of the house. To the left of the entrance lies the unused parlor; the room behind it serves both as living room and dining room, and there the Indians come all day. Behind this is the kitchen, the realm of the wife, and opposite are storage rooms. Behind "the guest room" a corridor leads eastward to a room which is a sort of anteroom for the school, the dispensary, and the shop. This is always filled with Indians. A small printing press is in the office, and the secretary of the missionary works here. From the porch one can enter a storage room which is also the toilet, and from there a corridor leads into the courtyard; from the courtyard a covered corridor leads into the church. There is school every morning from ten to one o'clock, but school is not taken very seriously.

Mr. Collinson is so busy with the daily affairs of the Indians that he has great influence over them. This is very fortunate for me. My informant was very unsatisfactory the first two days until I gave him a piece of my mind. Today he was all right. He was not punctual enough for my taste. This is a typical fault of the Indians. I am always very strict with them when I pay them. Today I collected some material on the Nass [Niska] language and hope to get a considerable amount before I go, especially since Dr. Schulenburg's grammar is of great help to me. My quarters are all right with respect to the room; I sleep very well, and during the day I sit in their living room, which I have almost to myself. But the food! This is not the worst thing, of course, and the people do their best. Darling, I will be satisfied with everything when I come home! I wish I were at home already.

*Sunday, October 14:* In this pious place I had to let my work rest today and even had to go to church. It interested me greatly to hear services in the Indian language. It is interesting how accessible the Indians are to religious ecstasy. Movements like the Salvation Army, especially, have a great influence on them. Every few years there are movements in various places where the people have visions and see miracles. The great drum of the Salvation Army exercises a strong influence here and has helped convert whole villages, especially because in their own beliefs the drum is supposed to attract supernatural help. Mr. Collinson told me today about several such movements here. I know about them myself from Fort Rupert and from the Fraser River, and Indian history is full of it. This shows how susceptible they are to religous concepts and how Christianity blends in with their old religion. Previously it was the duty of every man to bring about visions by fasting and self-castigation. The protecting spirit of his life announces the visions to him.

This morning I copied almost all my measurements and hope to finish with it tonight. Unfortunately I don't have enough paper and have to stop with the measurements in order not to completely run out. Today I had lunch with the Collinsons and we talked about etymology. I told him that my interpreter is not good in this field at all, and I explained it to him with a few examples. Mr. Collinson could not help me either, because he doesn't know the language well enough, but it turned out that his little boy, eight years old, knows it very well. I will try tomorrow to get some information from him. He speaks the language all the time and hears it a good deal, so that he has a strange feeling for it. Of course, he has to be guided by questions.

I heard that the *Danube* is expected tomorrow or the day after. Therefore I must send this letter to the post office on the Nass River, which is about six miles from here. Maybe I will receive some letters also. It seems an eternity since I got any. Of course, I left Victoria two weeks ago.

Goodnight now, sweet wife.

Your husband

Kinkolith, October 16, 1894

My dear Wife,

The *Danube* is not here yet but is expected any moment. However, it is not clear whether or not she made a little side tour. If so, she will not come for a week. At any rate, I mailed my letters and hope that she will take them with her.

I wanted somebody to tell me a legend tonight, but I am so tired that I just won't go and would rather stay at "home." Yesterday I once more tried the boy who belongs to the tribe I am looking for, but I had no success. He does not know enough. The rest of the day I worked on the Nass grammar and got a lot of material. Tomorrow I will finally start to collect texts, which I have not done yet. I am going through the whole of Schulenberg's grammar with my informant, and sometimes I make excursions into unknown regions. There is much more to learn of a language than Schulenberg published. It is much easier to learn from the people than from books. I still have to learn a great deal of the structure of words because my knowledge is for the time being restricted only to prefixes, which are very numerous. My informant is not very good. He is also lazy. This morning he didn't appear until nine o'clock, and if he does this again I will have to let him go, although this is dangerous because I don't have anybody else. Last night we had a heavy snow which melted during the day. At the moment, however, it is snowing again in big flakes. Last night we went out to measure the men, but I found little enthusiasm for it. They were very contrary and I got only one. I must try my luck again with Mr. Collinson. There are not many, perhaps six at the most.

There is nothing else to report. I will be glad to leave in two weeks. This little village is very uncomfortable. I am afraid that the old Indian of the Tsetsaut tribe won't appear. He could have been here yesterday but just did not come. I really wish he would! I can use my time in other ways, but the work on this tribe is the most important thing I hoped to do here. If it is possible I shall mail these lines also on the *Danube;* they will otherwise go on the same boat as I. I am anxious to get letters, since I have been away from Victoria two weeks now.

*October 17:* Last night it snowed again and today there is some frost. The countryside looks really beautiful. This morning the interpreter came to tell me that his wife is sick and he cannot work today. That was only an excuse, I am sure. But since I don't have any one else, I just let him go without saying a word. I then went to an old man and let him dictate texts to me all day long, and I shall continue with this tomorrow. I want to translate the texts later with my informant. I know so few words that I don't understand anything, and the old man doesn't know any English and very little Chinook. It was terribly cold in my little house, and I went to the mission in the evening to get warmed up a bit. The house is never warm; the strong east wind comes in through the windows. No wonder the Indians always have colds. The Tsetsaut has not come yet. I have almost given up hope. There is nothing I can do about it and I am only glad that I did not go after him.

Besides the work with the Indians, it takes me two to three hours to prepare myself for the next day. That keeps me very busy. Although the result is quite satisfactory I am not getting just what the British Association is most interested in. It is a good thing that the material I have won't be troublesome to work over; if everything goes along this way, it will be easy to write my report. This happened every time because I always have so much material. The

*Danube* has not appeared yet, and I suspect that she really went to Rivers Inlet first. If so, you will probably have to wait even longer for a letter.

*October 19:* Just now I hear the *Danube*'s whistle. How I am looking forward to my letters! Adieu for today.

Your Franz

October 21, 1894

My dear, dear Wife,

The day before yesterday the *Danube* arrived, and when I heard her whistle I quickly left my Indian for a few minutes and closed the letters. Mr. Collinson and I asked an Indian to take them to the ship. This sketch will show you how it looks here. The *Danube* was

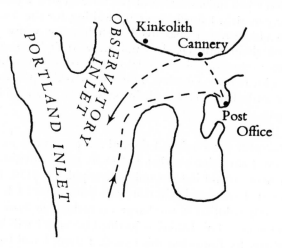

just opposite us when she blew the whistle; the bay is about two miles wide here. The boat crossed over to the post office, which is about five miles away. In the meantime the wind started and the boat had to wait until evening to return. I received a lot of mail. Your letters up to October 3 and your short one of September 24; the checks from Dawson and one from Yormans [?], whose letter you did not enclose however; the . . . ; the letter from the National Museum, which you should rather have sent directly to Schiff [?]; a letter from Hale; and Dawson's telegram from Ottawa authorizing me to use another $100. I have let him know that I think I don't have enough money for my trip.

Mr. Teit, from Spences Bridge, about whom I wrote you before, promised in his letter to send me a description of the tribes along the Thompson River. You probably remember that I found him very well versed and had asked him to write such a report for me which I want to incorporate in my own report, as much as feasible. He also wrote that he would help me with the measurements. Various printed material which you mentioned in the letters has not come yet. The people in Victoria are very slow with things like this. You can imagine how happy I was to get all these letters.

I wrote you that on the seventeenth and eighteenth my interpreter did not appear and that I collected texts during those two days. On the nineteenth he worked with me again but showed no interest. I wanted to send him away, but unfortunately did not do so, and yesterday he quit himself. I found a half-breed Indian who was at least happy about the job and showed interest. Yesterday I was quite satisfied with him, and I hope he is going to stay with me. Unfortunately he has a bad inflammation of the knee so that I won't be surprised if he gets sick. I finally gave up waiting for the Tsetsaut, but I found an old man who has lived with him for many years and knows much about him. He does not know their language but can give me some ethnographic material on the tribe after all. I cannot start with him before Tuesday, however. I ordered a model of a house from an Indian. I can use it in New York if something should develop there.

*Monday, October 22:* Tonight I figured out how much money I will still need, and I am quite worried. If I really stay in British Columbia until December 20 and if I get only the stipulated $150, I will have only $250 left. I see that I will still need $145 before I leave Metlakatla. The only solution is to charge everything in Fort Rupert to the two museums.[3] This I think is justified because I will be working for them there. By following this course, I think I will have enough money. Putnam will have to okay more money for me as he promised. Now I have to be very thrifty nevertheless.

Today I had a rather good day. My new informant does not know English as well as the old one, but he has more perseverance and energy. This morning we first worked on the language, then he interpreted for me old folktales which an old man had told me. I wrote down a few songs and collected some material on their customs. The latter are not very different. Of course there are legends

---

3. Apparently he is referring to the United States National Museum and to the American Museum of Natural History.

too. I hope to get a few mourning songs and others which promise to be interesting.

Today it poured again after it had been beautiful a whole week. During the nights, of course, it is freezing. The dogs finally leave me in peace. They now think I belong to this place, and I can go out without a stick and a pocket full of rocks. There were a few occasions about a week ago when about five dogs attacked me at one time. However, I hit around me wildly and hurled my rocks at them, so that they finally gave up. That was the last attack. I got a hole in my pants from the tussle, that's all. Since then I sometimes throw rocks at them when they come near.

My bed seems to get harder every day. It is just a soft cushion, not a mattress, so that I can feel the hard floor through it and my hips start to get numb, as during my Eskimo period. When the east wind blows, it comes in through the window, and how! This doesn't make it more comfortable, you know. But I will stick it through, if only there are enough Indians. The day before yesterday there were none in sight, and yesterday a man told me that the people don't like my presence here at all. And today they all smile at me again; the people are like children. A few of them think that I was sent by the government, that I am spying for the government because it wants to take their land, and that I am getting a great deal of money for the material I am collecting (I wish it were so). As a result, of course, they want more money from me. I have plenty of material to work on for tomorrow: in the morning, the language; in the afternoon, customs; and in the evening, Tsetsaut customs.

*Wednesday, October 24:* This afternoon, very unexpectedly, the old Tsetsaut appeared. You can imagine how happy I am. Now I can satisfactorily pursue the main work I had in mind for this place. I will probably stay here now until the *Boskowitz* comes back on her next voyage. I hope this man will be patient, so that I can get from him what I have in mind. As I wrote before, I had a lot of material to work on yesterday. I started at 8 A.M. and didn't stop until 9 P.M., so that I had no time to write you. How I will schedule the days from now on depends on the patience of my man. I want to be really careful not to wear him out. My interpreter is very patient and attentive. He does not know enough English, but I can get along with him very well even in matters of grammar. I wonder how it will go with the Tsetsaut, since we have to give up the Nass language now.

I will not be surprised if the *Boskowitz* comes tomorrow or the day after. I really should like some mail again. Darling, these days

I think again so much of our poor little child. I don't know why. I saw before my eyes how Christina held it in her arms, how it hit around with its little hands, and how I held it in my arms—the poor, poor little thing.

*October 25:* My first day with the Tsetsaut was a great disappointment. The man talks so terribly fast that I cannot get any proper material out of him. He may learn to speak more slowly if I insist on it, but I doubt it. I have to try my best, however. I worked the whole afternoon to learn the old habitat of the tribe and its relationship to the neighboring tribes. I am clear about it now, although it is a very slow process with him. He also gave me two legends and some linguistic material—vocabulary only. It is clear that I have to construct whole sentences to get anything out of him; I cannot ask him about grammatical forms as such. That makes the work much harder. I assembled a fairly complete grammar of the Nass language; not enough to enable anyone to speak the language correctly, but enough to give a clear picture of the language, the structure of which is not simple. I must try also to collect some material on their customs and usages. If I could spend the rest of my time here, I could do it, but this way it will again be piecemeal. I think I can risk keeping this letter here and carrying it to the boat myself.

*October 26:* I must close this letter today because the boat may come. If it does not, I can write a few extra words. Adieu for tonight, dear wife. This week I was really longing for you! It is eight weeks today that I have been away, and half the time is not even over. And it will be six weeks until I get back to Victoria. Well, time will pass somehow. Kiss the little ones for me.

Your husband

Kinkolith, October 27, 1894

My dear Wife,

As was to be expected, the *Boskowitz* has not come yet. If it comes later in the day, I can still send these lines with her. I did not accomplish a thing today because there was great excitement in the village all day. A girl was married. She was the maid in Mr. Collinson's household, and therefore she had to partly help with the feast. The breakfast was set for 11 A.M., and my interpreter and the Tsetsaut were so excited that I couldn't get anything done with them. I let them go at eleven o'clock. The interpreter came back after a little while, and we worked on Nisga [Niska] words. Friend Levi, the Tsetsaut, also came back, and he was really angry. "Now I lost two hours with just waiting," he said, "let's work now." As soon as we started the bell rang and the work was over again.

I went with them to the church, since I had been invited, and saw the happy couple getting married, entirely European fashion with orange blossoms, white veil, and white dress; the groom had no top hat, however. It was truly comical to see how out of place the bride and groom, the bridesmaids, and the best man felt. We went to the wedding feast in the schoolhouse, which was completely cleared of school furniture for the occasion. It was all decorated with cedar branches. In the middle of the room at the main table sat the married couple, their friends and some chiefs, and the white persons—Mr. Collinson and I. The relatives, meaning the clans of the bride and the groom, did the serving. They were the members of the Eagle and Bear families. Along the sides of the room were other tables at which the other guests sat. The tables consisted of long boards which lay on legs. Everyone had a soup plate, a cup, and an apple and candies on a plate. Soup, tea, and apple pies which the bride had prepared the day before the wedding were served. The meal, at which men, women, and children of all ages participated, was eaten in dignified silence.

After the meal there were speeches. I was sorry that I could not understand them and that I could not say anything either. Mr. Collinson translated for me the following speech, given by the uncle of the groom: "When a man gets married his wife must watch his canoe to see that it stays wet when the sun shines on it. If she does not do this, the canoe will split. But even then it is not lost altogether. If the husband sews the split together and ties a rope around it, the canoe can be used again. Thus the wife should help her husband because her negligence would be to the disadvantage of both of them. If she makes a mistake, however, the husband should not just stand and scold or mistreat her but try to help, because when both work on it together, everything will soon run smoothly again."

At noon my hostess let me know that she wanted better pay or I would have to move. I flatly refused, since $1.25 is more than enough. I did not see her personally. In the afternoon she told me herself, through the interpreter, that I could leave the same evening and look for other quarters. I told her that I paid her more than I would pay a hotel and explained to her how much money she would lose if she would not keep me. I also told her that Mr. Collinson wanted me to stay. So she finally gave in. Events like this do not contribute to my comfort, needless to say. There is no other place where I can stay, however. I cannot go to Collinson; he did not want me at the outset, and besides his wife has no help now. There is nothing else new today, except that it is pouring again.

*Sunday, October 28:* Nothing new again today. It is still pouring and pouring. I didn't sleep well and therefore overslept, so that I only came to breakfast at 8:30. I prepared myself a bit for tomorrow and then went to the Collinsons for Sunday dinner. When I came back I found the house full of Indians, but they went on to church. I lay down and slept. Now it is 5 P.M. and I don't know what I will do the rest of the evening. Sundays are always bad here. The boat has not come yet, although it may come any time now. I will have been here three weeks the day after tomorrow! Although I have a lot of work I am not satisfied. If only I could get more out of my good Levi! I wonder whether he could make a collection for me; that is, whether he and his . . . , who is not here, could make models of old clothes for me. I now know the distribution of his tribe. This considerably changes the ethnographic map of this territory. I will make such a map for P—— when I come back. BAAS would not print a decent map anyway.

*October 29:* I am able to write once more, since the trip of the *Boskowitz* is taking so long. I am sure that the captain is lying at anchor instead of going on during these dark nights. The boat will probably appear tomorrow and I will mail these lines then. I am so impatient to get letters! My Tsetsaut is quite exasperating. I get some words and legends, as well as a few interesting notes on customs, but the language! The following example will explain my difficulties. I ask him through my interpreter, "How do you say in Tsetsaut: 'If you don't come, the bear will run away?'" I could not get him to translate this. He would only say, "The Nass could be asked a thing like this; we Tsetsaut are always there when a bear is to be killed. That's why we can't say a thing like this." I also asked him, "What is the name of the cave of the porcupine?" His answer was only, "A white man could not find it anyway and therefore I don't have to tell you." Thus it goes all the time, and you can imagine how slowly I progress. Tomorrow I want to try another method. I cannot let him speak Tsetsaut because he speaks much too fast. Therefore, I shall try to tell his stories back to him and let him translate them for me, sentence by sentence. I don't know if this will work. He wants to leave on Monday, and so I shall try to go with the *Danube* to Metlakatla. I am not sure however. I should like to get measurements from there, but should like on the other hand to get some more material here. I will have to see how it goes this week.

Darling, I have thought over all the possibilities for next year once more, and I have an idea, about which I wrote McGee. He wants me to write the second booklet about the Chinook as soon as possible. I need more material on this and thus proposed to him that I would go at my own expense once more to . . . if he would guarantee $450 for the manuscript. Since I can get the material together in one week, this seems to be a very good plan. The connections here are so poor that I do not expect an answer to my inquiry before the beginning of December. This plan would, of course, delay my return somewhat. If I can do this, I will not have to think of becoming a substitute for Seler [?], which would have been very uncomfortable. How terrible all this insecurity is. Goodnight, dear wife. Two months have finally almost gone by. And this is half of the time. Maybe I can add a few more lines tomorrow.

*October 30—Evening:* The boat has not yet come. It poured so hard this morning that the boat probably remained in some port. Now it is beautiful again. The days are very short here. It is already so dark at five o'clock that one can hardly see anything. I am glad that I don't have to be here later in the year; the days are already short enough. Adieu now, sweet wife, I want to close this letter.

Your husband

Kinkolith
Wednesday, October 31, 1894

My dear Wife,

I was so sure that the boat would arrive yesterday that I closed my letter and put it into the envelope with the previous one. I am really impatiently awaiting the arrival of the boat because its delay also means that my return will be delayed, and I have no time to spare because my funds are very low. I would give anything if I could leave with this boat and return to you. This has been a very unsatisfactory day and, after such a day I always feel great discontent. This morning I tried to let the old Tsetsaut tell me a story in his own language. I think I get better results this way, but the work is so slow that I will have almost no progress to show. If it were a language like the Nass, there would not be any difficulty. But this language is extremely difficult, especially the verbs, which are irregular; I cannot find any form of the verb with sufficient certainty that I can say what it means. Today I wanted to get, "I am tired," but all I could get was, "It is late in the evening." I obtained a few worthwhile facts, and I will acquire enough to write a little sketch of these people. I have quite a number of myths again. I should like to hear the D—— but have not yet persuaded the man to talk.

Yesterday a man came down from a village fourteen miles above Kinkolith and brought me the model of a house which I had ordered from him. He constructed it very nicely, and it will serve to give a good description of the way houses of these tribes are built here. The houses are far more different from the Haida houses than I had thought. I had noticed this in Gyitqatla [?] [Kitkatla?] earlier and therefore ordered this model. The man also brought me a few stone axes and a mortar, which I bought from him. I intended to write you that I wanted to buy the David G—— book to read, but that in Victoria, the only copy cost $2, which I thought too much to pay. Now I have written one hundred and seventy pages about the Nass Indians, fifty-five about the Tsetsaut, and seventy about the Kwakiutl, and I have two hundred and thirty-four measurements. Not all of this material will go into the report, of course. I hope, Marie, that you sent me a reprint of my lecture on the Anthropology of the North American Indians, for which I asked. I need this for my lecture in San Francisco. It is possible, however, that I will not give this lecture, because I may not be there before Christmas. If only I were there now!

The more I think about the idea of visiting Cultee, the better it seems to me, and I hope that McGee will agree to it. This would make me completely independent for the summer and would make it possible for us to stay over there without worry all summer. Darling, the main reason for my wanting to send Ann the money was to show my parents that I feel responsible for the well-being of my sisters. Since Mama did not say anything we don't really know everything that is going on over there. But if we can give any relief to the situation, it is worthwhile. But now I must close. There is no more ink in my pen and I am writing on Mr. Collinson's table. Goodnight, darling. I wonder whether you have my letter which left here on the eighteenth?

*Thursday, November 1:* The long delay in the arrival of the boat is starting to make me angry. If the schedule is changed so that the boats come every three weeks or even only once a month, as it seems now, then all my figuring will go to the dogs, and I don't know how I shall manage my time. I would not want to leave right now, yet it is impossible for me to stay till the end of November. It seems that I have learned everything my friend the Tsetsaut knows. Now I must obtain some information on the Nass, and I should like to get some measurements of the Tsimshians.

I just don't know how I can stay here with these uncertain boat schedules. It could well be that a boat will leave Victoria on November 1, and another on December 1. Therefore I packed my things tonight and will be ready to leave tomorrow if it must be. I almost hope that the boat did not leave until today, although this would mean a big gap in my letters. I cannot tell you how unhappy I am that I cannot say when you will get my letters in the next seven weeks. Do not worry about me even if there are long intervals between letters. If there is too long an interval I shall telegraph from Victoria. Goodnight now, dear wife. I have not slept well the last few nights. You probably have been in bed for some time already. Just now the boat is arriving. Adieu. I think I shall stay here.

Your husband

*November 2:* What a disappointment! It was not the *Boskowitz* but a small steamer from Port Simpson which is going up the Nass River. Mr. Collinson says the boat belongs to the Methodist Mission and is bringing a missionary to a village above us. I am not yet sure what I shall do if the boat comes tomorrow. If it does not, I shall go to Fort Rupert as soon as it leaves here again because I cannot stay here all December. I would find enough work here, but I must go to Fort Rupert, not so much for the English as for my arrangements with Washington and New York. This morning I heard a very old tale from the Tsetsaut. It is identical with one known in Nova Scotia! This afternoon he made a marmot trap for me. These traps have important significance, because he made special ownership marks on this one which I did not expect to find here. Unfortunately he did not know what they meant; they were just old conventional marks to him. Thus I got some of my best materials on the Tsetsaut today. I want him to make a whole series of traps for me because they seem to reveal a lot about Tsetsaut art. In addition, I obtained some very interesting facts on the Nass, so that I can be well satisfied with my day's work.

How I was looking forward to my letters! But now I think it would be best if the boat didn't come before the middle or even the end of next week. If it actually left only yesterday, it would change all my plans. I would then go to Fort Rupert next week and stay there until the boat comes back again. It is also possible that the mail won't come to this place at all but will go to Port Simpson. In any event, this uncertainty is most uncomfortable. The evenings are starting to grow very long. It is already dark at 4:30, especially when it snows, as it did today and yesterday. My materials are so large in bulk that I don't know what to do with them out here without further study. So I am reading *Daniel Deronde,* which I borrowed from Mr. Collinson and which I like much better now than before. Deronde is not a figure likely to exist. I must look around for more [George] Eliot books, for which I formerly had no sympathy.

Darling, what are you and the children doing? As long as I knew you were still on the farm, the thought of you was not such torture, since I knew approximately how you were living. But now for three weeks you are living somewhere in the world and I don't even know where to look for you. Sometimes your picture becomes so clouded in my mind's eye that I become worried. Do you do things regularly with Helenchen? You know how important that is for the child. And what does my little fellow do? I am sure he will almost have forgotten his Papa when I come back. Darling, if only you would take life easy so that you will stay healthy and strong. Do you always take your medicine? My headaches and my . . . are completely gone and I am feeling quite well. Only the rheumatism is giving me trouble now in this cold and wet climate, especially during the nights when I can't get warm. But since I started putting on the warm underwear and the flannel shirt every night, I feel much better.

*Sunday, November 4:* I am in a very uncomfortable situation owing to the long absence of the boat. Because the Tsetsaut was not here at the beginning of my stay, I collected a great deal of Nass material. Now I have still more, including twenty-two pages of untranslated texts. But I can't stay here any longer because I will run the risk of not being able to leave before the end of December. I am not worrying too much about it, though, because I cannot change things. If it were not for the complications with Washington and New York, I would stay here until the next steamer comes. I need measurements from Fort Rupert for my English report, however, and so I have to go. This way I will again have much incomplete material about a new tribe. I was afraid that this would happen again, but it just can't be helped.

Yesterday morning I worked with the Tsetsaut again but did not get much from him. Yesterday afternoon I had an old man here who told me a story in Niska which was so long that he could not finish it in four hours. I hope I will get the rest of it today in spite of its being Sunday. Last night I went to Collinson's house, where I keep my trunk, and asked him for a wooden box to pack my collection. I had packed it in a suitcase first, but I was afraid that it wouldn't be strong enough. We found a box and packed everything and nailed the top on. I have already packed the things I used here, with the exception of some underwear and my blankets. These I can put into the suitcase at the last minute when the boat comes. I have to tie it with a rope; the bottom is almost out. When I am in Fort Rupert I will be much closer to you. I will send a telegram to Victoria for you and my parents because you have not heard from me in so long. This will shorten the time when there will be no letters. Seven days for you and three weeks for my parents! I long so much for letters, and yet I hope that the boat won't come before the middle or the end of the week.

*Monday, November 5:* I am curious to know how the boat story will end! I think it will come some time this week. Since there is good moonlight these nights it might travel during the nights too, if there is calm weather. I am only sorry for you and my parents that you have to wait so long for a letter. I hope you are not worrying. I wrote you that the connections from here are very uncertain. I worked yesterday afternoon, and today I wrote like mad. I should like to get as much done here as possible. I have an old man now who can tell stories very well. Today I bought a very expensive head piece, but the money is well spent because I obtained the myth that goes with it. I paid $10 for it. I now have a great deal on the language. Besides grammar and vocabulary, I also have ninety-seven pages of text, and if the boat does not come before Thursday I can get another fifty pages. This makes enough material for a description of the language. I also made a few measurements during the past days. It happens that my interpreter is taking the same boat to Victoria, so that we will be able to translate some on the boat. I hope that I will have three more working days here.

Last night, guess what? I started to write my Gies [?] report, but I did not finish. I am so glad that I finally wrote it, since I have wanted to do it for eight or nine years. I also wrote to Schulenberg and thanked him for his Tsimshian book. I can't sleep well here. I also do not like the food. For three weeks I have had nothing but pigs feet, potatoes, and tea—and oatmeal at breakfast. Yesterday I had some deer meat, which was a nice change, and last week there was some leaf cabbage which did not look very good. Well, one just shouldn't look! So many things go through my mind during these nights. I wish I were finally back in Victoria! There will be five or six long weeks until then. I wish I had some letters from you. I am honestly getting depressed.

*Wednesday, November 7:* No boat yet! If it doesn't come by to-morrow, we will have reason to believe that something happened to it. Darling, I am so anxious to get some letters, and I am so sorry that you have not heard from me in such a long time. If I didn't have to go to Fort Rupert because of my income for next year, I would give up the trip there. It is really too bad. I don't know how to best utilize my time here. I really fouled up this day. I wanted so badly to get one of the old songs of the chiefs and I did get three-fourths of it, but it turned out to be so difficult and unintel-ligible that I could do nothing with it. It is almost worse than my Eskimo texts because the Indians don't understand it themselves. The greatest difficulty seems to lie in the fact that the songs all came from Port Simpson, where a different dialect is spoken. This morning I translated, after making some measurements, and then collected new texts. There is still a great deal to do here, but I am ready to leave. I cannot imagine why anything should happen to the *Boskowitz.* She has been traveling this route for a long time and always lies at anchor when the weather is bad. I am sure she will come tomorrow or the day after. If only I would get news from you, the children, and my parents.

As I said before, I made some measurements today of people who refused to let me do it before but who know me now. An old man would let me measure him only if he could also tell me a story. He knew that I pay 25 cents per hour. He told me a story tonight which was not worth much but which included a very beautiful song. This noon I tried a few of the songs on an organ and they really sounded good. I must send this to my friend Fillmore in Milwaukee; he does not think very highly of the music here. One of the songs very strangely reminded me of Chopin's Funeral March! I will play it for you and *sing* it when I come home. Last night I didn't write because the old Indian was here. Tonight I have to work, however, because I did not do much during the day. I wake up very early, about 4:30, and am always tired in the evening. I go to bed at about 10 P.M. If I have to stay here much longer I will become very impatient. Of course, there is still a lot of material I could get which I could use later very well.

*November 10:* I didn't have time to write for two days because I was so busy. The nights were so miserable that I was too tired to do anything evenings after I finished with my work. On the morning of the eighth I had "old Moses" here again to tell me stories. In the afternoon and evening I translated. Yesterday morning I had some-one dictate some texts to me. And just as I sat down again to work on them there was great excitement outside; the boat was in sight! I quickly swallowed some food and packed my suitcase; in the meantime the canoe was ready, and I carried my things down with the help of an Indian. The boat—it was the *Boskowitz*—had lowered anchor in the meantime and I went aboard.

I soon received my letters and started to read them. This took several hours. You can imagine how relieved I have been since reading the letters. I have yours up to October 24; Mama's up to October 15. I am glad you didn't go to Glens Falls, because I don't think you would have had the advantages of a country place there, and this was the only reason why you wanted to go. New York would have been too strenuous for you. I am glad that you extended your stay on the Lake [Lake George] until the end of this month. For the one month after this you will be able to arrange something in New York. I only hope that you won't go to your Mother; this would be very disagreeable for me because of K——. I am sure you will find something suitable near her. I think your stay at the Lake these two last months will be more satisfactory than anything else. You would not have as much time for the children anywhere else.

I hope that little Helene has gotten over her flightiness. I am happy about the way little Ernst is getting along and happy to hear what you write about little Ernst's ways of working. I am sure he doesn't get this from me. I have been impatient as far back as I can remember. Oh, how I wish I were with you again! How did the boy acquire all the endings with "-li"? He already said Papali when I left. Helenchen's little pasted-on figure is very nice and I am happy to have it. It will go with me to the Fort Rupert Indians.

I also got an answer from Seler. I had correctly interpreted his hint. This is what he wrote on October 9: "Upon my return from my vacation I received your letter of September 17. I must tell you that I did not delay writing you intentionally. The arrangement which you propose is according to my wishes. I should have liked it at a different time, however, and, especially, lasting somewhat longer. I can start only after the beginning of the rainy period. Therefore I would need more time; I should like to have fifteen or eighteen months rather than nine months. But it has always been my principle to take what I can get. Therefore I accept your proposal as it is, although I must ask you to arrange the nine months between April and December. I am charging M. [Marks?] 850 per quarter; that is, 2,550 per nine months. The purpose of the thing is, as you correctly stated, that you don't become high and dry. Please write as soon as you can whether you can come here."

I answered him promptly and told him that I could not make any decision before January. I don't know, unfortunately, what such a long stay in Berlin would cost. If I figure everything, it would mean $600 from the museum in Berlin, $600 from Washington, and perhaps $450 from the Bureau of Ethnology [BAE]. I am afraid I must ask Rudolf for advice. He understands, of course, that I won't make such a long trip if I don't know where I will go afterward. This is the basis of the whole plan. I don't know whether it is wise to tie myself down when we are over there, but for such a long stay I would have to make some money. And I definitely need some scientific freshening-up. I must see whether I cannot come to some agreement in San Francisco, Chicago, or with Putnam in New York. I got a letter from Wirt in which he writes that he was dismissed on November 1 and that Watkins has already engaged someone else. We can thank God that we did not stay there.

Yesterday a sad event took place here. A family from Port Simpson which was about to go with the *Boskowitz* to Victoria lost a child through an accident. Now they are on board with the body and are completely out of their minds. The wife just came aboard, and my heart aches to see her walking around with her other child in her arms.

I received the galleys and have partly read them. From your last letter it appears that Alice has left school. Please write me what caused it and what she has in mind now. Yesterday afternoon I could go only very quickly through my letters because the Indian interpreter who wanted to go with me to Victoria changed his mind and is leaving the boat in Port Simpson. We worked until 11 P.M.; I now have thirty-one pages ready and only nine left without explanations. I think, though, that I will be able to translate them myself, except for a few words perhaps. This morning I read the letters over more carefully, one after the other. I certainly had thought I would be in San Francisco by Christmas and have just written Jordan that it now seems doubtful. This prompted me to write to McGee about work with the Chinook. This work would bring me to San Francisco after Christmas because of the boat situation, but the situation looks a little better than a few days ago. It looks as if I may leave Victoria on [Dec.] tenth, but I don't think that I can write you before that. The slow time the boat is making indicates that it will take eight more days. If I am unable to write, I will again send you a telegram, but don't expect it before the fifteenth.

From Victoria I will go again to Spences Bridge and into the Nicola Valley. This will take about ten days, so that I will be back in Victoria on the twenty-fifth. From there I will go straight south, but I must try to see Otto Richter in Seattle. I may go from there to Shoalwater Bay, if I can be sure that I will get $450 for the bulletin. Then I go to San Francisco, for which two days may be enough, and then I should have eight days left for southern California. It might be possible then to be in Chicago on January 11. I will try to do this if I cannot be with you New Year's Day. The Chinook tour is, of course, quite doubtful yet. I want to find out if a Chinook book has been published. Newell has highly praised me again in his latest *Folklore Journal*. He has seemed to think it is his duty since the Chicago affair.

I hope to get many measurements in Fort Rupert, also several casts of faces as well as some linguistic material which I need for my article for the *United States [National] Museum Bulletin*. I have asked you and Uncle for a reprint of my lecture "Anthropology of the North American Indians." I need a copy badly for my paper in San Francisco.

Just imagine, two days are gone and we are still in the Skeena River! We will probably stay here all night. There won't be any delay tomorrow, and Wednesday we shall be in Fort Rupert. I hope the weather is good enough that I can go ashore there. I just talked at length with the captain; it appears that I cannot stay in Fort Rupert as long as I thought. I will not be too sad about it because it will mean I can be in Victoria by the fifth and possibly with you on January 12. I hope this will be true. If, however, the boat does not leave Victoria until the fifteenth as was intended, I don't know what I shall do. I won't have enough time to finish my article for New York there. The boat is terribly crowded now. I think we have thirty passengers, and there is room for only sixteen. I have my bed and sleep well these days because I am warm and sufficiently covered. It is really strange how things change; on the way out I fussed about the bed because it was too hard. Now after that hard "bed" in Kinkolith, it really feels good.

*November 12:* Today was a very beautiful day. It was cool but dry. There were only a few showers and I walked around on deck a greal deal. The countryside is very beautiful. All day we went along the coast, which is formed by high mountains covered with beautiful trees. Innumerable waterfalls cascade from the hills. In a few hours we will be in Milbank Sound. If the good weather keeps up, we will be in Fort Rupert tomorrow evening. I mailed forty letters with this mail, and am up to date now, so far as I can see. I have now definitely decided to go to Victoria with the next boat from Fort Rupert. Otherwise I am in danger of staying there until after Christmas. This is the result of my conversation with the captain. After December 1, please send my letters to Spences Bridge. I hope to learn in the next mail whether I am to go to Shoalwater Bay. Then I can send you my plans by telegram after my return to Victoria.

Please be sure to send the draft for Anna. From their last letter I take it that they are very hard up over there and that Julius needs all his money for his new store. Why don't you write me how Richard [?] is. I think of him often. Poor Mrs. Caspar [?] I am so sorry for her. Please first put your $1,000 into the savings bank in both our names. The best would be the Citizens' Savings Bank because they already have our signatures. If the reprints of the article in *Popular Science* have not come yet, please send copies of the magazine to Harper, Jordan, Law, McGee, and Dawson, and don't forget to mark the article. I wrote the postmaster in New York with respect to the books. I wrote Bauer [?] that I sold the collection and that he should not hurry [?] with the $100. I sent the article about the St. Louis children to the *Anthropologist.* I did not hear anything from Jordan. Don't forget to send me Alice's address. The foregoing is all in answer to your questions. I am writing it all down while rereading your letters. Oh, I will be with you in about seven weeks! I wrote Mason yesterday and told him that it would suit me best to arrange the group in Washington in January and February.

*November 13:* Now we are almost in Fort Rupert. Adieu, darling; see you in seven weeks.

                                        Your husband


                                        Fort Rupert
                                        November 15, 1894

My dear wife,

I have been here for two days already and have not had the time to write to you. I am afraid that my letters from here will be scarce because I am very busy. The Indians are just having a great winter dance; I consider myself very lucky for this reason. Unfortunately I came somewhat late, but I hope to be able to see some of the major parts. Day before yesterday the weather was very stormy in the morning. At noon, however, the wind fortunately subsided, and when we sailed through Queen Charlotte Strait there was almost no wind. It was, however, very rough, which made the boat rock considerably, but I did not become seasick. The captain was kind enough to set me ashore. After some whistling a canoe arrived. It was George Hunt, who had been on the shore when I arrived and had seen the boat. We went up to his house, which consists of one room. It has some kind of partitions, though. Considering the fact that he has six children, two of whom are married and also living there, you can imagine how crowded the house was.

*Saturday, November 17:* As I told you, I have had no time to write. Day before yesterday I was interrupted by a few Indians and therefore could not continue my letter. Hunt has another little house, built in the same place in order to have more room. I am sleeping there now. The house is not finished, except for the outside; there is no heater yet. The first morning we discussed what I planned to do, and I invited all the Indians to a feast, which took place in the afternoon.[4] That was a sight! There were about 250 Indians in the house—men, women, and children. They were painted red and black, and wore jewelry; each was dressed in his cedar bark cloak. The lower tribal units [?] came first, and when they were all here, the members of the secret societies arrived. When they arrived everything was dead silent. Their place is behind the fire in the back of the room. Welcoming speeches were held for me and I was given the name *Heï'ltsakuls*, "the silent one" [or literally, the "non-speaking one"].[5] Then the master of ceremonies called the singers and told them what to sing. Every tribe—there were three tribes present— sang two songs, after which my "feast" came: hard tack and molasses. Before we ate I made my speech. I said that I had wanted to come for a long time and that I was glad to be here now. Then I spoke to the people who had been in Chicago and gave them

4. Boas later published a partial account of the feast which is not quite the same as his description in this letter:

> Before the biscuits were distributed I had to make the formal speech depreciating my small feast and asking my guests to be happy and to eat to their hearts' desire. In return I was told that no feast like mine had ever been given and that I was a great chief. The figurative speech of the Kwakiutl Indians has it about like this: "You are the loaded canoe that has anchored in front of a mountain from which wealth is rolling down upon all the people of the whole world; you are the pillar supporting our world." And all this for a treat of hard tack and molasses. But the gross flattery of this speech must not be taken too seriously, as it is simply a stereotype formula used for expressing the thanks for a feast. [1896c, p. 233]

5. Boas later wrote in one of his publications, "On one of my later visits I had received an Indian name, Heiltsakuls, 'the one who says the right thing' " (1896c, p. 232). This translation does not agree with the one he wrote here to his wife. Moreover, according to Mrs. Tom Johnson, George Hunt's daughter, the name that Hunt gave Boas was really *hēï'Lakwalɔts* (personal communication).

their pictures. While everybody was eating one society after the other called, "The Whales are eating now, that is good"; "The . . . are eating now, ku, ku, ku." These are the names of the societies. One of the Kwakiutl said that a long time ago he had loaned some blankets to another man and that if he did not get paid he would have to "put down a mat [?]." That means that the mat would not be taken away until the blankets were lying on it. Next the Koskimo brought blankets and gave them away with appropriate speeches, telling the Kwakiutl that they were nice people and open-handed, etc. At the end he gave me a silver dollar, but I also had to make a speech, and of course I will have to give him $2 before I leave. The whole thing lasted four hours and cost me $14.50. Of course, I gained the good will of these people and received invitations to all the feasts which are taking place here.

The day before yesterday I started to measure; I got twenty-five adults without any difficulty. I hope to get 100 altogether here, and for this I need George Hunt. His help is of the greatest value. Since it poured all day long again yesterday I could not go out with my instruments. I translated and wrote all day long and revised Fillmore's music, which is not very accurate.

In the evening another feast was given which was about the same as the first with the exception that a *Nutlamatl* [Fool dancer], a member of a secret society who wanted to join another society, was mercilessly teased in order to find out whether he could be made "wild."[6] The *Nutlamatl* has a long nose and cannot bear to have it touched. They smeared food on it, beat it, and spit on it. Finally he was tied to a post and his nose was smeared with grease [oulachon oil?]. At last the other *Nutlamatl* came to his aid and licked off his nose! These are real jesters! Then a man got up and said he was a Haida [a pretense] and made a long speech with a Haida accent addressed to the giver of the feast. An interpreter translated what he said. The end of it [the speech] was when the daughter of the giver of the feast had to repeat his [the pretender's] name.

This morning I went out with Hunt again to make measurements and got twenty-seven; I now have fifty-two, all adults, including three half-breeds. I am planning to go out two more days to make measurements and will have 100. Altogether I have measured 298 Indians so far. I am also doing many other things; this is not the only result of my work. I only hope that the photographer will come next week so that we can get pictures for the museum. I have already

6. See Boas' *Kwakiutl Ethnography* (1966, pp. 179–241) for a more complete description of the winter ceremonial at Fort Rupert.

received a part of the things I wanted, especially garments and a few carvings. I hope to get a beautiful large chest free, which I think I will keep for myself; you could use it for storing things after it is well cleaned.

I do not live too well here—especially very irregularly because the feasts are held at all times of the day and I don't want to miss any; they are the main point of my stay here. I am impatiently awaiting letters, hoping that I will hear from McGee concerning my visit to Shoalwater Bay. In addition I should like to know whether my Chinook book is out. I now have almost all the proofs of my *Berlin Tales;* only five or six printed pages are missing. I should also like to include the ones I have collected now.

Today I corrected a few of the songs Fillmore wrote down in Chicago. Either the Indians sang very differently into the phonograph, or he could not hear them well. I am positive that I have written them down correctly now, and the difference between my rendering and his is immense. I have now had enough practice to write it easily.

I cannot find the time now to write to the parents and probably will simply copy this letter during my trip home. Nor is there time to describe to you my impressions of the strange surroundings and the feasts; all my free time is used for making stenographic notes, i.e., I make short notes and go over them the next day with Hunt and have him explain everything to me. I shall just have to tell you everything when I come home. This would make a nice article for Scribner or Century. If only the photographer would come! The way home from the feast always looks like a torch-light procession because everybody splits his baton and uses it as a torch.

*Sunday, November 18:* I do not work too much here because the whole day is taken by feasts and dances. My time is well spent, however. I get quite a different impression of these feasts, witnessing them, from that I had formed only hearing of them. I also hope to get a number of photographs this week, and if I do I can write a nice article for an illustrated magazine. I should like to do this because the topic is really attractive.

I am just coming from a feast at which a new Bear dancer was initiated. The entry of the secret societies is very interesting. The whole house is full of people all adorned with cedar bark ornaments. The door opens and in come two Bears in dancing coats, with huge bear paws over their hands. Then comes the *Tsonogwa* woman dancer, who, according to the legend, is always sleeping. She acts as if she were sleeping; instead of walking to the right around the fire, as the dancers should, she walks to the left. The animal people then lead her along a rope to her place. Then the "Fool dancers" come. While they are dancing one can hear a loud noise outside. The *Nutlamatl* (Fool dancers) hide their heads under their garments and flee to the rear. Then the "Finback Whales" [Killer Whales] enter—colorfully painted men with huge fins on their backs, huffing loudly and turning this way and that. They leave and come back again as Ducks, also turning this way and that and running back to their places. New songs are sung which were composed today in the woods and eighteen women dance at the same time. Then the Bear dancer suddenly appears, walking on all fours and scratching around a bit in the rear of the house until he is appeased by a new dance of the women. After this a new Bear is initiated, a little baby who is carried in his father's arms. The father dances for him and swings his arms while carrying him.

This noon there was a big seal feed in which I also participated. I ate only the meat because I do not like the cooked blubber. I am going to these feasts in a blanket and headring, since I am on very friendly terms with the people. I am much better off here than in Alert Bay because there are no white people here.

*Monday, November 19:* Every day brings a new feast. I could not have chosen a better time. Today David, George's [Hunt] son, gave one, serving salmon and berries. It was very interesting. David is a Hamatsa, and therefore he is the first of the tribe in the winter. He is the chief of the Seal Society. This morning the whole Society went around in the village with blackened faces, the Bears with their huge paws and with deep growls, not—as usual—with loud shouts. When a name was called which the Bears did not like, they pushed the caller [one of the Fool dancers] so hard that he almost fell to the ground. While the names of the inhabitants of all houses were called the Seals looked around angrily. Usually the names were called four times but the Seals call only twice. The second time the Seals came with sticks, spears, and long ropes and drove everybody to the dance house by stretching the ropes ahead of them. At 3 P.M. they called the second time. We also went inside but did not stay long because we belonged to the friends of the hosts and therefore had to help.

Since David is a Kwakiutl, the people of the other tribes had the place of honor while the Kwakiutl sat at the left of the entrance. As the hosts, the Seals stood at the door. They barred the door with big boards so that nobody could leave. Then big kettles were put on the fire and the guests, two tribes [Koskimo and Nakoaktok], sang two songs each, after which the Seals brought the salmon. The Bears wore their big paws; the *Nutlamatl* had their clubs and spears, and the Bear was always led on a rope so that he would not become unruly. During the singing a [Nakoaktok] woman in the background got up and danced.

One of the Nakoaktok promised a feast, and the speaker of the tribe got up. He held a ring made of cedar bark in his hand. Everybody was as quiet as a mouse. He spoke—I don't know yet what he said. Then he walked around the fire, leaving the fire to the left, and went to the back of the room, turning around only once. He next put the ring on the young man who wanted to give the feast and blew on him in his capacity as medicine man. The singers then started another song. The young man came with two others into the middle of the room and danced. When he was finished the speaker of the Nakoaktok got up and held an arm band in his hand. He spoke a long time and gave the arm band to his son-in-law as a token that his daughter would give her husband four arm bands. Then he took a blanket and also gave it to his son-in-law. The latter answered and sang a solo, a song of happiness.

In the meantime the salmon were all cooked and placed on platters. These were long flat platters like those one can see in museums. Olachen [oulachon] oil was poured over them and we started eating. You really should see me in my blanket, eating with a spoon out of a platter together with four Indians! I do not want to make my coat filthy on occasions like this, and without a wrap it is much too cold. When somebody did not eat, the *Nutlamatl* and Bears came and pushed him and hit him. During the whole feast a very hot fire was maintained, so that the roof started to burn several times and somebody went up to extinguish it. That is part of every good feast!

The Seals ate in front of the house after everybody else had eaten. They were teased by everybody while they were eating. After everything was eaten the *Nutlamatl* wanted to make a speech. It is the custom, however, never to give him the opportunity to say something. Then they sang again. The word "ghost," or "dead man," occurred in one of the songs. As soon as this word was heard a Hamatsa of the Koskimo jumped up and yelled "Hap, hap hap"— the song broke off and his attendants jumped all around him and encircled him. Everybody beat the floor with his stick, and the drum was beaten as loud as possible. The Hamatsa tried to jump at the people but was prevented by his attendants, who had completely surrounded him. His hands trembled and he walked slowly around the fire. After one and a half rounds he left through the door. He is possessed by the *spirit* until another dance is held for him in four days.

The four large salmon which the Hamatsa was to receive were brought in. Again the *Nutlamatl* tried to make a speech, and again he was interrupted. In the meantime the berries were brought in. Large, carved bowls were placed in a row before the fire. They were filled with berries and the [oulachon] oil was poured over them. There were at least ten large barrels full of berries. While the bowls were being filled a man got up and made his old Haida jokes. He called the *Tsonogwa*, and a boy always brought in the wrong person. Now the speaker of the hosts spoke. He pointed out the various bowls and told about their meaning, etc. I do not know the details, of course. His mother stood next to him because he derived his greatness from her. Then they started to eat. I could not eat the stuff because the smell of the rancid [oulachon] oil made me sick.

As soon as all the bowls were empty, the Seals placed another barrel in the middle of the room with loud calls of "Ku, u, u, u," as if it were very heavy—which it really was. Then huge three-foot-long wooden bowls were brought in [sketch included]. They were also filled. Every chief received a spoonful which he had to drink. Actually he only acted as if he were finishing it all, but drank only a little bit and poured the rest into the giant bowls. When the spoons were brought to the chiefs their names were loudly called. This so vividly reminded me of the procession of the students around their dens. The Koskimo ate the most quickly, and soon there was a loud cry of "hu," indicating that a bowl was empty. The bowl was held up high and refilled by the Seals. When everybody had eaten enough there were more speeches, and then the Kwakiutl gathered around their chiefs at the entrance where the board had been placed and where the drum was. They sang, praising the host. This was the end of the feast. Tomorrow I will have Hunt translate the speeches for me.

*Wednesday, November 21:* Yesterday I could not write because I was too tired. The feast lasted too long. In the morning, I recorded with Hunt the speeches which were given the day before. While we were working a little steamer suddenly appeared, and a few minutes later another one. The first was a seal hunter which came to hire Indians for the trip, and the second was an Indian agent, and I was trembling with fear that he wanted to engage Hunt. Fortunately, though, he left this morning, but all this excitement yesterday was not good for me. I hope that tomorrow everything will go smoothly again.

Yesterday about six o'clock we were called to a feast by the Koskimo. First they gave away Nakoaktok blankets, and then speeches were held to thank them for the blankets. Then a man got up holding a copper in his arms, and he spoke lengthily about its value. He said he wanted to buy it and also said other things which I do not understand yet. Suddenly we heard whistling and much noise outside, and the same Hamatsa who had gone wild the night before stormed into the house with his companions. They danced around the fire and went out again. Then the Koskimo speaker asked the Kwakiutl and Nakoaktok to sing. The Kwakiutl sang their usual two songs, as did the Nakoaktok. The latter, however, sang out of time, and the head Hamatsa of the Kwakiutl jumped up and yelled "Hap, hap, hap." His nine companions ran toward him and they danced around the house and then around the fire with wild jerks. The whistles sounded wild. More speeches were held, and again the whistles and the yelling of the Hamatsa sounded from outside. Soon he came back, completely naked except for the dancing ornaments and two cedar bark rings crosswise over his shoulders and over his head. He danced the regular Hamatsa dance.

*November 22:* This morning I obtained a few more items concerning last night and also wrote down a few folktales. I wish I were away from here. George Hunt is so hard to get along with. He acts exactly as he did in Chicago. He is too lazy to think, and that makes it disagreeable for me. I cannot change this, though, and have to make the best of it. He left at noon with some excuse and returned only after several hours. He knows exactly how I depend on him.

*Sunday,* [November] *25:* The past days were so exacting that I did not even have the time to write you my notes in letter form. The day before yesterday I went to bed at eleven and got up at five the next morning. The *Boskowitz* arrived on the twenty-third and brought me your letters up to November seventh and letters from over there up to October 24. The photographer from Victoria, Mr. Hastings, also came as we had agreed. He took twenty-six pictures, quite good in view of the rain and snow around here. This morning the Koskimo brought two Hamatsas, and we made two pictures which show the bank of the [river?], but the people were very small. This morning it seemed at first as if it would be difficult to take pictures, but it turned out quite all right.

These pictures have given me the idea of writing popular, or maybe a semi-popular book on this part of the country. As a matter of fact I have developed such a plan in my head, and I think it could be quite a good book. When I come back I will try to sell the pictures to Scribner or to another magazine, and in this way find a publisher for the book. I am sorry that Mallory died, but he had been ill for some time. I wonder whether his replacement will keep his promise and will offer me a position? The *Boskowitz* is going to Queen Charlotte. I do not expect her back before the fifth or sixth. What I do afterward depends on the news I find in Victoria. I am glad that I have the photos. The news you sent is pretty good.

This morning at eight the announcement was called twice that the Koskimo would have their ceremony. Soon afterward they appeared—a boy and a young girl at the river bank, naked, ornamented with amulets and a strange little ring of white branches on their head bands. They jumped back and forth—hop, hop. The Koskimo came out of their singing house right away. First the three women and a boy, the *Tox'wit*. They were closely followed by a group of men and one woman who carried a board on which they beat while they sang. At a little distance came another group of men who carried a drum and beat the tact while the others sang. Finally the women came in [button] blankets, and they also sang. When they heard the Hamatsa they all started to run until they caught the two Hamatsas. The men then sat down and learned the new song of the Hamatsa, and the women danced and sang to the time. (I am enclosing a picture of this.) The old Hamatsa woman [wife?] danced too. After three rounds the girl was dressed in a blanket. Now the Koskimo and the Kwakiutl gathered on the [river] bank and sat there in a square. A grandson of *Wā'las*, a Koskimo, bought a copper from his grandfather and used 400 blankets as a down payment; they were piled up in the center. The full price is 1,200 blankets, which will be paid later. Speeches were made, and a woman danced for the grandfather, *Wā'las*, for whom the whole gathering sang songs of joy. At the same time the *Nutlamatl* and *Nane* [Bears?] of the Kwakiutl ran through the whole village, throwing rocks around and breaking [things]; then they danced.

I busied myself the whole day with taking pictures. We took several pictures of Indians and groups of Indians, from a flat rock along the shore. I took also two pictures of the purchase ceremony of the copper.

Yesterday in the morning a new . . . (winter dance) of the Kwakiutl took place. [Hemlock branches?] were brought, and everybody made head bands out of them. I have one too. Then all the women were tied to a rope which was held by a man. The Bears were also tied together; so were George and I. Now a square was formed. The men sang, and a woman, a *Tox'wit*, danced in the middle of the square. First, however, the speaker of the tribe called the spirit of the winter dance, while he danced halfway bent to the ground, his hands placed together and trembling. Then the woman danced the same way and suddenly caught the supernatural power between her hands and threw it toward all the people. They shook and shook and called, "Hi, hi, hi, hi" like the *Nutlamatl*. This was repeated four times. Next they all went into the village in a long procession from house to house into four houses. There we were standing . . . , and the master of ceremonies stood at the door. A woman sang a secret song, and the *Tox'wit* put something into the fire. While she was throwing it, everybody bowed low, then straightened up again and also called "Hi, hi, hi." They ended at a signal of the master of ceremonies which sounded like "ū," first high and then lower.

Immediately following there was another dance, a feast which lasted through the afternoon. In the evening a man distributed blankets which were ordered in the afternoon. The ordering was a very interesting process. But I will not describe it now. When this was over, everybody went into the house. After a general welcome the Hamatsa entered and danced. After the third and fourth time [he danced] with a cedar [Chilcat?] blanket; his assistant carried the blanket. He was accompanied by six men, four of whom carried [wore?]. . . .

*November 27:* The past days were so wearing that I did not find the time to write. Day before yesterday the Koskimo brought back their second and third Hamatsa. They appeared naked on the shore and were brought in with great pomp by the Koskimo, who were divided into four groups. I took two pictures of this ceremony. A man also bought a copper (plate) in a ceremony, of which I also took a picture. I was busy taking pictures the whole day quite successfully—after some initial difficulties. The great dance of the Koskimo, which lasted from 8 P.M. to 8 A.M., was in the evening. I stayed all night, although it was sometimes quite boring. But on the whole it was very interesting. First came the war dance, during which a woman was hit on the shoulder from the back with an oar so that it looked as if the shoulder were split by the blow, and she was led around bleeding. The oar was, of course, very cleverly cut beforehand so that the onlookers thought it was really broken. Then a man was pierced by a spear so that it stuck out on one side. This was also done very cleverly. I wish I could have taken pictures. You can imagine how tired I was in the morning! I slept one hour and then went out with the photographer to take some more pictures. We got several. In the afternoon we went down to the river where several . . . landed, and we started to take casts. I had asked Hastings to bring some plaster of paris for this purpose. We got a number of pieces. I was so tired in the evening that I went to bed at eight and soon fell asleep.

I pondered about your question how we should answer little Helen's questions about church. I have not found the right answer yet. The answer about Jesus is easier than the one about God. With respect to Jesus we could say that once a good man lived who set the example for everybody and taught the people what to do and what not to do and that, therefore, all good people loved him. Some think of him all the time and do what he taught them. Others come together with other people, and they let the preacher tell them how good he was; and in order to think of him all the time they have pictures of him—just as you look at dad's picture when he is away, that's how they look at Jesus' picture. This should somehow explain the differences of opinion. As analogy you could tell her about a child who loves its mother and tells it to her all day long; and then, there are children who also love their parents but who don't talk much about it and just do what they want them to. With respect to God one could maybe say: See the world around you! How was it made, who told the leaves to grow and drop in the fall? We don't know. We only know that spring is beautiful, and so is winter when it snows. We are just happy about it, and we don't want to make anybody sad; we want to thank somebody for the beautiful world because we enjoy it as we enjoy the presents our parents give us. We all feel like this. For some people this means to thank God; others call it to enjoy the world. That is the same thing. The manner of explaining it depends on how her reasoning develops, and this you have to find out. I think this method may work.

I slept until 8 A.M. and woke up full of strength. We took pictures all day and also made some casts. Nothing is going on tonight, but tomorrow we will have to stay up all night again. I hope I will get some pictures again. This afternoon there was a secret meeting of the Kwakiutl in preparation for tomorrow's big dance. It seems that a mask broke during the performance the other night. That happened while Wanuk's little boy danced. Therefore the latter [Wanuk] has to give this feast. Today he made a speech in which the poor devil said approximately the following: "Oh Kwakiutl, grant my son a long life. Once I tried to make my son a Hamatsa, but the deadly effect of *Baxbakwalanuxsiwe* hit him and he died." Then he was almost overcome by emotion and continued: "When he died I decided not to let another one of my kids become a Hamatsa. Now, however, since the mask broke I will let him become a Hamatsa. I will. But grant him a long life." Then Sē'wite [Si'wid], a blind man, cried: "Don't overdo it; let him have only two songs."

This was supposed to indicate that if he got four songs, as a Hamatsa should have, he would die soon. Then they all closed on the child and pushed him around [?], and next they decided how many dances were to be danced and how much they would cost.

I hope I'll get some good pictures and casts tomorrow. Up to now we have about sixty-five good pictures. I'll finish the casts tomorrow, I think.

*November 28:* This was written yesterday, the twenty-seventh, not on the twenty-sixth. I got all mixed up with my dates because of all that's going on here and the lack of sleep. Tonight and tomorrow we'll have to be up again all night. They will be dancing to bring back the new Hamatsa whom they had expected when Wanuk's mask broke.

This morning I invited everybody to an apple feast, for which they especially decked themselves out. Before that I took a few pictures of the village and of some carvings. While the people were on the way to the feast we got some quick shots. I will have to take a few more pictures of the women and some group pictures and then, I think, I will have enough. When it stopped raining we also made some casts of the rock sculptures. Unfortunately, they broke when we carried them home! Now it is almost 7 P.M., and I have to go to the feast soon. There is never a quiet moment here. I will be glad when this is all over. I am longing to get back to civilization. Then I can enjoy everything I have done here. I am anxious to find a letter from McGee in Victoria. I think the boat will come Tuesday or Wednesday. This morning all of a sudden our old friend Togra was announced. She will come back tomorrow as the new dancer. Her clothes were found on the shore this morning. This is, of course, all make-believe.

*December 1:* In the evening of the twenty-eighth a dance started again which lasted all night. I won't describe it now because I have no time. Right afterward the novices were to be brought in, and so I got up at 8 A.M. to take pictures of the ceremony. We had to wait till noon, however. In the meantime I went to bed again but was soon awakened by George, who was afraid that I would miss out on something. So I went to wake up Mr. Hastings. But unfortunately we were too early again. The people still had to compose their new songs and make their hemlock head ornaments.

At about 1 P.M. a group came leading the young Hamatsa; then another group, the *Nutlamatl,* which lead the new *Q'ominō'qa,* who was a friend of Togra's. I succeeded in taking four pictures. They

stopped and all the women came to meet them. The Hamatsa danced
toward the new *Q'ominō'qa*, who was covered all over with blood.
She was surrounded by all the other *Q'ominō'qa*, who danced for
her. They all danced in a round. Unfortunately George was not
here, and so I did not know what was going on—especially when the
new *Q'ominō'qa* danced with skulls in her hand. The Hamatsa
danced ahead of her, and after a while he took the skulls out of her
hand and put them down after he had licked them and eaten the
[something like maggots?]. The people were afraid to let me see
this. In the afternoon we took some more pictures. I was in bed at
7 P.M. and slept till 8 A.M. That was on the twenty-ninth.

Yesterday morning I had a few women sit for me while I took
several pictures for the New York group. I got a woman rocking
her baby and spinning at the same time. I also got women making
mats, baskets, preparing . . . , and a woman ready to go into a canoe.
If the plates turn out all right I will have really good group pictures.
In the afternoon I took more group pictures so that I will have quite
a good collection.

Right now one can hear the whistling and yelling of a Nak'wa-
tok [Nakoaktok] Hamatsa over the houses and trees, and so I'll just
disappear. The people are gathered at some feast right now, and
allegedly he will appear right afterward. Last night there was
another big dance in order to [initiate?] the new Hamatsa and the
*Q'ominō'qa*. They invited all the people to it, and at about 8 P.M.
everybody was there. After some short speeches we heard the
whistles from behind the curtains at the left from the entrance of the
house, and right away the singing started. Then the *Q'ominō'qa* appeared in the same manner as yesterday in her sleeveless shirt. Apparently she was supposed to be naked. She held her hands as if she
were carrying skulls. And the Hamatsa danced in front of her. A man
accompanied them with rattles. All the *Q'ominō'qa* danced again.
I could see everything very well. After two songs and two rounds
of dancing they disappeared behind the curtains. Then they returned
wearing ornamented head bands and dressed in blankets with big
neck rings around both shoulders and long strips of red cedar bark
with white stripes in the middle. They danced again past the fire.
After a short speech the little Hamatsa came out. It was Wanuk's
little five-year-old boy. The poor little one did not know what to
do. He is a Hams-hamtses [*hamshamts!ES*], not a real Hamatsa. All
Hamatsas danced around him. This was the right thing to do, according to Hunt's and my information. He disappeared after one
dance, and then a big mask of *Baxbakwalanuxsiwe* entered and
danced once around the fire. This was very beautiful. The dancers

were all naked but covered all over with red cedar. They did a good job. Then the boy came once more. Finally, the spectators formed little groups, each of which sang a song of its own. They are called the *Hēilikya*[?] singers. Before this a *Hēilikya*[?] had also accompanied the young Hamatsa's dance. His hands moved like the Hamatsa's, but he jumped with his feet together. All dancers always put their feet flat to the ground and the dance motion consists of a turning and jumping which is very strange. When this was over, arm bands and blankets were distributed to the Nakwatok [Nako-aktok] and to the Koskimo; and all the Kwakiutl went home to sleep.

I had to laugh yesterday. The people are curious to see the pictures from the back of the camera. I was just about to photograph a woman when somebody noticed that the picture was upside down, and he ran away telling everybody that her clothes had fallen over her head.

Today is packing day. I have not done much, though. The casts are packed. George and I went out to get some skulls. An Indian came our way, however, so we could not do much. I tried again in the afternoon, but this time a Hamatsa came and I had to give up. So I still don't have them. But something has to be done about it!

*December 3:* Since there was no dance last night or the night before, I went to bed early. The nights are now terribly cold, and it is also very wet. It is very uncomfortable and I cannot get warm. Yesterday at 6 A.M. I suddenly heard a steamer and quickly jumped out of bed. I had hardly packed at all and did not know how I could leave. It was not the *Boskowitz*, however, but a little fishing boat. But we were so alarmed by its sudden appearance that we were all packed by evening. I have fourteen boxes in all—two for Washington and twelve for New York. In the evening George and I went out again to get some skulls. This morning we measured some children and took some more pictures. All our plates are used—180! There are about twenty-five for which I don't care—some of Hunt's family, and some are spoiled. I hope I really have enough material for one article in a nice journal. I wish you had sent me a copy of *Popular Science.* Now everything is ready and I'll be glad when the steamer comes tomorrow. I only wish I knew the exact time of my return home.

*December 6:* I am closing these lines now. I wrote a special letter to you which I will send tomorrow. I will copy these papers for the parents so that they too know what I did here. Keep them well, be-

cause this letter is at the same time my report from Fort Rupert.
I won't be finished here by tomorrow, I think, so I won't close this
letter yet. Darling, when shall I be with you and the children again?

Your husband

On Board the Boskowitz,<br>December 6, 1894

My dear Wife,

We are now between Nanaimo and Victoria, and I hope to be
able to mail these lines tomorrow morning. I am so glad to return
after such a long trip. My stay in Fort Rupert was not at all agreeable, although I saw and learned a great deal. I hardly had time to
write you because I was so busy, and so I just described what took
place from day to day. I should like to copy this letter, since it is
for my parents; that is why I shall keep it a day longer. I will send
you a telegram tomorrow, and also one to my parents, because three
weeks have passed again without your getting a letter. It is so late
in the year that I cannot finish all the work I had wanted to do. If
I should find a letter from McGee tomorrow saying that I should
go to Shoalwater Bay, then I will give up the trip into the interior.
If I should not go to Shoalwater Bay, then I will make the trip. It
seems now that I could be in New York on January 5; however, it
is not definite yet. Tomorrow I shall be able to be more accurate.
I will be so happy to join you soon. I hope to get good news from
you and from over there tomorrow.

My trip from Fort Rupert is very disagreeable. The boat is
very crowded again and the weather so bad that one can hardly go
outdoors. On Tuesday, the fourth, we lay anchored in Fort Rupert
because there was a very bad storm. Yesterday it was beautiful again
and I finished the translation of my texts from the Nass River. Today
it is awful again; it is storming and pouring and I was very close to
getting seasick this morning. We have been in calmer waters again
since noon, and it seems we will stay there for a while. In Fort Rupert
I finally saw the entire winter dance. It was extremely interesting.
I also made one hundred and forty-four good pictures there, which
makes me think that I should publish something popular, perhaps for
Scribner or for Century.

Just these few lines for today to tell you that I am all right.
I wish I could return to you this minute. The time is beginning to
drag.

Your husband

Victoria, December 7, 1894

Dear Wife,

After I mailed your letter I received my letters, which had gone to the Canadian Pacific Navigation Company—those of November 9, 12, 16, 18, 23, 24, and 26. And I got the letters from over there of November 5, 12, 15, and 19. I also got a letter from Bauer announcing the birth of a little daughter; a letter from Fritz, who wanted to know something; the enclosed bill; and a letter from Jordan in answer to mine saying that I can come only at the end of December. He writes that he will be in Mexico from December 8 until January 15. Nothing from McGee or the National Museum, whose letters I had awaited very anxiously. I therefore sent a telegram to McGee today, and one to you stating that I shall send you my addresses tomorrow. I also telegraphed over there. From Jordan's note I take it that there is nothing behind the gossip [?] yet. I do not know what the silence from Washington means. I definitely have the blues today. I more or less gave up the trip into the interior. I might go to . . . and Spuzzum, instead. Cultee is in Bay Center, and I am sure that I will find him there if I should go. My work is so unfinished again that I don't even have the desire to go to the Fraser River any longer. I couldn't do very much there any more.

With respect to the money problem, don't forget that I have $500 here from the collection as well as the $100 which belongs to us; that Bauer has $100 and that the British Association owes us $200. I hope that you will write in your next letter exactly how much money you still have. Please pay the enclosed bill. You are right, the money for Anna will be very late. But why didn't they explain the situation more clearly? Did my Chinook bulletin appear? The reports from New York are not very encouraging. I hope nothing will interfere with the planned work for Washington. If so, we could go over there right away. Mama asked whether I was leaving you in New York. That would be the limit! I plan to leave here Monday or if possible Sunday evening. I hope to be with you again the first week of January. That is five more weeks! Today I copied a great part of the long letter to you but have not finished it yet. My parents will have to be satisfied with what I am sending them. Maybe, if you have time, you would send them a copy of the interesting part on page 6. I finished everything up to that page. I also received Uncle Kohn's letter. Please thank him for it; I don't think I will have the time.

*December 8:* This morning your letter of November 30 arrived. At noon a telegram came from McGee: "Can make no promise not subject to congressional action; but if appropriation recommended is granted, will purchase Chinook manuscript. Letter sent today." This telegram is ambiguous. Yet I think I will go. Last night I felt so blue that I wanted to go straight back. Today I am more reasonable. I will go to Spences Bridge Monday evening as planned and will expect McGee's letter when I come back here. If it is somewhat satisfactory, I will go to Bay Center, Washington, and then come back here. I feel I should take advantage of all opportunities out here, in view of the uncertainty of our future. If this were not so, I would return right away. I will get another $75 for the half month, and have the hope of getting $450 from the Bureau of [American] Ethnology. By the way, I am sending you my account as of today. Since I don't know how much money you have left, I must charge you with your figure of September 1. You can see from the account that I shall bring back from this trip the amount of $310.55. Since, however, I am buying the rest of the collection for the New York Museum on my account, and will charge them more for it, I shall bring back $460.

I had to buy a trunk because mine was falling to pieces. I paid $10 for it. If you only had a better boarding house. I wrote to Washington and asked them to look for a family for us. No word from Putnam. I think this very inconsiderate.

Adieu for today. I still have a lot of work to do. Kiss the children for me. I will write them tomorrow maybe.

Your husband

Victoria, December 8, 1894

Dear wife,

Today I forgot to tell you two things: First, that I sent you a small package with manuscript by express mail today, which you had best put into our safe deposit box. Do you have the things in New York? Take good care of them; they represent the major part of the results of my trip. I don't want to leave it in my trunk either. Second, I have just now decided to stick it out here, for the sake of despicable money, hard as it may be for me. Therefore you have to pay both life insurances, which are due on January 7. Please don't forget! They have to be paid on or before that day. If you don't want to pay them in person, send a check or a money order on the fifth. For the due date of the third, I will probably be there myself. I am feeling well after my bath and a hair and beard cut. The day after tomorrow I will have to put on my wool shirt and the dirt.

I sent a telegram to Spences Bridge so that my companion will be ready. I cannot be there before that. I hope I shall be finished there in one week. I have telegraphed you my further addresses: in Victoria until the twelfth, in Bay Center until the twentieth. If McGee's answer does not turn out satisfactorily, then I shall not go there, of course. I cannot arrange it differently. For the sake of our future I have to get as much as I can out of this trip. As I wrote before, I shall have $450 left when I return. I only wish you would write me how much money you have as of a certain date. I have asked you repeatedly for this information. Otherwise I will never be able to figure out how much we really have.

I am desperately awaiting a letter from Mason. I am disappointed that I won't see Jordan. I won't be able to give my paper because there will be vacation just then. I will visit F—— anyhow. Please send him a copy of my article in *Popular Science*. As far as I can tell now, I shall be in Spences Bridge on the twelfth; on the fourteenth I shall be back there again, and will leave there on the fifteenth. On the sixteenth I shall be on North Bend, the seventeenth and eighteenth in Spuzzum, and back here on the nineteenth. On the twenty-first I shall arrive in Bay Center. I can be in San Francisco from January 1 to January 5 and can leave Los Angeles on the tenth for home, so that I shall arrive home on the fifteenth. If only I could come earlier than that!

*Sunday, December 9:* I have to close now. I want to send the photos to both museums. I hope I find some letters from you in Spences Bridge.

Your husband

Vancouver, December 11, 1894

My dear wife,

I was very happy about your telegram which I received the day before yesterday. At least I got the most recent news. Of course I am expecting letters from you in Spences Bridge. I will be there late tonight and hope I will get them tomorrow morning. It is good that I can hear from you regularly now. The intervals won't be greater than a week now. I exchanged my ticket so that I don't have to return to Victoria but can go from Mission Junction directly to Seattle, where I have to spend one night. I wrote Otto Richter and am looking forward to seeing him. I had lots of work these past days. I had to straighten out bills, order photographs, take care of the shipping, and make a few calls. In short, I was busy all day long.

The weather is terrible now. The evening we left Victoria it stormed so badly that I could hardly sleep. We reached the protection of the islands before I became seasick, however. Later it became very calm. This morning it poured again. I made the final bills for Putnam and the National Museum this morning. I am enclosing a new one which should take the place of the previous one. I have time here until 2 P.M. I charged the New York Museum only $150 for my work, which is really very little for the good results I achieved. I think that I will go to Bay Center unless McGee's letter is too negative. Darling, it is very hard for me now that I have finished all the work I undertook, now that I have done my duty, to go into the interior again and work on the Chinook! However, it has to be.

I don't know what I wrote you last. I have written so much these past days. Write me to Bay Center until the twenty-second, then until the twenty-sixth to San Francisco, General Delivery; until January 1 to Los Angeles, and then to Chicago, care of Donaldson, but put the letters in an envelope with your address on it. Kiss the children for me, dear wife. Don't be too "blue" at Christmas! I will try not to be, either.

Your husband

P.S. The bill is not completely accurate because I did not have the final sums with me.

Vancouver, December 11, 1894

Dear Parents,

Once more I send you my love. I am on my way again to the interior, where I hope to make a few hundred more measurements, if possible. I hope that this will not take more than a week. Then I go to my old friend Charlie Cultee in Shoalwater Bay and return via San Francisco to New York. I hope that everything will go smoothly and I will be in Chicago on January 11.

The last weeks of work out here are very sour for me. I have completed everything I took upon myself, and if it were not for the despicable money, I would go to California and New York right away. But with our future so insecure, I have to take everything I can get. Today only these few lines. I did so much writing these past days that I don't even know what I wrote you the last time. I changed my ticket so that I don't have to go back to Victoria. Adieu for today. Thousand greetings to everybody from your

Franz

Lytton, December 14, 1894

Dear Parents,

I am using a spare half hour to send you my love. I have been in the interior since day before yesterday and am very glad that I came because I can make my former work here more complete. I am only making measurements. Monday night I left Victoria. I had ordered the same informant I had in the fall, with two horses, and we went around all day long up the hills and down the hills, from house to house, to make measurements. In Spences Bridge I received two letters from Marie. Monday I hope to get something from you because I will be in a place to which I have had my mail forwarded.

We only returned here Wednesday evening at ten and took the train to this place at three o'clock. Yesterday and this morning I worked busily, and this afternoon we are going to a village about two miles from here. Tomorrow we will go a little farther up the Fraser River. Tomorrow night we are going to North Bend, and on Tuesday I hope to wind up my work in British Columbia. What I shall do from then on is not certain yet. I expect a letter in Spuzzum where I shall be Monday or Tuesday. The contents of this letter will direct my decision. Enough for today. I am too busy to find leisure to write.

With all my love,

Your Franz

Lytton, December 15, 1894

My dear wife,

Again one place is behind me. I worked here busily for three days and with rather good success. I have measured, all in all, one hundred and twenty-three Indians since Wednesday, and if I have the same success tomorrow, Monday, and Tuesday, I will be glad that I went to this place and that I am virtuous. But I am impatient now to be with you again, and my impatience grows stronger every day. I hope you received the four packages and the various papers I sent you. Yesterday I also sent copies of measurements by registered mail which I hope will arrive safely. I have now made four hundred and sixty-two measurements in all. Day after tomorrow I hope I shall hear from you again in the beautiful place of Spuzzum. If only I could spend less time traveling. Wednesday morning, the nineteenth, I think I will leave Spuzzum and shall be in Seattle by evening. There I want to see Otto Richter [?]. I don't know yet whether I can leave for Bay Center on the twentieth. In any event, I'll try to be as fast as I can, you can rely on that.

This morning we crossed the Thompson River, then the Fraser, where there is much floating ice now. I finished my work in a little village about two miles from here. Then we went three miles up the river to another village. The snow-covered countryside looks much more beautiful now than in summer. The snow brings color and change, whereas in the summer everything appears grey and bare. The river flows through a deeply cut ravine between high mountains. The bottom of the ravine is filled with sand and gravel through which the river has gnawed its way through the centuries. Although it was very cold I got really hot walking up and down mountains. We arrived in the village at noon and ate our lunch. The chief was very nice. He called all the members of the tribe into his house, and after a few speeches in which he . . . I merrily did my measuring. We had to stop at 3:30 because it was getting dark early, and we did not want to be late for the ferry. Now I have . . . and . . . paid and to-morrow morning at five I go to North Bend, where I want to mail this letter. My informant is a very nice man. He comes from the Shetland Islands and has bummed around here a lot in all kinds of capacities. He is very much interested in the Indians and is writing a report for me about this tribe which will be very good, I hope. He will also make a collection for me. His name is James Teit. Good-night now, dear wife.

Dear kids, papa is so busy now that he cannot write you special letters. Every day the Indians tell me so many things that I don't have time to write you. Are you looking forward a little bit to my coming home soon? I bet you will have a lot to tell me when I come back. Papa has been away for such a long time. It is very cold here. The mountains are covered with snow and the rivers are full of ice. The wind is howling terribly. Are you cold too? Isn't it nice that little Ernst is going to kindergarten now and that Helenchen can talk to him now and then. Remember well everything that goes on at Christmas so that you can tell me when I come back. Goodnight! Today I send a kiss to each of you. Guess for whom each of them is.

Your papa

# PART THREE

---

# RESEARCH FOR THE JESUP EXPEDITION (1897–1901)

EDITOR'S INTRODUCTION.—*In 1897 Morris K. Jesup, president of the Board of Trustees of the American Museum of Natural History, organized and financed an expedition to the North Pacific Coast at the suggestion of Boas and F. Ward Putnam. Boas was placed in charge of the research, and he was accompanied to British Columbia by Livingston Farrand and Harlan I. Smith. This team was assisted in the field by George Hunt, James Teit, and Fillip Jacobsen (Boas 1898). The purpose of the expedition was to clarify some of the issues regarding the origin of the Indians raised by nineteenth-century scholars, that is, to determine whether American aboriginals crossed the Bering Strait into the New World. The expedition was also designed to explore other issues such as the period of occupancy of various parts of the Northwest Coast and the changes in the physical characteristics and culture of the inhabitants there, to study the geographical distribution of the types of men along the coast and their relationship to those of neighboring areas, and to investigate the languages and cultures of the coastal tribes with particular reference to the question of the distribution of culture.*

*Boas described the purpose of the project as follows:*

> It seems to me well to make the leading point of view of my discussion, on the one hand an investigation of the historical relations of the tribes to their neighbors, on the other hand a presentation of the culture as it appears to the Indian himself. For this reason I have spared no trouble to collect the descriptions of customs and beliefs in the language of the Indians, because in these the points that seem important to him are emphasized, and the almost unavoidable distortion contained in the description given by the casual visitor and student is eliminated. [Boas 1909, p. 309]

*The Jesup North Pacific Expedition continued for five years, from 1897 to 1901, but Boas made only two field trips during this time, in 1897 and in 1900.*

# 8

---

## Family Letters (1897)

Vancouver, British Columbia
June 3, 1897

Dear Wife,

Today upon my arrival I found your second letter with the enclosures. I am glad to hear that the paperhanger came. That will make it possible for you to leave soon. I hope to find a letter in Spences Bridge tomorrow telling me when you will leave. It seems like an eternity since we left, and even more of an eternity since we arrived in Seattle. I have seen all the people I wanted to see and hope that we will be able to start work tomorrow. Farrand was very surprised to learn how well known I am in Victoria. We saw all my friends and did a little shopping; and I got all my letters of credit for the trip. Last night I was invited to dinner by Dr. Newcombe, an enthusiastic natural scientist. Besides myself there were also the superintendent of Indian Affairs and a lawyer named Martin. It was a very nice evening. Just imagine, the letter I wrote to Dr. Newcombe about the potlatches led to a bill to cancel the law. I only hope that it will pass. The doctor goes to the Queen Charlotte Islands and has promised to collect certain things for me there, especially a large totem pole.

I did not get around to writing you yesterday; I was dead tired in the evening. We went to bed on the steamer and arrived here this morning. This afternoon the trip goes on, and at 11:00 we shall be at Spences Bridge. Mr. Hill-Tout here gave me five skulls this morning; one of them very valuable. I am very impatient now to get to work. I found out that the mail goes down the Fraser River every week; you will therefore hear regularly, and that is a great comfort to me. I hope that you all are going to have a good time. Today I have to buy a pair of shoes because I need something to change into. You must not forget to send the instruments which I put aside to Seattle [?] to the Museum.

I wonder what will come out of this trip? Please be so kind as to send a reprint of my article in the Bulletin of the Museum which just came out before my departure, to Mr. J. Vowell, Superintendent of Indian Affairs, Victoria, British Columbia. He asked for it. Adieu for today. I want now to write to my parents. Please always tell me a lot about the children.

Your husband

Spences Bridge, June 5, 1897

Dear Wife,

We can be satisfied with the results of our first two days here. If it only will continue this way! We have measured ten people and have photographed them, and I bought a small collection of ethnographic artifacts. It was not much effort, though. Teit had prepared everything for us very well. The Indians were ready for us promptly yesterday afternoon, and we could not work quickly enough to finish with all of them. I think the material turned out all right and will be usable, I hope, for the Museum as well as for our scientific report. I hope that the trip to the northwest will also turn out well. At the moment my plans are to go with Farrand to Kamloops and do the same work there as we do here, especially making measurements. I need a great number of measurements of the Shuswap Indians who live there.

The weather here is, of course, very beautiful because we are in the dry zone. Clouds appear in the afternoon sometimes, but it never rains. Today I finally received the galleys of the last tables of my Washington book. I want to finish them today and send them back. I didn't get anything from you today, neither a letter nor the pictures which you promised to send. I wonder if these lines will reach you in New York. That is all for today. Kiss the children for me. I only noticed yesterday that I did not send you the pansy of baby's grave [?]. Goodnight. Many greetings.

Your husband

Spences Bridge, June 6, 1897

Dear Wife,

Today only a short greeting. I am always so dead tired that I do not feel like writing. We seem to be finished here with the castings. I let Farrand and Smith make the casts ready for shipping. This afternoon Jimmy Teit and I went down to the village and collected melodies. The phonograph works very well, and we got ten good songs. The rhythms seem to be rather difficult, although the songs themselves are very simple. The few hours in the village were very interesting.

The singers became ecstatic and acted out all their old stories and ceremonies while they sang. One of them sang a prayer. While singing he danced and reached out to the sun with both arms while looking upward. Then he brought them down slowly, looking to the ground. Before that he had crossed his hands in front of his chest with the palms outward, moving them to the left and to the right as if he wanted to embrace the celestial body. An old woman danced the [Bear?] dance, by which a mother was supposed to be cleansed from having had twins. Twins are thought to be the children of grizzly bears, and the song is addressed to the bear. There were two women whom I could not get to sing at first. They did sing, after all, when all the men had left the house. I can really be satisfied with my first few days here. We got eleven casts and many photos, a few measurements and three songs. . . .

Darling, please write me regularly. Yesterday I worked out the entire travel plan. We plan to leave here Friday for the north. That is the eleventh. I hope to arrive in Bella Coola on the fifteenth. Unfortunately I have not heard from George Hunt. If he prepares the way for me in Bella Coola as well as he did here, the work will be easy. Kiss the children for me and give my regards to Mother. For you, dear old one, I send many greetings and kisses.

Your husband

Tomorrow I won't be able to write because we are going to a village five miles from here.

Spences Bridge, June 6, 1897

Dear Parents,

I might say that I can be satisfied with the first few days of my work this summer. We have been here three days and have been busy casting faces of Indians. Altogether we made eleven, and we also took photos of the people. I have become an experienced plaster-of-paris worker. The casts turn out quite well.

I finally have finished planning the trip for the whole next month. From here we shall go up north along the Fraser River for the next three weeks and then across a pass to Bella Coola. I will stay along the postal route for some time, so that you can expect a letter from me every week. It could be of course that I will miss a connection, but that is very improbable. The singing this afternoon was very interesting. The Indians here have a very . . . way. While they sang they acted out all their old stories and ceremonies. An old woman sang the song into the phonograph which serves to "cleanse" women who had borne twins. She took bundles of fir branches and hit her shoulders and breast with them while she danced. The song imitates the growl of the grizzly bear because they believe that the children derive from the grizzly bear. An old man sang an old religious song to the sun, a prayer. The gestures were very expressive. He raised his hands up high and looked at the sun. Then he lowered them slowly, pressing them against his chest while he looked down again. The singing was a great deal of fun for the villagers. Some of the people were bashful, especially the women, who did not want to sing until all the men had left the house.

The scenery here is very beautiful. The river flows down deep into the valley. Toward the south a tall mountain rises on the far side of the river. I will show you photos of it. Everything is very dry, however, because it is a country of eternal sunshine, at least in the summer. This is all for tonight. I am rather tired. I hope that the weather in Sassnitz will be all right.

With deepest love,

Your Franz

Fifteen miles below Lillooet
June 14, 1897

Dear Wife,

This is the first day of our trip. Tomorrow we shall be in Lillooet and I can mail this letter there. The trip is very good for me. We are outdoors all the time, and I have no intellectual work worth mentioning. I am not going to write about the trip because I want to write this to the children. If only I had some news from you! That is the "not so nice aspect" of this trip into the wilderness. Nature here is very beautiful. This morning we rode horseback through a valley about 2,000 feet high which looked very much like the Alps. Far off you can see the snow mountains. Today we descended again to the Fraser River valley. Now we are riding along the river toward the north. Horseback riding is not as hard on me as I thought. We go very slowly because the heavily laden horses cannot go fast on these steep trails. Only my knees and the lower part of my . . . are a little weak. This is also true for Farrand.

Smith left us the day before yesterday in Spences Bridge. He is supposed to go for several days to Kamloops to take pictures and to. . . . I am really worried about him because he does not look well and coughs all the time. The other night when he took down the songs he had a fever and was not feeling well at all. The climate here is good [?] for him. I hope he will get rid of the cough! It is dry, warm, and not too high. Our results this time are quite different from those before. The most interesting things we got are the explanations of the designs of the woven baskets, the materials, the jewelry, and the masks. We won't be able to do much in the next few days because we are traveling.

Best greetings for today.

Your husband

*June 15:* It is evening, and we are about six miles from Lillooet. It rained all day, and traveling is no fun this way. The valley here is very beautiful, but at various places the trail is really awful, steep down about 1,000 feet to the Fraser River! The walls of the canyon are vertical, and the trail goes directly along the rim. Now, however, we have passed the worst places and will soon be at the bottom of the valley.

Good night.

Your husband

Near Lillooet, June 15, 1897

Dear Parents,

We have been on the trip on horseback for three days. I have wanted to write you a long letter about the beauty of the countryside through which we are traveling, but now I cannot do more than send you my love and tell you that we are. . . . We rode across the mountains between the Thompson and the Fraser rivers, following the trails of the Indians. Nature is magnificent here. Ahead of us we can see the snow mountains of the coast range, and deep down below the Fraser River is roaring. Now we have crossed the mountain chain and are on a plateau which stretches from here toward the northwest. We have four riding horses, five pack horses, and three guides who walk behind us because. . . . In the evening we set up our tents and cook our meal. Then I try to get as much as I can out of the Indians. At nine o'clock it gets dark and we go to sleep. In the morning we get up at 6:30, cook breakfast, and load the horses. This takes until about 8:30. And then we keep going until evening, 4:30 or five o'clock, that is. Since the horses are heavily laden, they only walk, so that we cannot cover more than four to five German miles.

If there is some work to do, Farrand and I stay back while the others go on. Then we catch up with them again. Yesterday was a very trying day. It rained constantly so that we are still wet today. I hope it will improve soon. I can stand the horseback riding better than I thought, although I am getting a bit tired. Up to now we have not really done anything, but I hope that we will be more lucky in the villages which we will soon reach. (It is now 6 A.M.) Farrand is quite a nice traveling companion, unassuming and gay. There is not much occasion to talk with each other during the day. The evenings are always very agreeable. We both try hard to handle the horses. I can already saddle mine, but I cannot load them the right way. That is very difficult.

I am sorry that I cannot write you in more detail, but I have to go to work again. I hope this trip will be very good for me. Always in the fresh air and no hardships and no intellectual work—that is just the right thing for me. If only I were not so cut off from the world. And no letters! I won't be able to get any until the twenty-seventh.

With many greetings to everybody.

Your Franz


[No location cited]
June 18, 1897

Dear Wife,

The past days have been terrible. It rained incessantly, and only this morning it slowly started to clear up. You can imagine how completely wet everything was. The day before yesterday we arrived in Lillooet and I went immediately to the Indian village. Farrand and I started off early in the morning ahead of the others and so gained a few hours. Unfortunately the Indians are so scattered all over the countryside that we did not find very many at home. This will make the trip less profitable, although I got along very well with them. The same happened yesterday when we worked in another village. Farrand went on a side trip yesterday. I engaged an Indian to guide him. I hope he will be successful. He will join me again on the twenty-sixth.

I will be very happy when I find letters from you at Soda Creek. It is very disagreeable to be so long without news. My letters to you will also take very long because it is difficult to find connections with post offices. We will reach one the day after tomorrow. Then this letter will go. After that we will pass a post office every day, but the mail leaves them only once a week. There is an Indian village one mile from here which I want to visit tomorrow morning. I am rather unhappy that so much of our time is spent on the trips. But there is nothing one can do about that. I hope you are well. I long for news!

Your husband

Kelly Lake, June 21, 1897

Dear Wife,

Since I did not find a post office yesterday I gave my letters to a man riding by who will pass a post office today. I hope he will mail them. These greetings will be mailed in Big Bar. My life is very monotonous, and if the surroundings were not so beautiful, it would be boring. The night before last we reached the little Indian village, Paws Horn [?], where I made some measurements. In the morning after the pack horses had left, I went there again to make more measurements but did not get as much as I wanted because the Indians are so widely scattered.

We are now on a regular road, which we will follow for about two weeks. It left the Fraser River yesterday because it goes across a big mountain. Tonight we shall reach the river again. The way up the mountain was magnificent. The weather has cleared up again and one could see the high mountain range near Lillooet with its snow mountains and glaciers behind the valley of the Fraser River. Toward the east there were lower mountains, at first here [?] and then at North Thompson. The road winds up the mountain and every turn was beautiful again. When we reached the top, we found ourselves on an open plateau where there were many (three or four) ranches. Then down we rode again. On the other side we could see down below the deep valley with the lovely lake, and there we are now. We hope now to reach Big Bar by evening. I like to ride alone behind the pack horses because it is boring to go along with them in one line. I will be an experienced horseman when I come back. Yesterday, however, I was thrown when the horse suddenly shied.

Baby is now more than two months old! How I should love to get news from you. I will have to be patient for ten more days. I don't even know if you arrived safely at the farm. The mosquitoes are terrible.

Your husband

Hanceville, July 6, 1897

Dear Wife,

The weather was so ghastly these past days that I did not get to write you. Our life is so monotonous that there was really nothing to write about. Today the sun came out for the first time. It is cold and windy, however, and the mosquitoes leave us in peace. We came here a few days ago to be with the Chilcotin. I find it very hard to get along with these people. I doubt that I will be able to get many measurements. But let's start at the beginning!

We crossed the Fraser River on July 1 at Soda Creek. There used to be a ferry boat, but it has been abolished in favor of a steamer which goes up the river from there about eighty miles. So we had to wait for this steamer which was due at 6 A.M. but only arrived at eleven. I could not resist the temptation of sending you a telegram, which I hope you received. Farrand went to measure the Indians in the Indian village while I waited for him with the horses on the other side of the river. He arrived in a canoe. We could not make many measurements because the [saddle] horses were waiting for us; the pack horses had gone on. We then rode for two and one-half days across a high plateau to the Chilcotin River, or rather to the Riske, a little river north of the Chilcotin. The first village of that tribe was there. The measuring went on all right, although all the twenty-year-olds absolutely refused to be measured. If I had known how difficult it would be here, I would have tried to measure those in the mountains. Our camp was about four miles from the village. We left the pack horses behind, and Farrand and I rode once more to the village in the evening after dinner was over. At Soda Creek the plateau is quite wooded. When approaching Riske Creek one rides through open country again. They have less rain than other areas, and here too there is less. From Riske Creek it took us two days, in pouring rain, to reach Hanceville. There are not many Indians here, and they are very contrary and hard to handle, so that I don't know if we will get anything that will be worth mentioning. Farrand and I rode ahead again. Mrs. Hance, who has a store and runs the post office, invited us to her house. There we dried ourselves and had dinner. It was very nice to have fresh vegetables again instead of bacon and dried beans. The young woman, whose husband was on a trip, was very friendly and tried to persuade a Chilcotin who works for her to have himself measured. He agreed at first, but then his wife or mother-in-law seems to have scared him and he disappeared. I came here again this noon and had a long conversation with him. He said that if he were measured he would die within three months. I had the opportunity to acquire a few very good pieces for the Museum, and so we did have some success. I also found a good-natured young Indian who agreed to be measured and cast. Today we want to go to the other side of the river. I asked a German trader who knows the Indians very well to go with us, and he promised to do so.

I will be very glad when we finally reach the coast. I might be able to send you my greetings before that once more, but I am not sure. There will then be an interruption of about two weeks, or even three, depending on the steamers which we will meet at the coast. Bella Coola gets mail only twice a month, and since we shall arrive on about the twentieth, we will probably have to wait until August 1 to get connections. It is therefore possible that I won't get any letters into the mail until August 6 or 9. If it takes very long, I will have them send you a telegram from Victoria. I am very impatient to get letters but it will take until some time in August, and depends on the boats. I am fed up with these trips into the wilderness. I hope Farrand's and Smith's trips will be the reason that I may stop soon. I had news from Smith in Soda Creek. He seems to have had some success. If he were only well! I will close this later before we leave. The mail does not leave until July 9.

*The same afternoon:* This morning we went to the Indian village on the south shore of the Chilcotin. It is three miles from here. When we arrived we found it completely deserted, and so I could not accomplish a thing. In the afternoon I was on my way again to Mr. Hance's ranch, where I wanted to work on the young Indian whom I almost got yesterday, when I met on the way a young man who agreed to be measured and also promised that I could make a cast. Since my plaster-of-paris was at the ranch, I had to go one and one-half miles for it, and I left Farrand to watch over the Indian. Teit, who was with me, carried the plaster-of-paris back while I stayed and quickly worked on the old Indian until he finally promised that I could measure him and make a cast this evening. With this I will have exhausted my activities here and we will ride on to . . . which is about eight miles from here.

Adieu for today. How I should like to get news from you! And how I should like to be with you! A year ago we had our first beautiful days on the farm. I miss much of the development of our children by being away. I won't even recognize baby Gertrude. I hope all of you are well. My last news from over there came on May 30. I would also like to know how they are.

Adieu dear wife. Kiss the children for me.

Your husband

Keep the stamps for Ernst. They will be rare some day.

Puntzi Lake, July 12, 1897

Dear Parents,

As I thought, it is possible to send you some greetings from here. We are now one hundred and fifty miles from Bella Coola and I hope that we shall reach there on about the twentieth. Then you will have to wait about two weeks for a letter. It could be a little longer if a good steamer does not arrive. I am terribly itchy for some news from you. I have heard nothing about you since the end of May. I had my last news from Marie as of June 12. How happy I will be when we arrive at Port Essington! And I will get some letters again! To-day is Mama's and Toni's birthday. I wonder whether you are in Fort Brandenburg? I hope you are spending a very happy day. For a few days we are having beautiful weather again. Finally! The first weeks of the trip it rained a great deal; we were awfully muddy all the time. I will be so glad when we reach the coast. . . .

I found the tribes here so interesting that I decided to leave Farrand here for at least one month. He will then follow me to the coast. I hope he will be lucky and get good results. I am glad I can give him the opportunity of working completely independently for a while because that makes the trip more advantageous for him. These past days we rode along the Chilcotin River. The country is becoming very beautiful again. We can see the snow mountains of the coast range in the distance, while around us are green forests and many lakes. The few white people who live here are very nice to us. They do whatever they can to help us. Here lives the last white man until we come to the coast. He is a doctor who built himself a block house for sports and trades with the natives. He is not here at the moment. One can find all sorts of quaint persons, and Farrand and I love to figure out their motives. Of course I have no idea what is going in the world. We are completely cut off from the outside world. Fortunately I hired a guide to take us to Bella Coola, and I don't doubt but that we will get there without difficulty, especially since a group of Indians arrived here yesterday without trouble.

My work here has turned out successfully, against all expectations. At first it looked as if I would not get any measurements, but then I hired an interpreter and everything went as well as possible. The last two days were very nice. We rode through the woods from one little village to another. The Indians live here . . . , and we saw all the Indians who live along the road. It was really funny how they all accompanied us and how we finally arrived with a cavalcade of twenty horses. Here we left three of our horses be-

cause we don't have so much to carry any more. I hope to find
George Hunt in Bella Coola and hope he has collected a lot.

Adieu for today. These are only short greetings, but the way
we are traveling makes it hard to write.

Your Franz

Bella Coola, July 20, 1897
My dear Wife,

This afternoon I finally arrived here after a long trip which took
almost seven weeks. Just when we arrived we heard the whistle of
the steamer, which leaves tomorrow at 4 A.M. and won't be back
for two weeks. The pack horses are not here yet, and therefore a
few lines for . . . and for. . . . George Hunt is here; he seems to have
worked very hard and well. I am sorry that I can send only a few
lines to go on the boat for tomorrow morning, but it is already 8:30.
I have no light and just want to send you a token that I am still
alive.

I have eaten enough beans and bacon. I will stay here now for
two weeks, and you won't hear from me again for two weeks because there won't be another steamer before then. I am sending you
a telegram today which I will have sent from Victoria. I will do
the same in two weeks. Please send the telegrams on to my parents.
To my great surprise and joy I found many letters here for me, although I did not order any to be sent to Bella Coola. Please don't
forward any more printed matter to me. From my last letter you
will know that I left Farrand in Chilcotin. He will follow me in
four weeks. Adieu dear wife, I should like to continue but cannot
do it tonight. Kiss the children for me.

Your husband

Today must have been your birthday! Dear old one! I wish I
could be with you and tell you how I love you and kiss you! Did
the children have little surprises for you? I shall have to bring a
birthday gift to you in person. What do you think about a grizzly
bear skin? Write whether you want one. Or rather something from
the Indians which you can then put in (or on) your. . . . Grizzly
skins are really a bit too expensive.

Your husband

Bella Coola, July 21, 1897

Dear Wife [and Parents],

It won't happen again that the steamer comes and I am not ready with my letters. The trip on horseback through a mosquito-infested country makes letter writing difficult. Now I am leading a regular life again and can write you every day about what I am doing. Yesterday I could write only a few greetings to you and my parents, and some important business letters. I got a letter from Ernst G— from Freiburg. He wrote the book about the beginnings of art, which I found very good. It was an answer to my sending him the pamphlet on the art of the . . . Indians from around here. He was very glad to have it. He wrote that this work has solved many puzzles in the simplest and most surprising way: "Not only ethnology but also and foremost the science of arts should be grateful for this excellent treatise."

I have letters from over there up to June 14, and a very nice letter from Hete. Mama does not seem to be very satisfied with father's health. I am really worried about it. But there is no use worrying now. I hope that Ernst is completely well again. I hope that you all stay well during the summer, and later too of course. I miss so much not being able to watch the children grow. I enjoy their little letters so much! Now let me tell you about myself during these past days. I wrote you from Puntzi Lake on the twelfth. We left there at noon—our guide Teit, with his horse; our Indian Sam, with four pack horses, and I. The first day the path went slowly up the valley until we reached the plateau, which is about 3,500 feet high. The scenery there is desolate. The trees, all Scotch pines, don't grow big because of the cold climate and the bad soil. They are very dense, however, and the trail is so overgrown that it makes riding very difficult. The forest is even partly burned down [?], and so the trails are even rougher. I arrived here completely scratched up.

Many little creeks are on the plateau, and they flow very slowly and form little swamps and lakes here and there. The swamps are covered with grass, but there are deep holes into which the horses sink quite easily. Three of our horses got stuck in one of the swamps, and we had a terrible time freeing them. We rode three and one-half days through this disconsolate landscape. Then we came to a little river through which we had to wade. There was a fish dam (trap), and we found several tents in which there were three women with their children. The men had gone hunting into the mountains where elk are supposed to be abundant. The women live on the fish which they catch at the dam. We stayed overnight because I hoped to measure the women, but I could not persuade them. The women were very anxious to get bread and sugar, and we to get fish and other fresh items. While we put up our tents, the women sent a little boy with fish for us. We sent them sugar and flour in return. After a while more children came with more fish, which we also exchanged for sugar and flour. Thus we will have fresh food for several days. You cannot imagine how hungry one gets on trips like this and what enormous quantities one can wolf down. The next morning it rained so hard that I was afraid we could not go on, but at 10 A.M. it cleared up again. Traveling with pack horses is extremely difficult when it rains. Everything becomes totally drenched. The trail was very difficult because the wind had strewn huge trees across the path over which the horses had to climb.

At noon we reached the divide (watershed) between the Bella Coola and the Charlotte rivers. We stayed at a little lake overnight, where there were lots of mosquitoes. There an Indian caught up with us. He had returned from hunting, and the women had told him about us. He gave us a message for Bella Coola. In the evening another Indian came with his family; he had trapped some animals during the winter, and he wanted to sell the furs in Bella Coola. From then on we traveled with him; that is, we had different camps but made all the difficult parts of the trail together. On the sixteenth we could already see the snow mountains quite close. Ahead was an apparent deep incision in the coastline, or rather a broad break in the mountain range. A river comes out of it, along which we rode. From here we could easily look over the vast plateau which we had just crossed. It spreads out without interruption as far as the eye can see. Toward the north one can see three distinct groups of mountains and in the south and southwest are the foothills of the Coast Range. The valley gradually rises and becomes more and more narrow. Finally in the afternoon we saw the most wonderful snow mountains in the southwest. Toward the north the country has the character of a plateau. The higher we went the swampier the ground became, from the waters of the melted snow which could not drain off. In the evening we camped, with a wonderful view of the snow mountains. The air was as clear as could be and the evening sky was magnificent.

The next morning pouring rain awakened us again. We got up at 4:30 and left at 6:30. It cleared a little, but we did not have a distant view; the view was poor all day long. The valley became more and more narrow. We now went down along a river which goes into the Bella Coola Inlet. Finally, about three miles from the Bella Coola River the valley narrowed into a gorge. We left it and rode along the northern side of the mountain until we arrived at the foot of a pass which leads into the Bella Coola valley. There we made camp, about 4,000 feet high. In the evening it poured, and the wind blew so hard that it threatened to blow our tents away. How happy I was when the sun shone again the next morning and the wind abated. In two hours we reached the summit of the pass. The trail went across snow fields and meadows. We saw right before us the most beautiful mountain country. Deep in the valley was the Bella Coola, and we rode slowly toward it along the side of the mountain. The view was gorgeous. There were steep mountaintops with huge glaciers, and in the valley a sea of clouds through which one could see the river. The landscape was magnificent. We caught a marmot which served us as dinner. If I had the time and the desire, there would be plenty of opportunity to hunt. There are hundreds of fresh tracks of elk, black bears, and grizzly bears. Our guide shot at a grizzy bear, but he got away. We also saw a few mountain goats.

Then came the descent, which was easy all the way. In four hours we descended about 5,000 feet and found ourselves in a completely different climate. It was warm and humid, and we were surrounded by the dense forests of the coast. In order to cross the river, which is very broad and dangerously swift, we had to make a float on which an Indian crossed over to get a canoe which was on the other side. All our things were shipped in it to the other side. The horses were herded into the river to swim across. It was all very exciting. We urged the thirteen horses into the river by using sticks and by shouting. At first they managed to break through our line and had to be rounded up again. We camped that night on this side of the river in pouring rain. Early the next morning, on the twentieth, we started out again. The weather was very beautiful. The trail went first through a very dense forest but at 11 A.M. we reached a regular road. Here in the valley is a Norwegian settlement, about two years old. We passed all the houses, the first sign of civilization in two weeks. I rode ahead alone because I wanted to be sure of arriving that evening. I had written to George Hunt that I would arrive between the fifteenth and the twentieth, and I wanted to keep my word. I was glad to find him here and to find that he had everything well prepared. That assured the success of my trip. I hope that Smith was lucky too and had collected all the material he was supposed to.

It took me a few days to get organized. Teit let the horses rest for two days and left the afternoon of the twenty-third, since it rained heavily in the morning. Until then I stayed with them in the tent, and also slept there. The trader, a Mr. Clayton, was kind enough to offer me a bed in his storage building where he had all the provisions for his general store; that is, yard goods, hardware, glass, pots and pans, canned fruit and meat, etc. Now after seven weeks I am sleeping in a bed again! It feels wonderful to stretch out on it in the evening. Today, the twenty-fourth, I also got my clean laundry, which an Indian woman washed for me, and I feel like a new man.

During the day I stay in an Indian house where George Hunt cooks for the two of us. Our daily food now is salmon, which is an agreeable change from beans and bacon. The whole first day I spent settling our finances with Teit, giving Farrand instructions, and making my own plans. On the twenty-second I went over the whole collection Hunt had made; I got the names of all items, and a number of stories, etc. On the twenty-third I started going over all the old Kwakiutl manuscripts with Hunt. This is a great task because I have to write out two hundred and thirty pages of manuscript after his dictation, in addition to all the other work I have to do. I cannot write more than fifteen pages per day. The greatest difficulty here is the lack of interpreters. Nobody knows English and everything has to be done in very bad Chinook. Today I had a few old people here, and the prospects of getting good material are fine. I only wish that I had my old Bella Coola manuscript here. The tribe is very interesting. I wish I had a good interpreter and could stay here for a long time.

*July 27:* I am making rather good progress but life is very uncomfortable. I sleep very well in Clayton's bed, surrounded by fruit jars, axes, patent medicines, buckets, and what not. I get up at 6 A.M. and George Hunt has breakfast ready in the filthy Indian house. The house is on stilts, and in the middle a place for the fire is built up. Previously the privy, if I may mention it, was in a corner so that all the filth went under the house. Nowadays a platform is built for this purpose behind the village. The weather is cold and unfriendly, and all this makes it not too nice here. Also, the food is not very good, but we have a little more variation than in the interior. I am now so far advanced in my work that short visits to the various tribes do not lead to anything. First I would have to study the language thoroughly and collect material, as I did with the Kwakiutl. My next task will probably be to work out the Kwakiutl material very thoroughly. Every morning George Hunt dictates his material, which he had sent to me in New York, so that it gets into decent shape. And I try to improve his orthography. The information I am collecting here is very interesting. This tribe is a real psychological puzzle. They built up a highly developed and very complicated Olympus [Goetterwelt] out of the mythology of the neighboring tribes, which is a mess of ghosts and spirits. The whole thing is connected with the calendar and seems to be the beginning of a highly developed religion. I got some rather good information on it, but it will take years to get to the origin of it. This probably will be the most interesting result of my trip. Since I had some previous information on it, I could try to come right to the point. I have to stay here ten days and hope to really achieve something.

*July 30:* I have some time today because the Indian with whom I worked ran out of information. I will use this time to send you my love. I am making good progress, and I think I will have good results from my stay here. The tribe is very interesting. Their mythology had aroused my interest before, but I did not know that they had such a highly developed system of gods. All around they have merely ghosts and spirits, but this tribe has veritable gods who live in Walhalla and to whom are entrusted the lives and the fates of men as well as nature. I start my day every morning with George Hunt, who dictates texts to me. We are about halfway through. It is quite boring. At nine I go to the Indians. For the past few days I have had a good interpreter (female), only for Chinook, but everything goes ten times as fast. Almost all my information comes from an old man who took pride in trying to surpass everything that was ever told to me before. I am trying of course, by cross-examination, to find out whether everything he tells me is really true. Thus far I have found him very reliable. I am only sorry that I don't have more time for these people. My interpreter speaks the language so clearly that I get a lot out of it. I work with the Indians until about 6 P.M. During the first days I also worked evenings, but I soon gave this up. Yesterday I wanted to get the Man Eater tale from the old man, but he hesitated. I hope, though, that I will still get it.

I walk now with George every evening for two hours. I miss the exercise of the past weeks. However, I am catching up with the sleep I missed during our ride. I go to bed at 9:30 and get up at 6:30 in the morning. That gives me nine hours. This should be enough. I have to stay here for one more week. If only I could quickly get a boat to Port Essington! I long for news from you. It is awful not to get any mail. I only hope that the children are all right. I should have written Anna with the last steamer. Her birthday letter will probably be one week late. But the letters which went with the last boat had to be written in such a hurry that I should not have had the time, even if I had thought of her birthday. It was pitch dark when I ran to the landing that night to mail my other letters.

*August 2:* The weather has been beautiful again since yesterday, and I used the beautiful evening to climb one of the mountains. The mountains here are really beautiful. One has a view way up the valley, to the place where we came down. The mountains are about 9,000 feet high and rise straight up from almost sea level. From down here one does not see many glaciers, only snow fields and sugared peaks. I am finishing all my letters today to be ready in case the ship should come. I do not believe, though, that it will arrive before the fifth. I hope I won't have to wait too long for a steamer to the north. If Smith were not waiting for me there, I would not be so anxious, because the time I have scheduled for this place is very short. Six weeks from today I shall be in Victoria again. How happy I shall be to be home again! Tomorrow is Marie's birthday. How I should love to be with her!

*August 3:* Today I finished my work, as I was afraid it would happen. The man with whom I have been working is completely squeezed dry; there is nothing more I can get out of him. And since the boat will arrive tomorrow or the day after, I don't want to start anything new. I am quite satisfied with the results of my work here, however. Today is Marie's birthday. How I would like to be on Lake George with her! It is awful that I have to be away every summer. From now it will be at least eight weeks until I am at home again. I am also very anxious to get letters again. I don't think that I will have any before the twelfth. There is nothing I can do but wait. It will be more than a week.

*August 5:* The ship is expected this afternoon, and I am quickly adding another greeting to this letter. From now on I will be able to write you four times a month. I will be on a regular boat route. The departure times are not very regular, though. I will send you news, however, as often as I can. I plan to stay in Port Essington until the twenty-seventh. From there I shall go until September 16 to Rivers Inlet, and then home I go! These lines might reach you on the twenty-eighth, your wedding anniversary. Please, dear parents, accept my sincerest congratulations. Many happy returns. In a few years, when we celebrate your golden wedding anniversary, your grandchildren will be real little people already. Adieu for today.

Your Franz

Bella Coola, August 2, 1897

Dear Wife,

Today I copied all my bills and am enclosing them. I have been worried for some time that I did not make copies of them. Up to now they balance exactly right. But I am really careful in writing everything down. There is not much news to tell. Since yesterday we have been having good weather and George [Hunt] and I climb a mountain every evening, not as far as the top but just a few hundred feet. These are not high mountains, but we enjoy the view. The countryside is really magnificent. We can see the high mountain range over which we came, and to the north the snow mountains. I don't think that I will be able to do much in the last two days here. I have achieved as much as one can in the direction I wanted to go and anything new I might start could only be fragmentary. The material I have now is *very* beautiful. After I leave on Thursday George Hunt will stay another two weeks and collect some more. I think I will then have a very good collection. He also promised to busily collect for me all winter. I hope he really will do it! I have now copied two hundred pages of his texts and have thirty-one more to do. How happy I shall be when I am finished!

How I wish I were with you! Last night I vividly dreamed of you and the children, crazy things at that. What is baby doing? Are you all well? Sometimes I go intermittently hot and cold when I think how long I have no news from you.

*August 3:* Today is your birthday, and I am afraid that there may not be any congratulations from me. I hope you got my telegram on the twenty-eighth, and I think you should have my first letter from here today or very soon. Darling, I would like to be at home with you, and yet I have to wait for many long weeks. I should not start counting yet, but in the last few days I have been figuring: six weeks of work and then I go to Victoria, and if everything turns out all right I can go home from there. I don't think that Smith will stay much longer than we, because money is getting very low. I still have $2,000, but collecting material is expensive. If only Smith has success!

Well, I wanted to congratulate you on your birthday, but here

I am again with my Indians. But all the time I think about you and when I shall be with you again. That will be at the best in eight weeks minus two days. That's long enough for me. I hope that you all are well. I am getting more and more itchy for news from you. I will send you a telegram again from Bella Bella. It will be really Namoh [Namu], but since you don't know where that place is, I say Bella Bella. I hope I don't have to wait too long for a steamer. I will also have to write Jesup from there. I don't want to do it, though, before I see Smith, because I want to report on everything. I wonder whether I shall hear something about Dorsey.

What are my children doing? Will they recognize their Papa when he comes back with a big beard? Kids, how I would like to play with you! Just imagine, I lost one picture out of my medallion in the mountains. It got caught on a limb. It is a miracle that I did not lose the whole thing. It apparently fell into one of the saddlebags and I found it the next morning. How happy I shall be when I am with you again. I hope that from now on I can send off a letter every week, but the steamers don't run on an exact schedule so that I never know for sure when the letters will leave. I am afraid that there is nothing for me to do for the rest of the week.

*August 5:* Just one more greeting to you and the children before I close. I hope that the boat will come this afternoon. I finished the texts with George Hunt, two hundred and forty-four pages, and a number of songs on seventy-two more pages. That was really hard work. I am anxiously waiting for the steamer now. In one week I shall have letters from you! My plans now are to stay in Port Essington until August 27. Then I will stay in Rivers Inlet until September 2, and then home I go.

Adieu, dear one.

Your husband

Namoh [Namu], August 7, 1897

Dear Wife,

I am sitting here waiting for the steamer which should bring me to the Skeena River. We arrived here last night, and I heard that a steamer will come tomorrow. I hope that it will really come. Everyone here is crazy about the gold discovery in Alaska. The whole boat traffic has been changed and I will not be surprised if this letter leaves here together with my previous one. Four steamers now go to Alaska, and one along this coast. I heard that one of the Alaska boats is going to land here to pick up the mail. I hope it will really come. Thousands of people go to Alaska in order to become rich quickly. There will be famine there. How poor and disappointed most of them will return! I just finished a letter to Jesup, and one to Putnam. I reported my progress to Jesup; I did the same to Putnam, but to him I also wrote that I needed a raise of $1,000 in the fall. I was very firm. I hope it will help.

I am terribly anxious to get to the Skeena River to receive your letters. Sometimes I go hot and cold when I think that I have had no news from you for seven weeks. I hope I will get your letters up to July 26. The last one was dated June 21. I hope that you all are well. Mama's last letter about Papa worries me all the time. I went on the boat the night before last and slept on a board in the hold. In the morning at 4:30 we started off. The day was beautiful and the countryside magnificent. We made quite a detour. The captain had to pick up the fish from all his storage places. We went up the entire Milbank Sound and then back to this place. We arrived at about eight. A Mr. Drainey lives here with his family and the workers of a cannery; that is, Indians, Chinese, and Norwegian fishermen. The people are very nice to me. Mr. Drainey has eight children, for whom he has a teacher. Last night I had to accompany his songs on the piano and then I played dances for the young ones. That's how to make yourself useful and agreeable. I slept in a little guest house behind the warehouse, the first time in a real bed since June 11, with a good mattress but this time without sheets and with my blanket as a pillow. The food tasted ten times as good when served on plates and at a table instead of on the ground or on one's knees. They had new potatoes and eggs. What a treat! Don't think too badly of me, but I am craving decent food and fresh vegetables. The whole place was built only a year ago and still looks quite unfinished. Tree trunks are still lying around. But there are window boxes with sweet peas, geraniums, and other flowers! This is Mrs. Drainey's touch. I am closing this letter now because the boat might come tonight.

Adieu, dearest wife. I wish I were with you. Kiss the children for me. I will write more from the Skeena River.

Your husband

Dear Wife,                           Namoh [Namu], August 9, 1897

Here I am, still waiting for the steamer to come. Yesterday was an eventful day. At 4:30 the steamer *Islander* arrived back from the north. When it landed I saw a few friends from the Chicago Museum; first Jimmy Deans and then Dorsey, and other acquaintances from Victoria.[1] They were on a collecting tour. They came ashore and we had a very friendly conversation for about twenty minutes. Then the boat left again. I wish it had left for the opposite direction. I heard that Smith has been in Port Essington since the fifth and that he was very successful with his digging.

I am angry at myself, but this trip of Dorsey's annoys me very much. More than I can tell you. I am mad at myself because there is an element of envy in me which I despise but which I cannot suppress altogether. It does not help that one behaves decently when inside oneself one is as shabby as the next fellow. What makes me so furious is the fact that these Chicago people simply adopt my plans and then try to beat me to it. Well, little Dorsey won't have achieved much with the help of that old ass, Deans. He was in Montana on May 31, then went to Victoria; from there to Fort Simpson, then to the Charlotte Islands, then up the Skeena River and down again. He is now on the way back to Victoria. Half of his time must have been spent traveling. When I was in Chicago they assured me that Dorsey would not be here at the same time as I. I don't really think that his trip will interfere with my work, but this treacherous way of acting makes me awfully angry. Well, one cannot change people. I ask myself often whether I would inform Fewkes or Cushing if I wanted to go to the Southwest. I am sure I would have told them what I intended to do, and I would have asked them for all the information, especially if I had known that they were there. One is very much inclined in things like this to judge oneself differently from how one would judge others. I can understand that if we wanted to make a collection from the Pueblos or from New York, the people who live there would be asked many questions, but that is quite another thing.

Well, I do not want to think too much about this matter so that I won't get too angry, and I also will not act toward these people as if I were angry. I really believe that I am unselfish enough with respect to my scientific work that I wish everyone the most progress. Otherwise I would not have taken Farrand and Smith with me. It seems to me, though, that everyone who is serious should seek and take my advice and not just run out here at random. In any event I don't think that Dorsey acted honorably. He told me that he wanted to go to Fort Rupert, and Deans asked me

1. Boas had been appointed temporary curator of the Chicago Field Museum in 1894. Because of conflict with some of the other administrative staff at the Museum he resigned. The following year was a very difficult one for him while he searched for a permanent position.

whether I had seen George Hunt. I was mean enough not to tell them where he was, and I have written George Hunt that he should not do anything for them. I have to do this to protect myself. I will write Putnam about it so that Jesup will see how urgent and important the publication of my results is. Dorsey told me also that there is a whole box of letters for me in Port Essington. I wish I had them here!

At about one o'clock a steamer arrived from Port Essington. It brought back all the Bella Coola. The canoes of the Indians were tied to it, and the boat towed them. When they arrived there was much confusion. The Indians made their camps on the beach, and soon their fires burned briskly. This morning at 5:30 they steamed on. There were also some Bella Bella canoes around, which were shipped this morning with the boat owned by the cannery. The night was terribly noisy. First the Indians made a lot of noise, then a thunderstorm came, and in the morning one could hear the steamer's whistle. I get up every time I hear a whistle because I am anxiously awaiting the *Princess Louise*, which will arrive some time today. I am glad that my letters left so soon. The *Islander* will probably be in Victoria tomorow, and you will have my telegram tomorrow or the day after. How happy I shall be when I am with you again! I can hardly stand my impatience at least to get letters from you. Just imagine, I have not heard from you since June 21! I will probably leave these lines here so that they can go south with the next boat. We no doubt will meet it between here and Port Essington. Adieu, dear old one.

*August 10:* Yesterday after I stopped writing this letter a steamer appeared, and then another. Both went to the south, however. In the afternoon still another steamer came in sight which looked like the *Princess Louise*. Fortunately I found a spy glass and could see that it was not. That boat also passed us by. Finally at four o'clock the *Princess Louise* arrived, and I quickly and happily went aboard. Tonight if everything goes well, I will probably get my letters. How I look forward to them, and how excited I shall be until I have seen your latest one and know that you all are well! I always look first at the last letter to find this out quickly. I did not leave my letters in Namoh [Namu] after all because the next steamer won't leave there before Friday. So you will hear from me from the Skeena River again. It was very foggy last night, and I don't think we got very far. Well, I think I will live through this day somehow. Only seven more weeks and I shall be with you and the children. I am going to write Winger [?] with the last steamer, asking him to bring our passports from St. Paul to New York. That is an awfully big expense! You can see from my writing how the boat rocks. I will close this letter in Port Essington.

*August 11:* Port Essington. Last night at nine o'clock we finally arrived. Smith was on the dock in pouring rain. He looks well, and he has gained eight pounds. I hope he is really well. Of course I ran immediately to get my letters. Thank heaven, you all are all right! The news brought me up to July 27. You must have received the telegram about my arrival in Bella Coola a few days later. From my parents I got letters up to July 17. You can imagine how happy I was about the letters. Thank the children for their letters. I have to answer many letters now, so just these few lines today. Adieu, dear wife. How happy I shall be when I am with you again! The *Danube* will come today. On the fourteenth the *Princess Louise* will arrive. I will send another letter on it. Smith was very successful. From Farrand I had letters up to July 27.

Your husband

Port Essington, August 13, 1897

Dear Wife,

The *Danube* has still not arrived, and so I can send you more greetings. I have been here now for three days and we are working hard. Smith started right in to make castings, and since yesterday I have joined him. We already have sixteen—partly Haida, partly Tsimshian, and one Tlingit woman. Smith is photographing. I spend the rest of the time with a Haida painter whom I got just in time. He was ready to leave for Fort Simpson the day before yesterday when I quickly engaged him. I am showing him all the photographs which I had made in New York and Washington, as well as in Ottawa, and I am able to identify many objects with his help. I am very happy about this because our collections from now on will be much more [complete?]. I will be busy here probably until the end of this month. I want to send Smith to Bella Bella on the twentieth to make castings with Farrand. Then he should go with me to Rivers Inlet and do the same there. From there he will go on September 1 to the Fraser delta and cast there. I shall see Farrand in Bella Bella on my way back south from Port Essington and then not again until we return.

On my first evening here I devoured your letter and those of my parents, starting with the last one, and then I read one by one from the beginning. How happy I am with the picture of the children! Baby looks quite different from the others. Yesterday I slowly reread the letters in proper order. You cannot imagine how relieved I am that I finally have them! I also got many other letters, one from the Museum. Winser shows himself again in his splendor. He is going to keep back $350 from our money for the freight, he writes. That about makes me bankrupt, especially since Dawson did not send me any money either. I wrote him a very urgent letter and hope that the money will still arrive. If not, I am going to pack my things and go home. This money business made me very angry.

I also got a letter from this Mr. . . . , who writes that he cannot go to Asia because there was some row about it. This shabby fellow S—— must have had his hand in it. I have not answered him yet and will not do it even in time for the next boat. The Dorsey business angers me no end. What he is doing is definitely not in the interests of the Chicago Museum, as I understand the interests of the Museum. The only explanation is that he wants. . . . He has engaged some people here to collect things for him. If I should want something, I would have more difficulty getting it. Fortunately I do not want to collect anything here at all; I came here only to study! And then his *Science* (?) article! . . . In short, he is a mean guy. This does not make me too angry, and it should not make you angry either.

The first night here I was so excited about all your news that I could hardly sleep, but now I am on my feet again. I wrote Jesup a long letter about Smith's activities and took the opportunity to praise his tact in dealing with the Indians, and also his energetic work. When I come back to Bella Bella I will write him about Farrand and hope that I can praise him also. The few large arrows I wanted to buy here I have to forget because of the money situation, but that cannot be helped. I wrote this to Jesup. I am so happy that I heard from you and the children. I can't write the children today because I am too busy. The steamer may come at any time. I must also write a short note to my parents.

Adieu, dearest one! How sad about the death of Mrs. Goldmark! Thank . . . for the generous gift! . . . Last night a cannery steamer brought the news that the *Danube* is in the Nass River and that it will arrive today. Adieu! I was very surprised with Ernst's German letter. I send you many kisses.

Your husband

Port Essington, August 15, 1897

Dear Wife,

Today is Sunday, and since I am with the pious Tsimshians I can't work with my Indian. I have therefore worked on my finances and tried to figure out how I can manage best. I have $1,720 left of the money granted me. Of this amount, however, Winser has $350, and Dawson owes me $375. If I don't get this money, I will be in a great mess. I can't understand why Dawson did not send the money. All my plans depend, of course, on the money situation.

I am rather satisfied with the results of my work here. We now have twenty-five castings, ten Haida and fifteen Tsimshian. I have also measured all these people. Although I should like to get more measurements, I think that the ethnological work is more important, and so I cannot use much time for measurements. I made a very interesting series of face measurements, fifty-six altogether, which give me, as I expected, interesting clues to the meaning of the local ornamentation [?]. I am more successful than I expected with the explanation of objects. I have up to now identified twenty-five objects for New York; some that belong to Washington and some to Ottawa. I don't have anything from Berlin that would come from this neighborhood. I think I will stay here two more weeks. I have not decided yet when Smith is going to leave. I want him to go. I want to send him to a village, Gitqatla [?], to take a few photos, but the place is very hard to reach and I don't know how we can arrange it. He will subsequently follow me to the south.

I am very comfortable here. The house Mr. Cummings owns is a veritable hotel and even has a bathtub and a real water closet. These are unusual treats. The two weeks in Rivers Inlet will be quite disagreeable again. But at least I can see the end of the trip coming nearer and nearer. Six more weeks and I think I will be with you. I hope to leave Victoria on September 20, but I am not sure I will be able to because the steamers here are so irregular. Last week many came, and since then there has been a great interval. But maybe there will be one again on Tuesday on its way to Alaska.

Today I will write a few lines again to the children. I have some news for you which will be a surprise. The night before last Smith came to me and told me that he wanted to do something which I would think was very stupid. He wants to get married on the way back. He thinks he could live with a wife on $60 a month. He wanted to know my opinion. Still waters run deep! He said that he had thought over everything carefully and that he has been engaged for many years and now he wants to get married. I told him what difficulties he would have living on such a small amount and that his chances for a major raise were very slim. I told him I could not argue with him, that I could only warn him of all the problems he would have, but that I was convinced he would do whatever he wanted anyway. He asks whether you think that he could make ends meet. I don't think you should tell Mother about it because he does not want to make the matter public before he decides what to do.

*The same evening:* I killed the day as well as I could, filling the time with letter-writing, walking and making order in my notes. I even slept a little after lunch. Tomorrow work starts again. I do hope that we will get some Tsimshian women! The closer it comes to the end of my trip, the more anxious I am to be with you again. It is almost a quarter of a year that I have been away from you. I long for you and the children, my sweet wife. I don't want to think of all the work I shall have this coming winter, and of all the difficulties I have to overcome in order to be able to go over there during the summer of next year. Will I succeed in getting a three-to-four-month vacation from the Museum? I hope so! It would be a terrible disappointment for my parents and for us if we could not make the trip.

*August 17:* There was a veritable exodus of the Indians here during the past days, and Smith has nothing more to do. He will take the next boat to the south, work with Farrand in Bella Bella for a few days, and then go to Rivers Inlet. We probably will arrive there at the same time. The next steamer from the north will quite likely arrive tonight or tomorrow morning. That is why I am closing this letter now; I will give it to Smith. The steamer is not a mail boat, but the customs officer will take the letter, I think, and mail it in Victoria. Tomorrow or the day after a steamer will come from the south and bring me letters.

Adieu, dear wife. I am quite satisfied with my work here. I obtained some good material about Indian art and have also identified many objects. In six weeks I shall be with you!

Your old man

Port Essington, August 15, 1897

Dear Parents,

I am planning to go a few days to Lake George before returning to the city. I won't stay longer than three days. The nearer it gets toward the end of this trip, the more anxious I become to get home. Time passes fast enough in view of the successful work I am doing here. It is much more enjoyable, however, to be back with one's own people.

The trip agreed with Smith very well. He gained eight pounds, and he is looking much better. He is a very nice young man. He has had to fight against so many odds that he could not finish his university studies; therefore his education has many gaps. But he is a man with his heart in the right place, and he is absolutely reliable. I do not think he will ever become a great scientist, but this is not necessary so long as he is successful in some direction. My plans for the immediate future are very vague. Smith will go south with the next steamer to work for a few days with Farrand, who is expected on the coast within a few days. From there Smith will go with me to Rivers Inlet, and a few days later he will go to a place called New Westminster, where he will cast again. I will go to Rivers Inlet by the end of this month, from there to Victoria until the middle of September, and return home from Victoria.

I am quite satisfied with my progress here. I met just the right man and got excellent material from him. My purpose here is to collect more material on the art of the Indians, about which I wrote in my article. As I said before, I was really successful. I hope my man will keep on. We are also successful with the castings; I now have fifty-seven, quite a nice number. They will give me a good foundation for further studies. We are almost completely cut off from the world. I have read with the greatest interest the few newspapers you sent me. The only thing going on here is the gold fever. You cannot imagine how crazy the people are! Loads and loads of people go to Alaska. There will be a famine this winter. We never know when a boat will land here because they all go straight to Alaska to bring the gold diggers there. The boats are terribly overcrowded. Some of the people sleep on deck or wherever there is space. All of them hope, of course, to return laden with riches.

*August 17:* I am quite satisfied with my progress here. I got exactly the material for which I came. I should like, in addition, to get some castings of women, but they are so contrary that there is little hope of getting any. Adieu, you old ones. Greetings to all the sisters. Love.

Your Franz

Dear Wife,                                   Port Essington, August 19, 1897

I hope you will get the letter I gave to Smith to mail yesterday. In the evening at about 8 P.M. the steamer *Coquitlam* came in sight, back from Alaska. Because during all these last days we have obtained only one casting with little chance of getting more, I sent Smith to Bella Bella; he will arrive today. I hope that he and Farrand will be successful there and get good material. I have gathered much interesting data here, but I am not satisfied yet with the identification of the photos from the Museum. I should have more than this one man, to feel safe. I cannot get any explanation from him about masks. His own drawings are very good, and I did get the main thing I wanted to learn about.

Suddenly today two women came and wanted their faces cast. I did it, of course, but I cannot get their photos now. They were so nervous that they did not keep their faces still and one of the packs crumbled. The castings, however, can be used after all. Unfortunately, the facial paintings are all collected. My Haida friend takes so long to do a painting that I lose a lot of time. I cannot do anything else while he is doing it, and I have some free time. In between I let him tell me things. Since his Chinook is rather limited, however, the conversation is very difficult. For a few days the weather here has been very beautiful. I don't think I ever saw it so beautiful on this coast. I am longingly on the lookout for the *Princess Louise*, which is expected these days. It is supposed to bring me mail. I will probably stay here until the twenty-sixth. The *Coquitlam*, which took Smith to Bella Bella, will be here again in a week. Then comes my last stop, Rivers Inlet. There will be plenty of work.

*August 21:* The boat finally arrived toward evening. It brought my letters: three from you, dated July 29 and August 2 and 3. The first had little Helen's enclosure. I will have to send her birthday greetings with this mail because the ships are so irregular here. You can keep the letter for her. Yesterday the *Tees* arrived, Monday the *Princess Louise* is expected, and at the end of the week the *Coquitlam* comes again. The latter is not a mail boat. The *Tees* will go south tomorrow, the *Louise* and the *Islander* probably on Wednesday. I am rather worried that I don't have a letter from you of a later date. The steamer left Victoria on the sixteenth, and your last letter arrived there on the tenth. You usually write more often than that.

The situation in the Meyer family is really rather sad, but no one can do anything about it. Theo's illness can't be helped, of course, but so many other things could be different. I am awfully sorry for Helene. I think if she had used more energy in addition to her good judgment, many things would be different. As you said, she just lets things run their course, and that is not right. To give in is good in minor matters, but it is bad when important things are involved. It is also wrong that they are not raising Walter in the right way. I am convinced that all the bad experiences with Ernst will repeat themselves later with the boy, if they don't deal more strictly with him now. He has many nice qualities, but his bad temper and dictatorial ways will get worse with the years. Be sure to try to protect Ernst from bad influences like these. If I could only instill sound judgment and a strong will into my children! I am quite aware in what respects I fail, and I would like something better for my children. I have perseverance in many things, but quick decisions and certainty of actions are lacking.

Yesterday I wrote a long letter to Putnam on behalf of Smith. Smith wrote him that he wants to get married, and Putnam is very much worried about it. One cannot give Smith advice because he is going to do whatever he wants to do. Putnam told me about a letter Smith had written to Winser. I wish Smith would learn certain things, especially to hold his tongue with respect to some people. I don't know but I have doubts that he will ever amount to anything. His education has many gaps, and it will always be apparent because he does not have the mind to spur him on and help him try to fill the gaps. He likes mostly activity which he can do with his hands. He is clever and resourceful, etc., but where theoretical work is involved, he lags behind. His attitude in all possible fields is very naïve, and frequently the questions he asks are unbelievably simple. I often tell him to think it over himself and then give me the answers to his own questions. On the other hand he is such a nice fellow that I really feel sorry for him. Well, maybe he will succeed yet. He is only twenty-five years old. But if he really should get married with an income of not over $60, I don't know what will become of him.

I have to answer Putnam and give Smith a piece of my mind about his letters. Don't worry, I answered him saying that I urgently advise him against. . . . I warned him about the Columbia College job because it is only a low clerical job. He is a hopeless case.

Today is little Ann's (Aennchen's) birthday. I wish the little one would not be so lazy about writing letters. Her letters always give the impression that someone forced her to write, and that she does not enjoy doing it. It really shows that we are nine years apart; when I left home she was only nine years old, and afterward we were never together for any length of time. Toni's letters also seem forced, but there are other reasons involved. She feels that many, many events have made strangers of us, events about which we have had different feelings and toward which we have reacted very differently. I wish I could change this; when I think of our earlier relationship, it really depresses me. What can I do to change things? Only with Hete do I feel a real brotherly relationship.

I decided today to go south with the *Princess Louise*. That might be on Wednesday; she left Victoria yesterday. I hope I will get some recent news from you. I am wasting too much time here. My work progressed during the first few days I was here, but now, since my man makes paintings of a different kind, everything goes so slowly that I myself don't. . . . Today I made the last casting. I have no more plaster-of-paris. We made thirty-two altogether here. That is quite a nice number.

*August 22:* I must close this letter today because the steamer might come this evening or during the night and I don't want to delay these lines. You can expect another letter soon; I will take it with me to Bella Bella and finish it on the steamer. . . . Last night I dreamed that I had begun my teaching at Columbia.[2] I am not looking forward to it because I have not prepared myself at all. There will be an awful lot of work! Yesterday I wrote a long letter to Putnam about Smith. Putnam had asked me what I thought of him. That was a difficult thing to write. If only Smith would get a raise! And he wants to get married on $60 a month. Adieu, dear old one [Olle]. I want to try to make friend Edensaw finish the story about the Raven. Kiss the children for me. Another five weeks to go.

Your husband

On board the *Tees*, August 26, 1897

Dear Wife,

The last days were terrible. We were expecting the arrival of the boat from the south, which was due on Monday, and of two boats from the north, also due on Monday. Nothing came, however. Finally in the afternoon of the day before yesterday the *Tees* came in sight, on her way to Victoria. She came about one hour after high tide and before she knew it, she rammed with full force into a sandbank. There she had to wait until the next high tide. This happened at night and she proceeded to the cannery and arrived in Port Essington yesterday toward noon. Since nothing was known about the *Princess Louise*, I decided to take the *Tees* south. Al-

2. In 1896 Putnam appointed Boas assistant curator of ethnology and somatology in the American Museum of Natural History. Boas was also appointed as a lecturer in physical anthropology at Columbia University.

though my Indian was busily painting for me, there was nothing I could do, and that made me very nervous. Of course I was very unhappy to leave without the letters which the *Princess Louise* was supposed to bring, but it seemed to me that I would not be fulfilling my obligations if I stayed on; hence I left. You can imagine how I hated to go, since I was worried about my mail which might have left Victoria on the thirteenth. However, we had not left Port Essington for more than a half hour when we met the *Princess Louise!* She also had to wait for the tide and probably arrived in Port Essington at 11 A.M. I think she will come to Rivers Inlet on Monday, so that I can get my letters then.

I hope that I will catch Smith this morning in Bella Bella. I will then continue with him to Rivers Inlet. I wonder whether Farrand will be there and how successful he was. I think that Hunt might go with us to Rivers Inlet also. I made a few more castings during the last days, so that my supply of plaster-of-paris is all used up. After Smith had left I got three Haida women and one Haida man. I was successful in obtaining drawings and paintings. You might remember that I planned to collect paintings done on hard-to-decorate materials in order to study the symbolism of the Indians. For this purpose I chose face paintings and paintings on edges of blankets. The results are very satisfying, because I found just what I had expected; that is, strong stylization and stressing of symbols. A big group of people waited for the steamer in Port Essington. Four were from Spokane, Washington, who had explored mines on the Skeena River. They arrived a half hour after the boat which took Smith south had left. They had to wait eight days for the next boat. They are typical Westerners. Quite nice in a way, but at the same time very rough. When I arrive in Rivers Inlet, I will have to have a good talk with Smith. If one could only make him a little more independent. He is. . . .

I am not quite sure how regularly I will be able to write during the next weeks. Not all steamers can get into Rivers Inlet and I don't know when mail is going to leave from there. Don't worry if the mail doesn't come regularly. In just three weeks I will be in Victoria, and from there I go home! How happy I will be when I am with you again.

*The same afternoon:* We are just leaving Bella Bella. Smith came aboard. He had only moderate success. He got nine masks altogether and the relevant photos. Farrand only arrived the day before yesterday. I did not have more than five minutes to talk with him. He seemed to have been quite successful in Chilcotin, although the people are hard to handle there. George Hunt allegedly got everything we wanted in Bella Coola. He will probably be waiting for us in Namoh [Namu] and then come aboard. I have to close now. Up to now the whole trip has gone according to plan. I only hope it will continue on this course. I hope to be able to find good work in Rivers Inlet. I am very anxious to see all of you soon!

Adieu, dear wife. I wish I were already with you.

Your husband

Rivers Inlet, August 28, 1897

Dear Wife,

You must already have my last letter which I sent on the *Islander*. It seems that all the steamers land here, and so you will hear from me often enough. I received only *one* letter from you, although the steamers cover the period from August 10 to 22, that is, leaving Victoria. I am really worried. All I got from you was written on August 9 and 13, and then a letter from Helenchen of August 11, in which she tells me about Wing Point—that the land cost $800. I am very happy with your letters, little, dear girl. You are writing German very nicely now. I could not find any mistakes even after looking hard for one. Four weeks from today I shall be with you again. Won't that be wonderful? Today is my parents' wedding anniversary. I hope they got my congratulations in time. I am doubtful about it because I was still in Bella Bella when I wrote them. I hope to get letters on September 3.

Yesterday Mr. Cunningham was on the steamer from Port Essington, and he had brought all my boxes. I have already sent everything collected by Smith to Victoria, and now I will get together all my stuff and send it also. There are very few Indians here. I am collecting as many castings as I can as long as Smith is here. However, he is supposed to back to Victoria with the next boat to take up his archaeological work again. It also does not look as if Hunt and I will be able to do very much here, but I am not sure yet. We made three castings, and I am hoping for four or five more, or even more than that. The women have not agreed to it yet, but they act as if they will. We met a young man from Washington on the boat, a Mr. Preble, who is collecting mammals for the Department of Agriculture. He was also on his way to this place, and we invited him to camp with us. We are sleeping in an empty . . . Indian house which, however, is built like a house for white people. We sleep on the floor and cook over an open fire. Our boxes and cartons serve as table and chairs. I think Smith will leave tomorrow at the same time as this letter. There is also a missionary here who makes himself very agreeable; not that we need him, but I am always glad when these people are nice to us.

There is nothing else to report except that I should like to know how you are. I hope to find good linguistic material here. This afternoon we made three more castings of women, and toward evening I met an old acquaintance, one of the Bella Coola who had been in Berlin with Jacobsen. He recognized me right away and I am going to make his casting tomorrow. The man is . . . here. I have to keep this letter short so that I can mail it when the boat comes tonight. If it does not come I will add a few lines tomorrow.

*August 29:* The steamer did not come so I am adding a few greetings. You asked me when I am coming back. I cannot really say for sure because the steamers go very irregularly. I think there will be one on the fifteenth and then I could be in Victoria on the seventeenth. I will leave there approximately on the nineteenth or twentieth. I won't stay in Chicago any longer than absolutely necessary. I have not heard from Donaldson at all and should like so much to know how he is. I do not think that I will stay overnight. This way I could be with you on the twenty-fifth. It could be a few days later, however. Breakfast is ready now and I have to end this letter. Kiss the children for me. I wish I were with you.

Your husband

Dear Wife,                        Rivers Inlet, August 30, 1897

I have been here now for four days and have actually done nothing. Yesterday the *Princess Louise* arrived, and Smith promptly made ready and went aboard. Last night we had an earnest conversation in which I urgently advised him to wait with his marriage. I told him he would get more money after January, I am almost certain. I also told him that I thought it was dangerous to get married on $60. I could see that all the time he talked with me, he was thinking about his letter to Putnam. I told him not to be so reluctant to talk his affairs over with me. . . . The last thing he said when we took leave of each other was that he did not know how to talk freely about his affairs, since it was not his nature to do so. I will write my mother about it again. I wish I could force him to open up. I am not a talker myself, but such isolation must be awful! It is not easy for me to talk like a father to him, since we were always good comrades. I should be surprised if he accepted my advice. I hope he will be good in his future work. I wanted him away from here because there was not much for him to do, and every day during this season counts for his work. I only hope that Putnam won't ask Jesup to leave Smith here over the winter. I spoke out against this and would never permit it because. . . . I think he could stay here until December but no longer.

We made eight castings and I might get three or four more. Yesterday I tried to find a few people to tell me stories, and finally I found two whom I could use. They were, however, so contrary [?] that I could not do anything with them. All day long today I tried desperately to make them dictate to me but with very little success. Tonight I finally gave the Indians a speech in my house, saying what a great friend of theirs I was and what good things I have done for them![3] I *hope* that tomorrow I shall get some promises, otherwise I don't know what I shall do here all the time. I cannot even think of buying things here because the people ask huge prices for everything. It is very difficult to get started with them.

The village lies on both sides of the mouth of a big river. A very gracious missionary lives on the other side. I crossed over in a boat today to ask him whether he could help us somehow. He really spoke to the Indians, but without success. I wonder how it will be tomorrow? In your letter of the ninth you asked when I will be back. That is not known yet for sure. I don't know the time the steamers are arriving. I should like to leave on the fifteenth, if possible. I hope that I will get letters from the boat which arrives on Friday.

*August 31:* Today I was more successful, thank God. With the help of the missionary, I got a man today who is willing to tell me stories, and I took down twenty pages. I hope this man will hold out. Of course I have no translations yet and must find somebody to help me with them. George Hunt does not know the dialect well enough. This missionary is really unusually nice. He made a special trip this morning to tell me that the man was willing to tell me stories. Unfortunately he lives on the other side of the river, so that I have to cross over every day. But I am really happy that I have found some work. This afternoon four men came who wanted their faces cast. It really gave me great pleasure. I don't know when this letter will leave, but I will close it tomorrow morning anyway. The *Danube* might come tomorrow morning. The next boat south will then be on the eighth. You will have to wait a week for the next letter. I am

3. In a letter to his parents on the same day he wrote, "I also used my oft-used trick and invited all the Indians to a feast."

already in the stage of counting the days and hours until my return. Two more weeks here, and then I go to Victoria. . . . If the boat is not here by tomorrow night, I will add to this letter.

Your husband

Dear Parents,                            Rivers Inlet, August 30, 1897

Today you will get only a greeting. I am tired from doing nothing. The Indians are very unfriendly, and I could not even begin my linguistic work. Yesterday, after looking around a good deal, I finally found two who said they were willing to dictate to me. They have not done so yet. It is annoying to sit around with nothing to do while being surrounded with the most interesting material. Up to yesterday noon we had made eight castings, and the chances of getting more seemed very bad. Therefore when the steamer appeared I told Smith to pack and go south. He should take up his archaeological work again. He should look through the piles of shells along the lower Fraser River.

There is also a missionary here who apparently has had very little success in his six years of missionary work. He has very nicely promised to help us and has also brought some fresh bread and salmon. Whether or not we will be successful with his help will be seen tomorrow. I have employed my oft-used trick: inviting all the Indians to a feast. I will give a speech and will then, I hope, gain their confidence. The people are very difficult to handle. For tomorrow one had promised to tell me a tale. I will be surprised if he does come.

Smith boarded the steamer yesterday. It stayed here until 1 A.M. because it was loading salmon. I have not seen him since then, however, because the steamer anchored on the other side of the river. I will close this letter now because the steamer will probably come tomorrow. If it does not, I will stick another letter into the envelope. The next steamer after this one comes on the eighth, and you would have to wait another week. Today I finally had a little success. This morning we went to the other side of the river and found a man who told us stories quite well. I wrote down twenty pages but have not translated them yet. This afternoon another young man came who wanted his casting made. I gladly made it, and now think I will get four or five more. Therefore I am feeling much happier today than yesterday. Everything looks better today. The missionary who is so friendly came over this morning to tell me that he had spoken with a few people who seemed willing to have their castings made.

It is really very gracious of this man that he tries so hard to be of help. I wish I could somehow reciprocate his kindness; maybe by not working on Sunday! At least not with his Indians.

I am counting the days to my return now. I will probably leave here two weeks from tomorrow. The weather is awful. We are actually wet all day long, partly from the rain and partly from having to step from the boat into the water to pull the boat ashore when we cross the river. Otherwise we are quite comfortable. Mr. Preble is good company. We both have our work to do and don't disturb each other. How happy I shall be when I am back home! I am at present really tired of traveling. The unfriendliness of the Indians during these past days reflects itself in my mood.

Greet the sisters for me, dear Old Ones, and be greeting yourselves from

Your Franz

Rivers Inlet, September 1, 1897

Dear Wife,

The month which will bring me back to you has finally started. I can hardly believe that I might be with you three weeks from Sunday. If only the steamer's schedule won't cheat me out of a day or two. These lines will not go with the *Danube*, which is coming tonight. I am really busy now. This morning at eight I started to translate. From ten until three o'clock I took dictation, and afterward I made a few castings. That is how I like to work! Sunday and Monday, however, were very slow. Now the people come of their own accord to have castings made. For tomorrow I have four reservations, since I cannot do all of them at the same time. I will have to go down and get more plaster of paris, which is stored at the salmon cannery. Today it rained only half the day, which is considered good weather here.

Two weeks from today I leave! Mr. Preble is going to take the steamer which leaves here Sunday. I hope it won't get stuck. He has a young wife in Washington and has been away from her since April. The Indian who dictates to me is very good, but the translation is going very slowly because Hunt is unbelievably clumsy [?] with it. I have to rely on my own studies, although this takes much more time than having someone explain it to me. If everything goes on this way I will be content with the results here. The Indians now want to sell some of their things to me. This makes me very happy. On the other hand, George Hunt has to go up the river for a few days. However, I don't mind too much because I think I can do without him. I might even go up there myself, if it should be worthwhile. It has been very cold since yesterday, so that my woolen blankets don't keep me warm on the floor. I hope it will warm up again.

Darling, I can't tell you how I look forward to my return. I hope you all are well. How much baby Gertrude must have grown! I do not care that the people want $800 for Wing Point. It would have been nice to have a bit of land there, but I am not too disappointed. We would not have the money to build a house there now anyway. Are the children looking forward to my return? I wish I knew what to bring them, especially Ernst. I thought I might find something here in Rivers Inlet, but there is absolutely nothing. I have the same problem with respect to you. I don't know what to bring you. Helenchen is writing nice letters now. Are they copies of a draft or does she just write them down? I don't think I can get an answer to this letter unless it does go with the *Danube*. I must say that when I think of my classes, I am quite worried because I have not prepared them at all.

*September 2:* My Indian is dictating quite well, and I am getting a good amount of texts every day. I hope that he doesn't become impatient before the two weeks are over. The people now also come on their own to have the castings made. Today I made six castings and wrote eight pages of new texts and eleven translations of old ones. My Indian cannot dictate more than four hours, whereas I can write them down for any length of time. It is terribly cold at night, so tonight I will keep my pants on. . . .

I hope I will get some letters tomorrow or the day after. I long for news because I have had none for about three weeks. I am expecting a telegram from Winser about our money business. I wrote you about the $350 which he is withholding. Anyway, we live very cheaply here. I wish we could live in New York like this! You would not like the food, though. We do not need more than twenty-five cents per day. There is nothing new to tell you. Each day I tell myself that there are only so and so many days left! It is three weeks from tomorrow! I will send you a telegram from Victoria about the exact date when I shall arrive. Kiss the little children for me. How I look forward to seeing them. I hope that all of you are well. I am feeling fine.

Goodnight, dearest. I will be with you soon.

Your husband

Rivers Inlet, September 2, 1897

Dear Parents,

The *Danube* has not come yet and if it does not by tonight, this letter can still go on it. I am now really well set up here. If there is no disturbance, I will be very well satisfied with the results. The people seem to have shed their meanness. Money has started its attraction and they now come of their own accord to have castings made. I had six today and will soon have enough to be able to establish their types, of these local Indians. Since Smith left I have made nine castings. Besides, I am very busy now collecting linguistic material; I get my portion of it every day. I hope my Indian will last until I leave.

Unfortunately the Indians whom I am casting are all on the other side of the river. Since the one who tells me stories also lives there, I have to cross over every day. This is quite good because at least I get some exercise. This is not so important while I make the casts, because this work keeps me moving around enough. I am very anxious to find out whether Jesup will be satisfied with the results of my trip. I think he ought to be, because I am. I am honestly afraid of the winter because I will have so much work to do. I am especially afraid of my lectures, having made no preparation for them whatever. At Columbia College it is the custom for a professor to give the same lectures year after year, but I cannot make myself do this. It is just not my way. I will of course use some of the same material I used last year; yet I hope to bring new material into it. I wonder if I shall get my old course together again? Besides, I have all sorts of new plans for the Museum. I will write you later about them when they are fully developed in my own mind.

All my attention is focused on the Indians now. This makes my travels so relaxing for me, that I am able to concentrate completely on one subject and forget everything else. At home there is always something that needs my attention, so that I never feel at rest. I often think it would be better to concentrate more on one thing, but if there is so much else to do, is it not better to do one's duty? I hope to find the new wing of the Museum almost ready to receive everything. My gallery is supposed to be finished by May at the latest, and then away we go to you! But first it *has* to be finished. This really spurs me on. But enough for now. I am tired tonight. Casting is not too easy a job. Take my love, dear Old Ones, and greetings to the sisters.

Your Franz

*September 3:* It is evening now and no steamer yet. Maybe the *Danube* passed us by. I think, however, that the *Coquitlam* will come on Sunday, at the latest. Our Washington guest, about whom I wrote you before, wants to leave with the next steamer. After this, George [Hunt] and I have one and one-half more weeks to endure. Work is progressing. Today I made four more castings and got some texts. The day after tomorrow is Sunday. I won't write down any texts then, but I will fill my moulds. That takes most of the day because I have to go so far to get water. My last castings turned out very well. Little by little I am becoming a good plaster of paris worker. My collection is rather voluminous already. We now have ninety-five castings altogether. Tonight the steamer will probably come. I hope it will bring good news.

*September 5:* The *Princess Louise* is just arriving, and it is 5 A.M. I hear that she is going to turn around here and. . . . I hope I shall arrive in Victoria on the fourteenth; after a few days of work there, I shall go home!

 In great haste,

Your Franz

Rivers Inlet, September 3, 1897

Dear Wife,

 I hope the *Tees* comes tomorrow morning and will bring me mail. And I hope the letters will contain good news. The closer it is to the time of my return, the more restless I become. I cannot enjoy my work any more and I think only of how I would like to be with you again. I am, of course, doing my duty, but my enthusiasm has gone. Today I made four more castings. There are twelve empty moulds left which have to be filled, and I think I will use Sunday to do it. I thus lose a whole day; the fresh water is so far away that I waste much time getting it. The missionary and his wife came to see me yesterday and asked me to come over today to get some fresh bread. These people are so friendly that I could not [refuse?] them. She said that she was very sorry for the way we live here. It is really not beautiful: bedroom, dining room, . . . room and plaster of paris shop, all in one. Everything is brown and sandy because the Indians come and go with their dirty feet. We are so used to this kind of life, however, that we do not pay any attention to it. Goodnight for now, I am very tired.

Your old man

*September 5:* Just now the *Princess Louise* is coming in. It is 5 A.M. I went down to find out about departure times and found that the *Louise* is turning back here today; so there won't be a boat on the fourteenth for me. Therefore I will have to take the *Tees* in about one week. This way I will be in Victoria on the thirteenth and shall be with you on the twenty-fifth. I will use the few days I have in Victoria to make a visit to New Westminster. I will leave from Seattle on the twentieth. I am closing now in a hurry so that these lines can leave in time. Mr. Preble is leaving with this steamer. Well, not even three more weeks to go. Hurrah!

Your old man

Kiss the children for me.

Rivers Inlet, September 5, 1897

Dear Wife,

Do you know how nice it is to get news that is not too old? The *Princess Louise* did not stay very long today. When I mailed my letters I found out that she had made a special trip up here to pick up all things from Rivers Inlet. There are five packing companies here. She took on people at all the different stops and then steamed home again to Victoria. She will *not* come back. Therefore I have to take the next boat to Victoria. I heard that this will be the *Tees*. She was expected today and really steamed in at noon. When we saw her coming, we took our canoes right away and went to meet her. She carried many letters for me. The bank wrote that they received $340 for me from New York. They must have telegraphed the money after my energetic protest. No letter from the Museum. There was also a letter from Dawson [?] in answer to my inquiry about why *he* did not send me the $375 which he owed me for my work here. He said it will come, but it is not here yet. In addition, the photographic plates came, as well as the phonographic cylinders which had been lost.

There was also a letter from Laufer, the [German scholar?], accepting my offer. He had written me first to Victoria, U.S.A., and the letter went back to him. Darling, will I get the $1,000 raise? No, but maybe half of it. Unfortunately I did not get anything for my collections here. That's too bad, but can't be changed. The people just have nothing to sell here, and many are away. Today I filled moulds all day long. I could not finish, however, because I do not have enough plaster of paris. The barrel is on the other side of the river. Little by little all my material is piling up in Victoria. I now have twenty boxes there, eight here, fourteen in Namu, and eight in Alert Bay. I hope that they will all arrive safely in New York.

I also received a few lines from Smith, who is happily established, and warm, on the lower Fraser River, and he is finding everything satisfactory there. It seems to be very promising. I hope he will be successful there. You probably will be disappointed in having to wait so long for the letter I sent you today; I was annoyed to have to wait so long to be able to mail it. The *Danube* did not come as far as here, and so the letter could not leave. This letter you will have in one week. According to plans, before I leave Seattle I will go for a few days to New Westminster. I will probably have to stay at least half a day in Chicago. I want to go to the cemetery and also see Donaldson; I have to stay with the M——. Will I get a letter from you there?

Today I also had word from Teit, who finally arrived happily in Spences Bridge on August 18. Regarding Putnam and Association: Putnam wants to extend my tenure by five years. This probably means success for his enemies who wanted him. . . . I assume that Cattell and others are behind this. I don't think Cattell uses good judgment all the time; he is hot-headed and wants to go with his head through the wall. I will probably hear more about these things when I come back. Cattell . . . for anthropology. . . . The German whom I wanted to hire for our expedition, a Dr. Laufer from Cologne, accepted my offer. That means this work will start next year. Just now the *Coquitlam* is steaming in, September 7.

Your old man

Rivers Inlet, September 5, 1897

Dear Parents,

I am too clumsy to write popular articles, and I do not have enough time for it. You are exactly like Marie, who always asks why don't you do this or that to make money. I can't do more than work however. We often laugh about these "opportunities to make money." The last one was an offer by Appleton, a New York publisher, to write a popular book about this part of the Pacific Coast. I should like to do this very much but cannot afford to do it, unless I get $1,200. It would cost me too much time. Since I cannot expect more than $200, I cannot do it unless I could make a set of lectures out of it which would be well paid. Well, one cannot do everything! I made a rule a long time ago to write nothing that cannot also be used as a lecture. That is why I do not write much for journals besides some side products of larger works for which I don't have any room there. I am really looking forward to a return to civilization. I only hope that I get a lot done this week.

The weather here is almost always awful. Today it is not so bad, although it has rained intermittently. One has to get used to it. You will be disappointed not to have heard from me for so long. I am also disappointed that no steamer is coming. I will take this letter with me to Victoria and will mail it there.

*September 7:* The *Coquitlam* is just arriving. I will have to close.
　　With all my love,
　　　　　　　　　　　　　　　　　　　　　　Your Franz


　　　　　　　　　　　　　　　　　　Rivers Inlet, September 7, 1897
Dear Wife,

Today I have more or less finished my collecting. I still have to translate all collected texts and pack them. I also have to finish the castings and pack them and give Hunt instructions. Tomorrow morning I have two more castings to make. Altogether this will make twenty-seven castings, nineteen of which I made myself after Smith left. I hope they will all arrive in one piece. By the way, Dorsey's collection was not on the *Mexico*, which sank. This was an error of the newspapers. We will have sent back altogether one hundred and twenty-five boxes. I hope Smith will add to this figure. Not included are a few large things which I collected. They will arrive later in Victoria, and Smith will ship them. I was glad when this morning the *Coquitlam* arrived so that I quite unexpectedly could mail my greetings to you and the parents. I thought that the steamer had passed us by.

We expect the *Tees* on Friday or Saturday, and then back she goes to civilization! I don't have any presents for the children and won't get anything before I reach Victoria. I had figured on finding something here but there is nothing to be found. I didn't buy anything for the collection either. I am so glad that the trip is nearly over. Two weeks from yesterday we will leave Seattle for home. Therefore there are only a few working days left; the rest is traveling. How happy I shall be when I arrive two weeks from Saturday at home. Every day here now is one too many.

*September 9:* In the evening: All my castings are ready to go on board now. I have asked for a house on the other side where we are going to sleep from now on, to be sure not to miss the boat. The landing place is about three-quarters of a mile from here on the other side of the bay, and the crossing during the night would not be very convenient. I am feeling very well because most of my work here is now wound up. I don't know whether I shall do some work in Victoria; this largely depends on the answer I get from New Westminster. In any event I do not have more than three or four days of work left. The results from this place are quite little, and I am glad to get away. Toward the end my work never seems very interesting to me. All I want is to go home, to go home. The steamer might come tomorrow or perhaps the day after. The nearer it gets, the more impatient I become. I don't want to, or rather can't, write anything any more. I am afraid you have not received many satisfying letters this entire season. I have always been in a hurry to get back to work. During the last few days the weather here has been good, but now it does not look very good. I hope that I will have nice weather on the farm. I am very anxious to know what kind of luck Farrand had in Bella Bella.

[No signature]

Aboard the *Tees*, September 13, 1897
My dear Wife,

I did not write these past days because we impatiently waited for the steamer. We were in no mood to work or to write. On the evening of the ninth we brought all our things to the west side of the river and camped there in an old house. The owner of the cannery invited us to eat with him, which we gladly accepted. On Fritz's and Helenchen's birthday I wrote a long text which my Kwakiutl Indian [George Hunt] dictated to me, and by Saturday noon I was finished. How I would have liked to be with you at the birthday dinner! We waited for the boat all night from Friday to Saturday, which made a very restless night. The steamer only came on Saturday in the evening. Farrand was on the boat. My Bella Bella collections had been put on board in Namu, together with the collection from Rivers Inlet. Then off we sailed.

That night I talked a very long time with Farrand, whom I had hardly seen since July. He did *not* do very much but has assembled quite a few things. He will tell me more on the train. Since it was very foggy at the mouth of Rivers Inlet, we stayed there until yesterday morning. We were in Alert Bay at once. The things which Hunt had collected for me were there. Unfortunately sad news waited for him there. One of his children, an eight-year-old boy, was very ill, and possibly already dead at the time the news finally reached him. His sister had written him several times about the boy, but from the letters he could not guess how ill the boy was. With the last steamer his brother-in-law sent an Indian to him to tell him, not about his sick son, but about a copper mine [?] which he had found. I am very sorry for him, but I could not help him. If the people had written more clearly earlier, I would have sent him home, of course. It is always annoying to work with Hunt because I cannot make him understand certain things.

We are now between Comox and Nanaimo and will probably arrive in Victoria late in the evening. From there I will ship all my boxes, fifty-two altogether. That will take me two days. I don't know yet whether I shall do something else there. I should like to measure the Indians in prison, if I get the permission. I will leave Seattle at the latest on Sunday, the nineteenth. I will stay twelve hours in Chicago. There I will find out the train schedule and send you a telegram, probably on the twenty-fifth. If there is nothing for me to do in Victoria, I will leave two days earlier. How I look forward to seeing you again. I will mail this letter tonight so that you will get it as soon as possible. Tomorrow morning I will get my mail and then write you again. Before I leave Victoria I will send you a telegram. Only one and one-half weeks!

Your husband

Oriental Hotel
Victoria, September 14, 1897

Dear Parents,

Now I am finally in Victoria, and since there is nothing for me to do here I will depart for home the day after tomorrow. I hope that I shall be with Marie and the children on the farm in one week. You can imagine how I am looking forward to it. The nearer the time comes, the more impatient I become. Tomorrow I will ship all my boxes, fifty-three altogether. That will take quite some time. But I have already done most of the work. I was not quite in the mood to write lately. There was so much work in Rivers Inlet until Saturday. We moved our camp to the other side of the river and waited there for the boat. I still did some work on Saturday, but there was too much commotion. Tonight I am tired again because I ran around all day. The people near me talk so much that I cannot collect my thoughts. My next letter will be from Chicago.

With all my love,

Franz

# 9

## Family Letters (1900)

[Vancouver], July 1, 1900

Dear Wife,

I really hoped for a letter from you yesterday but it did not come. I received letters, however, from Mama, Farrand, and Mc-Gee. Now I won't be able to hear from you for the next eight or ten days, or until the next steamer comes to Alert Bay. I spent a lot of time yesterday trying to get a check cashed. Since I don't know anybody here in Vancouver who I could ask to endorse a check for me, I had to telegraph the bank in Victoria to send me money by telegram to the local branch. When I went to the bank the last time, I met Dorsey and Cubier on the street. They were back from their trip to California and Utah and were returning to Montana. Did I write you that I weighed 158 lbs. when I left . . . ? Cubier introduced me to a gentleman from Philadelphia last night whom he had accidentally met at the hotel. He is a Mr. Balch, who is making a pleasure trip to Alaska. I invited them both to eat with me.

Since I've been here it has, of course, been raining. I feel very uncomfortable in my light suit because it is made only for good weather. The trip inland was very hard on my winter suit. I don't know yet whether I should leave the two suits here or not.

Adieu for today. Now I want to answer Farrand's [?] letter and then go on working.

Your husband

[Vancouver], July 2, 1900

Dear Mama,

I thought that I would be on the waters of the Gulf of Georgia by this time, but the boat is just leaving tonight, so I still have time

245

to send you my greetings. From now on my letters will be rarer, although at regular intervals. As far as I can tell, there are three steamers a month going to Alert Bay which take mail. I finished all my correspondence here in Vancouver and completed a short paper on the Eskimo which I had started before my departure from home. I also took many walks, did some shopping, ate and drank and slept.

This is a very nice hotel. The food and everything else are excellent. From here on I take my leave of all civilized food. Now there will be salmon, salmon, and more salmon. I have met a few people here with whom I run around. It has made the time pass quickly. I brought only French books with me this summer. I have to go to Paris when I get over there, and my French needs some improvement before my arrival. Up to now I have regularly read one hour of French every day; [now he wants to work on more Indian material]. I hope everything in Alert Bay will turn out well so that this trip will be a success.

I am growing a beard again this summer. I last grew one three years ago, but this time it has turned out completely gray. We are not young anymore! Adieu for today. Next time I'll be able to tell you what luck I have with my work.

Your Franz

Alert Bay, July 5, 1900

Dear Wife,

I arrived on the evening of the third and started to work right away. I have been lucky up to now. I found a good interpreter immediately, as well as a few old people who tell me stories and a good painter who explains paintings to me. Thus I work more than twelve hours a day, with little time left for letter-writing. I am very well taken care of. Spencer, whom I already knew from my first trip, is good to me. He is the owner of the local cannery. During the day I have a little "cavern" where I work with my Indians. A cavern is a little one-room house. . . . I eat and sleep, however, in the house [Spencer's house]. I have a bed in a pleasant little room upstairs, where I am writing just now. The food is also good. Spencer's wife is a sister of George Hunt. It is cool here, so that one can always work outside. It rains once in a while, of course, but at least not all the time. George Hunt and his whole family are here, of course. They are all working in the canneries.

The length of my stay depends on how quickly I tire out the

people. If my interpreter can stand it, then I'll stand it into August. Then I plan to go to another village in the neighborhood. Tuesday, the tenth, the *Tees*, on which I arrived, will go back again and take my letters. It seems that there are boats coming each direction every week. They usually meet here on Tuesdays.

*Continued on the eighth:* I won't be writing many letters from Alert Bay. I get up at 6 A.M. Breakfast is at 6:30. At 7:00 my interpreter comes and I work with him until noon. I eat lunch and at 1:00 P.M. he comes again. Work is resumed until 6:00. Then there is dinner. After dinner another Indian comes who, at present, explains paintings to me. We work until 9:00, and by that time I am tired and do not want to write any more. Life is very uniform this way, but I am happy to be getting good results. Up to now I am very satisfied. I am slowly beginning to understand the grammar of the language [Kwakwala]. It is terribly complicated. The painter with whom I work evenings is very good, and his teaching helps me a great deal in understanding the art of these tribes. For the time being I see George Hunt only evenings and Sundays.

Physically I feel well. I weigh myself from time to time in order to see whether I am gaining enough. Upon my arrival here I weighed 159 pounds. I do hope that I will receive a letter from all of you on Tuesday (the day after tomorrow).

Your husband


Alert Bay, July 8, 1900

Dear Mama,

The work here is not exciting. With the help of the Indians, I critically revise texts which I collected in previous years. This will take at least six weeks. At the same time I have to ask many questions about their grammar. Fortunately I have a good interpreter. During the next weeks I will have to work hard. I use the evenings to perfect myself in Indian art; that is, I have paintings explained to me. If my people can stand it that long, I'll accomplish a great deal. The first four days were promising. When the weather is good, as it was yesterday and the day before, I sit outside all day except when I have to eat. The view here is beautiful—when there is a view. Most of the time, though, there are clouds over the mountains.

Mr. Spencer has quite a nice house. On the first floor there are two bedrooms, a dining room, a parlor, and the kitchen. Several bedrooms are upstairs, one of which is mine. Mr. Spencer is married to a half-breed Indian, a sister of George Hunt. Mr. Hunt is one of our best collectors out here. They have five children, two of whom are in school in Victoria. The other three will also be sent to school in Victoria during the winter. Two sisters of Mrs. Spencer have also married men who work in the canneries. Because I have known all of them for years, I am very well taken care of. I lived here once before, on my first trip in 1886.

*July 9:* Yesterday, Sunday, I did a great deal of work carefully revising old texts with George Hunt. It is a real pleasure to be able to work absolutely without disturbances. In New York there are so many administrative duties that often I cannot even think of work. I frequently try to arrange my work differently, but without success. The Museum and the students take most of my time.

   With all my love,

                                     Your Franz


                                     Alert Bay, July 10, 1900

Dear Wife,

   The day before yesterday the entire Canadian fleet, consisting of one ship, arrived in this port! The captain came ashore and was kind enough to take my letter with him. Therefore you will receive a letter. . . . I know that a steamer is going south today, so I send you these greetings. I have nothing new to tell except that my work progresses. As was to be expected, the weather is hideous. It has been raining constantly since yesterday.

   Up to now I have worked only in the language field, and the language [Kwakwala] is terribly hard and complicated. The Chinook and Tsimshian are easy in comparison. I am really happy because I can look forward to working without being disturbed by all sorts of other things. All in all I haven't felt as well and strong as I do now, for a long, long time. I sleep better than before, and that probably has some influence on my well-being. The laziness of last spring and the weakness after the operation are completely gone, and I enjoy my work more than I have for ages. I hope that there will be letters from you today. Since the twenty-ninth and the thirtieth I haven't received anything, and I do not like these long intervals. I hope you have nice weather. I bought something to read and to . . . in Chicago, but at the moment I have no time to read or do anything else because I work all day long. I don't know yet how far I'll get into the language. Such work cannot be done in a short time because one must study all the collected material.

How are the children? What I would give to have them here with me or to be with them there. Heini will have forgotten me. I've been away from you four weeks now. Shall I still come to see you at the lake? That will depend on my progress here. Please write me everything about the children. The letters of the . . . do not contain much.

Your husband

Alert Bay, July 14, 1900

Dear Wife,

The mail boat finally came Thursday the twelfth, and I got your letters of June 18 and 22, and several from the children. Since the mail boat was late it will only be here on its way back in about eight days, so there won't be any regular mail to Vancouver for about fourteen days. I hope, however, that these lines will be taken by a steamer which passes tomorrow.

I am making nice progress with my work. The Kwakiutl is much harder than I thought. It is the first Indian language I have worked with which has irregular verbs, etc., and they are terribly difficult to handle. I am not working on the language all day long now. I work on the grammar in the mornings; in the afternoons old fellows tell me stories; and in the evenings, when George Hunt is free, I revise the texts with him. If only I can finish everything I have planned! I am really in true Kwakiutl country [?]. A painter paints for me, and his works are very useful for understanding the art of the people. Now I work exactly eleven and a half hours every day; from seven to twelve, from one to six, and 7:30 to nine. You can imagine that I do not have either the time or the desire to write. It is a miracle that I do not have a cramp in my hand.

As a matter of fact, I am ashamed to admit that it is a weight off my mind that we won't have another baby, because it is so hard to educate them properly. Except for this reason it would not make any difference, and I should like to have many more. I hope that the children are really all well, and you also. That Heini had to . . . again. I only hope that he is sleeping better now. I have gained another one and a half pounds since last week and now weigh 160½. I sleep well and feel normal in every respect. Yet I take the . . .

regularly twice a day. I hardly have any exercise, of course, but am in the open air almost the whole day unless it pours. I sit with my people in front of the house on the dock and enjoy the ventilation. If I have to be in the cavern, I have the windows and the door open.

*July 15:* Yesterday I had no more time to write. Today, Saturday, breakfast is at eight, but since I am used to getting up early, I have been down here since seven. I want to write to Mama this morning, and to the children and to New York. The children will be last. Yesterday I wrote a few lines to Laufer. Of course this . . . mess disturbs all my plans for him. Miss Andrews [?] wrote me that I received a telegram for my birthday from the Geographical Society from Berlin, and from London from the Anthropological Institute. I had seen . . . , the president of the Folklore Society. Did the Bureau of Ethnology do something? A letter also came from Vladivostok from . . . , who had met there with Axelrod [?]. Time flies unbelievably with all the work I do. It gives me great pleasure that I am able to apply all my energy to one subject for a change. If all goes on like this I hope that I will have all my material and . . . together next winter. I got all birthday letters on the twelfth, from you and the children, Marie, Toni, and Hete.

That's all for today. I hope to get some letters the day after tomorrow.

Your husband

Alert Bay, July 19, 1900

Dear Wife,

I can't tell you my feelings upon receiving your letter of the seventh, yesterday. I felt like giving up everything here and going home. That such a thing should happen to you! I feel as if a great hope has not been fulfilled. In addition there is the worry about you, that perhaps you are not really sick but upset. And I don't know the cause. Please don't mention anything, and say that you are not sick. I can't tell you how helpless I feel in my remoteness. I cannot get any letter until next Thursday, the twenty-sixth, and cannot be patient until then! I won't mention anything in my letters abroad because I don't know whether you have written them about it. I am terribly *upset* about it. Nevertheless I am busily working, but my thoughts are not with my work. I am getting on all right. Every morning I work on the language, and in the afternoons on ethnology.

*July 20:* I wrote this last evening before my evening subject came. His arrival interrupted me. From 7 P.M. until dark I take dictation. I now understand the structure of this language quite well. It is the . . . which I have started. I think it is even harder than Eskimo. I'll continue this work until the end of this month; then I don't know what I shall do. I need George Hunt for the revising, but he is still working in the cannery, and I have not asked Mr. Spencer whether I can have him in August.

Alert Bay, July 20, 1900

Dear Children,

I thank you many times for your letters. It is too bad that I was not there on the Fourth of July. I should have liked very much to shoot off fireworks with you. That was just the day when I started my work here. I have so much to do that I don't have time to tell you everything or as much about it as I should like to. Alert Bay is a little bay on an island. A little river coming from a lake about half the size of Lake George empties itself into the sea exactly across from it on Vancouver Island. The lake lies between high mountains which are still covered with snow. The whole territory is covered with dense woods so that one can hardly get through. There is much brush, and the trees are very high. Fallen and half-decayed trees lie around everywhere. They are all needle trees: . . . and fir trees of all kinds.

Fishermen live in a little house at the mouth of the river. In July the salmon swim upstream in order to spawn in the cold water of the lake which gets its water from the glaciers. The fishermen put out huge nets and often catch over 1,000 fish per day, each weighing six to eight pounds. Yesterday they caught almost 5,000 fish. Then all the boats come over here, and the fish are put into cans, such as we often have Sunday evenings. You should see how many people work on this, and how many machines. First the fish are unloaded and put into a huge wooden building where they are cleaned and put into the cans. This building stands on legs in the water, and the floor has half-inch spaces between the boards so that the blood and the intestines can easily be washed through. The fish are put into a heap at one end of the room. From the heap a man takes a fish and puts it on a table. A Chinese worker takes it and cuts off the head, the fins, and the tail with a sharp knife. First, however, he opens the belly and takes out the intestines. Then he throws the fish to the left to another Chinese who removes the scales and throws it into a large wooden rinsing tub where it is cleaned. Then they are cleaned again and given to an Indian who has a little machine consisting of four knives. . . . At the end is a handle. The fish is put under the machine and cut into four parts, each just as long as the can in which it is to go. The distance between the knives is as large as the can is tall. Then the pieces are pushed along and two Indians take them and halve them exactly in the middle so that the right and left halves are separated. Then the pieces are again thrown into a big rinsing tub from which they are poured into buckets. The Indian women sit on the other side of the shed ready to put the fish into the cans. Each has a little wooden rack on which twenty-four cans are placed. They fit exactly into the holes so that they can stand flat. First the cans are salted. There is a board with twenty-four holes which is fixed above the rack with the cans, and salt is poured through the holes. The women then take the fish pieces and put them into the cans. They have to weigh exactly one pound. Now all the cans are brought into the adjoining room on a little cart. Here they are first weighed. This is done on a machine which automatically rejects the cans that are too light. Then those that are too light are sent back to be filled up. I cannot describe this machine. Then the cans are placed on a long tape which runs over wheels and passes the cans on to another machine which puts the tops on the cans, and on to still another machine which solders the tops on. Then about 144 cans are put on an iron frame. A Chinese comes with a large hammer and makes a tiny hole in each top. Then the whole frame is picked up with a large . . . and put into a boiler. The purpose of the little holes is to let the air escape during the cooking. When the fish is done, a Chinese worker closes all the little holes again. Then the whole frame is placed into a long bath in which all the fat is removed from the cans. Finally they are rinsed in hot and then in cold water. Then it goes into the cool room, and finally labels are stuck on the cans by the Indians. They are packed, forty-eight cans into one box. That amounts to about eleven salmon, and on some days up to 400 boxes are filled. The boxes are sent to Victoria at the end of the season and sold there. Many go to England and to Canada. None go to the United States because the duty is too high. The salmon that comes from Alaska and from the Columbia River, which is as good as the above-mentioned, sells much cheaper in the United States. The merchants in Victoria, who are the agents for the fishermen, sometimes sell all the fish even before they are caught. For example, they promise to sell one buyer all the fish they will catch. At present a box costs $4.50, and at 400 boxes a day, this makes a daily value of $1,800. While the fishing season is on, the people make a lot of money, but the season lasts for only six weeks.

The heads and intestines of the salmon are thrown into the sea and little dog sharks come and eat them. You should see the number of sharks that are around on days like this. They come only in the evening—during the day they are in the deep water and. . . .

With many kisses.

Your old papa

Alert Bay, July 21, 1900

Dear Mama,

Time flies just unbelievably here with the regular work I do, and when a week is over I can hardly believe it. The first part of my work, the language part, progresses very well. I hope that I'll have the same luck with the ethnological part, which I have now started. If everything goes on as it now seems, I shall be able to return by September 10. As interesting and attractive as my work is here, the long distance from my family and the belated news do not make life very enjoyable. I wrote you last Sunday, but they say that there will be a steamer again tomorrow which takes mail. I got a letter from Marie and one from Anna on Tuesday evening. Uncle Jacobi is probably with you now. I hope you will enjoy these few days.

I think that Uncle will be glad to be finished with the. . . . It must have been a wonderful feeling for him to be honored from all sides. I am feeling fine. I sleep well and am in the fresh air all day long, though I should like to get more exercise; it is impossible because my day is filled with work. I think, however, that this will change in two weeks when I start with another kind of work. Then I cannot let the Indians come to me but will have to go to them.

The weather was beautiful all last week. In the mornings it is always foggy and wet, but the sun always comes out during the day. In the mornings one can stand a fire, so there is always one lighted in the house. I wish I had finished a big job which I have to terminate here. It is the revision of old material which I gathered here years ago—my language texts, which have to be carefully examined according to sounds. I estimate that this will take eighty hours of hard work. I cannot do this more quickly and still do a good job. I have spent at least four hours every day on it for three weeks. But enough for now. I have to go back to my work. Give my love to all my brothers and sisters.

Lovingly,

Your Franz

Alert Bay, July 23, 1900

Dear Wife,

The mail boat left only yesterday and took my greetings on the twentieth to you. Nevertheless I am writing again today because, presumably, the other steamer will come by tomorrow. Whether it will really come is hard to say; last week they were not on schedule. I shall not be surprised if we don't get any mail this week. This could mean that you won't get a letter for two weeks. I do hope, though, that such won't be the case. Therefore, I have to send you my best wishes for your birthday today. I do not feel like it at all, especially because I have a load on my chest since your last letter. I am waiting impatiently for news about you. If I have to wait another eight days for a steamer to come, I don't know how the time will go by. If only you and the children are all right!

There is nothing new here. My work progresses slowly, but well. The most laborious part is the revision of the texts which I am doing with George Hunt. I can't do more than eight papers per hour, and I cannot stand this pace very long. I have now revised 187 pages and still have 495 to go. I hope I will finish the work before my return. As of today I have been away from you for six weeks. Will I be able to leave here in seven weeks? That would be September 10. I am feeling fine. Yesterday, Sunday, I worked all day with George Hunt. In the afternoons I keep busy with the menus, and the preparation of food. I have made myself a form [?] out of old newspaper in which I put the plants which the Indians use. If I did not have so much to do, it would be very boring here. This way, time flies. I am now wearing my corrective glasses. My eyes would become too tired otherwise. Spencer's children, the ones who go to school to Victoria, are here for their holiday. He has five boys, aged twelve, ten, nine, eight, and seven. The two oldest ones go to school.

Please write me extensively about everything; about yourself and the children. Be patient with the little worms and make life easy for them so that later they will think back with pleasure upon their home.

Your husband

Alert Bay, July 23, 1900

Dear Mama,

My last letter left only yesterday, but I have to write again today because presumably the next steamer is going to come tonight or tomorrow morning. It is possible that after this there will not be any mail for two weeks, since the steamer which arrived one week late messed up everything. Yet I hope there will be the possibility of sending a letter. It is unpleasant not to receive any letters for two weeks. I left Lake George six weeks ago today. I should like to go there again for a few days after my return, but I do not know whether it will be possible. It all depends how my work progresses here. For the moment, I am quite satisfied with it but would like to have more time. My life here is so monotonous that there is absolutely nothing to tell. I cannot entertain you very well with my grammatical discoveries. I am very tanned and feel fine. In spite of the work, I am gaining weight.

*July 25:* The regular boat has extended its voyage to Alaska and is therefore not coming by until tomorrow. I am itching more than ever for some letters.

*July 26:* With my regular work it is very hard to take the time to write letters. Every time I sit down to write, my Indians come back and I have to go again. Except for the first week, the weather has been fine. In the mornings it is very foggy, but it clears up during the day so that I can sit outdoors and enjoy some fresh air. I am curious to know how Mr. Jung's [?] seventieth birthday turned out. Upon my instigation he received many congratulations from European scientific societies. I do hope he was happy about them. I hope to employ George Hunt full time starting a week from Monday. Then I will leave my linguistic studies and start to collect customs, etc. During the past days I spent my afternoons interviewing women on the gathering and preparing of food, and having them tell me about their medicines. Here comes my Indian now, and I have to finish in case the steamer comes by. . . .

With love,

Your Franz

Alert Bay, July 26, 1900

Dear Wife,

You are better off than I. The *Tees* went to Alaska on its voyage and has not come back yet. We are expecting it back tomorrow, and you will get these lines near your birthday. Well, my most sincere congratulations again. Oh, if I only knew how you are! I will probably have to wait several more days for letters. I received the last news from you on the seventeenth, the day you had to go to bed. What are the little ones doing?

Sunday I asked Mr. Spencer whether I could have George Hunt, who now works in the cannery, by the fourth of August. He promised that I could. With his help I will be able to get everything I want. I am gathering food samples and medicinal plants used by these Indians. I won't be able to get all of them now, though. I did not work the last two evenings because I could not get any Indians to work with, and also because it was too much for me. I do not get any exercise so I want to use a few evenings to run around. It is dark now at 8:30. After dark I can't work by artificial light. I think Miss Andrews [?] will take her vacation in August. I hope it will do her much good. The revision of the texts is a terrible job. I wish I were finished with it. I took dictation all afternoon and my hand is completely stiff. Adieu for today. I hope you and the children are well. Were you gay [?] on your birthday?

Your husband

Alert Bay, July 28, 1900

Dear Wife,

This morning the steamer finally came and brought my letters. I got yours and those of the children of July 7 to July 15. It was a load off my chest to hear that you are feeling better, but my heart is still heavy and I wish I could be at home. Are you really all right? I am writing these lines in a great hurry because this morning a second steamer arrived which goes to Victoria, and I hope that I can send this letter with it. Unfortunately, my glasses have broken, and this is hard on my eyes. I hope that I can somehow repair them.

There is no news other than that my work is progressing. I also heard from Farrand [?], and I wish I would hear from Kroeber. Not a word from him yet. Besides, I had a letter from Laufer from Berlin today. Please take care of yourself. I worry about you and your well-being. Last night I dreamed all kinds of nonsense about you and father; there is hardly a night now in which I don't dream of father. Kiss the little ones for me.

Your husband

Alert Bay, August 1, 1900

Dear Mother,

Tonight I have a few free moments and I want to use them to send you these greetings. We have had beautiful weather these past weeks so that my Indian friends and I could always sit outdoors. This has changed the past few days though, and it rains all the time now. I hope that I can start with my ethnographic work on Monday. It is time for it now because my interpreter is losing his pleasure in this monotonous work. Time flies unbelievably fast when working so hard. During the past days I always had a . . . still after 8:30. The lighting conditions here are very bad so that I cannot work any more after it gets dark. The latest I can now work is nine o'clock, what with the dusk and the lamps. I am upset that I did not bring a small lamp with me, a thing I should have done. I am glad that I could send you word last week. A little steamer arrived here unexpectedly and took my letters. I hope that there will be letters again the day after tomorrow.

There is really terribly little to tell. I see nobody but the Indian with whom I am working. I see the other people only at meals, which are very short and unimportant. [Sunday evening at nine o'clock there was some entertainment.] A Scotsman who is an engineer here sang solos. I accompanied him on a little organ. Since I did not know his songs we finally had to sing children's songs, for which there was some music, and the English National Hymn, etc. Fishing was very poor in the last few days because there were no more salmon. All of a sudden another kind of salmon appeared today, the ones which are caught in August, and everything is in full swing again. The quantity of fish caught here is hard to believe. Today there were about 18,000 fish caught with the nets. . . .

*August 2:* Today it cleared up at last, but it is still cool and damp. I always wear my heavy suit and do not feel too warm at all. I am glad that Dr. Laufer has called on you. He is a very witty man. To-morrow is Marie's birthday. I wish I could be there with her in-stead of fooling around here with my Indians. I am sure you are already thinking about your return to the city. When we are over there next year, we all could go to . . . for some time. I should like so much to go there once with my children, although you interest me more than they. There is time enough to talk about it next year. A winter of strenuous work lies in between. I again dread my lec-tures. How many hours one has to read every week! Now, goodbye for today, dear old one. I still want to write to Marie. I should also like to write to Anna, sending it by this ship so that she will get the letter on her birthday. However, I don't have her address here, and so I want to send her letter to you.

With all my love,

Your Franz

*August 3:* I got your letter of the ninth today.

Alert Bay, August 2, 1900

Dear Wife,

I don't have anything to tell you. The weather was awful all week, so that I had to sit in this hole all the time. The salmon were very scarce all of a sudden and the cannery did not work for a few days. Today there were a great number of fish and everything is going again. Nevertheless, I hope that I can have George Hunt from Monday on. My interpreter is becoming rather dumb these days, probably because of the constant work on the same subject. I still have so many old texts to revise, however, that I will not be finished with him for some time.

Please write me about our finances by the end of this month, especially whether you could put something away in August and September. You know that we have to buy many things in October for which we have to save now. I shall be happy if you have a lot left. I myself use very little. When the time comes I think that I will not have spent more than $40 all summer. There were a few things for which I could not charge the expedition. I am longing again for letters. Maybe there will be some tomorrow. Although time passes very quickly, it seems an eternity since I have heard from

you and the children. I have to stand it another two months and.
. . .

Tomorrow is your birthday. I wonder where you all will spend it. Did my congratulations arrive on time? What are you going to do? Did the children figure out something for you?

Your husband

Alert Bay, August 7, 1900

Dear Wife,

Yesterday, Sunday, from two to five, I finally had George Hunt at my disposal and worked with him. Today, however, there were so many fish again that I could not have him, and I am sure the same will be true for tomorrow and the day after. This is terrible because I now want to stop with my linguistic work and work on ethnology. I have so much to do in this field that it is high time that I start.

If only I would get my raise of $1,000 next year. It will be very hard to make ends meet without it, especially with our trip to Europe. I am so worried about you. I am sorry that I did not write to the children again, but I am always so tired in the evening that I do not even feel like writing to you. Work here is really no fun. I have learned a lot, linguistically, but otherwise I have not accomplished very much. I worked my way through the medicines of these people, and their food; that is, the vegetation and some of their industries, but there is still so much to do that I don't know how I will finish, especially if I can have George Hunt as my "interpreter" for such a little time. My language interpreter cannot be used for such work. Now and then I get good news from Farrand [?]. I have not heard from Kroeber [?] at all; so I wrote him the other day and asked him to write. I don't know anything about Swanton [?] either. I have learned so much here that I think I can publish the texts when I come back. I want to do this in . . . though, and not at home if I can avoid it. . . . It would be good to tell me about it soon.

*August 8:* I just want to add a greeting. If the steamer comes during the day I must carry my letter down right away. If it comes this evening, however, I might add some more.

Your husband

Kiss my little ones for me. It has become evening in the mean-time. Work did not progress well. I spent the whole afternoon over the tense of a verb [?], a very complicated business. I am unhappy that I cannot have George Hunt at my disposal because I finally want to stop working on the language. It does not lead to anything more. Good night for today. Fortunately I can use my glasses as they are.

Your old man

Alert Bay, August 7, 1900

Dear Mother,

Tomorrow or the day after, the steamer is expected again and I am sending you my love. I think my letters from here are very meager. My life is monotonous, and in the evenings I am so written-out that I do not feel like writing long letters. I stopped my lin-guistic studies day before yesterday; I want to pursue only eth-nology. For this I need especially good informants, however, and since the canneries are still working full time, I do not get as many as I want. I hope that next week there will not be as many fish caught as now. That would leave me enough to get what I want. In about four weeks I will strongly consider concluding my work. I should like to be back on September 20, and not go back to my university work right away.

Ernst has to go to a bigger school this year where he can stay un-til college. We want to send him to Adler's school, which starts on September 23; we must be back in town at that time. You probably know that Felix Adler has a good school. It is not as expensive as other schools and has a very good reputation. I do not think that we can do any better for the child. The school costs $150, whereas other private schools cost $300. Best of all, however, there is no snobbish atmosphere in this school. About one-half of the students go there free, so that there is a good mixture of the poor and the rich. Even Laura Jacobi's school is too stuck-up.

I hope you enjoyed the days which Uncle Jacobi spent with you. We are also looking forward to the time of our visit. You need not be afraid that a baby will upset our plans. This is not very probable. I do not think that there will be more grandchildren for you from our side. I hope that we will make good people out of the children we have. Oh, how I miss them! Baby won't know me any more. He always liked to be with me very much. When nobody could handle him, when he did not want to go to sleep, he was always content with me. Now he walks all by himself. Good night for today. Maybe I can add a greeting tomorrow.

*August 8:* The steamer is not here yet and I have a minute to close my letter before my interpreter comes. I sent greetings to Uncle . . . and Kaufman. I hope they will be on time for their birthday and wedding, respectively. It would have been nice if you had celebrated them all together. Please give my love to all my sisters.

Love,

Your Franz

Alert Bay, August 16, 1900

Dear Wife,

This morning I got your letter of August 2. I was disappointed that I did not get a second letter, since the steamers now run on a schedule that will not bring the next letters before the twenty-fourth or twenty-fifth. I hope that Heini is completely well by now. Your letter was mailed on the fourth, although it was dated the second. This time you, too, will have to wait over a week for a letter, because the steamers run so terribly irregularly. I always have to finish my letters one or two days before the alleged arrival of the steamer; otherwise I would miss the opportunity when it arrives at night.

The past two weeks were rather unsatisfactory. I had counted on getting George Hunt at least four days a week but the cannery was so busy that I had him only one day besides Sundays. Mr. Spencer, however, finally promised to dismiss him completely on Friday. Now I think I can finish my work here in about four weeks. That would be September fourteenth or fifteenth. About eight days later I could be with you. You will have to notify me, of course, whether you will be on the lake or in town. I still feel I should like to spend a few days with you on the lake, but that is far off as yet. Make your plans regardless of me. Write Mrs. Donaldson [?] where you will be at that time and write me by the end of the month about our finances. I still have much to do here; however, I hope that George Hunt will be able to do by himself many things which yet have to be done. I revised much of what he had done and can see that he does everything properly and that he does not pull my leg. I find him quite dependable, more than I had thought. The result of this summer should be that I can publish in their original text the tales which I have collected during the past years. I want to start with this right away after my return. And then I want . . . , in case I should give a speech as a new member at the meeting of the National Academy in Providence, to give them an outline of the language. I now understand it quite well, and it is very interesting. It is also unbelievably complicated. In addition, I can now prepare a description of the way of life of this tribe, and perhaps have it printed next year. The material which I have obtained for this is interesting and diversified. Then, I think, I will have finally finished with this tribe.

Adieu for today. Many kisses from

Your father and husband

Alert Bay, August 16, 1900

Dear Mother,

Today's steamer did not bring a letter from you. With this steamer I also sent a letter to Rudolf. I wish I could write him more often, but I don't want to sit down and write him a rush letter. Last winter there was rush and work all the time. I am glad I had the operation after all. I am sleeping much better now and, as a consequence, feel much better in general.

About my work here: there is nothing good to report at this time. I was not idle, of course, but did not achieve what I wanted during the past two weeks. The cannery had so many fish that I could not get hold of any Indian and therefore had to continue to work on the language. I had hoped to start with the ethnological work on the fourth. I did some of it, but by no means all I wanted. Beginning Friday, the cannery will have less work because all cans will have been filled. Then I hope I will make some progress with my work. I don't think it will take me longer than four weeks, so that I will be able to be at home on September 23. I am really looking forward to this moment because the separation from the children and the irregular news are very unsatisfactory; but this has to be expected with my kind of work. The scientific result of this summer is most satisfactory. I will finally be able to publish the [Kwakiutl texts?] which I have been collecting for six years. I will start with this right after my return while the language is fresh in my memory. Then I hope I will have enough material to make a detailed description of the manners and customs of the Indians. That will be a very peculiar work of culture [?]. What museum pieces I shall get I don't yet know myself. I leave this to my man here, to whom I gave a whole list of what I want. I also have enough material for the language part, but the editing of it will take years, of course.

. . . Enough for today. I look forward to the next steamer. With many greetings to all of you.

Your Franz

Alert Bay, August 23, 1900

Dear Mother,

I chucked my linguistic work last week, the eighteenth, and am now working on the customs of the Indians. Now I can see clearly how long the work will take me; I hope to be finished by the middle of September. This way I actually will be able to go to Lake George for a few days. I want to be back home between the twentieth and the twenty-third. I am getting restless. The long absence and the bad postal service do not suit me at all. This time I will have to wait two weeks for the mail to come, and I should like very much to know how Toni is getting along. I last got news when the Uncles were in Berlin with you, about August 2.

So far I am quite satisfied with the progress of my work, although my present informant is a very touchy guy whom one has to treat with kid gloves and who may leave whenever he feels like it. It is difficult to be dependent on someone like this. Last Sunday I made a little trip by canoe, the first since my arrival. In the morning I rode with an Indian to a river on Vancouver Island which empties into the strait right across from this island. The strait between here and Vancouver Island is about four kilometers wide. I wanted to see the salmon works [?] and a few old houses, as well as some old Indian graves. I was fortunate to have chosen that day because since then we have had terrible weather—rain and nothing but rain. I should very much like to make a two-day tour, but this is impossible with this kind of weather. I really don't have much to tell you. My work is monotonous, interrupted by nothing. I have been away from New York for ten weeks now and am counting the days until my return. I really miss the children. My first weeks here were so interesting that I was completely absorbed by my work. But the more I learn, the less daily progress I seem to make. In the evenings now I always have the interpreter, with whom I work on the language; he instructs me during the day on the customs and manners of the Indians.

I wonder whether Anna got my birthday letter in time, and also whether Toni is completely well now. I am impatiently waiting for the next mail, which might come Saturday the twenty-sixth. My present letter is very unsatisfactory. I think the terribly dark weather is the cause of it. It kills all one's courage. All-in-all, I am very well and spry. I have gained weight here and am as tanned as a gypsy. I wonder how the Chinese affair will develop. The last newspaper I read was that of August 7. I am afraid this will spoil my plans for Laufer. I would rather not think about all these things until I come back. I was told that all sorts of changes would be made this summer in the Museum. I have not heard anything about it yet, and I should be surprised if the . . . was painted. All administrative things take an awfully long time there. I wonder what students I will have this year. My old ones are all gone. One of them, who now has a job in California, is going to come back for his doctorate, probably around Christmastime. A young fellow from Harvard will come, and one from New York, and one from New Haven. That is all I know with regard to my special students.

Adieu for today, dear old one. I am too stupid to write a reasonable word. Please give my love to all the sisters.

Affectionately,<br>Franz

[Alert Bay, August 23 or 24, 1900]

[Dear Wife,]

The steamer is not here yet so I am adding a few more lines. Instead of clearing up, it started to pour, and it is so unbelievably cold and humid here that it cannot even be described. The work has progressed rather well during the past days, but I shall be surprised if I can finish it. I could, of course, go on working here, but sometime the joke must end. I still have so much material left that I don't really know what I have done so far. I think I will have to go through it and sort it. The governor general of Canada is expected one of these days. He is on an inspection trip. Everything here will probably be topsy-turvy so that I won't be able to work much.

I think I should get some rest before the tough winter work starts. I probably won't get any answer here to these lines because of the boat connections. Please write to me at Victoria, however, about your plans for the end of September so that I can make up my mind whether it is still worthwhile for me to go to the lake. If it were for a whole week, I would do it. I think I am coming through Binghamton, where I could take a train to Albany [?]. Did you ever get back the 1,000 m. ticket? Adieu for now, though. I have to work.

Your old graying one

*August 25:* The steamer is still not here. Therefore one more greeting. Today was a beautiful day again. I hope there will be more to come. I can finally see the end of my work. I wonder whether the steamer is coming tomorrow. I am hoping for a letter from you.

Your husband

Alert Bay, September 7, 1900

Dear Mother,

I am finished here with my work and am waiting for the steamer to take me to Victoria. The connection is very bad, and it is annoying to see so many boats going by to Alaska and not be able to go with them. Because of the customs matter these steamers cannot stop here.

These last days I have cast Indian faces in plaster-of-paris. I was annoyed because it was so hard to persuade the men to let themselves be cast. Now my collection is being packed. I do not want to start something new because the boat may come any time between today and the eleventh. I only hope that it will bring me some letters. I have not had any for two weeks. The last letter I got from you was dated August 7, and from Marie August 12. I hope there will be a steamer from Victoria tomorrow which will bring something. The end of such a trip is always very tough on me, as funny as this may sound. If only everything is all right at home. I wonder whether Trudel is going to recogize me. This could hardly be expected of Heini, though. There is less news than ever today. I worked very hard here all the time and did everything I had planned to do. . . . The weather was beautiful all the time; I was very lucky in this respect because it usually rains here quite a lot. Although I have the time today to write you, I don't feel like it. I'll leave the letter open until I have news from you. The letter will go to Vancouver on the same boat I am taking to Victoria. When you receive it, I will be in a civilized place again. I am counting on being home for sure, in two weeks.

*September 9:* The mail finally came this morning, bringing me your postcard of the ninth, your letters of the tenth and twentieth, and Marie's letter of August 28. Now I can't wait for the steamer to take me to Victoria. I plan to stay there only one day and then proceed home. I hope that your stay on Ruegen with Toni was really nice. I am so glad to get away from here. My work is finished; the trunk is packed so that I can take the steamer as soon as it comes.

When it finally does come! This sitting around here is very boring. I have a little left-over work to do in order not to have to think of this terrible steamer all the time. My next letter will probably be from St. Paul. The one day in Victoria will not leave me time to write. There will be a greeting from the lake, I hope, before we go back to New York. I had a nice letter from Laufer from Heidelberg today.

Adieu for today. You will see from the Vancouver postmark on this letter when it was that I finally left here. It takes the steamer about twenty-four hours to get there from here.

With love,

Your Franz

# PART
# FOUR

---

# INDEPENDENT
# RESEARCH
## (1914–1931)

EDITOR'S INTRODUCTION.—*Boas' last five field trips to the coast, from 1914 to 1931, were independent of any sponsoring organization. Consequently he was free to do the kind of work he wanted without being constrained by the aims, goals, or policies of some outside organization. He apparently did not maintain a diary during his last trips, and many of his letters are no more than suggestive of what his activities may have been. Nonetheless they reveal that the general character of his field work during these trips was entirely consistent with his earlier work. During these years he also worked in Puerto Rico (summer, 1915) and in the pueblos of New Mexico (summers, 1919–21).*

*Little information is available regarding his sources of financial support for his last five trips to the North Pacific Coast. Apparently Elsie Clews Parsons financed some of his research, as she did for many of his students, but he undoubtedly had other sources of support as well.*

# 10

---

# Family Letters (1914–1931)

August 6, 1914

My dear boy [Ernst],

I have not heard from you in a long time. I have been under way since last Friday, and shall finally arrive [tomorrow] in Cranbrook. At the moment I am on a stern-wheeler on Lake Arrow. You can imagine that I can think of nothing else than the unfortunate war and the danger to which our aunts and Grandmother are exposed. To me it seems like a terrible dream. I cannot visualize how reasonable people and nations which are "leaders of civilization" can conjure up such a terrible war. If Germany loses, such hatred will be created that it will stir up her nationalism for centuries to come; if she is victorious, such arrogance, that it will lead to the same consequence. If people would only realize what a source of hatred and misfortune the highly praised patriotism represents! That one cherishes one's own way of life is a natural thing. But does one need to nourish the thought that it is the best of all, that everything which is different is not good but useless, that it is right to despise the people of other nations? In our private lives we would not follow such an unethical rule; why should it prevail in our national life? If one only could exclude this "Patriotismus" from our schools and teach our children the good in our culture, and appreciation of the good in other cultures. Instead they artificially cultivate envy and rivalry.

Yesterday the English paper in Vancouver had a very anti-German editorial. It stated that England must free world trade from the fetters in which it is kept by the German fleet. For centuries England was leading in world trade, and now Germany is taking over. Thus everyone belies himself!

271

I can't think of anything else. Do you see Helen often? I do hope so. Now she has nobody in New York. Please take the time to write me what you are doing.

Your father

August 7, 1914

Dear Wife,

This morning I can send you greetings again, but with difficulty because the boat rolls so much. Today we are on Kootenay Lake. Yesterday I went down Lake Arrow, then by train to an arm of Lake Kootenay, and slept here on the steamer, which will leave at 6 A.M. At ten I shall be on a train again. This afternoon at four o'clock I shall be in Cranbrook.

I do hope that there will be letters for me. I have not received any word from you since a week ago yesterday. There were a few lines from Miss Andrews [?] in Spences Bridge. I hope that my work here will move ahead quickly so that I can go home soon. I don't feel like working at all. The terrible war drives me crazy. Why did Germany overrun Belgium and thereby lose the sympathy of all the world? There must have been a reason which we do not know. Did she want to beat France to it? Anyway . . . German arrogance, French lust for revenge, English envy, lust for power—these are behind the whole thing. . . .

Your husband

I wrote to Helen and Ernst today. I haven't heard from Helen since July 17.

St. Eugene, Cranbrook, British Columbia
August 15, 1914

Dear Heini,

You want to know what I am thinking about the war? First of all, I think that it is horrid and that there is no excuse for the people who bring such a disaster to mankind.

It is not easy to explain what I am thinking, but I shall try: If you play baseball against another school you are enthusiastic about your team and sad when your school loses. In accordance with the Ethical Culture School we tried always to impress on you that you should not only be interested in your team but you should give recognition of good performance on the part of your opponents, and also be happy about it. It is only a coincidence that you are in the same school with one boy one day; tomorrow you could be in school with another; and it does not make us better to be in school with the good players. The only thing that counts is the good play, and you can try to be as good as the good players. It is a sign of a bad school when its students are envious of other schools and are against them, just because they don't belong to them.

Now think what they told you in school about the flag; that you should carry it high and that there is nothing better than America. Of course it is right that we feel like this, and we should always try to contribute as much as we can to the community to which we belong and in which we live. At the same time, however, it is easy to forget one thing—the "school spirit" is good if everyone is doing the best he can for his school. It is bad if he belittles everything good which goes on in another school. Thus, although the need to feel like an American is impressed on you, we don't hear enough that there is the good and the beautiful also in other countries, that the people there strive also for the good and the beautiful just as we do, and that we should not be envious of them but give them their due. If we work and live as Americans, we are working for mankind and it cannot be justified that we begrudge others for what we did in our own country.

This false love for the fatherland other people call patriotism. They are forgetting that every country with its special features has to work together with other countries in order really to fulfill its duties and to be of use.

In Europe, it seems, the feeling is much stronger than here that everybody belongs to one nation, because there the languages are different and the whole history . . . is based on conflicting interests. There, even fewer people than in America think that they are world citizens rather than patriots. Thus Russia has only one goal, to become the largest power as leader of all Slavic peoples. That would mean about the same as if England or the United States or Germany wanted to be the leader of these three nations, plus Denmark, Sweden, and Norway, as well as Holland and Belgium, because these languages are related. Austria is a state which actually consists only of the former possessions of the emperor, which have very little in common because the people speak German, Hungarian, Czech, etc. In Austria the government has only one aim, and that is to defend Austria against all disturbing elements, the most important of which is Russia's desire to have all the Poles, Czechs, and Serbs for herself. Germany is proud of its successes during the last fifty years. She wants to have her own way, and has offended all her neighbors with her bad manners. France has had only one idea since 1870, and that is revenge on Germany. England is envious of the growth of German trade and wants to put an end to it. You see, it is altogether the same as with schools which are envious of each other and which fight with each other.

The various large countries have at times worked together in one matter in order to achieve an advantage in another matter which seemed to be of more importance to them at that time. Thus Russia and England always have opposite interests, but since Germany is just now in their way, they have united with France against Germany. And Russia is using the conflagration against Austria; France and England against Germany. This wrong and egotistic strife which separates the nations is, as you see, equally bad with all of them. It is less outspoken with Germany because. . . . However, the Germans are as guilty in this respect as all the others.

What led to this war just at this time nobody knows, because none of us knows what actually happened. The first step is clear: Austria believes, and she is right, that her existence is threatened. I am not the emperor of Austria and therefore might say that her existence should come to an end. If we want to understand these people, however, we must try to think as they think, and try to understand their actions and their aims. Austria says to Russia that she has to defend herself against the Serbs but that she does not want to deprive them of their independence. Whereupon Russia answers by mobilizing against Austria. What follows now, I don't understand. One might have thought that Austria would protest now and either declare war or let Russia declare war on her. But no. Germany is speaking for her ally instead. She asks Russia not to mobilize. And since the Russians don't listen, Germany declares war. At the same time, she asks France if she would stay neutral in a war against Russia. France answers that she will act according to her own interests. This is as much as a declaration of war. At the same time England asks Germany not to use her fleet, a request, of course, that is rejected by Germany. And there you have the whole story!

I cannot warm up for either side. If the war was unavoidable, the brutal actions of Germany can be explained by her emergency. But I cannot forgive them the breach of their contract with Belgium.

I like even less the fact that Germany apparently figures, in the event of a victory (which seems quite unlikely), that she will get the colonies of France and Portugal. Many people will say that this was the reason for which Germany started the war, but this is not true. I don't think Germany is that stupid. If one knows so little of what is going on, one should not forget that the Germans avoided war until now, although it had been very close many times before.

There is one lesson for all of us: one should kill false patriotism. . . . This is true of all things, from the small to the great ones: family pride, party hatred, etc. All this originates from the fact that we always consider the little group to which we belong better than the whole world, and therefore we always want the best for it. Instead, we should do the best we can for our own group and always appreciate what other people achieve also.

Try to understand this, if you can. In time you will have an understanding of everything I have written, my boy.

Kiss everyone for me, and a hug for you from

Your Dad

Cranbrook, British Columbia
August 15, 1914

Dear Wife,

Yesterday the mail finally came, five days late. I got your letter and cards of July 6, 7, and 8. Many thanks. I can't write much because I am too busy. There is nothing new here.

Today I finished work with my good informant and must now see how much I can translate. I did my work very differently from how I had originally planned it because I cannot get an interpreter. I really did not want to collect so many. . . . All in all I got about . . . pages, in addition to the ones for Chandler. The contents of the stuff are interesting and as far as this goes it is. . . .

Therefore just a quick greeting for you today.

Your husband

Cranbrook, British Columbia
August 25, 1914

Dear Mama,

I am writing again, not even knowing whether you are getting my letters. It is terrible for me not to know how you are. Your last letter was dated July 23. I have to think of all of you incessantly, especially of Walter and Hans. What a misery such a war creates. And to what end?

I am finally about to leave today. It was an endless summer. During the last week I could not write many letters because I worked too hard. I had some good Indians and the work progressed rapidly. I worked nine to ten hours [a day] with my Indians and then needed another hour to prepare myself. I hope I shall have good connections so that I can be at home soon. I really can't write you in an orderly fashion because my thoughts are always circling around the same point.

Your Franz

FAMILY LETTERS (1922)

[No location cited]

Dear Ernst,

I can imagine how busy you are, but we [Marie and F.B.] really would like to know how Helen and the baby are getting along. We had hoped to get a letter today but there was nothing. We stayed in Seattle five days in all and spent most of the time with the [Leslie] Spiers. I met many people and formed a committee for the Emergency Society. That took quite some time. Days on which I see many people are very hard on me.

This morning at nine o'clock we left and arrived in Victoria after 1 P.M. I haven't been here for twenty-two years! The place has really changed very much. First we went to our hotel, then to the post office, and then to the museum. There we met George Hunt. They gave me a room in the museum where I am going to work. I hope Mama will find something with which to occupy herself. Seeing the people again whom I know here makes me realize how old we are. A Dr. Newcombe, who does not practice and who is very interested in Indians, came to pick us up from the boat. We missed him, however, because there were many people and I did not look around for anyone. I met him shortly afterward in the museum.

Much love to all of you.

Your father

Give my love also to Father and Mother and Baby.

Spences Bridge, British Columbia<br>August 30, 1922

Dear Toni,

I am too tired tonight to write a serious letter. I worked very hard in Victoria, and Mama had a good time. We went together to the movies and to the real theater and made several little trips. At the end I even had to give a lecture. George Hunt from Fort Rupert and another Indian were here. I have a room in the library in which I do my work.

The visit here is very sad. An old companion of my travels is dying of cancer of the bladder. I spend much time with him trying to give him courage. Tomorrow we leave. Five more days of mountain climbing, and then we go home again. Both of us are very glad to get back again.

Greetings and kisses,

Your brother Franz

FAMILY LETTERS (1923)

Vancouver, November 13, 1923

Dear Wife,

I arrived here late last night. I was too tired to write and went straight to bed. Monday night I arrived at about 1 A.M. at Spences Bridge. The ride across the mountains was marvelous. It was a sunny day and light snow was on the mountains, and more of it in the Selkirks. The trees were covered with all sorts of frost formations. It looked like a fairyland; at the bottom the very dark firs, then various other trees, with rocks above those, and the snow topping it all. Early in the morning the shadows dominated everything. Outside in the last car it was so cold that one could not stay very long to admire the landscape.

I have some terrible stuff in my left eye, and it is all inflamed now. As I have had the same trouble since St. Paul, I went to an eye doctor today to have it examined. There is nothing really wrong and I am treating it with.... I did not dare go to Bella Bella without having it checked. I think I will have to wear protective glasses.

Then I went to Mrs. Teit who had come from ... with two of her children. I sat with her over some papers which she had classified and which she is going to send to New York. I am sending one to little Viaux (one of my students) to be finished by her, and some of it she is to change. The train was very late again; it came only at four o'clock instead of 2:30. We arrived on time here in Vancouver, however. During the seven hours it took, the train made up the missing one and one-half hours.

This morning your greeting from Alma Farm arrived, and also a few lines from Helene and Trudel. Erna [Gunther Spier] wrote that she will be there on December 18, and then I will see her. The other day I forgot to take the rest of the money with me. I am almost sure that I will need it. Please send me a blank check so that I can get the money from . . . , if needed. There is still $53.50 of my travel money in the bank. Unfortunately I have not heard yet from George Hunt. I am, of course, very anxious for him to be there when I arrive. Today it is foggy but quite warm. I have a nice room, am enjoying my bath, and have all my laundry washed here. The boat leaves tomorrow night at nine. I hope you got my postcard from my trip here.

Greetings to everyone. I wish I knew how things go with Kann [?] and Cecil [?].

**Your husband**

Vancouver, November 14, 1923

Dear Hete,

I still have some time before my boat leaves for Bella Bella, and so I will quickly send you my love. I haven't written to you since we came back. That is because Fritzi gets my letters first, which are not for her alone but also for Toni and Anna. The last news I had before I left Chicago was about the Munich Putsch. There is so little in the newspapers here that I don't know at all what is going on. I am sure, though, that it looks very bad. . . . And then I will be able to give you more money, since my income has increased. I arrived in Chicago at 4 P.M. I had dinner in the hotel with Hete and Oskar. Then we went to the parents Yampolsky. You probably heard that the father suddenly came to New York where one of his nephews had died. On Thursday Hete came and we went together to the cemetery, then for a few hours to the museum, and at noon back to the Yampolskys. . . . It seems that Oskar will get a position as a teacher of arts and crafts in the high schools. That would solve all the difficulties for him. I wish Cecil were that far! As botanist he has not much chance for advancement in a reputable university because he is not considered a 100 per cent American. The botanists seem to be politically prejudiced, strange as it may seem. At least the . . . guys I know, with few exceptions.

I was in Spences Bridge from Sunday night until Monday. I looked through and brought to order all the papers Teit left there. He has many notes, which I have sorted. I shall let a few of my students sort these things. For instance, Erna Gunther Spier (Fritzi knows who she is) is finishing the Puget Sound stuff of. . . . I am really curious about how I will get along. I have no idea how I will live at Bella Bella and what I will find there. It will turn out all right, I am sure, if only I have luck and find good and reliable people from whom I can learn. I am well prepared and know the problems, but it depends so much on good informants. Thirty years ago it would have been easier. I am so glad that I can work a few more weeks and that I don't have to concentrate on administrative matters. How easily one can rid oneself of these worries! I am curious to know how my endeavor to get money for the German schools is getting along.

In Chicago I got a letter from Fritzi with some encouraging words. Now I have to wait until the twenty-third for my next mail. I am really far away from everything. The trip through the Rocky Mountains was very beautiful. It was a very clear day, and the light on the snow mountains was wonderful. It was very cold, however, and one could not stay outside long without getting cold feet. Here it is quite warm, and it drizzles and rains all the time. It will be even wetter in Bella Bella. I wonder how Fritzi gets along with her work. I hope it will be all right. I told someone in New York about her work the other day and was told that she could get very good teaching positions when she has finished her studies—positions that would give her enough time for her research. That would be really wonderful.

I should like to know how all of you are. The . . . must really be terrible. If you could only be spared it. But enough for today. I have to go down to the boat.

With love,

Your brother Franz

Bella Bella, November 17, 1923

Dear Wife,

I have time for only a few words. The steamer arrived yesterday at 9:30 and landed at the salmon fishery. The Indian village is on the other side of the island and there was no boat to get me there. After an hour a man with a little gasoline engine boat came and brought me here. And here was George Hunt! I found lodging in a little hospital for Indians; there are six nurses; the doctor was not there, but he will be there today. They are all very nice but unbelievably quiet (mute). I already found a young man this afternoon to work on the language. Up to now everything has turned out fine. George Hunt is very depressed. Just when he left to come here one of his daughters died, his oldest son has cancer [?] of the spinal cord, and his oldest sister suffered a stroke.

It rains incessantly. I am quite well taken care of. I sleep in an empty ward with four beds. There is no table and I am writing on one of the beds. There is also a washroom which cannot be locked.

This is a great embarrassment for the nurses. Everything is a little difficult, but it is all right. I only hope that the Indians are and remain communicative. The first thing to do, of course, is negotiate for the price. The boat trip was very nice and so was the weather. It is unbelievable how the coast has changed. Alert Bay looks like a European or, rather, an American village. The steamship lines go up and down the coast. I did not have to wait around for a boat after all.

Don't write "via Canadian Pacific" on your letters any more. They don't take mail now. Write only "via Vancouver." The post office is about two miles from here, and one has to grab the opportunity when a boat goes. But don't expect regular mail. None of my letters to George Hunt arrived.

Kisses and greetings from

Your husband

Bella Bella, Monday, November 19, 1923

Dear Toni,

I have been here since Friday and really have had good luck. I had sent my interpreter from Fort Rupert ahead to this place. He had told me that it wouldn't be hard to find people here who would give me the desired information on the language, the customs, the tales, etc. I hope it goes as well as that! But one never can tell how suddenly the people will become contrary and how other unexpected difficulties will develop. As a matter of fact I am already counting the days until my departure. In view of the abominable conditions over there I hate to be so absolutely cut off from everything. There is mail once a week here, but it is a matter of luck if they find the people who are to get the mail. The post office is on another island.

For the time being I am quite well set up here. I have a whole ward, that is, a room with four beds in an Indian hospital. It is maintained by the Methodists, who are more concerned with prayers than with health. There are two regular nurses, two who are still learning, a doctor who is also the preacher, and a young Chinese and his wife, who are the cooks. There are prayers after dinner and in the evening a chapter is read from the Bible. Then everyone crawls under the table and prays. It is very hard for me to do these things, but as long as I am their guest—paying guest of course—I have to cooperate and may not hurt their feelings. There is hardly another place here where I could live. All the Indians live in modern houses, which are unbelievably dirty in comparison with their old houses. The windows are never opened, and the people themselves say that the new houses bring them the diseases. Of course, if someone has tuberculosis, tuberculosis is in one of these houses and everyone gets it.

Outwardly all the people [Indian] are Methodists, but their former Weltanschauung is still deeply anchored in them. My informant does not know these things, of course, and I am not telling him anything. Up to now I work on the language during the day and on their customs in the evening. As soon as I know the language a little better, I will change this schedule. Nowadays . . . I sit all day long with my informants in the house and work. Now and then we talk about things in which they are interested, in order not to tire them out. Up to now it has rained all the time, but today it seems to be clearing up. A board walk runs all through the village, and it is so slippery that one slips with every step. The old canoes have completely disappeared. The people use gasoline engine boats! The changes which have taken place since I was here the first time in 1886 are almost unbelievable.

Well, now my people are coming and I have to stop. In . . . weeks I shall be home again.

Greetings to all of you. In Vancouver I wrote to Hete for the last time.

Your brother
Franz

Bella Bella, November 20, 1923

My dear Wife,

I have to write in spite of not knowing when the letters will leave here. The steamers seem to go quite regularly, but there is no way to get the letters there in time. Up to now I have fared quite well here. On Friday I got a young man who was quite good for my language work. He came again on Saturday but vanished afterward. On Sunday I was in the house of an old man who gave me good information on the various tribes, etc. This is the hardest nut which has to be cracked here. The language work is rather easy because the language is closely related to the Kwakiutl. But also in this field some difficulties remain which have to be overcome. I spent Sunday with the old man because the language fellow went hunting. We worked the same as on any other day. George Hunt is invaluable for me because he knows the people and can get them much more easily. Here it is the same as everywhere on the coast: everyone is afraid to tell something that does not belong to his family. That makes my work hard.

First of all I am revising my Kwakiutl with George Hunt. You can imagine how busy my day is. I really don't have a minute's time except for meals. After all, I also have to revise the material I get. I never go to bed before twelve o'clock. Up to now I am set up quite satisfactorily. The nurses are really funny, at mealtimes especially. When the first nurse (head nurse) comes in, they all get up, and when the doctor, who is now back, comes in, all of them including the head nurse get up. They don't speak a word to each other [during the meal] but when they are outside of the [dining] room they start fooling around with each other.

Yesterday I got an unexpected letter from Tegger [?] but nothing else. My Thursday instruction was wrong, if only by one day, as much as I can find out. I must say that I never hated so much to be away. I am already counting the days until my departure, although I find my work very interesting. That I don't hear anything of world events is quite good for a change, although last night I could not get out of my mind how Germany is suffering. I wonder how Fritzi is getting along? I should also like very much to get news from Ernst. As a matter of fact I have not heard anything from them since I left.

Just now, at 8:15, the sun is rising right before me in a clear sky with little clouds to the northeast against the dark islands. It is a wonderful sight. I can't wear my khakis here because the people are too elegant, but I wear the shirts anyway. They are all right for this place. The greatest inconvenience is the washroom. There is only one little washroom, which is connected with the operating room. The first thing I shall do when I get back to Vancouver is to take a wonderful big bath!

Enough for now. I have to start work. I wonder how all the little ones and you big ones are getting along and how Heini has settled his affairs.

Greetings and kisses to everyone.

Your husband

Bella Bella, November 23, 1923

My dear Wife,

I think I never counted the days as much as on this trip. But the results are worth all the worries and work. Much that was completely unclear to me in Fort Rupert has become clear to me here. I am working very hard, from 8 A.M. until about 11 P.M. Since George Hunt came everything has gone easier. I feel like a spider in a web toward which everything is flying. I tell Hunt what I want and he brings the people to me. I am also making great progress with the language; it is easy for me because I know the Kwakiutl so well.

For a few days now I have shared my room with a missionary. He is on a temporary trip. He is a half-breed Tsimshian. Fortunately he is very seldom in our room because he is visiting Indians [?] and tries to. . . . I also heard from the faculty [?] and Bubl [?]. I still have to write today about our budget for next year. Yesterday I received a telegram (by mail of course) in which they asked for some recommendations for summer school. I had offered it to Spier and Speck, but both of them refused. I hardly know whom else I should recommend, since we pay so miserably. I telegraphed back (again by mail of course) recommending Michelson, with some misgivings. At least he has teaching experience.

There is really nothing else to tell, and I hardly have the time to write now. I wrote Fritzi with the last outgoing mail. She should hear from all of us regularly. What is going on in the world, I don't know at all. I am sure there is nothing to be pleased about. It is really sad that Max Köhler died. He was supposed to be very efficient. I often feel very strange when I think of all the young, promising people who formerly approached me, and whose work I am now finishing or having someone else finish!

Enough for now. I am glad that the end is near.

Your husband

Bella Bella, November 28, 1923

Dear Wife,

Today a steamer is due which takes mail, and I want quickly to send you my greetings, although there is really nothing to tell. The missionary is unfortunately still here. He still shares my room, which disturbs my work a bit because he is always running to and fro. However, I don't pay any attention to it, either on Sundays or weekdays.

My work progresses well but it is almost too much. I start at 7:30, right after breakfast, and don't get to bed before midnight. I take very little time out for meals. I end my work with the Indians at 9 P.M. and then have to prepare myself for the next day. Since I know the problems here so well, the material is in good order and can almost be used as I take it down. I only have to file it in the right place. The result is quite satisfactory. I don't bother with details, but the entire social structure and its transferability come out very clearly here. Many points which were obscure on Vancouver Island are much clearer here.

I think I already wrote you that I got a telegram from Columbia. They want recommendations for next summer, since Spier and Speck have declined. I answered by telegram that they should ask Michelson. I don't like to take him on, but I don't know anyone better right now. I myself am all right. I don't get any exercise, except the walking on the board walk of the village. Afternoons I always have people who have to tell me things. I see the funniest things! What do you think of an Indian house with a player piano, an organ, or a billiard table? Everything is in the kitchen, of course, and not well taken care of. On the other hand they don't love the dirt. Everyone here has good gasoline lamps with incandescent mantles. This helps the light problem, since the days are very short. I have to use artificial light until 9 A.M. The weather is strange. Every day it changes several times from snow or rain to clear skies. The lawns are green but the annuals are all dead.

Enough now. Greetings and kisses to all. I hope there will be a letter again tomorrow.

Your husband

Bella Bella, December 3, 1923

Dear Wife,

This week I had a letter from you, one from Hete, and from Trudel and Ernst who also sent me F——'s letter. I sent one to Gladys [Reichard?], who had written me quite extensively. I must say that I am very tired. I haven't worked this hard for a long, long time. The result is quite satisfactory, although everything here is so thoroughly lost that it is very hard to find out anything reasonable. The young people have even lost much of their language, but not as much of the grammar as of the vocabulary. I speak Chinook [Jargon] with all the people except my main language. I speak the Chinook [Jargon] quite well, although there are always . . . words that pop up. I take it down in shorthand, everything they tell me.

The weather is just awful; it rains and storms all the time. Many boats were thrown ashore and badly broken up. The house shakes as if from earthquakes. Last night the doors suddenly flew open, forced open by the wind. All in all it is hellish weather. . . . We have to thank God that we are still alive. This week I wrote to the captain of the ship that I want to go back next week. Otherwise he won't stop here. Three weeks from today I shall be back with you. Oh, I am looking forward to it. How worried I was about you! We know more about the children only after they are gone.

There is really not much to tell. The missionary is gone, thank goodness, and I am again alone in my room. What is . . . doing? Is she very busy in the nursery? Of course, I should not ask any questions because I won't receive answers to them any more.

Greetings and kisses.

Your husband

Bella Bella, December 8, 1923

Dear Wife,

I am only going to send you greetings today. My work here is going along. Last night I slept like a log until a quarter to eight this morning, when it started to become light. On the previous nights sleep didn't want to come because I had too much on my mind. There is still so much to do here. Fritzi's letter sounded on the whole quite satisfactory. I am glad that she is finally opening up toward us. I almost have the feeling that we are only now getting to know her. That Heini does not write is really. . . .

One of the nurses here, a Miss Newsome, wants to know whether there is a postgraduate course in a hospital in New York where she can study the nursing of children. She would like to go to the Lying-in Hospital if she can find a good course there. Would you please try to find out? We can write her when I come home. I am sorry that Julius' pension is really going to stop. I wonder what happened. It was only promised for the time until. . . .

Maybe I can write once more. The steamers are very irregular here. The last one did not come at all. I hope. . . .

Love,

Your husband

Bella Bella, December 11, 1923

Dear Wife,

This is the last greeting from here. I must say that I am glad I will finally get away from here, although there is still much, much to do. Let someone else finish! I have not heard from you since

Thursday, but I am still hoping for a letter this week and then one in Vancouver. This week the steamer was late one day. I hope that this won't happen next week because I want to be at home on the twenty-fourth.

Yesterday afternoon I couldn't do any work. There was a big wedding. A young couple got married last Sunday and the big feast for the whole tribe took place yesterday. The whole village was invited. We had to sit at the door of the bride and. . . . I can't describe the feast today because I am too busy. I started to write you this morning but had to stop when my Indian came. I have to use every minute these people are with me, to bring together loose ends and to learn anything I do not yet know.

All in all, I think I can be satisfied with the result. However, it was a very expensive trip. I don't think that I will have $1,000 left. George Hunt is not of much help any more, but I am going over the Kwakiutl material with him every night. My hand aches from all this writing. I work from 8:30 in the morning until 11:30 at night with the pencil always in my hand. I take very little time out for eating. How is everything with you? I am counting the minutes until the twenty-fourth! Greetings and Kisses.

Your husband

Vancouver, December 18, 1923

Dear Toni,

Well, here I am again. I really cannot say that the trip back from Bella Bella was beautiful. First of all my steamer didn't come and I had to take another one. I had to pay again and must now try to get the money back. It was cold and rainy. In Queen Charlotte Sound I was seasick, and then a drunken group of lumberjacks came on board. They turned everything upside down until the mate finally almost literally carried them up on deck where they could cool off in the rain and wind. Then the screw propeller got caught in the chain and it took ten hours to get it loose. Finally there was a big storm in the Gulf of Georgia and we arrived here at midnight instead of at 11 A.M. My boat had already left and thus I lost one whole day. It is still possible that I will be at home on Christmas Eve if the snow is not too bad in the mountains and on the passes.

Today the floor is waving under my feet, and my hand is all cramped from the continuous writing in Bella Bella. My shorthand was really a great help. I wrote all my notes in shorthand. I hope that I will be able to read them. I am quite satisfied with the results of this trip. I did not lose any time, because I had George Hunt with me. He would always find my victims, whom I then pumped dry. When there was nothing else to do, I worked with him. As a Kwakiutl, he was invaluable in my language work since he could give me, in interesting cases, the Kwakiutl equivalent. I really feel that I learned a great deal and that the trip was worthwhile. It was, however, not as cheap as it was thirty-seven years ago. Because I was so stingy with my time, everything cost much more.

I have no idea what is going on in the world. Did you get my second letter to the . . . *Times?* I was very surprised that they printed it because it was contrary to their attitude. I wonder whether there is also going to be a change. The only news on Germany I have had in a long time is that the food prices have gone down 50 per cent. Is this true? The attempt to get money for the school has also slowed down since I left. According to the last report I received, the circular brought in only $3,000. This is not enough, by far! I did not hear anything of. . . . But there will be mail in New York. I did not let them forward anything because the mail to Bella Bella was not reliable. I am so glad that I am away from the prayer atmosphere of the Bella Bella. The eternal praying and crawling under the table to talk to the dear Lord was very hard on my nerves. I wonder whether these people think at all? In all other respects they were very nice and I am glad that I was so well taken care of. . . .

But enough. Tonight I am going to Seattle. The day after tomorrow I go home via Chicago. I think Hete will also be there if she is still in New York. Greetings and kisses to everybody. With all my love,

Your brother Franz

FAMILY LETTERS (1927)

Oakville, August 17, 1927

Dear Wife,

Today your letter of the thirteenth arrived, which was very quick, and one from Ernst which had gone first to Berkeley. These few days here are still very strenuous. I am working mornings from eight to twelve with Blanche [?], who learns quite quickly. At noon a bus picks me up. At this hour it is too hot to walk in the sun. This way I am there at 12:30 and work with Jonas (the . . .) until 6 P.M. Then I walk back, which takes me one and one-half hours. I am. . . .

It has been awfully hot here these past two days, 104 degrees in the houses and not a bit of breeze. Even at night it hardly gets cooler. Tonight however is nice and cool, and one feels relieved. I still have to prepare myself for tomorrow, so that I really don't have time to write letters. I have yet to write to Gladys about her work.

I want to stay one day in Seattle and shall be in Victoria on Tuesday, the thirtieth. I think three days will be sufficient, and I will leave there on the second. I shall be with you on the sixth. I will be very glad when the time is that far along. I am looking forward so much to being with you again. I should like to be with Ernst as much as possible. We will be together with Helene all winter, and the trip to Ernst is so very far.

Your husband

Oakville, August 19, 1927

Dear Wife,

Today I am sending you only a few greetings; you can't expect much more this week because I am very busy. I have to use these last days to get as much material as possible, and the connections are very bad. I am always terribly tired in the evening when I come back. Then I still have to work about two hours in order to be prepared for the next day.

I wrote to Ernst yesterday. I hope he can take his vacation a little later so that we can be together in the country for some time. I have to be back at school on September 26, but we could have three weeks together in the country [before that time]. I hope the weather will be good. Here it is nice and cool now after the great heat last week. I am enclosing a nice letter from. . . .

Greet everyone for me. I wish I had a little kiss from you again.

Your husband

FAMILY LETTERS (1930–1931)

Fort Rupert, October 24, 1930

Dear Toni,

Only a greeting to let you know that we [F. B. and Julia Averkieva] arrived well and are stationed comfortably. Civilization has infringed badly on the lives of the Indians. We are living in a good frame building; that means a wooden house such as Cecil's or Ernst's house [?]. We have good beds and good food. In other words, there are no more hardships. Everything is strange. There was a radio on the steamer. On the twenty-second the announcer said it was the birthday of Liszt, the greatest musical genius who ever lived, and that they are going to perform a concert in memory of Liszt—the *Hungarian Rhapsody*, etc. They also played Schubert and (just think of it) the *Erlkoenig*, etc. After arriving in Hardy Bay we had to wait eight hours until a boat came to bring us here. I now send you just this quick greeting because someone is going back to Hardy Bay.

You will hear from me again soon. I found peace and rest . . . in Hardy Bay.

Your loving brother,

Franz

Fort Rupert, October 27, 1930

Dear Toni,

Yesterday I received your dear letter of October 4, and one of Anna's in Port Hardy last Thursday, on the twenty-third. It is very nice to hear from you out here. Before I talk about anything else I must set you at ease about my "hardships." The village here has greatly shrunk, but George Hunt's nephew and family live here. His father is an American and is married to a woman from Montana. They have a big house, in which we have two rooms with good beds. We are getting good food and are well taken care of—as well as in any small town. It is very wet here but not cold. The grass stays green all winter, and the few cows owned by our hosts can stay on the pasture all winter. Since Thursday, when we arrived, it has rained hard every day except yesterday.

There are very few Indians here now. They have all been out fishing, but they are gradually coming back. For the time being I have to work with George Hunt, to revise everything and to answer grammatical questions. This means hard labor in his case because he has no understanding of grammar. His wife teaches Julia Averkieva women's work: weaving mats, making boxes, etc. The kid is a very nice girl, . . . and industrious. Now she chiefly has to learn the string games. My phonograph is busily at work. I have already recorded, in addition to the string games, one war song and one Potlatch song.

Today a man told me a long story. I have to let several people repeat a story to me in order to control Hunt's style. Otherwise I can't get a picture of the linguistic feeling of the natives, and I am very anxious to get a picture of their style. It seems that we are lucky. There is a rumor that a winter ceremony will be held this year in secret, because the feasts are forbidden by the government. But if there is nobody to watch they do whatever they like. The interference with the Indians on the part of the government is really scandalous. The way they administer the law, everyone who has formal knowledge [of the winter ceremonial] would have to go to jail. I read in the paper here (in Port Hardy) that Bruening prevailed after all and that the Reichstag took a vacation. Thus it went over better than I feared. I have the *Nation* . . . sent to me at this place. Otherwise I would hear nothing from abroad. But enough for now. I hope this letter will leave here tomorrow.

    With love, your brother

Franz

EDITOR'S NOTE.—*Boas' letters during the month of November, 1930, are missing. Fortunately Helene Boas Yampolsky had abstracted several of them before she died, and so a partial record of Boas' activities in Fort Rupert is still retrievable. I am also including abstracts of several letters to Ruth Benedict to help round out this record.*

Fort Rupert, November 9, 1930

[To Benedict]

    We [Julia and I] are getting on quite nicely now. Julia is making friends with the women and has been learning matting and basket making. Now she is learning cat's cradles, of which there are hundreds here. She is picking up village gossip, etc. The language comes pretty hard to her. I talk with difficulty and understand only after I write it; I follow conversation only partly. It goes too rapidly, but I am getting into it again. There are now feasts without end. Day before yesterday I gave a feast to the Indians, and according to custom they gave us presents, which make me poor because I have to return the value with interest. . . .

    The question of song and dance rhythm was not complicated. The feet and hands move with the time-beating; but time-beating and singing are a tough problem. There are at least four different styles of song; text as well as time are of different styles. I am getting texts from different informants. The literary style of all agree fairly well so far, although there are minor differences. Yesterday we had a mourning feast, with eating, mourning songs, speeches, and a song to drive away sadness. There is a Comox Indian here. I wonder whether you or Ruth Bryan could find a Comox vocabulary and texts in the Salishan vocabularies in one of the files in my room. If so, please, send it by registered mail. I might get time to revise it, although I am not sure. He says there are only six Comox left.

Papa Franz

Port Hardy, November 13, 1930

[To Benedict]

We are getting along well. Almost every day brings a feast with songs and dances. Julia danced last night with the crowd and has her first formal dancing lesson tonight. We are getting quite a little acculturation material. It is marvelous how the old life continues under the surface of the life of a poor fishing people. I am getting some more rather interesting data regarding the development of the whole modern system. I think even the order of seats among the bulk of the tribes is less than a hundred years old. Julia is gradually getting some data on their modern economic life. So far she has learned blanket work and is still collecting cat's cradles, the distribution of which is not uninteresting. I am getting texts from different informants. The style is partly uniform, although some people have their individual mannerisms. The dance problem is difficult. I hope that the films will give us adequate material for making a real study. In music there are a number of quite distinct styles; summer songs, mourning songs, love songs, winter songs, but I shall not unravel that problem while here. The language also has baffling problems. There is no *good* informant, because all of them are satisfied with a variety of forms. I rather think this is due to the merging of several dialects into one, which is not equal in all individuals. I am mindful that this is an acculturation problem and I hope we shall get enough on that point! Here it is either raining or cold, generally the former.

Fort Rupert, November 18, 1930

[To Ernst]

I had a council with the Indians, who are really suffering because of the stupid persecution of their customs by the government. I can do nothing about it, but promised to do my best in Ottawa.

I am not at all certain what I can do, because the missionaries here are behind it all. It goes so far that the children in school are not allowed to draw in the traditional style of their people but according to prescribed models. . . . I have used up all of my films and phonograph cylinders, and am borrowing more. I am anxious to thoroughly work out the various aspects of the Kwakiutl and I need the material for this purpose. Julia is learning the dance, but I believe it is too difficult to learn quickly. At any rate, through the criticism she receives I learn what it is all about. You can imagine what a relaxation it is to have to think of only one thing. The distractions in New York are terribly wearing in contrast to this.


November 18, 1930

[To Grandchild, Nornie]

The Indians gave me a nice mask with ermine skins and a carved cane. I gave them some presents too. They gave me a funny name. I do not believe you can say it; I will try to write it: Mullmumla-eelatre. That means, "If you put water on him the southeast wind will blow." It is a big rock nearby here, and the Indians believe that if you sprinkle water on its southeast side the wind will begin to blow. But anyway I am with love and a kiss. . . .


Port Hardy, November 24, 1930

[To Benedict]

Yesterday we were at a feast again—dried salmon and fish oil—when a boat from a village about twelve miles away came and invited the whole tribe. They are all gone today except a few old women. I did not want to go because the return is too uncertain and I have my work pretty well laid out. There will be no interruption. I already have a good deal of material for this style-motor question. But I want some more from different people. Julia is getting the life history of a few women, particularly their marriages. She has more than fifty cat's cradles. She is a pleasant companion.


Fort Rupert, November 26, 1930

[To Benedict]

Julia is trying to get the confidence of the women. I have so much to revise and fill in that I find it hard to see as much of the individuals as I should like to. Still, there are a few souls with whom I chat now and then, sometimes purposefully, sometimes not. Julia dances a few of the dances quite well. She is an expert at cat's cradles. I am worrying now about the style of oratory because I do not yet know how to get it down. Most orators talk so rapidly that I cannot follow it, except now and then. Anyway, I have my troubles with ordinary conversation. I can understand narrative quite well, if they talk distinctly, but many have the Indian habit of slurring over the ends of their words—whispering—and that makes it difficult. . . . Life is pretty full here.

Fort Rupert, November 27, 1930

[To Ernst]

Last night a deputation came from the Newettee [Nawiti]. In the darkness from the boat a speaker spoke with the voice of thunder. They had come to give a name to a child who is now a few months old. The chief answered from his house in an equally loud voice. The entire front room was then rearranged and dinner was cooked for the visitors. There was singing and dancing. This afternoon there was name-giving in an old house—i.e., in old Indian fashion. A large fire was burning in the center and we all sat along the wall in the old fashion. The singers sat in a circle in front of the fire while a girl danced, adorned with a headdress and skins of ermine. Then all the guests received presents. Julia was happy to be at a feast in an old house, but it was nothing compared with former times. There were only thirty people there. The old bedrooms and storerooms which made the house livable were gone.

Port Hardy, November 28, 1930

[To Ernst]

Julia and I took a vacation and went into the woods. We had to do a lot of climbing through salal berries and other brush, through swamps and over rocks. It is quite beautiful about a mile from here—tall old trees quite untouched. The weather was nice and we walked a few hours until we were quite tired. Yesterday morning I took pictures of a Shaman woman. Yesterday evening there was another feast: dried salmon and fulod [?] bread and tea! Suddenly a boat from the opposite coast (a distance of about twelve miles) arrived in the village. They invited the Indians to a potlatch. Speeches were held and each messenger was given one dollar. The chief was angry because the invitation interfered with his plans, and so he stayed here. Otherwise the village is empty again. I hope there will be no wind so that they can return tomorrow. If it should be windy they cannot cross the open sea in their boats. This afternoon a message came from Alert Bay that an Indian woman died. The chief is going there to the services. I wrote so much yesterday and today that my hand is lame.

Fort Rupert, December 8, 1930

Dear Toni,

On the second I wrote to Anna, but the letter is still here. Since November 26 there has been so much wind, fog, and rain that no boat dares to go out. Since no news from me can go out for two weeks, I wanted to send a telegram today but the line is interrupted. So we are sitting here really shut off from the world until the weather improves. We have not received anything either, of course.

There were all sorts of feasts here during the past weeks, especially the wedding of a couple who have been living together for several years. Last Tuesday (I think) there was a "feast," in the only still usable old house, to which the father of the groom invited all families . . . of the tribe to "make war" with him against the bride. Then everyone got up and said what he wanted to do. One of them said: "I have a copper boat that runs by itself and with it I conquered the . . . of all tribes." This is a reference to the family legend. Thus everyone had his say and then presents were distributed to everybody. The next day the wedding took place. The family of the bride awaited the groom and his gente in the feast house. Then the persons who invited everyone made their rounds, and everybody went into the house of the bride's father. There they were all fed. They all brought their . . . which were needed for later. Then the events began.

First came the speaker, a very imposing-looking man reminding me of Papa and Uncle Solomon [?]. The group stopped in front of the house, and the speaker sang a song and beat tact against the wall of the house with his staff (no speaker may speak without a staff), and said "uh! uh!" with it. This is the call of this particular gentes. Then he proceeded into the house with his companions, showed the huge double-headed snake, and made his speech, saying that the snake would get the bride.

Then a second speaker came, who said that his ancestor had the arrow which hit everything he wanted it to, and he still has two pieces, one as an arrow and one as a bow. He then went around the fire and pretended to hit the bride. And he called out, "I got her." Now another man came with a long spear that used to be his ancestors' and which allegedly hits everything he wants. To the right and to the left of the bride were two copper plates, one of which he pierced [broke?]; he then called, "Now I got the bride." Then a man came with a . . . , one with a mountain goat, and caught the bride. One after the other came—a man with the Thunderbird, a whale, a killer-whale, and so forth.

After each of them had "got" the bride, the father made a speech, in which he talked about his copper, and gave ten pieces to the brothers of the bride, who represented the family. Each piece represented one thousand blankets, that is, $500. Then came the . . . speech of the family which had received the money and had given the father of the bride two coppers, which represented approximately the value of what was given by the father of the groom. Next the bride was led to the father of the groom and two women danced with the coppers. After this a big dinner is supposed to be given by the father of the bride, at which the bride is . . . for the first time. Since one cannot buy anything in this place and there was not enough fish and oil, the feast had to wait for good weather.

In the meantime another house, in which the feast will be held, is made ready. Unfortunately all this makes a very shabby impression because the house is only a shell. All trunks and chests, seats, bedroom furniture, and supplies which used to fill the house are gone. The people are dressed like poor workmen, [the men] with caps on their heads, the women in skirts and sweaters. Fortunately they wore blankets because it was cold.

My work is progressing very slowly because everyone is busy with the preparations for the feast. But it is very interesting to watch because I have not yet seen a wedding here. A few days ago there was also a commemorative feast for a man who was drowned in the spring. His sister gave the feast. Everyone received money, including me, and the women got material for dresses. Her brother made the speech. He spoke about all great . . . with their ancestors. There was also a feast at which a child was given a name. There are always family stories told at those occasions.

Now about myself. You asked me the other day why I wanted to leave Germany in 1885. The main reason was probably that I saw no future there and that I wanted to get married. But there was more behind it. The anti-Semitism during my university years, the intrigues in Berlin when I wanted to habilitate myself, and the idea that America was politically an ideal country seem to have been the main motives. The draft probably also had a part in it. One recognizes the good only when it is lost. Until 1898 I was glad to have left Germany. Then my disappointment with America started, which grew worse and worse. At that time, and more so after the war, I felt that I was emotionally through with America. This has mellowed a little, but I realize that we are in all fields thirty years behind Europe. The people here don't want to see the necessary socialization of society because the country is so large. But the misery of the working class [?] is as bad here as over there. Even here in British Columbia one can always read in the newspapers about the problem of unemployment. I am fully convinced that the Russian revolution will force some progress. It will take some time, but it will happen, as in the French Revolution. The demands of our civilization will remain. The way it is now, things cannot go on!

Enough for now! I wish your letter would come. . . .

With all my love,

Franz

Fort Rupert, December 14, 1930

Dear Children [Ernst],

Yesterday's greetings cannot be counted as a letter, but I wanted to send a few lines because one can never tell when the next postal connection will be. Yesterday the weather was good and a boat came from Hardy Bay and returned right away. In the evening it started to rain again and since then it has been raining and storming all the time.

A year ago today I went to Chicago not knowing what fate had in store for me. I said goodbye—goodbye forever—to your mother under the viaduct over the 125th Street! You lost a dear mother, and I cannot find myself since then. When my work is done, my thoughts always concentrate on the same thing—Mama, Trudel, Heini, Baby! Oh you all know it! I will find myself eventually and do what has to be done, but the real enjoyment of life is gone. You all are my dear children and grandchildren, and you will not be angry with me when, in addition to you, I think of all our beloved ones who are not with us any more.

My work here is going along so-so. There are many interruptions—dances, dinners, speeches, etc. I am now collecting speeches, which is extremely difficult because they are so filled with metaphors and really don't say a thing. The speakers talk themselves into veritable ecstasy—at least so it seems—and when they talk too long the whole company starts to converse. But the speaker continues until finally "the food settles in his stomach." Then he is content and sits down.

Yesterday I took pictures, from eleven to 2 P.M., of all sorts of games which are hard to describe. I hope they turned out all right. I need four more cases [of photographic plates?], but don't know whether I can get them. The phonograph cylinders which I ordered came yesterday. I want to get enough to record all the music styles they have here.

Yesterday there was quite a mess. The chief, who is hated by everyone, gave a great feast. A cow was bought and butchered, and the meat distributed. There were speeches, and he made his adopted grandchild the heir of his son. And then around the brat, a real good-for-nothing, copper plates were placed which were to prevent anybody from saying anything against him. A copper plate was placed above his head which meant that he breaks it to show his greatness. A speech was given while the meat was distributed. He [the chief] said, "This bowl in the shape of a bear (is) for you, and you, and so on; for each group a bowl." The bowls, however, are no longer here. They are in the museums in New York and Berlin. Only the speech is still the same. In the same way a child was supposed to be named, and they said . . . , but these are only words. It is strange how these people cling to the form though the content is almost gone. But this still makes them happy.

Three weeks from today we are supposed to leave. I will stay, however, for eight days in Alert Bay and shall be in Vancouver on January 12. You can write me there. I will probably be in Victoria on the thirteenth and fourteenth, and in Seattle on the fifteenth. Then two days at Bessie's and in Berkeley, and then home!

I am looking forward to seeing you again, kids. Lovingly,

Your father


Fort Rupert, December 25, 1930

Dear Toni,

This will probably be one of my last greetings from here. The Indians are invited to a neighboring village; almost all of them are leaving tomorrow. I will have only two or three days more here and then will go to Alert Bay. I have to wait and see how it turns out.

Yesterday was Christmas Eve. I have had it in mind to invite the Indians once more and, after some debating, I was asked to do it. Well, I had fifty-five guests. I served salmon with fish oil, tea, hardtack with jam, and apple sauce. The Indians used this opportunity to celebrate Christmas; that is, they had entertainment in their old style, in which the men and the women in groups make fun of each other. The men sang first, then the chief gave a speech challenging the women to speak in turn. The speaker always holds one of the staffs in his hand, and the challenge consists of throwing the staff on the floor, near the person who is supposed to talk. At first the women did not want to participate, but after some time they also became gay. They sang, and a few danced to the songs. Then the groups gave each other presents. The women now entered with teaspoons tied to long sticks and they danced with them in their hands. After this every man made a speech, including me, and received a . . . spoon. Now the men, after more dancing and more speeches, gave the women fish angles and fish. . . . Then the women came with dead pigeons, with which they executed a lively dance. Thus it went on, from 5:30 until 1 A.M.

Today I recorded some more songs on my phonograph. All in all, I now have one hundred and forty-five, which, as far as I can tell, include all existing styles of music and poetry, feast songs, boasting songs [Renommierlieder], games, love songs, dance songs, religious songs, etc.

This afternoon all the important men came to see me in order to ask that I intervene for them with the government so that they won't have to fear the government's interference with their feasts. The policy of the government toward the Indians is very stupid, in my opinion. The most harmless deeds are punished with two to three months in jail, and this is done very arbitrarily. Some people are punished and some are not.

Yesterday I sent you a telegram which you probably received this morning. Your telegram arrived on the sixteenth. I knew that you would think of me on that day and I was very pleased. I am glad that I shall be back a month from today, and yet I am dreading my return into the house, which is so empty now. Now I must stop. All the work comes at once, especially at the end, and there is still much to do.

Your loving brother,

Franz

Alert Bay, January 5, 1931

Dear Children, [Ernst]

The past days were not at all nice here. On the thirty-first I got a telegram from Berlin with New Year's greetings. In the evening we were up until midnight with Mrs. Cadwallader, our landlady. Her husband and his sister had walked all the way to Port Hardy because the weather was so bad. His wife apparently thought that we wanted to celebrate the coming of the New Year with her.

The weather was terrible all week. When it unexpectedly cleared up on January 2 we rode quickly with all our luggage to Hardy Bay, arriving at noon. Two sisters of George Hunt live there, one the mother of Mr. Cadwallader. Since the next morning (January 3) was fair, we drove in a car across the whole island to the west coast, about eleven miles. We walked back, and while we were under way it started to rain again. The walk through the woods was very beautiful nevertheless. I took a few pictures, but I don't know how they will turn out because the light was not good. The quiet; the deep green of the cedars, the hemlocks, and the fir trees; and the dense green foliage of the . . . trees was wonderful. Since the path goes up and down, there is much climbing. In the evening it started to storm again and the houses shook and trembled. At about eight o'clock it cleared again and we arrived here at about 11 P.M. A married granddaughter of George Hunt who lives here invited us to stay with her. Thus we are living in a . . . house. Everyone is away; they went to the same feast as the Fort Rupert people. I went immediately to see the Indian agent, to be polite, and right away we had a controversy over the fact that I notified Victoria of the dysentery epidemic, against which nothing was being done. In any case, I accomplished this much—that the water from the latrines may no longer run into the drinking water. Then I visited the . . . female interpreter, and this week I plan to work on the grammar again. Today I worked with her again; it went very well, the only difficulty being that she is not familiar with some old forms.

Today I received your postcard of the twenty-eighth. I am glad that my telegram to Aunt Helene arrived on time. I had heard that you would all be there. Please thank . . . for her letter, about which I was so glad. I have so little time now that I cannot write any letters except to you children and to Berlin. I am sure that you have heard that I was elected president of the AAAS. I do not like this at all. I would rather withdraw from everything but, since anthropology has not been up for its turn for some time, I was afraid that this would happen. I could not very well refuse because of anthropology as . . . Miss Berger [?] congratulated me by telegram. I should say an expression of sympathy, rather, is in order. When such events occur I am always sorry that my parents and Uncle Jacobi are not alive any more. They would have been made very happy. Mama used to see such things through my eyes, although she was always very happy when I was honored. What do I care about honors today?

Helene, would you please put the $2,700 which you got from Ernst in my "non-drawing account"? When I come back I want to talk over with you what I shall do with the money. In the meantime I should like Ernst to find out whether the hospital into which Mama was brought is a decent one and whether it is therefore indicated that I give them money. If it is a bad hospital, I should prefer not to do it. I want to settle the whole matter as soon as possible.

A Finn came today from a Finnish village near here, and invited Julia to go there. She promised to be back tomorrow, and so I let her go. She had wondered how she could get there. But enough for now. Thanks for the letters and newspapers. The one Fritzi [?] sent never arrived.

Greetings and kisses to all of you.

Your father

On Board *Princess Alion* [?]
January 11, 1931

Dear Children, [Ernst]

Now the work is finished and we are on our way to Vancouver. My last letter left from Port Hardy last Saturday. I do not know any longer what I wrote. It stormed all week, and when the weather cleared up on Friday we went to Port Hardy. This is probably the last time that I will see George Hunt. He is seventy-six years old and quite frail. I still had a few questions on the last morning! We went to Hardy Bay and I made yet another photo of . . . . The next morning we rode by automobile to the west coast and walked back, eleven and one-quarter miles.

Well, I have written all this already. How beautiful and quiet the large forest was; how huge the trees. The next morning, Sunday, we rode to Alert Bay, about twenty miles away. The steamer, the same as the one we are on today, is very beautiful, a real ocean passenger boat, of 1,845 tons, two decks, and elegant salon, etc. I wore a woolen shirt and no tie and was out of place because all passengers had dinner [dress]. In Alert Bay we wanted to go to a so-called hotel, but a young Indian woman whom I knew and who knew that we were coming awaited us and invited us into her house, where we had two rooms one flight up. Her husband was at a potlatch in another village, but he returned on Thursday (today is Sunday). We had everything we needed, however. My bed was so hard that my old hip bones revolted against it. The washing facilities were not very good either, because there was only one little wash basin for the whole family in the kitchen. Tomorrow, however, I shall go into a bathtub!

I worked all week with the official lady-interpreter and cleared up some items. [Boas criticizes the interpreter. He mentions that the woman systematizes the language improperly and makes mistakes in English too.] The people say of her that she talks like a child, and right they are, since she makes this kind of mistake. Julia is collecting more string games, etc. There is a big school in Alert Bay. The children sleep eighty to a room, packed like sardines, but the place is well ventilated. The building was finished only last year. The principal seems to be quite a reasonable man. I have lectured him at length on potlatches and marriage customs. These are the two customs for which the Indians are so unreasonably persecuted.

Friday we were invited by the missionary, and we had to accept. He seemed very decent in comparison with the former missionary. I have written to the [lieutenant] governor of British Columbia and asked him for an interview. If I can see him, I want to inform him of all these matters. I don't know for sure whether it will be of any help.

Today is the anniversary of the death of our little Hete. Such days of suffering one does not forget. It was thirty-seven years ago. Today I received a letter on the boat from Aunt Hete and Aunt Toni. Now Rudi has also been fired, although he had been with . . . for ten years. They are paying his salary for another four years, however. This is very decent.

Ernst, I have asked Helene to ask you to make inquiries about the hospital Mama was brought to. If possible, please have the information when I arrive. I do hope I will get a letter from you tomorrow. I shall hurry with my visits here on the coast because I would like to be in New York on the twenty-sixth or the twenty-seventh.

Love,
Your father

# APPENDIXES

# APPENDIX I

---

# GENEALOGICAL PLATES

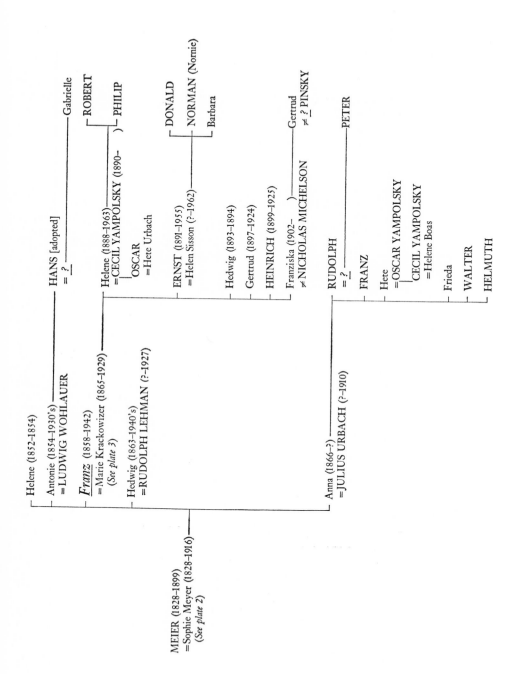

307

PLATE 2: *Meyer*

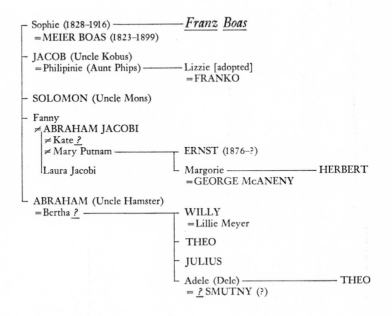

Sophie (1828–1916) ———————— *Franz Boas*
  =MEIER BOAS (1823–1899)

JACOB (Uncle Kobus)
  =Philipinie (Aunt Phips) ————— Lizzie [adopted]
                                   =FRANKO

SOLOMON (Uncle Mons)

Fanny
  ≠ABRAHAM JACOBI
    | ≠ Kate *?*
    | ≠ Mary Putnam ——————— ERNST (1876–?)
    | Laura Jacobi
                            └─ Margorie ——————————— HERBERT
                                 =GEORGE McANENY

ABRAHAM (Uncle Hamster)
  =Bertha *?* ———————————— WILLY
                             =Lillie Meyer

                            THEO

                            JULIUS

                            └─ Adele (Dele) ——————————— THEO
                                 = *?* SMUTNY (?)

PLATE 3: *Krackowizer*

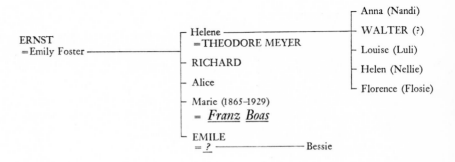

ERNST
=Emily Foster ——————— Helene ——————————— Anna (Nandi)
                        =THEODORE MEYER      WALTER (?)
                                             Louise (Luli)
                        RICHARD              Helen (Nellie)
                                             Florence (Flosie)
                        Alice

                        Marie (1865–1929)
                          = *Franz Boas*

                        EMILE
                          = *?* ——————— Bessie

·308·

# APPENDIX 2

# Franz Boas: Chronology of Principal Activities and Events (1858–1942)

*Major Activities*

*Field
Trips*

1858 Born July 9, Minden, Westphalia, Germany.

1877 University of Heidelberg, Spring; University of Bonn, October.

1879 Accompanied principal professor, Theobald Fischer, from University of Bonn to University of Kiel in October.

1880 University of Kiel.

1881 Received Ph.D., University of Kiel. Thesis: "Contributions to the Understanding of the Color of Sea Water." Principal interests at this time were physics and geography.

1881–82 Served as a "one-year volunteer" in the German army.

1883 Field trip to Baffinland; partially financed by the German newspaper, *Berliner Tageblatt*. Traveled to Baffinland to study the geography of the region and to obtain ethnographic material on the Eskimo.

1884–85 Visited the U.S. and New York City for the first time during part of the winter.

309

*Major Activities*

1885    Appointed assistant to Adolph Bastian at the Royal Ethnographic Museum, Berlin.

1886    Arranged a period of leave from the University of Berlin to embark on first field trip to British Columbia. En route to the Pacific Coast, attended a midsummer meeting in Buffalo of the American Association for the Advancement of Science and was made Foreign Associate Member.

1886    Northwest Coast field trip between September 18 and December 16. The purpose was for general reconnaissance; collected artifacts for the museum; studied folklore; "ethnogeography" (ethnographic map of Vancouver Island); language study; collected skulls.

1887    Returned to New York. Became assistant editor of *Science* in January. Married Marie A. E. Krackowizer on March 10, 1887. Resigned from the University of Berlin and decided to become a U.S. citizen.

1888    Resigned from *Science*.

1888    Northwest Coast field trip between May 31 and July 24, under the direction of the BAAS Committee for the Study of the Northwestern Tribes of Canada, E. B. Tylor, Chairman. Purpose of the field trip was for reconnaissance; description of customs and beliefs; partial listings of the Northwest Coast tribes and languages; anthropometric measurements; collected skeletons; photographed prisoners.

1889    Northwest Coast field trip July 18 to September 14 (?), directed by the BAAS. Worked especially with the Nootka, Salish and Kwakiutl; collected almost complete list of "tribes, septs, and gentes [numinas]" of the Kwakiutl.

1889    Appointed by G. Stanley Hall as docent in anthropology at Clark University, Worcester, Mass., at $1,500 (?) a year.

1890    Northwest Coast field trip from late May to mid-September, directed by BAAS. Filled in omissions of previous trips, including ethnographic and linguistic map; anthropometric measurements.

*Major Activities*

1891      Northwest Coast field trip July 5 to early September, directed by BAAS. Collected Chinoook texts. (Limited information available.)

> 1892     A. F. Chamberlain received first Ph.D. in America in anthropology, at Clark University under Boas. Boas resigned from Clark University; appointed chief assistant, World Columbian Exposition, Chicago.
>
> 1893     At Chicago Exposition. Trained George Hunt in the rudiments of phonological transcription.
>
> 1894     Appointed curator in Field Museum, Chicago—a temporary position; searched for a permanent position part of the year.

1894      Northwest Coast field trip September 10 to December 20 (?), sponsored by the BAAS. Anthropometric measurements among Interior Salish; made plaster casts and took photographs; studied Tsetsaut (Athapascan) and Niska (Tsimshian) languages, customs, and bodily measurements; observed and recorded songs and customs of Kwakiutl winter ceremonial.

> 1895     Searched for a permanent position much of the year. After leaving the Chicago Field Museum "a difficult time followed, in which he was befriended by W J McGee, until Putnam (in 1896) called him to the American Museum of Natural History as Assistant Curator of Ethnology and Somatology" (Kroeber 1943).
>
> 1896     Received appointment at AMNH as assistant curator in ethnology and somatology; appointed lecturer in physical anthropology at Columbia University. (Cattell, a psychologist, was apparently influential in obtaining this appointment.) Salary was $1,500 a year.
>
> 1897     The Jesup Expedition, created at Boas' suggestion, began with Boas in charge of the research.

1897      Northwest Coast field trip June 3 to September 14, sponsored by the Jesup Expedition. Investigated physical characteristics of Indians on banks of Fraser River north of Lytton; customs and physical characteristics of Chilcotin;

*Major Activities*

Bella Coola customs and beliefs; graphic art of the Haida; and physical appearance of Haida and Tsimshian. Pursued limited language study.

1899    Appointed professor of anthropology at Columbia University for a term of two years at $2,500 a year, effective July 1. This later became a permanent position.

1900    Northwest Coast field trip June 21 to September 9, sponsored by the Jesup Expedition. Revised texts; worked on Kwakwala grammar and Kwakiutl ethnology; studied Indian art; studied customary techniques of collecting, preparing, and using plants among Kwakiutl; recorded tales; cast Indian faces in plaster of paris.

1901    Appointed curator of anthropology at the AMNH on January 1, after Putnam left the museum to continue his work at Harvard and to assume the directorship of the museum at California. Also appointed honorary philologist of the Bureau of American Ethnology.

1905    Resigned from the AMNH.

1908    Editor of the *Journal of American Folklore* until 1925.

1910–12    Instigated the founding of the International School of American Archaeology and Ethnology in Mexico, where he lectured and conducted archaeological and linguistic research.

1914    Northwest Coast field trip August 4 to August 25. Collected linguistic materials, including texts from the Kootenay; anthropometric measurements.

1915    Conducted field work in Puerto Rico during the summer—five weeks after his facial operation.

1917    Founded *International Journal of American Linguistics*.

1919–21    Conducted field work in pueblos of New Mexico part of each summer.

1920–28    President of the Emergency Society for German and Austrian Science.

## Major Activities

Field
Trips

1922    Northwest Coast field trip August 15 to August 30. Worked on linguistic problems among the Interior Salish. He was accompanied by his wife, Marie. (Limited information available.)

1923    Northwest Coast field trip November 13 to December 18. Cleared up doubtful linguistic and ethnological points, including Kwakiutl winter ceremonial and social organization, social organization of Bella Bella, and "Eagle" of Fort Rupert; Bella Bella folklore.

1927    Northwest Coast field trip about June 29 to about September 2. Largely linguistic work, especially in Washington. Students did ethnological work. (Limited information available.)

     1928    President, International Congress of Americanists.

     1929    Boas' wife, Marie, died.

1930–31    Northwest Coast field work October 21 to January 12, 1931. Acculturation; motion-picture photography and sound recordings; corroboration of Hunt's material; style of storytelling of different people, including songs and oratory; revision of texts with Hunt; descriptions of feasts and wedding.

     1931    President of the AAAS.

     1936    Professor emeritus-in-residence at Columbia University, stipend of $6,000, effective June 30.

     1942    Died in New York, December 22, 1942, while attending a luncheon given for Paul Rivet.

# APPENDIX 3

---

# LOCATIONS VISITED BY BOAS DURING HIS NORTHWEST COAST FIELD TRIPS

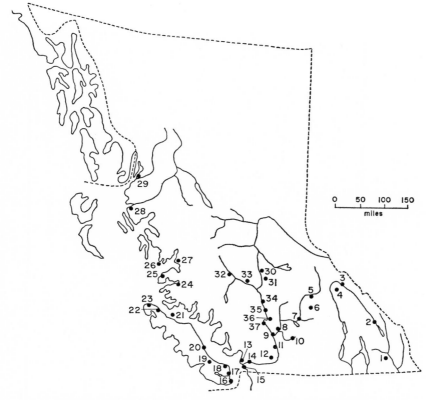

FIG. 1.—Locations visited by Boas in British Columbia: 1886–1931. Figures 1, 2 reprinted, by permission, from *Pioneers of American Anthropology: The Uses of Biography*, ed. June Helm, © 1966 by the University of Washington Press.

*Key*

1. Cranbrook (St. Eugene)
2. Windemere
3. Golden
4. Glacier
5. Sicamous
6. Enderby
7. Kamloops
8. Spences Bridge
9. Lytton
10. Coultee, Nicola Valley
11. North Bend
12. Harrison Hot Springs
13. Vancouver
14. New Westminster
15. Ladners Landing
16. Victoria
17. Cowichan
18. Nanaimo
19. Alberni
20. Comox
21. Alert Bay
22. Fort Rupert
23. Nawiti
24. Rivers Inlet
25. Namu
26. Bella Bella
27. Bella Coola
28. Port Essington
29. Kincolith
30. Soda Creek
31. Williams Lake
32. Puntzi Lake
33. Hanceville
34. Kelley Lake (?) (Alkali Lake [?])
35. Big Bar (?)
36. Fountain
37. (18 mi. below Lillooet)

317

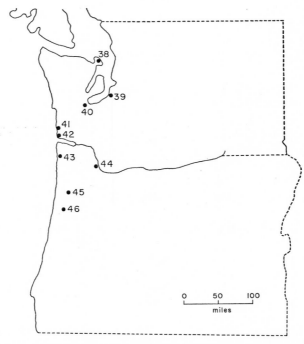

FIG. 2.—Locations visited by Boas in Washington and Oregon: 1886–1931.

*Key*

38. Port Townsend, Washington
39. Tacoma, Washington
40. Oakville, Washington
41. Bay Center, Washington
42. Ilwako, Washington
43. Seaside, Oregon
44. Portland, Oregon
45. Grande Ronde, Oregon
46. Siletz, Oregon

# REFERENCES

Benedict, Ruth

1943     Franz Boas as an ethnologist. *Memoir of the American Anthropological Association* 61:27–34.

Benison, Saul

1949     Geography and the early career of Franz Boas. *American Anthropologist* 51:523–26.

Boas, Franz

1887*a*   Anthropology in the American and British Association for the Advancement of Science. *Science* 10:231–32.

1887*b*   Museums of ethnology and their classification. *Science* 9:587–89.

1887*c*   Review of Bastian's *Die welt in ihren spiegelungen unter dem wandel des volkergedankes. Science* 10:284.

1888     The Indians of British Columbia. *Popular Science Monthly* 32:628–36.

1889*a*   Aims of ethnology. Lecture given before the Deutschen geselligwissenschaftlicher verein von New York, March 8, 1888. New York: Herman Bartsch. Reprinted in revised form in *Race, language and culture*, pp. 626–38. New York: Macmillan.

1889*b*   Unpublished letter to Horatio Hale in the Library of the American Philosophical Society, Philadelphia, July 6.

1893     Notes on the Chinook language. *American Anthropologist* 6:55–63.

1896*a*   The limitations of the comparative method of anthropology. *Science* 4:901–8. Reprinted in *Race, language and culture*, pp. 270–80.

1896*b*   Review of Chamberlain's *The child and childhood in folk thought. Science, n.s.* 3:742.

1896*c*   The Indians of British Columbia. *Bulletin of the American Geographical Society* 28:229–43.

1897     The decorative art of the Indians of the North Pacific Coast. *Bulletin of the American Museum of Natural History* 9:123–76.

1898     Operation of the [Jesup North Pacific] Expedition in 1897. *Publication of the Jesup North Pacific Expedition* 1:1–12.

1909     The Kwakiutl of Vancouver Island. *American Museum of Natural History, Memoirs*, vol. 8.

1935    Unpublished letter to A. L. Kroeber in the Library of the American Philosophical Society, Philadelphia, August 28.

1966    *Kwakiutl ethnography.* Helen Codere, ed. Chicago: University of Chicago Press.

Brinton, Daniel
1896    The aims of anthropology. *Proceedings of the 44th meeting of the American Association for the Advancement of Science for 1895* 44:1–17.

Cushing, Frank
1896    Exploration of ancient Key Dweller's remains on the Gulf coast of Florida. *Proceedings of the American Philosophical Society* 35:329–425.

Dawson, George M.
1887    Notes and observations on the Kwakiool people of Vancouver Island. *Transactions of the Royal Society of Canada* 5:2.

1894    Unpublished letter to Franz Boas in the Library of the American Philosophical Society, Philadelphia, May 28.

Gallatin, Albert
1848    Hale's Indians of North-West America, and vocabularies of North America with an Introduction by Albert Gallatin. *Transactions of the American Ethnological Society* 2:xxiii–clxxx.

Gruber, Jacob
1967    Horatio Hale and the development of American anthropology. *Proceedings of the American Philosophical Society* 3:5–37.

Hale, Horatio
1882    A lawgiver of the stone age. *Proceedings of the American Association for the Advancement of Science for 1881* 30:324–42.

1888a   Unpublished letter to Franz Boas in the Library of the American Philosophical Society, Philadelphia, April 30.

1888b   Unpublished letter to Franz Boas in the Library of the American Philosophical Society, Philadelphia, May 21.

1889    Unpublished letter to Franz Boas in the Library of the American Philosophical Society, Philadelphia, July 13.

1890    Unpublished letter to Franz Boas in the Library of the American Philosophical Society, Philadelphia, May 21.

Haven, Samuel
1856    Archaeology of the United States, or sketches historical and bibliographical, of the progress of information and opinion respecting vestiges of antiquity in the United States. *Smithsonian Contributions to Knowledge* 8:1–141.

Henry, Joseph
   1858    Report of the secretary. *Annual Report of the Smithsonian Institution for 1857*, pp. 13–37.
Johnson, Mrs. Tom
   1964    Personal communication (taped interview).
Kluckhohn, Clyde, and Prufer, Olaf
   1959    Influences during the formative years. *In* Walter Goldschmidt, ed. The anthropology of Franz Boas. *American Anthropological Association, Memoir* 89:4–28.
Kroeber, A. L.
   1943    Franz Boas: The man. *American Anthropological Association, Memoir* 61:5–26.
McGee, Anita Newcomb
   1889    Notes on American communities. *Proceedings of the American Association for the Advancement of Science for 1888* 37:322–23.
McGee, W J
   1898    The Seri Indians. *Fifteenth Annual Report of the Bureau of American Ethnology for 1895–96*, pp. 1–344.
Mason, O. T.
   1887    The occurrence of similar inventions in areas widely apart. *Science* 9:534–35.
Mathews, Washington
   1897    The study of ceremony. *Journal of American Folklore* 10:257–63.
Morgan, Lewis Henry
   1851    *League of the Ho-dé-no-sau-nee, or Iroquois.* Rochester: Sage and Brother.
   1876*a*    Ethnical periods. *Proceedings of the American Association for the Advancement of Science for 1875* 24:266–74.
   1876*b*    Montezuma's dinner. Review of Bancroft's *Native races of the Pacific states*, vol. 2. *North American Review* 122:165–308.
   1877    *Ancient society, or researches in the lines of human progress from savagery, through barbarism to civilization.* New York: Henry Holt & Co.
Powell, John Wesley
   1877    *Introduction to the study of Indian languages with works, phrases, and sentences to be collected.* Smithsonian Institution, Bureau of American Ethnology.
   1879    Mythological philosophy. *Popular Science Monthly* 15:665–808.
   1881    Report to the director. *First Annual Report of the Bureau of American Ethnology, 1879–1880*, pp. xi–xxxiii.

1887    Museums of ethnology and their classification. *Science* 9:612–14.

1891    Indian linguistic families north of Mexico. *Seventh Annual Report of the Bureau of American Ethnology for 1885–86*, pp. 7–14.

Powers, John Stephen
1877    Tribes of California. *Contributions of North American Ethnology*, vol. 3.

Rohner, Ronald P.
1966a    Franz Boas among the Kwakiutl. In *Pioneers of American anthropology*, June Helm, ed., pp. 213–22. Seattle and London: University of Washington Press.

1966b    Franz Boas: Ethnographer on the Northwest Coast. In *Pioneers of American anthropology*, June Helm, ed., pp. 149–212. Seattle and London, University of Washington Press.

1967a    The Boas canon: A posthumous addition. Review of Boas' *Kwakiutl ethnography. Science* 158:362–64.

1967b    *The people of Gilford: A contemporary Kwakiutl village.* Ottawa, National Museum of Canada Bulletin 225.

n.d.    An anthropologist's anthropologist: George Hunt's influence on the ethnography of Franz Boas. In manuscript.

Stocking, George W., Jr.
1965    From physics to ethnology; Franz Boas' Artic expedition as a problem in the historiography of the behavioral sciences. *Journal of the History of the Behavioral Sciences* 1:53–66.

White, Leslie
1963    *The ethnography and ethnology of Franz Boas.* Texas Memorial Museum Bulletin 6.

Wilson, Daniel
1878    Address of Professor Daniel Wilson. *Proceedings of the American Association for the Advancement of Science for 1877* 26:319–34.

Wyman, Jeffries
1875    Report of the Peabody museum of archaeology and ethnology. Harvard University.

# INDEX OF PERSONAL NAMES

Hale, Horatio Emmons, ethnologist, philologist, BAAS member, xvii, xxi, 81–82, 99, 103, 106–9
Hall, Reverend Alfred James, missionary in Alert Bay, B.C., 43–46, 112
Hance, Mr. and Mrs., store owners at Hanceville, B.C., 208–9
Hastings, photographer in British Columbia, 88, 147, 183–84
Haven, Samuel, lawyer and archaeologist, xvii
Hedwig, Boas' third child, 157 n
Helene (Bublichen) Boas Yampolsky. *See* Boas, Helene
Henry, Joseph, scientist, xxvi
Herigon, Ned, British Columbia trader married to Indian, 31, 38
Hills, George, Anglican bishop, 27
Hill-Tout, Charles, Canadian anthropologist, 201
Hunt, David, son of George Hunt, 180
Hunt, George (Kwakiutl), Boas, principal informant, xxiii, xxviii, xxix, 91, 177–83 *passim*, 199, 211, 215–19 *passim*, 236–37, 243–44, 246–66 *passim*, 276, 279–86 *passim*, 289, 290, 300

Itlkakuni, Bella Coola informant, 20, 21

Jacobi, Abraham, Boas' uncle, 17, 65
Jacobsen, Captain Adrian, exhibitor of Bella Coola Indians in Berlin, Germany, 20, 92
Jacobsen, Fillip, Bella Coola informant, 66–67, 199
Jesup, Morris K., president of board of trustees, American Museum of Natural History, 199, 234
Jonkan, Father, Catholic missionary in Victoria, B.C., 90
Joseph, Chief, chief of Slaa'n Indians, 86–87

Krackowizer, Marie, Boas' wife, 17, 296

Krause, Aurel, geographer, studied Tlingit Indians, 6
Kroeber, Alfred, anthropologist, xvii

LeJeune, Father, Catholic missionary in British Columbia, 138, 141
Levi, Tsetsaut informant, 163–70 *passim*
Lomas, Indian agent in British Columbia, 53, 65–66

McDonald, W. J., Canadian senator, 147
McDonald, female Indian informant in Victoria, B.C., 88
McGee, W J, anthropologist, geologist, hydrologist, xxvii, 167, 191, 192
Marie. *See* Krackowizer, Marie
Martin, lawyer in Vancouver, B.C., 201
Mason, Otis T., ethnologist, xix
Mathew, Tsimshian informant, 23–25 *passim*
Matthews, Washington, physician, ethnologist, philologist, xxv
Meyer, Jacob (Uncle Kobus), brother of Boas' mother, 44, 143, 146
Morgan, Lewis Henry, anthropologist, lawyer, xix, xxv–xxvi
Morris, Mr. and Mrs., traveling companions of Boas in 1888, 97
Morrison, Mrs., interpreter in British Columbia, 93

Newcombe, Charles F., natural scientist in British Columbia, 201

Oppenheimer, German with Indian wife at Spences Bridge, B.C., 140

Parsons, Elsie Clews, anthropologist, 269
Petermann, August Heinrich, German cartographer, editor of *Petermanns Geographische Mittheilungen*, 49
Petrock, Mr., Indian agent, 60–61

# INDEX OF SUBJECTS